Morga

Morgan

HOW THINGS WORK

AN ILLUSTRATED ENCYCLOPEDIA

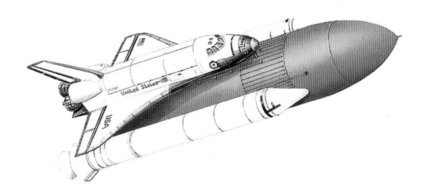

HOW THINGS WORK

AN ILLUSTRATED ENCYCLOPEDIA

*Find out about the technological breakthroughs and
brilliant inventions that have shaped the modern world*

CONSULTING EDITOR:
CHRIS OXLADE

BACK**PACK**BOOKS
◦
NEW YORK

CONTENTS

INTRODUCTION....8

INVENTIONS AND DISCOVERIES....10

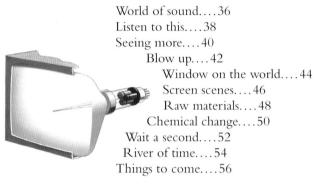

MACHINES....58

CAMERAS....114

COMPUTERS....174

SHIPS....236

TRAINS....298

CARS....358

AIRCRAFT AND FLIGHT....418

INTRODUCTION

How often have you looked at an amazing machine, such as a jumbo jet, a computer games console, or even a dentist's drill, and wondered how it works? Have you also wondered who invented it, and who designed all its parts? This book answers your questions. It tells you about a huge range of machines and devices, from vast ocean liners to machines so small they can be seen only with a microscope; about simple machines that open cans to machines that contain

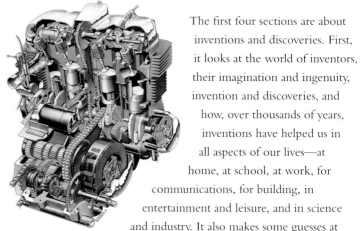

The book is full of neat revealing illustrations such as this car engine, which offers a great view of the mechanisms inside.

millions of moving parts; machines of ancient design to machines that use incredible modern technology; and machines that help with everyday household tasks to specialized machines for science and medicine. It will tell you when they were invented and how they were developed, often from simple ideas thought up thousands of years ago. For example, who invented the wheel, and why? Why did ancient people build wheeled carts? Who built the first motorized wheeled vehicle? Where else are wheels used in cars and other transport machines?

This book can roughly be summed into two halves.

You most likely own or have ridden a bicycle. But have you ever stopped to examine exactly how the gears on it work? Have a look!

The first four sections are about inventions and discoveries. First, it looks at the world of inventors, their imagination and ingenuity, invention and discoveries, and how, over thousands of years, inventions have helped us in all aspects of our lives—at home, at school, at work, for communications, for building, in entertainment and leisure, and in science and industry. It also makes some guesses at what might happen in the future. Then it looks at machines that make our lives easier, starting with simple machines such as levers and pulleys, and moving on to the incredibly complex machines used in industries. Along the way it looks at the science of machines and the special materials used to make them. It also looks closely at two specific inventions—cameras and computers.

Computer technology has come a long way from when something with this Imac's capacity would need a whole room to fit in.

The last four sections cover the world of transport on land, at sea, in the air and in space. It looks at all aspects of cars, trains, ships, planes and spacecraft. It examines how they have developed into the amazing machines they are today, how they move, how their engines work and how they are

very important safety aspects of transport and some examples of where and why things have gone wrong, such as the sinking of the Titanic in the early 1800s. Along the way, there are some fun items, such as famous cars that have appeared in Hollywood films, unusual designs, record breakers and famous voyages.

Did you know that without the invention of trains life as we know it would be unimaginable? Trains were the first mode of transport that allowed us to travel great distances quickly.

used for mass transport and for sport and leisure. It also investigates how machines have spread around the world, their infrastructure, such as roads, railroads, bridges and waterways, and their effects on society and the environment. It also looks at the

Many people value cars as the simplest means of traveling quickly whenever and wherever the impulse takes us, but there are important environmental concerns to consider.

About the projects

This book has more than 100 different projects for you to do at home. Some are experiments, some show you how parts of machines work, and others are working models of machines. All the projects are designed to help you to understand just how things work.

Before you start a project, always read through the instructions carefully and gather together all the tools and materials you need. Work on a large, flat table covered with a protective cloth or mat, and don't rush. You will need an adult to

MAKE AN ARCH

You will need: 2 bricks, ruler, sand, 6 wooden toy blocks, builder's plaster, water, plastic spoon, plastic knife

1 If using anything other than a table specifically for recreation, it is be a good idea to cover it with newspaper first. Place the two bricks on the table. They should be about 8 in. apart.

2 Pile up sand between the bricks and smooth it with your hands to make a curved mound. Place the wooden blocks side by side across the sand. The bricks should touch the outer blocks.

This project, taken from the Inventions and Discoveries section, will give an excellent demonstration of how pedestrian bridges manage to stay up and stay strong.

help you with some of the stages in some of the projects. Always take care when working with sharp knives and scissors and hot objects.

PART ONE

INVENTIONS AND DISCOVERIES

Civilization and the way we live today come from the human being's seemingly endless desire to create something new. The mortar (cement) that held Roman buildings together and the computerized medical technology that can make pictures of the human brain are examples of how inventors have worked hand-in-hand with discovery to find new ways to enrich people's lives. Invention is about constant improvement. Beside the Hubble space telescope, Galileo's telescope seems little more than a small, hollow tube, yet without that tube, the space telescope would have been impossible.

AUTHOR
Peter Harrison
CONSULTANT
Peter Mellett

SHAPING OUR WORLD

MANY things you do, from reading this book to flying in an airplane, would be impossible without the work of inventors. Without Johannes Gutenberg who, in the mid-1400s, invented the first printing press in Europe, this book could not have been printed. In 1903, the brothers Orville and Wilbur Wright were the first people to build and fly an airplane successfully. The airplane that takes you on vacation could not have been built without their pioneering work.

Human beings have been inventing things for thousands of years. The wooden wheel was first used as a means of transport 5,500 years ago. Inventors have also improved on existing inventions to shape the world we live in today. Nowadays, trains and cars travel on wheels made of metal and rubber at speeds of up to about 120 mph. This book is about how inventions have formed today's world.

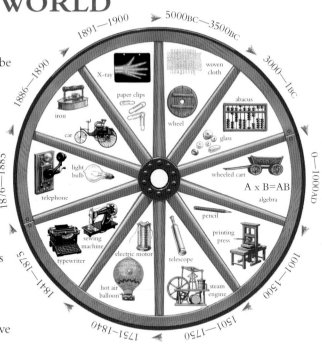

1891—1900 · 5000BC—3500BC · 3000—1BC · 0—1000AD · 1001—1500 · 1501—1750 · 1751—1840 · 1841—1875 · 1876—1885 · 1886—1890

X-ray · woven cloth · paper clips · iron · abacus · wheel · car · glass · light bulb · wheeled cart · telephone · A x B=AB algebra · pencil · sewing machine · printing press · typewriter · electric motor · telescope · hot air balloon · steam engine

Moving on

In this wheel are some of the objects invented from 5000 B.C. to A.D. 1900 that have fundamentally changed our lives. Follow the arrowheads to see the progression of invention through the ages.

Clean and dry

In the past, people washed clothes by putting them in a tub of hot water and rubbing them with soap. William Sillars invented the first machine for washing clothes in 1890. By turning the big wheel on the lid of the tub, a person could turn the long pegs on the underside of the lid. The moving pegs swirled the clothes around in the tub and washed out the dirt. The first electric washing machine was invented in 1901 by Alva J. Fisher.

1890 washing machine

modern washing machine

Flyer 1

jet engines

416 passengers
on board

tail fin

Boeing 747

Big Brother

The Wright Brothers' first airplane, *Flyer 1*,
was only about 30 feet long. A modern
Boeing 747 is over 10 times bigger, and is
almost 230 feet long. Only one person could
fly on *Flyer 1*, while a *Boeing 747-400* can
carry 416 passengers. Most modern passenger
aircraft, such as the *Boeing*, are powered
by jet engines. The jet engine was invented by
Sir Frank Whittle in 1930.

It's good to talk

People can make telephone calls from wherever they want using a modern
cellular phone, such as the one seen here (*right*). The first telephone was
invented by Alexander Graham Bell in 1876. He is seen in this engraving.
He is testing the first telephone line to run between New York and
Chicago in 1892. Bell's telephone sent voice messages along wires. To make
a call, the user's phone had to be connected to a telephone wire. Cellular
phones use radio waves and do not need wires.

MAKING LIFE EASIER

WITHOUT the development of bricks and mortar, it would not be possible to build the houses we live in today. People in modern houses, schools, offices and factories can turn on lights and heaters at the flick of a switch, turn taps for water and look out through windows. In the 1700s and before, people had to fetch water from wells. Today water comes into buildings in pipes under the ground. Before there were electric lights, people used to light candles or lamps burning olive or whale oil.

The wires and pipes that supply electricity, water and gas to buildings today were invented in the 1800s. Many different people took part in their invention. The first electric power station was built in New York in 1884, based on the ideas of Thomas Edison. In the early 1800s, William Murdock, a British inventor, was the first person to set up a factory that produced gas for lighting streets and buildings. In the 1800s too, many people in cities were affected by diseases, such as cholera, that were caused by poor hygiene. Sewer pipes were built to carry drain water away from cities to treatment plants.

Straight and narrow
People used bricks to build gateways such as this 5,000 years ago in the part of the Middle East now called Iraq. These bricks made strong walls that could stand for many years.

Built to last
Gates in the German city of Trier (Trèves) were built almost 2,000 years ago. The mortar (cement) that holds the stones in the gates together was invented by the Romans, who then ruled all of France and parts of Germany. The long-lasting strength of mortar is an important reason why so many ancient Roman buildings have survived to this day.

Onward and upward
People are lifting blocks of stone on a winch, standing on scaffolding and cutting stone at the top of the tower in this illustration from the 1400s. Winches and scaffolding made it easier to lift heavy weights and keep stone in place.

Dangerous metal

Lead was used for centuries to make the pipes through which water flowed from reservoirs to houses and public buildings such as baths. Lead dissolves in water and harms the health of the people who drink it. Since the 1950s, plastic water pipes have been used as a safer alternative.

Letting in light

Roman glass tiles, such as this one, were made 2,000 years ago. Ways to make sheets of clear glass for windows were not found until the 1200s. In the 1800s, the British scientist Michael Faraday invented ways of making really large panes of glass.

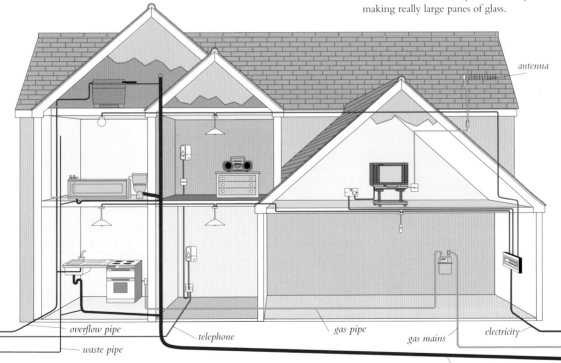

antenna

overflow pipe

telephone

gas pipe

gas mains

electricity

waste pipe

water mains

The modern home

A cross-section of a modern house shows some of the amenities that make our lives comfortable. Electricity and telephone wires often run underground but can be carried on poles and pylons from power stations.

BUILDING FOR STRENGTH

A PLATFORM bridge was one of the earliest human inventions, and was probably first used tens of thousands of years ago. People laid a tree trunk or a single slab of stone across narrow rivers or steep gullies to make traveling across easier. Many modern platform bridges are hollow and made of steel. The model here shows how thin folded sheets make a strong, hollow platform. If you stand on a simple platform bridge, the downward force of your weight makes it sag in the middle. Too much weight can snap a flat wooden plank or crack a stone slab.

Arch bridges, however, as the second project shows, are not flat and do not sag when loaded. They curve up and over the gap that span. The Romans were among the first to build arch bridges from many separate stone blocks more than 2,000 years ago. The shape of the bridge holds the stone blocks together. Pushing down on the center of the bridge creates forces which push outward so that the load is borne by the supports at either side.

A strong bridge
The Rainhill Bridge spanned the Liverpool and Manchester railway in 1832. It was made by putting stone blocks around a wooden scaffold. The bridge could support itself when workers hammered the keystone at the very top into place.

MAKE A PLATFORM

You will need: *scissors, stiff card stock, ruler, pen, 2 boards 8 x 8 in., modeling clay.*

Your platform is stronger than a platform bridge because it is supported on four sides. Without this support it would sag in the middle.

1 Cut out four strips of card stock 16 x 4 in. With a ruler and pen, draw lines ½ in. apart across each strip. Fold each strip back and forth across the lines to form zigzag pleats.

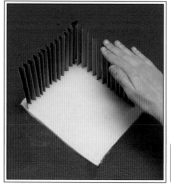

2 Lay one board flat on the table. Stand a piece of pleated card stock upright along the board's edges. Repeat for the other three sides. Use modeling clay to secure each corner.

3 When all sides of the platform are in place, lay the second board on top. Push downward with your hand. Pleating the card stock has made the platform very strong.

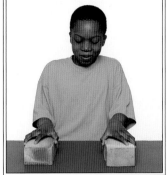

MAKE AN ARCH

You will need: 2 bricks, ruler, sand, 6 wooden toy blocks, builder's plaster, water, plastic spoon, plastic knife.

1 Although it is not shown in this picture, it would be a good idea to cover the table with newspaper. Place the two bricks on the table. They should be about 8 in. apart.

2 Pile up sand between the bricks and smooth it with your hands to make a curved mound. Place the wooden blocks side by side across the sand. The bricks should touch the outer blocks.

Like stone blocks in real bridges, the wooden blocks make a remarkably strong curve.

3 Notice that the inner blocks touch each other and have V-shaped gaps between them. Mix the plaster with water until it forms a stiff paste. Use the knife to fill the gaps between the blocks with paste.

4 Make sure you have filled each space where the arch meets the bricks. Wait for the plaster to dry. Once dry, remove the sand from underneath the arch.

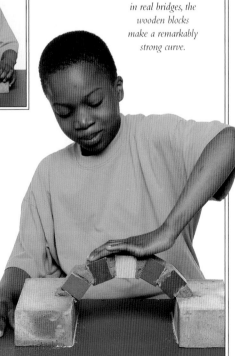

5 Push down on the arch and feel how firm it is. The weight that you are putting on the bridge is supported by the two bricks at the side. This bridge is stronger than the platform bridge and does not sag in the middle.

HOME IMPROVEMENTS

ARLY humans lived in caves or shelters made from stones, wood or soil. They first discovered how to start a fire by rubbing sticks together. Fire provided them with warmth and a way to cook. The earliest houses with permanent walls, roofs and windows were built in villages such as Catal Hüyük in southern Turkey about 8,000 years ago. People there washed with hot water, had fireplaces in the middle of rooms and slept on shelves built against the walls of the houses.

Furniture, such as beds, chairs and tables, was first made by the ancient Egyptians. The ancient Romans built huge public baths and even had central heating 2,000 years ago. The basic design of homes has not changed very much since then. However, houses in Europe did not have chimneys until the 1200s, and glass windows were unusual until the 1400s. It was not until the 1800s that many houses were built with indoor plumbing, and electric wiring was not built in the walls of houses until the 1900s.

Let there be light
This ancient Greek lamp is similar to those people used all over the world for thousands of years to light their homes. Lamps such as this burn olive oil. The flame they give is smoky and not very bright. Candles were also used for lighting homes as early as 5000 B.C.

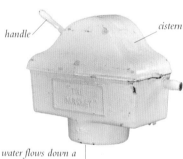

handle

cistern

water flows down a pipe into the toilet

toilet

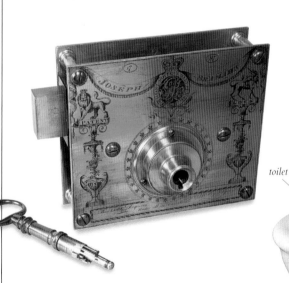

Finding the key
Homes need strong locks to keep valuables safe inside. The lock shown in this picture was invented by Joseph Bramah in 1787. It was the safest lock ever invented at the time. He boasted that he would give a reward to anyone who could pick the lock (unlock it without a key). It was 67 years before anyone succeeded.

Flushed with success
The earliest toilets that are known about are more than 4,000 years old. They were found at Harappa and Mohenjo-Daro in Pakistan. Joseph Bramah, who invented the lock, invented the first flush toilet in 1778. This glazed ceramic toilet was manufactured in 1850. It used water kept in a cistern (small water tank) above the toilet seat.

1910 vacuum cleaner

1993 vacuum cleaner

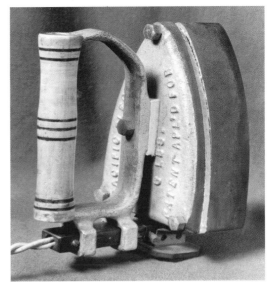

Crisp creases

For over 2,000 years, people have heated flattened pieces of iron to press onto clothes to smooth out wrinkles. In the past, people heated the iron on a fire or on a stove. In the late 1800s, inventors found a way to heat an iron using electricity. This electric iron was first produced in 1903.

Dust buster

Keeping homes clean has always been a concern. Prehistoric people threw their trash onto heaps at the edges of villages. In the 1900s, ways of using a vacuum (airless space) to suck in dirt were invented. This early vacuum cleaner, called the Daisy, was first made in 1910. It worked by using a bellows (pump for sucking out air). Modern vacuum cleaners, such as the 1993 Hoover, use power from an electric motor to suck dirt into a bag.

WEAVING

Almost every kind of cloth is made by weaving. Threads made out of plant material such as cotton, or animal fleece such as wool, are woven on a loom. The oldest pieces of cloth known were found in Switzerland and are estimated to be about 7,000 years old. Before people invented ways to make cloth, they wore the skins of the animals they hunted to keep warm and dry.

The cotton plant grew plentifully in Egypt and India 5,000 years ago. People there invented ways to weave it into clothing. In other parts of the world, clothes were made from the wool of sheep or goats. The flax plant was also used to make cloth called linen. In China, silk was woven as early as 4,500 years ago. In the 1700s, several inventions made it much easier to spin and weave both cotton and wool thread. These inventions allowed cloth to be made in much larger amounts than ever before. In the 1900s, artificial fibers such as nylon were invented that allowed new kinds of cloth to be made.

Secret silk
For centuries, weaving silk was a secret known only to the people of China. They learned how to create fine, richly colored cloth of the kind seen in this banner. It was buried 2,000 years ago.

1300s spinning wheel

Fine thread
Silk is made from the thread that forms the cocoon (covering) spun around themselves by silk moth caterpillars. The cocoons are gathered and washed, and then the thread is unwound. The threads are braided together to make strong thread for weaving. This Chinese painting from 500 years ago shows women spinning silk thread.

Spin me a yarn
The plant fibers or animal hair from which most cloth is made have to be spun together to make them strong. This is called yarn. In the 1300s, people in Europe first began to use spinning wheels such as this to spin thread. Experts believe wheels like this were first invented in India about 4,000 years ago.

20

1769 Arkwright spinning machine

Fast and furious

In the 1700s machines were invented that made it possible to weave cloth far more quickly than before. This meant that thread had to be spun more quickly. In 1769, Richard Arkwright invented a spinning machine that used horse power to turn pulleys and rollers. It spun thread much more quickly than on a spinning wheel.

Power weaving

A factory is outfitted with some of the first large-scale weaving machines. Large weaving machines powered by steam engines were invented in the 1800s. These machines produced much more cloth than was possible using older ways of weaving. However, the people who worked at the machines in factories like this had to work very long hours in conditions that were often dangerous.

Stretch and bend

Clothes made from wool or plant fibers can be stiff and heavy to wear. Modern clothes made from synthetic fibers are designed to be more comfortable. The clothes this woman is wearing for exercising are made from Lycra, invented in 1953. It is very flexible and ideal to wear when you need to be able to bend.

Lycra

Smooth and shiny

This boy is wearing a raincoat made from polyvinyl chloride (PVC), a kind of plastic invented in 1913. New ways of making material were invented in the 1900s. New kinds of thread called synthetic (artificial) fiber were made from chemicals, not from plants and animal wool. Two of these materials are nylon and polyester.

CLEVER COOKS

EOPLE cook food, especially meat, because cooking kills germs, which makes the food safer to eat. Until about 8,000 years ago the only way to cook meat was by roasting. People pushed a spit (metal rod) through an animal's body and held it over a fire while they turned the meat to cook it all over. The Chinese learned 3,000 years ago how to cook many different kinds of food using the Chinese *wok* (a metal cooking bowl). The ancient Egyptians knew how to bake bread in an oven 5,000 years ago. By the time of the ancient Greeks, people cooked using ovens, pans and frying pans. Not surprisingly, the first ever cookbook was written 2,300 years ago by an ancient Greek man, Archestratus. Cooking methods changed very little for the next 2,000 years.

Ways of preserving food by freezing were invented in the 1800s and have changed the way people eat. Foods that had only been available in certain seasons could be eaten all year round. Nowadays people can buy food cooked in advance and heat it up in a few minutes in a microwave oven.

Open-air eating
The Dutch artist Pieter Brueghel the Younger painted village people eating together in the 1500s. The huge cooking pot in the background of the painting was used to cook thick soups or stews over open fires.

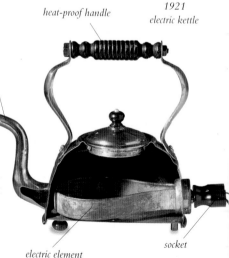

heat-proof handle

1921 electric kettle

spout

electric element

socket

Mass catering
In medieval Europe many people lived together in monasteries or castles. Cooking was done in huge kitchens such as this. Large fireplaces made it easier to feed many people quickly. These kitchens continued to be used up until the 1800s, as shown in this drawing of 1816.

A cup of tea
Tea was first mixed with boiling water as a beverage in China 2,000 years ago. It became popular in Europe in the 1600s and is now drunk all over the world. Boiling water in a kettle became much faster in the 1900s when electric kettles like this one were invented.

Long-lasting soup

People have known how to preserve food (keep it edible over time) for thousands of years. Meat and fish were salted or dried. Fruit and vegetables were stored in the dark or cooked and then sealed in bottles. In the early 1800s, the Frenchman Nicolas Appert found a new way of keeping food fresh. He sealed it in steel cans, as the men in this factory in the mid-1800s are doing.

Frosty food

Freezing keeps food fresh for a long time. Ice cut out from huge blocks was used in Roman times to keep food fresh, but melted quickly. A number of inventors in the 1800s found ways of using air and liquids to flow around a box and keep it cold indefinitely. Electricity was used in the first refrigerator in 1934.

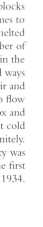

1934 refrigerator

Ready in a flash

Microwave ovens cook food faster than any ordinary oven. Scientists invented this way of using radio waves to heat food in the 1940s. By the 1950s, the first microwave ovens were being sold.

Instant oven

Before the invention of gas ovens, ovens had to be fueled with wood or coal each morning, which meant a lot of hard work. In the 1800s, inventors discovered how to make gas from coal and store it safely so that it could be fed through pipes to people's houses. Modern gas ovens like this one are linked up to gas pipes. The owner just turns a valve and gas flows into the oven where it is lit to provide instant heat for cooking.

YEAST FACTORY

Making drinks!
When yeast is mixed with sugar it creates lots of tiny bubbles. This is called fermentation. When yeast and sugar are combined they create alcohol.

Yeast is a type of fungus that lives on the skins of many fruits. People all over the world have used it for thousands of years for brewing beer and baking bread. Just a spoonful of yeast contains millions of separate single-celled (very simple) organisms. They work like tiny chemical factories, taking in sugar and releasing alcohol and carbon dioxide gas. While they feed, the yeast cells grow larger and then reproduce by splitting in half. Yeast turns grape juice into alcoholic wine and makes beer from mixtures of grain and water. When added to uncooked dough, yeast produces gas bubbles that make the bread light and soft. Brewing and baking are important modern industries that depend on yeast working quickly.

This project consists of four separate experiments. By comparing the results you can discover the best conditions for yeast to grow. Yeast grows best in wet places. Removing the water makes yeast cells dry out and hibernate (sleep). Add water to powdery dry yeast even after many years and it becomes active again.

FINDING THE BEST CONDITIONS

You will need: measuring cup, water, tea kettle, sticky colored labels, 4 small jam jars, teaspoon, dried yeast granules, sugar, scissors, plastic wrap, rubber bands, 2 heatproof bowls, ice cubes.

1 Half-fill a tea kettle with water. Ask an adult to boil it for you and then put it aside to cool. Boiling the water kills all living organisms that might stop the yeast from growing.

2 Label the glass jars one to four. Put a level teaspoonful of dried yeast into each jar as shown here. Then put the same amount of sugar into each jar.

3 Pour 5 fl oz of water into each of the first three jars. Stir the mixture to dissolve the sugar. Do not pour water into the fourth jar. Put this jar away in a warm place.

4 Cut out pieces of plastic wrap about twice each jar's width. Stretch one across the neck of each jar and secure it with a rubber band. Put the first jar in a warm place.

5 Place the second jar in a glass bowl. Put ice cubes and cold water in the bowl. This mixture will keep the jar's temperature close to freezing.

6 Place the third jar in another glass bowl. Pour in hot water that is almost too hot to touch. Take care not to use boiling water, or the jar may crack.

7 Regularly check all four jars over the next two hours. As the ice cubes melt, add more to keep the temperature low. Add more hot water to keep the third jar hot.

high temperature   warm temperature   cold temperature   dry jar

8 In the jar that was kept hot, the yeast is a cloudy layer at the bottom, killed by the heat. The yeast in the jar that was kept warm has fed on the water and sugar, and its gas is pushing up the plastic wrap. The jar that was kept cold has only a little froth on the surface because the cold has slowed down the yeast. In the dry jar, there are no signs of activity, although the yeast is mixed with the sugar.

Discoveries in the lab

Alexander Fleming, a Scottish scientist, identified the properties of the Penicillium mold. Chemists working in laboratories try to invent new substances such as plastics, drugs and dyes. They conduct experiments to see what happens when different chemicals and other substances are combined. Most of the apparatus (equipment) is made from glass so that the chemists can see what is inside.

STAYING WELL

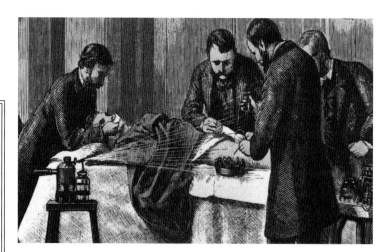

early stethoscopes

HUMAN beings have been seeking new ways to cure illness and take care of the sick for thousands of years. Today there are many drugs, machines and tools that doctors and nurses can use to fight disease. Yet in some ways little has changed. In ancient Egypt 4,500 years ago, a doctor would use compression (pressure) to stop someone from bleeding. A modern doctor would do exactly the same thing. In China 2,000 years ago, doctors knew a great deal about the human body. They also practiced a healing technique called acupuncture (inserting needles into parts of the body), which is still used all over the world.

By the 1500s Chinese doctors knew about some of the drugs that we use today. Medicine in the United States and Europe began to develop quickly in the 1800s. Techniques were invented to stop germs from infecting people and to anesthetize (make unconscious) patients in surgery. In the 1920s, the British doctor Alexander Fleming discovered, by chance, the first antibiotics (drugs that kill germs). Many more antibiotics have been invented since then which treat different kinds of diseases.

Sounds under the skin

The French doctor René Laënnec invented a hollow tube in the early 1800s that allowed him to hear the sounds inside a patient's chest and heart. It was called a stethoscope. Four different kinds can be seen in this photograph. A doctor can find out whether there is illness in a patient's lungs and heart by listening through a stethoscope.

FACT BOX

• The great Indian physician (doctor) Susruta first discovered that mosquitoes spread malaria and that rats spread the plague 1,500 years ago.

• Doctor Willem Kolff invented the first artificial kidney machine in 1943. Like a kidney, the machine removes poisons from a person's bloodstream. People whose kidneys are too damaged to work use this machine.

Keeping clean

Surgeons began to use carbolic sprays of the kind shown in this engraving whenever they operated on a patient. Far more people survived surgery because of this. Before the 1800s, many people died after surgery because germs infected open wounds. The British surgeon Joseph Lister invented a way of preventing many such deaths. He washed the wounds in carbolic acid, a chemical that kills germs.

ether inhaler

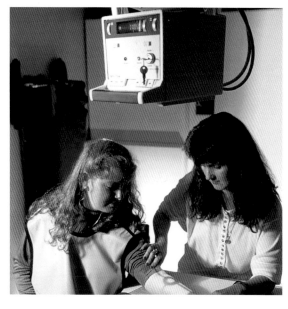

It's a knockout

When surgeons cut people open they are able to give them an anesthetic (drug that puts people to sleep) to stop them feeling pain. The first modern anesthetic was discovered in the United States by a dentist, William Morton. In 1846 he used the chemical called ether to stop a patient from feeling pain from surgery. Ether inhalers, like the one shown here, were invented to allow patients to breathe in ether before and during an operation.

See-through machine

A radiologist (X-ray specialist) uses an X-ray machine to photograph bones inside a patient's arm. Radiation (radio waves that pass through the air) from the machine passes through the patient and strikes a piece of film, leaving a picture of her bones. The German scientist Wilhelm Konrad von Röntgen discovered this special radiation by accident in 1895.

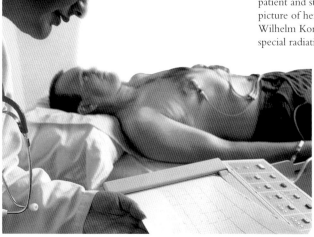

Just a pinprick

Many drugs are given by injecting them into a person's vein or muscle using a hypodermic syringe. Usable syringes were invented in the 1600s but they carried germs. In 1869 the French scientist Luer invented the first all-glass syringe. This was easier to keep germ-free. Disposable syringes became available in the 1970s.

Beating heart

Modern electrocardiographs (ECGs) such as this one can be used in hospitals everywhere to check patients' heartbeats and warn of heart disease. The Dutch scientist Willem Einthoven invented a way of recording the beating of people's hearts as a line on a piece of paper in 1901. However, his machine was very large and heavy. He was awarded the Nobel Prize for his achievement in 1924.

POWER TO THE PEOPLE

All charged up
The Italian scientist Alessandro Volta shows his invention to the Emperor Napoleon. He invented an electric battery and named it after himself. He used disks of copper and zinc piled above each other separated by cardboard disks soaked in salt water. When joined together, they produce an electric current.

Dᴵˢᶜᵒᵛᴱᴿᴵᴺᴳ how to make electricity was one of the most important steps human beings made in using energy for heat, light and many other purposes. Before this discovery, people relied on coal and wood for heat and muscle power for most other work. The ancient Greeks knew that rubbing amber with cloth produced static electricity, but they did not know why. From the 1700s, many scientists in Europe and the United States tried to understand how electricity worked and how to generate it. It was not until the 1800s that real progress was made. In 1829 Joseph Henry in the United States invented the first true electric motor, a machine that could use electricity to turn moving parts such as wheels and belts. In the 1870s and 1880s in Britain, Sir William Siemens built the first electric railway and the first electric turbines (machines that make electricity by using water force). The age of electricity began in earnest in 1884. The first electric power station, designed by Thomas Edison, was built in New York. In the modern world electricity is used everywhere.

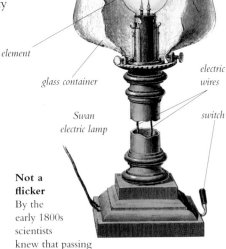

element

glass container

electric wires

Swan electric lamp

switch

Not a flicker
By the early 1800s scientists knew that passing electricity through a thin wire could make it heat up and give out light. But it took until the 1870s for Sir Joseph Swan and Thomas Edison to invent light bulbs that would light an ordinary room without quickly burning out. By the 1880s, the Swan electric lamp was being sold commercially.

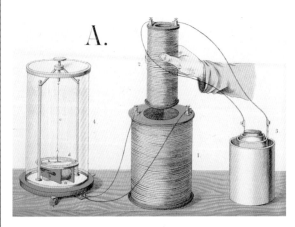

A.

Magnetic power
In 1831 Michael Faraday showed that a magnetic field could produce electricity. Since the 1700s, scientists had experimented to find out if this was possible. Faraday's device produced electricity using changes in the magnetic force of an iron wire. His discovery made it possible to build all later electric generators.

Six-bar sizzler

Electric fires make it very easy for us to warm up when it is cold. The first electric fires were invented in the late 1800s. This fire from the 1900s works in the same way as electric fires of today. Electricity warms up the wire, which is coiled around the bars of the fire to create heat.

1913 Belling electric fire

Bright as day

Electric power enabled work that needed good light, such as making detailed drawings, to be done at night. Before the electric light bulb was invented, people depended on candles, oil lamps and gas lights. They were inconvenient to use. The clear, steady light of electric light bulbs made work easier.

Power from the atom

A nuclear power station contains nuclear reactors that release energy, which generates electricity. The potential of nuclear power was realized with the development of the atomic bomb in World War II. Making electricity from nuclear power is more expensive than using coal. The radiation from the nuclear waste is also very dangerous.

Razzle dazzle

Big cities are full of neon advertisements such as the flashing lights of the Piccadilly Circus in London. In 1910, the French chemist George Claude sealed neon gas into a thin glass tube. He discovered that electricity made the gas give out a bright reddish-orange light. Soon after, ways were invented of using this brightly colored light on the front of buildings to advertise products.

CREATING ENERGY

Energy is needed to do work. Electrical power, steam power, and even horse power are all forms of energy. The two projects described here explore different ways in which energy can do work to make something move. The development of the steam engine and the electric motor in the 1800s provided completely new sources of energy. They used that energy to power ships and railway engines, for example, and to light homes and streets.

The turbine project shows you how the energy of water pouring out of a bottle makes the bottle spin around and around. It is that kind of energy on a much bigger scale that turns turbines in power stations, so generating electricity. The electric motor project shows you how power from an electric battery can turn a cotton reel around and around. Electric motors are used in many household appliances, such as vacuum cleaners and washing machines.

Reservoir power
This hydroelectric power station uses falling water to drive turbines that spin generators. The dam is built across a valley and stores water that comes from streams and rivers. Turbines and generators are inside the dam wall.

MAKE A TURBINE

You will need: scissors, plastic soda bottle, pencil, 2 wide drinking straws, tape, thin string, water.

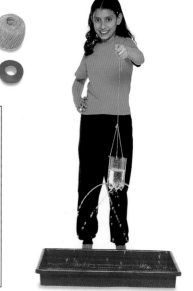

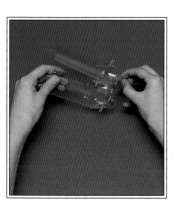

1 Cut off the bottle's top. Use the pencil to poke holes around its base. Cut the straws and push them through the holes. Use tape to hold the straws to the bottle.

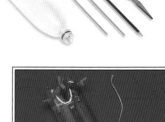

2 Poke three holes around the top of the bottle. Tie three equal lengths of string through the holes and join them to one long piece of string.

3 Hold your turbine over a tray or outdoors so the water will not make a mess. Fill the bottle with water. It squirts out through the straws, causing the bottle to spin.

MAKE AN ELECTRIC MOTOR

You will need: *awl, ruler, plastic modeling board ¼ in. thick, (blue) base 6 x 4 in., 2 (red) end supports 2 x 2 in., 2 (yellow) coil supports, 2½ x2 in., 2(white)coil support spacers 1½ x ½ in., 2 (green) magnet supports 1¼ in. high, glue suitable for sticking plastic, scissors, thin drinking straw, copper wire, aluminum foil, spool of thread, thin tape, knitting needle 6 in. long, 2 powerful bar magnets, 4 paper clips, 2 flexible connecting wires 8 in. long, thick tape, 6-volt battery.*

1 Use the awl to make a hole ½ in. from the top of each of the two end supports. Glue them to the base board, ½ in. inward from the shorter edges.

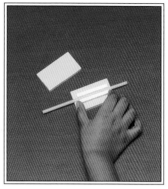

2 Cut a 4¾-in. length of straw. Glue the straw to one coil support. Put the two coil support spacers on either side of the straw. Glue the second support over the top.

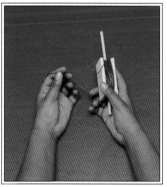

3 Strip ¾ in. of insulation from one end of the wire and 1¼ in. from the other. Wind the wire tight between the coil supports. Slide the reel onto the straw. Cut a strip of foil the width of the reel.

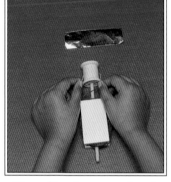

4 From this strip cut enough to fit three-quarters of the way around the reel. Cut it in half. Put the ends of the wire, which must not touch, against the reel. Tape a piece of foil over each wire so the wire is under the foil's center.

5 Stick the reel to the straw. Hold it between the end plates. Slide the knitting needle through the hole in each end plate. Secure the coil support with wooden blocks. Place the magnets on the supports so that the coil and reel spin freely.

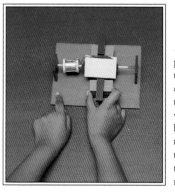

6 Unbend two paper clips to make hooks. Join one end of each to a connecting wire and attach to the base with thick tape. Using paper clips, join the ends of the wires to the battery. The coil should start spinning around.

KEEPING IN TOUCH

IN the modern world, printed information is found in books, magazines, newspapers and downloaded from computers. None of these would exist without writing and alphabets or without the printing press. The first alphabets were invented between 5,000 and 3,500 years ago in the Middle East, India and the Mediterranean. The letters that make up the words in this book belong to the alphabet invented by the ancient Romans 2,500 years ago. The Romans borrowed and altered the ancient Greeks' alphabet.

Before they knew how to make paper, people in Europe wrote on wax tablets or sheets of parchment (animal skins) or carved words in stone and wood. The Chinese invented papermaking almost 2,000 years ago. The Arabs introduced paper to Europe in the 1100s. The Chinese also invented printing on paper about 1,000 years ago but Johannes Gutenberg invented both movable type (cut-out letters) and the printing press in the mid-1400s. Today, the most popular forms of communication are the telephone, e-mail and the Internet.

Written in stone
The ancient Egyptians had no alphabet. They used written signs called hieroglyphs, such as these carved on stone, which illustrate people, animals and gods.

Leaves of skin
Before printing, books in Europe were written by hand. They were often richly decorated. Pictures and writing were made with brushes and pens on parchment.

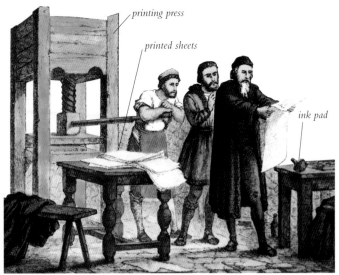

printing press

printed sheets

ink pad

Read all about it
Johannes Gutenberg examines a page from the printing press that he invented. On the table is a pad for putting ink on the type. The type was made up into words and put under the press. The words were inked, a sheet of paper was placed on top of them and the press was squeezed down heavily.

Sharp instruments

The easiest way to write on parchment or paper is to use a long, thin instrument with a nib that releases ink. For centuries, people used quills dipped in ink (sharpened goose or swan feathers) to write. By the 1800s, a way of making metal nibs, such as the one shown here, had been invented. These were much sharper and lasted much longer than quills.

1903
metal pen nib

1924 telephone

Neat letters

Documents written on typewriters are easier to read than handwritten ones because the letter shapes do not change and the lines are evenly spaced. Christopher Sholes, the man who invented the first typewriter, was a printer who wanted to find a way to use type for writing rather than printing multiple copies. Sholes's daughter is shown here in 1872 using one of her father's experimental typewriters.

Long distance calls

The invention of the telephone by Alexander Graham Bell in 1876 opened up a new means of communication to people all over the world. Instead of writing to each other, they could simply pick up a telephone and talk. In the 1960s, telecommunication satellites were launched into orbit above the earth, making it easier and much cheaper to talk to people in other countries, often thousands of miles away.

ON THE WIRE

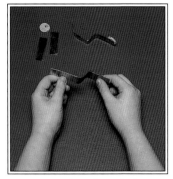

1 Cut ¾ in. from the end of each copper strip. Bend the longer strips to the shape shown here. Glue a circle of cork to one end.

UNTIL about 200 years ago, the best way to send a message was to write a letter and give it to a rider on a fast horse. In 1838 Samuel Morse invented an electric telegraph that could send messages over a wire. Morse installed the first telegraph line between Washington and Baltimore in 1844. The first telegraph cable to span the Atlantic Ocean was laid in 1866. Some people have called the telegraph the Victorian Internet. Morse also invented a special code to use with his telegraph. The code is just like an alphabet, but instead of symbols there are long and short bursts of electricity that make blips of sound.

You can make your own telegraph and use it to communicate with a friend. There are two symbols used in telegraph communication, a dot (.) and a dash (-). Each letter of the alphabet is represented by a different group of dots and dashes.

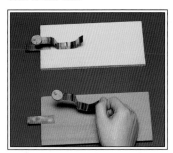

2 Use a drawing pin to attach ¾-in. copper strips to each baseboard. Put one copper strip with the cork on each of the baseboards. Position the cork just over the edge of the board.

MAKE A TELEGRAPH

You will need: scissors, 2 flexible copper strips 4 x 4 in., strong glue, 2 cork circles, 4 drawing pins, 2 pieces of fiberboard 6½ x 3¼ in., screwdriver, 2 bulb holders with screws, 2 bulbs, 2 batteries with holders, 2 paper clips, plastic-covered wire.

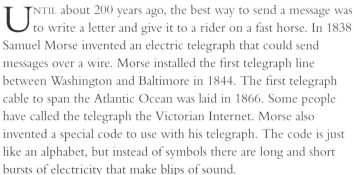

3 Attach each bulb holder to the opposite end of the baseboard. Using a screwdriver, turn the screws clockwise to make them bite into the baseboard.

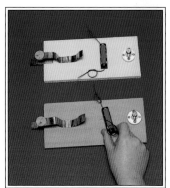

4 Glue a battery holder to each baseboard. Position it midway between the rear of the copper strip and the bulb holder. Remove ½ in. of insulation from each of the wires.

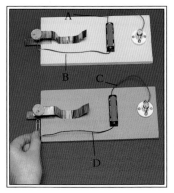

5 Attach the red wires (A and C) to the bulb screws as shown here. Attach the black wires (B and D) to the ¾-in. copper strip with a paper clip.

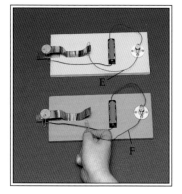 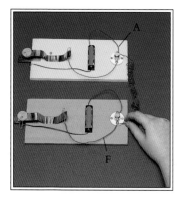 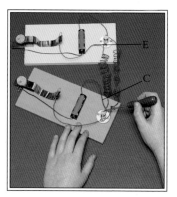

6 Use more wire to connect the rear end of each copper strip to one side of each bulb holder (wires E and F). Tighten the terminals on the holders to make a good connection.

7 Using a length of wire at least a yard long, connect wire A to wire F. Make sure the wires are tightly connected.

8 With an equal length of wire connect wire C to wire E as shown here. Again, make sure the wires are tightly connected.

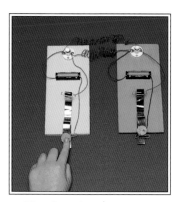

9 The telegraphs are now connected. Press one of the corks down to test whether your telegraph works. Both lights should light up.

10 To make a dash with your telegraph, hold down the cork for half a second, and to make a dot, hold the cork down for a quarter of a second. Now you can try sending messages to a friend. Remember that your partner will have to look up each letter, so leave gaps when sending letters.

Slow talking

A telegraphist of the 1880s could send and receive about 80 letters of the alphabet each minute, which would be about 12 to 15 words a minute. You speak at the rate of about 200 to 300 words a minute.

WARNING!

Please be careful when using electrical equipment. Always have an adult present.

WORLD OF SOUND

PEOPLE communicate by sound when they talk to one another, but if they are too far apart, they cannot hear each other. The discovery in the 1800s that it is possible to send sounds over long distances changed people's lives. It allowed them to speak to one another even though they were hundreds of miles apart. Sound can be carried long distances in two ways, along wires or through the air. When Alexander Graham Bell invented the first telephone in 1876, he used wires to send sound. Telephones continued to use wires for many years. In the late 1800s, an Italian named Guglielmo Marconi invented a device that sent sounds through the air. It was called radio. Today people all over the world communicate by radio. In the 1800s, machines were also invented that allowed people to store sound so that it could be played back after it had been recorded. The first sound recorder, invented by Thomas Edison in 1877, was called a phonograph. In the mid-1900s, ways were invented to record sound onto tape and plastic compact discs (CDs).

Radio genius
Guglielmo Marconi uses the radio equipment he invented. In 1901 he traveled to Newfoundland in Canada and there received the first transatlantic radio message. This proved that messages could be sent by radio over distances as great as the 2,900 miles between Europe and America.

Sound bites
On early phonographs such as this 1903 machine the sound was recorded on a wax-coated cylinder. Each cylinder could only play for three to four minutes. In spite of this, phonographs became very popular.

radio waves

antenna

antenna

radio station

radio

Carried on the air
Sounds such as the human voice are turned into electricity inside a microphone. The electric signal is then transmitted by an antenna as radio waves through the air. These waves travel to an antenna that passes the signal to a radio. The radio can be tuned to turn the signal back into sounds that people can hear.

Sound decorating

By the 1920s, radios and speakers such as this were being made for use in the home. The radio, which was finished in a black textured metal case, was originally designed for use on polar expeditions. The speaker, however, was designed to be as beautiful as a piece of furniture.

The Golden Age

By the 1930s, radio had become an entertainment medium (a way of communicating) that broadcast news and music all over the world. People often called the radio the "wireless" because it was not joined to the transmitting station by wires. Millions listened in on radio sets, like the one shown here, to national radio networks such as NBC in the United States and the BBC in the United Kingdom.

Dramatically vivid discs

This DVD (digital video disc) player offers a richness of sound and clarity of picture not previously available in other machines. Like a CD (compact disc) player, it uses a laser to scan across the surface of a plastic disc. The digitally recorded sounds on the disc are then fed into earphones through which the user listens.

Cool sounds

This type of radio became very popular in the 1950s. It used transistors, which are tiny electronic components that amplify (strengthen) weak radio signals. Transistor radios were also quite small and therefore portable. The transistor was invented in 1948 and is now used in many electronic devices.

LISTEN TO THIS

Play it again, Sam!
You can play deep notes or low notes on a guitar. The sound waves vibrate slowly with a frequency as low as 50 times each second; high notes vibrate much more rapidly.

Sound is energy that moves back and forth through the air as vibrations. These vibrations spread outward as waves, like the ripples caused by a stone dropped into a still lake. Inventors have created ways to communicate by channeling these sounds.

In the first part of this project, you can see how sound waves can be made to travel in a particular direction. Channeling the sound inside a tube concentrates the waves in the direction of the tube. By channeling sound toward a candle, you can use the energy to blow out the flame. The second part of this project shows how sound is a form of energy. Loud sounds carry large amounts of energy. Scientists say that loud sounds have large amplitudes (strengths). The last part investigates pitch (frequency of vibration). Low sounds consist of a small number of vibrations every second. Musicians say low sounds have low pitch, but scientists say they have low frequency. You can make a set of panpipes and see how the pitch depends on the length of each pipe.

HOW SOUND TRAVELS

You will need: plastic wrap, cardboard tube, rubber band, candle, matches.

1 Stretch the plastic wrap tightly over the end of the tube. Use the rubber band to fasten it in place. You could also use a flat piece of rubber cut from a balloon.

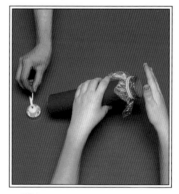

2 Ask an adult to light the candle. Point the tube at the candle, with the open end 4 in. from the flame. Give the plastic wrap a sharp tap with the flat of your hand.

3 You hear the sound coming out of the tube. It consists of pressure waves in the air. The tube concentrates the sound waves toward the candle flame and puts it out.

SOUND WAVES

You will need: *ticking watch, tube 2 in. x 3 ft long.*

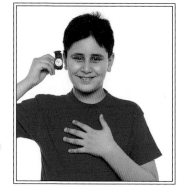

1 Place the watch close to your ear. You can hear a ticking sound coming from it. The sound becomes fainter when you move the watch away from your ear.

2 Place one end of the tube to a friend's ear and hold the watch at the other. The tube concentrates the sound and does not let it spread out. She can hear the watch clearly.

HOW TO MAKE PANPIPES

You will need: *scissors, wide drinking straws, modeling clay, card stock, tape.*

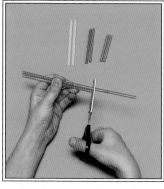

1 Cut the straws so that you have pairs that are 3 ½ in., 3 ¼ in., 2 ¾ in. and 2 ½ in. long. Block one end of each straw with a small piece of modeling clay.

2 Carefully cut out the card stock to the same shape as the blue piece shown above. Tape the straws into place with the modeling clay along the most slanted edge.

3 Gently blow across the tops of the straws. You will find that the longer pipes produce lower notes than the shorter pipes. The longer pipes have a lower pitch and the shorter pipes have a higher pitch.

SEEING MORE

Over the centuries, people have invented instruments that increase the power of the human eye. The microscope allows people to see very small things that are close to them. The telescope lets people see things that are very far away. Both microscopes and telescopes use lenses (specially shaped pieces of glass) to magnify the images that the eye sees. Eyeglasses help people with impaired vision to see clearly.

People knew 2,000 years ago that looking at something through a lens could magnify what they saw. At the beginning of the 1600s the Italian Galileo Galilei invented a tube with two lenses placed in it that allowed him to see details of the surface of the moon. This was the first telescope. Later in the same century, Robert Hooke in England and Antoni van Leeuwenhoek in Holland invented the first microscopes. Since then microscopes and telescopes have become more and more powerful. By the end of the 1900s, telescopes had been built that can let us see stars trillions of miles away. Microscopes now exist that let us see creatures as tiny as germs.

Double vision
In the 1700s Benjamin Franklin, the statesman, writer and scientist, invented bifocal spectacles. Eyeglasses are two lenses combined into one. They enable people to see clearly at both short and long distances.

Looking closely
This is one of the first microscopes ever made. It was invented in the 1600s by the English scientist, Robert Hooke. Through it he could see tiny objects such as the cork cells shown in the book on the left. Hooke shone light through the glass globe on the right to light up the objects he looked at through the microscope.

picture of cork cells

microscope

light focused through globe

Fivefold vision
Doctors soon used microscopes so that they could see the human body's parts in great detail. This microscope, invented in the 1800s, has five barrels to allow five different people to look through it at the same time. It was used in medical schools.

Double barreled

Binoculars such as these were invented in the early 1800s. Like telescopes, they use lenses to make distant objects seem closer, but they have two barrels rather than one. People using binoculars look through both barrels. Binoculars are shorter and easier to carry around than telescopes.

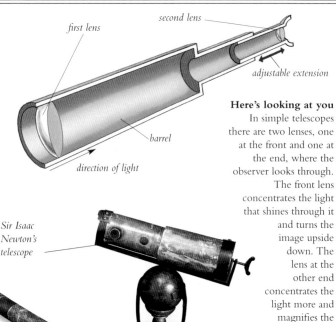

first lens

second lens

adjustable extension

barrel

direction of light

Here's looking at you

In simple telescopes there are two lenses, one at the front and one at the end, where the observer looks through. The front lens concentrates the light that shines through it and turns the image upside down. The lens at the other end concentrates the light more and magnifies the image more.

Stargazer

When the Italian scientist Galileo Galilei learned in the early 1600s about a telescope invented in Holland he decided to make one for himself. He had soon built a telescope through which he could clearly see the craters on the surface of the moon. Galileo's telescope allowed him to discover the four largest of the moons around the planet Jupiter, 370 million miles from Earth. The telescope to the right of Galileo's was invented by Sir Isaac Newton in the late 1600s.

Sir Isaac Newton's telescope

Galileo's telescope

FACT BOX

• The largest mirror used in a telescope is at the Mount Palomar Observatory in California. The mirror is over 16 feet wide and allows those using the telescope to see for enormous distances deep into space.

• Electron microscopes allow people to see objects as tiny as the individual cells that make up our bodies. These microscopes do not use lenses but beams of electrons (electrically charged particles).

Orbiting observatory

The Hubble space telescope was launched into space in 1990. It orbits Earth at a distance of 370 miles. Instead of lenses, it uses mirrors that move to see the stars. The first telescopes like this were invented in the 1600s. The Hubble telescope is much bigger than those. The larger of its two mirrors is 7½ feet wide.

BLOW UP

lens

screw

Inner world
Van Leeuwenhoek's microscope had a spike and a glass lens on a flat sheet. He stuck the object he wanted to view on the spike and turned the screw to bring the object opposite the lens. Then he turned the microscope over and looked through the lens.

THE earliest microscope was invented by the Dutch scientist Antoni van Leeuwenhoek around 1660. It contained a single round glass lens about the size of a raindrop.

If you look at an ordinary magnifying glass you will see that the two surfaces curve slightly. The curved surfaces bend light as it travels from the object to your eye. A window pane has two flat surfaces and so does not act as a magnifying glass. Powerful magnifying glasses have highly curved surfaces. Van Leeuwenhoek realized that a glass sphere has the maximum possible curvature. As a result, a spherical lens has the maximum possible magnification of about 300 times. The invention of this microscope opened up a whole new world. For the first time, people could see pollen grains from flowers, bacteria and the sperm from male animals. In this project you can make a copy of van Leeuwenhoek's microscope by using a tiny droplet of water instead of a glass sphere.

JAM JAR MICROSCOPE

You will need: *two large jam jars, water, a pencil.*

1 Fill a jam jar with water and place it at the edge of a table. Look through the jar with one eye and move the pencil back and forth behind the jam jar.

2 Find the position that gives the clearest image with the greatest magnification.

3 Place a second water-filled jam jar close behind the first one. Hold the pencil in the water in the second jar. Move the pencil back and forth.

4 You will find that the image is about four or five times larger than before.

WATER DROP MAGNIFIER

You will need: *small aluminum foil disk, metal spoon, candle, small nail, water, flower.*

1 Place the disk on a hard surface. Use the outer bowl of a spoon to flatten the disk. Stroke the spoon from side to side until the centre of the disk is flat and smooth.

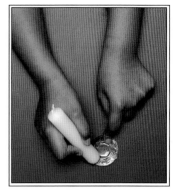

2 Rub the disk on both sides with the end of a candle. Make certain that both sides of the smooth center part are coated with a thin layer of wax.

3 Push the nail through the center of the disk to make a small hole in it. The hole should be perfectly round and measure about ⅛ in. across.

4 Collect water on a fingertip so that a droplet hangs down. Hold the disk flat and lower the drop onto the hole. The wax holds the water in a round lens shape.

5 To use your magnifier, hold it about ½ to ¾ in. from the object. Now bring your eye as close to the water droplet as possible. Look at how the flower is magnified.

The world in a grain of sand
This woman is using van Leeuwenhoek's simple microscope by pressing it against her eye. Unlike most later microscopes, this was not a heavy instrument that could not be moved easily but a light, portable object. By using this microscope, scientists were able to discover much more about the world around us, including the insides of our own bodies.

WINDOW ON THE WORLD

ONCE Guglielmo Marconi had invented a way to broadcast sound and people became interested in radio, inventors tried to find a way to broadcast pictures. John Logie Baird, a Scottish inventor, set himself the task of achieving this. Unfortunately, no one else believed it was possible to broadcast pictures and he was forced to work alone and in great poverty.

In 1926, Baird finally succeeded in sending a picture a few yards, but his way of sending pictures was not perfect. In the 1930s Vladimir Zworykin, a Russian electrical engineer, invented a better way to send pictures by using electricity to run through a cathode ray tube. Zworykin's invention was essential for modern television. The first public television programs were broadcast by the BBC in Britain in 1936, and by the 1950s, televisions were beginning to appear in every home in the United States and Europe.

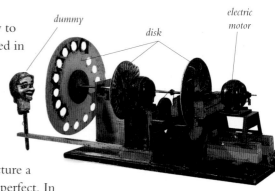

dummy

disk

electric motor

Spinning circle
The first picture to be captured as electrical impulses was a dummy's head. Baird placed three disks with holes in them in front of the dummy. These created flashing patterns of light that were turned into electrical impulses by a photoelectric cell (device for turning light into electricity).

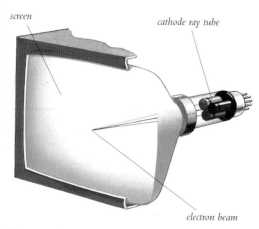

screen

cathode ray tube

electron beam

Tube travel
The cathode ray tube is the heart of a television. Pictures are received by the antenna in the form of electrical impulses. These impulses control a stream of electrons inside the cathode ray tube. The electron beam scans across the screen and creates the picture as points of colored light. This is the picture that the viewer sees.

Box in the corner
The televisions that large numbers of people first began to buy in the 1950s looked very much like this one. The screens were small and the pictures could only be seen as black-and-white images. Reception was also difficult because there were very few transmitters.

1950s television

Light in the gloom
When television was first widely broadcast, people saw it as something very new. Most programs were broadcast only in the evenings, and families gathered together to enjoy this new form of entertainment. Gradually more and more people bought televisions.

Moving eye
The cameras used in modern television studios are much more complicated devices than John Logie Baird's invention. This camera is on wheels and can move around the people or objects being filmed. It can move in closer and tilt up or down. Inside the camera, the image is changed into electrical impulses.

Super cool
Modern television screens are much bigger than those available in the 1950s and most are in color. Flat-screen televisions, such as this one, first became available in the early 1990s. These televisions do not have cathode-ray tubes. Liquid crystals display the picture on the screen.

SCREEN SCENES

THE picture on a television screen is made up of thin lines of light. Follow the instructions in this project, and you will also see that the picture consists of just three colors—red, green and blue. Viewed from a distance, these colors mix to produce the full range of colors that we see naturally around us. A TV picture is just rows of glowing dots of colored light. Fax machines work much like TVs, only more slowly. Feed a sheet of paper into a fax machine, and a beam of light moves back and forth across it. Dark places absorb the light and pale places reflect it. The reflected light enters a detector that produces an electric current. The strength of the current depends on the intensity of the reflected light. The electric current is changed into a code made up from chirping sounds that travel down the line to the receiving fax machine. The code controls a scanner that moves across heat-sensitive paper and produces a *facsimile* (copy) of the original. The last part of this project shows how a fax machine breaks an image into tiny areas that are either black or white.

Fast messages
A fax machine sends pictures or writing down the phone line to another fax machine in seconds. The first fax machine was invented in 1904 by the German physicist Arthur Korn. They became common in the 1980s, but they are slowly being replaced by electronic e-mail.

LOOKING AT A TV PICTURE

You will need: TV set, flashlight, powerful magnifying glass.

1 Turn off the TV. Shine the flashlight close to the screen and look through the magnifying glass. You will see that the screen is covered in very fine lines.

2 Turn on the TV and view the screen through the lens. The picture is made up of minute rectangles of light colored red, green and blue.

SECONDARY COLORS

You will need: *red, green and blue transparent cellophane, 3 powerful flashlights, 3 rubber bands, white card stock.*

1 Attach a piece of colored cellophane over the end of each flashlight. Stretch the cellophane tightly and use a rubber band to hold it firmly in place.

2 Shine the flashlights onto the white card stock. You can see the three different primary colors of red, green and blue.

3 Position the flashlights so that the three circles of colored light overlap in a cloverleaf pattern. Overlapping colors mix to give new colors.

DIGITAL IMAGES

You will need: *ruler, tracing paper, photograph, black felt pen.*

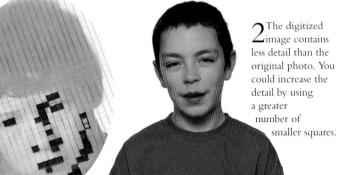

1 Measure lines ¼ in. apart to cover the tracing paper in squares. Put the paper over the photograph. Use the pen to fill each dark square. Leave each light square.

The picture is made from squares that are either black or white.

2 The digitized image contains less detail than the original photo. You could increase the detail by using a greater number of smaller squares.

RAW MATERIALS

Human beings have learned over thousands of years that it is possible to change raw materials to make them more usable. Between 6,000 and 3,500 years ago people discovered that they could obtain metals such as copper and iron by heating ore (rock that contains metals). The metals were then heated and shaped to make tools, weapons and ornaments. Metals are still used all over the world to make millions of useful objects.

Another breakthrough in the use of natural resources was grinding flour to bake to make bread. The Chinese discovered 2,000 years ago that tree bark, old rags and rope could be made into pulp and then dried to make paper. In the 1800s, from rocks deep in the earth, oil was discovered as a new source of energy. Later, people learned how to use oil to make plastics and other synthetics. Today oil is the greatest single raw material used throughout the world.

The age of bronze
About 6,000 years ago, in what is now the Middle East, people first learned how to mix metals to make an alloy. They dug up ores that contained copper and tin, and smelted them together. From this new metal they created tools and weapons such as this sword. Bronze was much more useful than pure copper because it lasted longer and could be sharpened repeatedly. Gradually, other people learned how to make bronze.

Mysterious knowledge
Lead cannot be turned into gold, but during medieval times many people, such as this alchemist, believed that it was possible. An alchemist drew on his knowledge of chemistry and magic to try turning lead into gold. People feared that the alchemists were magicians. Although the alchemists never made gold from lead, they did pave the way for modern chemistry.

A taste of steel
The Bessemer converter marked a new way of making steel in the mid-1800s. The British inventor Sir Henry Bessemer had been making cannons out of iron for use in the Crimean War, when he had the idea for the converter. Air is blown into molten iron inside the converter, taking away any impurities and creating strong steel for use in many different industries.

Brand-new material

In the early 1900s, the chemist Leo Baekeland invented a way of creating a thick liquid from chemicals which, when it hardened, became a new material that no one had ever seen before. He called this material Bakelite. It was long lasting and could be shaped to make many different kinds of objects, such as this radio case.

Strong and light

In the late 1800s, the electrolytic cell was invented as a way of using electricity to extract the light, strong metal called aluminum from bauxite ore. Aluminum is used when strong, light metal is needed, for example when building aircraft.

Riding on air

When motor cars were invented in the late 1800s their wheels were hard, like cart wheels. Charles Goodyear invented a process that made rubber hard and allowed people to make car tires from it. Inside the tires were inner tubes filled with air, which were first invented in 1845 by Robert Thomson.

CHEMICAL CHANGE

D URING the past 100 years, scientists have invented many substances that we take for granted today. Examples include plastics, medicines, detergents and fuels. These new substances are created by mixing natural substances that react to each other. These are called chemical reactions. There are just three main ways in which chemical reactions can happen: passing electricity through substances, heating them or combining them.

These experiments show the three ways in which chemical reactions can happen. In the first project, electricity breaks down salty water to make chlorine, which is a disinfectant used to keep swimming pools clean. In the second project, you heat sugar, which is made from carbon, hydrogen and oxygen, to create pure carbon. The third shows how to make the gas used in some fire extinguishers. This gas is made by combing baking soda and vinegar to create carbon dioxide.

Measuring
In a laboratory, this scientist is carefully measuring the exact amount of chemicals to add to a test tube in which the experiment will take place. In science, accuracy is very important.

ELECTROLYSIS

You will need: screwdriver, battery (4–6 volts), bulb and holder, wire, 2 paper clips, jar, water, salt.

WARNING!
Please be careful when using electrical equipment.
Always have an adult present.

1 Connect the battery and bulb holder with wires as shown here. Remove ½ in. of insulation from each end. Use the paper clips to join the wires to the battery.

2 Stir salt into a jar of water until no more dissolves. Dip the two bare wire ends into the mixture and hold them about ½ in. apart. Look for bubbles forming around them.

3 The bulb should light to show that electricity is passing through. Carefully sniff the jar from 8 in. away. The smell is like swimming pools.

HEAT CHANGES

You will need: old pan, teaspoon, sugar, stove.

1 Make sure the pan is completely dry. Spread one teaspoonful of sugar across the bottom of the pan. Aim for a thin layer an ⅛ in. thick.

2 Place the pan on a burner over low heat. After a few minutes, the sugar will start to melt and turn into an amber liquid. You may see a few wisps of steam.

3 The sugar starts to bubble as it breaks down and gives off steam. If you continue heating it, the liquid will change to solid black carbon.

MIXING THINGS

You will need: teaspoon, baking soda, glass bowl, vinegar, matches.

1 Place three heaping spoonfuls of baking soda in the bowl. Cooks sometimes add this white powder to vegetables such as peas and carrots. It helps to keep their natural color.

2 Pour vinegar into the bowl. As the liquid mixes with the white, powdery baking soda, a chemical reaction happens. The mixture bubbles as a gas is given off.

3 Ask an adult to light a match and lower the flame into the bowl. The chemical reaction has made a gas called carbon dioxide. The flame goes out when it meets the gas.

WAIT A SECOND

Shadow of time
An ancient Roman sundial is cut in the shape of a shell from a block of marble. Sundials were made in many shapes and sizes. People could judge the time by watching as the shadow cast by the sun moved from one line to another.

Sometimes we say time lays heavily on our hands. At other times we say it goes by in a flash. How do we know how much time has actually passed? The easiest way to tell the time is to watch the sun as it rises in the morning and sets in the evening. But people have always wanted to measure time more accurately. This led to the invention of the sundial. The oldest sundials known are Egyptian and are more than 5,000 years old.

Today we use clocks and watches to measure time. The first clocks were invented in the 1300s. They had wheels and cogs, weights and pendulums that worked together to turn the hands of the clock. Portable, pocket-size watches were invented in the 1600s, when people discovered how to use springs rather than big weights and pendulums to turn the hands of clocks. Watches became smaller but had to be wound regularly. In the 1920s the self-winding watch mechanism was invented. Most modern watches are now electronic, not mechanical.

The sun and stars
This clock in St. Mark's square in Venice dates from the late 1300s. At this time clocks were very large and often built in or near churches because they were too big to fit in homes. Its face is decorated with astrological images of the animals and gods that were used to represent the different seasons and months of the year.

Tracking the sun
Before the 1700s, ships' captains relied on quadrants to find out where they were. They used quadrants to estimate the hour of the day, which helped them to know where on Earth they were. This particular quadrant was designed by the English mathematician, Edmund Gunter, in the early 1600s.

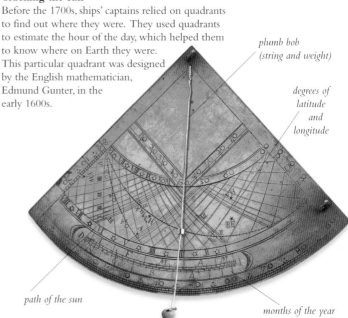

plumb bob (string and weight)

degrees of latitude and longitude

path of the sun

months of the year

At sea

Sailors far from land needed to know the time so they could figure out where they were. They needed accurate clocks to figure out the time it had taken to travel a distance. In the 1700s a prize was offered by the British government to invent a marine chronometer (ship's clock) that would keep accurate time on-board ships. John Harrison worked at the problem for 34 years and invented four watches. The last of them won the prize.

Precious object

A pocket watch was expensive to make and owned only by those with money to spend. A metal case protected the watch from bumps and knocks. This watch was made in 1759. Its many tiny wheels and cogs would have taken months for a skilled watchmaker to make and put together.

hour hand cog

winding cog

minute hand cog

All in one

Some modern watches use a liquid crystal display (LCD) to show the time in digital form. In addition to giving hours and seconds, the watch also displays the day of the week, the month and the year. Other functions can be used by touching the icons at the bottom of the watch face.

Split seconds

Willard Libby, who won the Nobel Prize for Chemistry in 1960, invented the atomic clock. An atomic clock tells the time using the extremely regular changes in the energy inside individual atoms. Clocks such as these can tell the time to within one second over thousands of years.

RIVER OF TIME

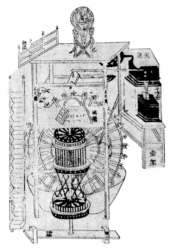

Water timer
This Chinese water clock was built in 1088. Water trickles into tiny buckets attached to the outside of a large wheel. As each bucket fills up, the wheel clicks around to the next empty bucket. Each bucket empties as it reaches the lowest position. The position of the wheel indicates the time.

THE Ancient Egyptians invented water clocks in about 3000 B.C. because the sundials they used could not tell the time at night. Water clocks use water that slowly drips from a bowl, and the level of the surface of the remaining water indicates the time. However, a water clock cannot tell the time until you have compared it with another clock. You can make a water clock in the second part of this project.

In 1581, the Italian Galileo Galilei studied how different pendulums swinging back and forth could indicate time. He discovered that the time depends only on the length of the pendulum. It is not affected by the mass of the pendulum, or how far it swings from side to side. You can repeat Galileo's important experiment in the first part of this project. In 1641, Galileo's son Vincenzio Galilei constructed a mechanical clock that used a weighted pendulum to control the speed of hands across a clockface. All grandfather and grandmother clocks work like this. However, pendulums are not always accurate because their speed can vary depending on changes such as heat.

MAKE A PENDULUM

You will need: modeling clay, string, stopwatch.

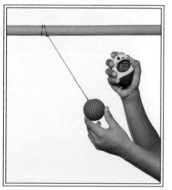

1 Roll some clay to make a ball 1½ in. across. Use string to hang it 12 in. below a support. Pull the ball out to the position shown. Let go and time 10 complete swings.

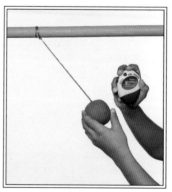

2 Repeat the experiment. This time, use a larger heavier ball with the same piece of string. You will find that the time for ten swings is the same despite the heavier ball.

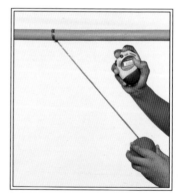

3 Increase the length of your pendulum by hanging the ball from a longer piece of string. You will find that the pendulum swings more slowly than before.

MAKE A WATER CLOCK

You will need: awl, aluminum pie pan, drinking straw, large plastic tumbler, scissors, water, pitcher, marker.

1 Use the awl to make a small hole in the bottom of the pie pan. The smaller the hole, the longer your water clock will run.

2 Place the drinking straw in the bottom of the plastic tumbler. It will act as a pointer as the water level rises. Cut the straw with a pair of scissors if it is too long.

3 Place the pie pan on top of the plastic tumbler. Make sure the hole in the pie dish is over the center of the tumbler.

4 Pour water from a pitcher into the pie dish. Keep adding water until the dish is full. As soon as water starts to fall into the tumbler, note the time on your watch.

5 After 10 minutes, use the marker to mark the water level on the side of the tumbler. As the water drips into the tumbler, mark the level at 10-minute intervals.

You can use your pie-pan water clock to time your eggs for breakfast.

6 After half an hour, you will have three marks up the side of the tumbler. Empty out the water, refill the pie pan and you can use your water clock to measure time passing.

THINGS TO COME

THE pace of invention has increased dramatically since the 1800s and there is no sign of it slowing down. Almost every week new inventions are announced. A recent invention for replanting trees by dropping saplings from the air could make forests grow again in many parts of the earth. Computerized map systems have been developed that make it impossible to get lost when traveling.

Many new inventions are things we hardly notice, such as the material Velcro that holds surfaces together and is sometimes used instead of buttons and zippers on clothes. Some inventions are useful only in special situations. Kevlar is a recently invented, bullet-proof material that is very valuable for soldiers and policemen but rarely used in everyday life. Understanding of the genetic structures of living organisms is increasing all the time. In the future people may be able to choose what color their baby's hair will be! One thing is certain: whatever happens, people will never stop inventing.

Electronic circuits
Semiconductors are essential for making many of the electronic devices that we use every day, from pocket calculators to personal computers. Semiconductors are used to make electricity flow through tiny circuits in complex patterns that control how machines work.

Solar energy
People are trying increasingly to find new sources of energy because the old ones, such as coal and gas, will be used up in the future. Solar energy (the heat and light of the sun) is one new energy source. This Russian space module, part of the international space station (ISS), is powered by the solar energy panels that fan out on either side of it. The panels convert heat and light into energy.

Russian space module

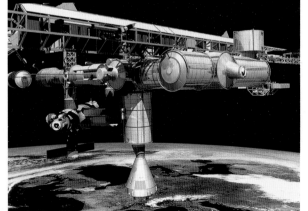

Village in orbit
The international space station is due to be completed in 2004. It is being built with the cooperation of 16 different countries throughout the world. They hope that having this permanent space station in orbit will allow scientists to make discoveries in space that will advance medicine, science and engineering.

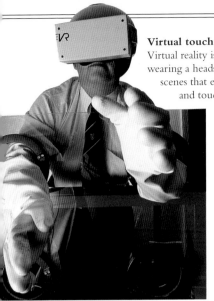

Virtual touch
Virtual reality is an invention that allows users wearing a headset and gloves to see and feel scenes that exist only on a computer. Looking and touching in this way can be a very helpful way of training people to use machines. For example, pilots can be trained to fly a new aircraft without actually going into the air.

Talk to me
A scientist is looking at a graph that shows the word "baby" on a computer screen. It is part of research into how computers can reply to human voices. If people could talk to computers, using them would be easier.

Safe energy
The biggest problem with energy produced using nuclear fuel is the danger of radiation that can kill people. Some scientists recently believed that they had found a way to generate energy using the cold-fusion process shown here. The process creates energy by nuclear fusion without making radioactivity. It is uncertain whether this process can be used on a large scale or even repeated easily.

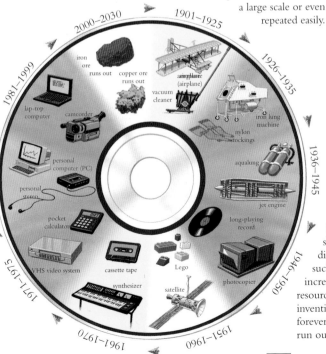

2000–2030
1901–1925
1981–1999
1926–1935
iron ore runs out
copper ore runs out
aeroplane (airplane)
vacuum cleaner
lap-top computer
camcorder
iron lung machine
nylon stockings
personal computer (PC)
aqualung
1936–1945
personal stereo
jet engine
pocket calculator
long-playing record
1976–1980
VHS video system
cassette tape
Lego
photocopier
1946–1950
synthesizer
satellite
1971–1975
1961–1970
1951–1960

Still turning
Some of the many inventions since 1900 are shown inside the circle of this CD (compact disc). In the last 40 years, electronic inventions, such as video and CD technology, have been used increasingly in homes everywhere. However, the resources on which people rely to make new inventions, such as copper and iron, will not last forever. In particular, copper ore will start to run out in 25 years.

PART TWO

MACHINES

However complex modern machines are, many
of them use very simple devices that have been
employed for thousands of years. The wheel, the
pulley and the lever all helped to build the ancient
pyramids of Egypt. Added to other simple
devices, such as the screw and the gear wheel,
they allowed people to make spectacular advances
in what they could accomplish. The engines and
motors developed in the 1800s allowed another
great leap forward, and the computers of today
are creating a revolution that may be even more
wide-reaching.

AUTHOR
Chris Oxlade
CONSULTANT
Graham Peacock

WHAT IS A MACHINE?

screwdriver

pliers

scissors

hammer

wrenches

Thousands of different devices can be called machines, from calculators and televisions to trucks and aircraft. Scissors and staplers are very simple machines, while computers and cars are complicated. All machines have one thing in common: they help us do jobs and therefore make our lives easier.

Think about what you did yesterday. Make a list of every machine you can remember that you used or saw, from when you woke up to when you went back to bed. Many things that we take for granted, such as opening a can, cutting paper and tightening a screw, can only be done with a machine. Other jobs, such as washing clothes, used to be done by hand but nowadays are usually done by machine. Machines are being improved—and new ones invented—all the time. We may find that tasks that take a long time today become much easier and faster to do in the future.

Simple machines
Tools such as these are simple machines that are useful to have at home. They each do a task that would be much more difficult without them. Can you think of a job for each tool?

Useful screws
The parts of this model helicopter are attached with screws. The screws are machines because they do the job of holding the helicopter parts in place.

Domestic machines
A microwave oven is one of the many machines that people use at home to make preparing and cooking food quicker and simpler. Other domestic machines include vacuum cleaners and washing machines.

Using tools
This girl uses a wrench to tighten the nuts on her model helicopter. A wrench is a simple tool that is used to tighten up, or undo, nuts. Using the wrench is more efficient than if the girl used her fingers alone, because the wrench can make joints much tighter and more secure.

FACT BOX

• Leonardo da Vinci (1452–1519) was an Italian artist and inventor. He drew plans for machines, such as tanks and aircraft, that were hundreds of years ahead of their time.

• Greek scientist Hero of Alexandria lived in the 1st century A.D. He invented a steam engine, a slot machine and a screw press.

Old farm machines

People use many different machines to help them farm the land in this picture, which was painted in about 1400. Some of the first machines ever invented were used by farmers. At the bottom of the picture is a plow, and halfway up on the right-hand side is a water-wheel. At the top, by a church, is a machine called a shaduf, which was used to raise water from a deep well. Next to the shaduf is a machine that was used for sowing seeds.

Calculating machine

Unlike most of the other machines shown here, a computer does not help lift, move or cut things. Instead it makes life easier by remembering information and doing calculations. Computers help us to work faster and more accurately. They can do amazing work—such as controlling the flight path of a spacecraft.

Construction machines

Diggers and cranes are used on a construction (building) site. These huge machines are clearing the site of rubble before the buildings are restored. Construction machines have powerful engines for moving and lifting heavy loads, such as soil, rocks, steel and concrete.

Travel by machine

To travel from place to place you need a machine to get you there. The space shuttle is a machine that transports people into space. Its powerful rocket engines launch it through Earth's atmosphere. Other transport machines, such as cars and trains, also have engines. Their engines are much less powerful than those on a spacecraft.

Chopping machine

A hand axe is used to chop large logs into smaller pieces. When the woman brings the axe down, the sharp blade slices into the wood, forcing it to split apart. The axe is a simple machine, but it is very effective. It does a job that is impossible to do by hand.

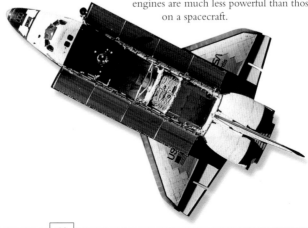

POWERFUL LEVERS

Six simple machines that were invented thousands of years ago are still the basic elements of all machinery. These machines are the lever, the wheel and axle, the inclined plane or ramp, the wedge, the screw and the pulley. The simplest, and probably the oldest, is the lever. A lever is a bar or rod that tilts on an object called a pivot. You only need a small push down on one end to raise a large weight on the end nearer to the pivot. Any rod or stick can act as a lever, helping to move heavy objects or prise things apart. The lever makes the power of the push into a much larger push. This is known as mechanical advantage.

Did you know that some parts of your body are levers? Every time you brush your hair or get up from a chair, the bones in your arms and legs act as levers, helping you to lift your limbs.

Shut the door
Closing a door near the hinge is hard work. It is easier to press on the handle because the door is a lever. Its pivot is made by the hinges. The door turns your small push on the handle into a bigger push.

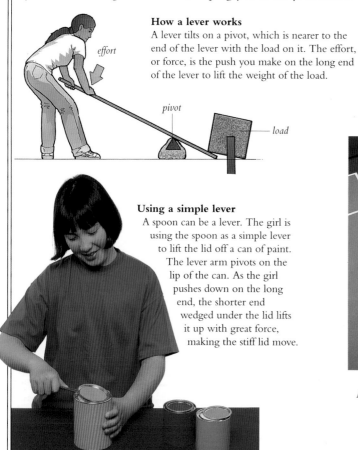

How a lever works
A lever tilts on a pivot, which is nearer to the end of the lever with the load on it. The effort, or force, is the push you make on the long end of the lever to lift the weight of the load.

effort

pivot

load

Using a simple lever
A spoon can be a lever. The girl is using the spoon as a simple lever to lift the lid off a can of paint. The lever arm pivots on the lip of the can. As the girl pushes down on the long end, the shorter end wedged under the lid lifts it up with great force, making the stiff lid move.

Levers in the body
A tennis player uses muscle-powered levers in her shoulders and elbows to serve the ball at high speed. Small movements of the muscles cause large movements of the racket, which gives the racket the speed for a fast serve.

LEVERS AND LIFTING

1 A ruler can be used as a lever to lift a book. With the pivot (the box) near the book, only a small effort is needed to lift the book up. The lever makes the push larger.

2 When the pivot is moved to the middle of the lever, the effort needed to lift the book up is equal to the book's weight. The effort and the load are the same.

3 When the pivot is near where the boy is pressing, more effort is needed to lift the book. The force of the push needed to lift the book is now larger than the book's weight.

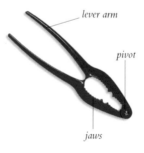

lever arm

pivot

jaws

The strong crushing action of the nutcracker's jaws is produced by pressing the two lever arms together.

Raising water

In Middle Eastern countries, farmers use a machine called a shaduf to lift water to irrigate their crops. The arm of a shaduf is a lever with a bucket on one end and a weight on the other, pivoted on the top of a wooden frame. The shaduf operator pulls the empty bucket down into the water using a rope. The weight at the other end acts as the effort, lifting the bucket of water (the load). The shaduf is an ancient machine, used by farmers for thousands of years.

Cracking a nut

A pair of nutcrackers, like a pair of scissors or a pair of pliers, has two lever arms joined at a pivot. Pressing the ends of the nutcracker arms together crushes the nut in its jaws. The levers make the effort you use about four times greater, allowing you to break the nut quite easily. Putting the pivot at the end of the levers rather than toward the center (as in a pair of scissors) means that the arms of the cracker can be shorter but still create a force just as great.

63

BALANCING LEVERS

Levers are used for lifting, cutting and crushing. A lever on a central pivot can also be used as a balance. The lever balances if the effect of the force (push) on one side of the pivot is the same as the effect of the force on the other. A see-saw is one kind of balancing lever. It is a plank balanced on a center post or pivot. Someone small and light can balance a much bigger person if they sit in the right position on a see-saw.

Outside the playground, balancing levers have other important uses. By using a lever to balance one force with another, the size of one force can be compared to the size of another. This is how a weighing machine called a balance scale works. It measures the mass (weight) of an object by comparing it with standard weights such as ounces and pounds.

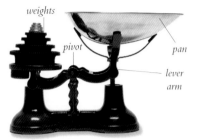

weights *pivot* *pan* *lever arm*

Weighing up
Balance scales like this one were once used for weighing things at stores and in the kitchen. To make the lever arm balance, the weights on the left must equal the weight in the pan.

Using a balance scale
An object, such as a pile of strawberries, is put in a pan resting on one end of the lever arm. Weights are added to the other end of the arm until the arm balances. Then the individual weights are added up to find the weight of the object. We call the result "weight" because we measure the force needed to balance the weight of the object. In fact, a balance scale measures pounds.

Balanced crossing gates
A grade-crossing gate is actually a balanced lever. The pivot is at the side of the road, with the gate to one side and a heavy counterweight on the other side to balance it. This means that only a small effort is needed from electric motors to move the lever up or down. The gates are operated automatically by electronics linked to the railroad's signaling system.

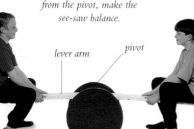

Two children of equal weight, the same distance from the pivot, make the see-saw balance.

lever arm   pivot

Balancing a see-saw

A see-saw shows the effect of moving a weight nearer or farther from the pivot of a lever arm. Two children of equal weight, the same distance from the pivot, make a see-saw balance. If another child is added to one end, the arm overbalances to that side. By moving the single child farther from the pivot, or the pair closer to it, the arm balances again.

By adding another child to one side, that side overbalances. The pair's greater weight easily lifts the lighter boy.

FACT BOX

• Stone Age people were probably the first to use levers. They may have used branches as levers to move heavy rocks.

• Balance scales were invented by the ancient Egyptians so that they could weigh gold. Gold was precious, so it needed to be weighed accurately.

• A trebuchet was a medieval war machine like a giant catapult. It was based on the lever arm. It was used to hurl boulders at the enemy up to ⅓ mile away.

By moving the pair nearer the pivot, their weight can be balanced by the lighter boy moving farther away.

Investigating balance

Make a ruler balance on a tube. Now put different-sized piles of coins at different positions on each end so that they balance. For example, you can make one coin balance two coins if the single coin is twice as far from the pivot as the other coins.

ALL KINDS OF LEVERS

Levers are very common machines. Look around you and see how many levers you can find—don't forget the levers in your own body! Each of the machines shown here has a diagram to show you where the pivot, effort and load are, to help you to see how the lever is working.

Levers are divided into three different basic kinds, or classes. The most common type is a first-class lever, where the pivot is always between the load and the effort, as with a see-saw, a pair of pliers or a spade. In second-class levers, the load is between the pivot and the effort. Nutcrackers and wheelbarrows are examples of these. In a third-class lever, the effort is between the pivot and the load, as with hammers, tweezers and fishing rods.

Spade work

A spade is a first-class lever for lifting and turning soil. A sharp blade makes it easy to push the spade into the soil. Pressing down on the handle is the effort, the pivot is your foot on the blade and the load is the soil. Pushing the handle down levers the soil up.

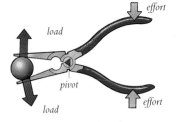

In a pair of pliers, the effort is pressing down on handles. The load is the resistance that an object has to being crushed in the jaws of the pliers.

effort

load

pivot

Lifting the handles of a wheelbarrow lifts a heavy load nearer the pivot, or wheel.

First-class levers
A pair of pliers has two lever arms linked at the pivot by a hinge. They are first-class levers because the pivot is between the load and the effort. The handles are on one side of the pivot and the jaws are on the other.

Second-class levers
A wheelbarrow does not look like a lever, but it is one. The lever arm goes from the end of the handle to the center of the wheel, which is the pivot. A small effort pulling up on the handles lifts the load in the barrow.

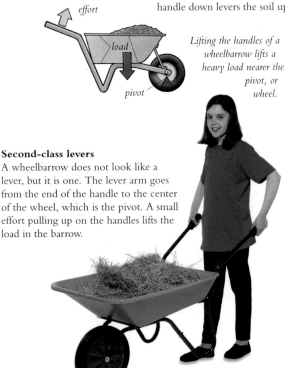

A hammer acts as a lever when you use your wrist as a pivot. Your fingers make the effort to lift the hammer's head.

Third-class levers

A hammer may not look like a lever, but it is. The handle joins with your hand to make the lever arm, with your wrist as the pivot. Your fingers supply the effort to make the hammer head move down. The load is the weight of the hammer head. The small movement of your arm makes a large movement in the hammer head to drive the nail into the wood.

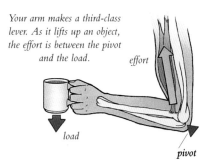

Gone fishing

A fishing rod is a third-class lever, similar to the hammer above. The pivot is at the fisherman's wrist. The effort is made by his hand, and the load is the weight of the rod and the fish on the line. An effort much greater than the load is needed to lift the rod. The advantage of the rod is that only a small movement of the fisherman's arm makes a large movement at the end of the rod. So a flick of the wrist casts the line which floats far across the water.

FACT BOX

• The longer a lever arm, the greater the force. Using a lever (it would have to be a strong lever) 30 feet long, with a pivot 4 inches from the end, you could lift an elephant with one finger!

• A piano is full of levers. Each key is a lever with other levers attached to it. When you press a key, the levers make hammers fly at the strings.

Body levers

The lower bones in your arm form a third-class lever with the pivot at your elbow. The muscle at the front of your upper arm is called the biceps. It makes the effort to lift a weight in your hand, which is the load.

Your arm makes a third-class lever. As it lifts up an object, the effort is between the pivot and the load.

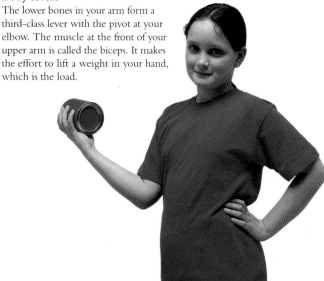

MAKING LEVERS WORK

MAKE A GRIPPER

You will need: short pencil, two pieces of wood each about 6 in. long, thick rubber bands, objects to pick up or crush such as candy or grapes.

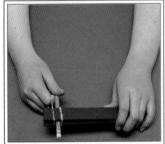

You can find out how to make two different lever machines in the projects here. The first is a simple gripper for picking up or crushing objects. It can act both as a pair of nutcrackers (a second-class lever) or a pair of tweezers (a third-class lever). In a pair of nutcrackers, the load (in this case a piece of candy) is between the pivot (the pencil) and the effort (where you push). In a pair of tweezers, the effort is between the pivot and the load. Draw a lever diagram that shows both ways of using lever machines to help you understand how each one works.

The second machine is a balance scale. It is like the ones used by the Romans about 2,000 years ago. It works by balancing the weight of an object against a known weight, in this case a bag of coins. The coins are moved along the lever arm until they balance the object being weighed. The further away from the pivot the weighted bag is, the greater turning effect it has on the lever arm. The heavier the weight being measured, the further the bag must be moved to balance the arm. The weight is read off from the scale along the arm.

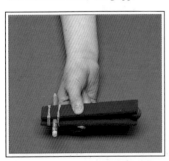

1 Put the pencil between the two pieces of wood, near one end. Wrap the rubber bands tightly around the pieces of wood to make a pivot. You have now made the gripper.

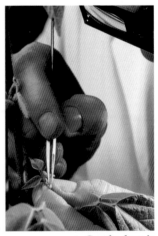

Gently does it
A pair of tweezers is used to pick up minute grains of pollen. Tweezers make it easier to pick up tiny or delicate objects. The tweezers act as a third-class lever, so the force that squeezes the object is smaller than the effort you use.

2 Hold the gripper near the pivot to make it act like a pair of tweezers. See if you can pick up a delicate object, such as a piece of candy or a grape, without crushing the object.

3 Holding the gripper at the other end makes a pair of nutcrackers. It increases the force you make. Try using the nutcrackers to crack a small nut or to crush a small sweet.

MAKE A BALANCE SCALE

You will need*: thick cardboard about 20 x 3 in., thin card stock, scissors, string, ruler, hole punch, 5-in. circle of cardboard, tape, 3¼ oz coins, felt-tipped pen, objects to weigh.*

1 Make the arm by folding the thick cardboard in two. Make a loop of thin card stock and attach it to the arm so that its center is 4½ in. from one end. Tie a piece of string to this support.

2 Make a hole ½ in. from the arm's end. Make the cardboard circle into a cone-shaped pan and tie it to the hole. Make an envelope and tie it to a loop so that it hangs over the arm.

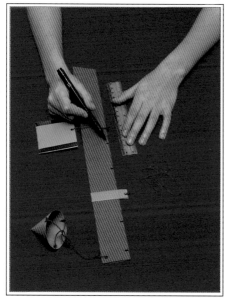

3 Put the 3¼ oz of coins in the envelope and seal it up. Starting from the center of the support, make a mark every 2 in. along the arm. This scale will enable you to figure out the weight of any object you put in the pan because each mark equals 1½ oz.

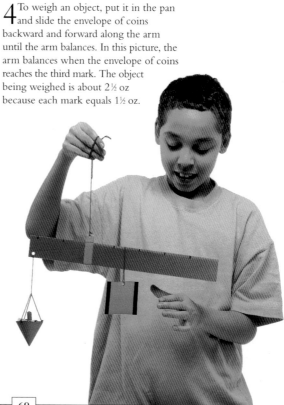

4 To weigh an object, put it in the pan and slide the envelope of coins backward and forward along the arm until the arm balances. In this picture, the arm balances when the envelope of coins reaches the third mark. The object being weighed is about 2½ oz because each mark equals 1½ oz.

WHEELS AND AXLES

The wheel is one of the most important inventions ever made. About 6,000 years ago, people discovered that using logs as rollers was a more efficient way to move heavy loads than to drag them. A slice from a log was the first wheel. Then people found that they could attach a wheel to the end of a pole. The pole became an axle.

A wheel on the end of an axle makes a simple machine. Turning the wheel makes the axle turn, too. It is a machine because turning the axle is easier using the wheel than turning the axle on its own. Wheels and axles increase mechanical advantage—turning the wheel makes the axle turn with greater force. The bigger the wheel compared to the size of the axle, the greater the force, making turning even easier. Wheels are used in millions of machines. One of the most obvious is in wheeled vehicles, which were in use more than 4,000 years ago and are still the most common form of transport today. Sometimes wheel and axle machines can be difficult to recognize. Can you find a wheel and axle in a wrench or a door key?

Pedal pusher
Pushing on the pedals of this child's tricycle turns the axle and drives the tricycle's front wheel.

handle

spindle

Winding up
The key of a wind-up toy has a handle that acts as a wheel and a spindle that is an axle. The large handle makes it easier to turn the spindle.

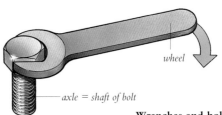

wheel

axle = shaft of bolt

Wrenches and bolts
A wrench and a bolt make up a wheel and axle system. The threaded shaft of the bolt is the axle, and the handle of the wrench is the wheel. By turning the wrench, it is much easier to tighten or loosen the bolt.

Lock and key
A key doesn't look like a wheel and axle machine, but it is. A key has a small handle on the end, which makes it easier to turn in the lock. The handle acts as a wheel. The key's shaft is the axle.

Putting the spoke in

A cart full of grapes is pulled by oxen in this Roman mosaic, which was made about 1,700 years ago. Using wheeled carts meant oxen could pull a much heavier load than they could carry. The first cart wheels were made from slices of tree trunk. About 4,000 years ago, the Romans hollowed the wheels out and added spokes to make them lighter. Vehicles could now go faster.

Potter's wheels

A potter in India uses a wheel to cast his pots. Casting pots was one of the first uses of the wheel. Simple potter's wheels are still used around the world. The massive wooden wheel can be turned either by foot or by hand.

Keep on spinning

The rim of this grinding wheel moves at very high speed as it sharpens tools. The wheel is very heavy, which means that it tends to keep spinning even when the tool is pressed against it.

Racing wheels

A racing car is moved along by its rear wheels (which are called the driving wheels). Each driving wheel is turned by an axle called a driveshaft. In most cars the driving wheels are the front wheels.

Driving in a screw

A screwdriver is a machine. Its shaft is an axle and its handle is a wheel. The handle increases the force on the shaft when it is turned to drive in a screw.

Steering wheels

A car's steering wheel is attached to the end of an axle, called the steering column. The wheel increases the force from the driver's hands, giving the driver enough force to control the car.

WHEELS AT WORK

MAKE A CAPSTAN WHEEL

You will need: *pencil, small cardboard box such as a shoe box, ruler, cardboard tube, scissors, dowel, tape, string, a weight, thin card stock, glue, thick cardboard.*

There are hundreds of different examples of wheels and axles. Some are very old designs, such as the capstan wheel. A capstan is a wheel on an axle with handles that stretch out from the edge of the wheel. The handles are used to turn the wheel, which turns the axle. Large capstan wheels can be turned by animals as they walk around and around, or by several people who each push on a handle. In the past, they were a familiar sight on ships and in dockyards, where they were used to raise heavy loads such as a ship's anchor. This project shows you how to make a simple capstan wheel for lifting a weight. At the end of the project, a ratchet is attached to the axle. A ratchet is a very useful device that acts like a catch. It prevents the capstan wheel from turning back on itself once you have stopped winding it.

1 Draw a line around the box about one-third from the top. Place the tube on the line, draw around it and cut out a circle. Repeat on the opposite side of the box, so the circles match.

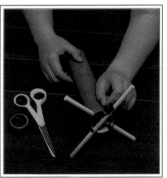

2 Cut four slots in one end of the tube. Lay two pieces of dowel in the slots so that they cross over. Tape the dowel in place. You have now made the capstan wheel.

3 Push the tube into the holes in the box. Tape the end of a piece of string to the middle of the tube inside the box. Tie a heavy object to the other end of the string.

Around in circles
Sailors on board a sailing ship turn a capstan wheel. The wheel turns a drum that pulls the ship's heavy anchor up from the sea bed. The longer the handles on the capstan wheel, the easier it is to turn the drum, but the farther the sailors have to walk. Pulling up the anchor by hauling in the cable would be much more difficult.

4 Stand the box on a table edge so the weight hangs down. Turn the capstan wheel to lift the object. Try turning the handles at their ends and then near the wheel's center.

5 To make a ratchet, cut four small rectangles of cardboard and carefully glue them to the tube at the opposite end to the capstan wheel. These will form the ratchet teeth.

6 From a piece of thick cardboard, cut an L-shaped piece. Bend one of the legs of the L at a right angle to the other leg. This will form the part that locks into the ratchet teeth.

7 Glue the cardboard L to the top of your box so that the end hanging over the edge just catches in the ratchet teeth. Let the glue dry before trying your ratchet.

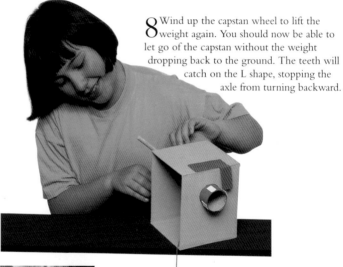

8 Wind up the capstan wheel to lift the weight again. You should now be able to let go of the capstan without the weight dropping back to the ground. The teeth will catch on the L shape, stopping the axle from turning backward.

Crushing the grapes

A wine press crushes grapes from a vineyard to release the grape juice that is used for wine-making. The press is operated by turning a nut at the top that forces a screw thread downward into the tub. The horizontal bar on the nut works like a capstan. Pushing in opposite directions on its ends turns the nut. The longer the bar, the greater the turning force on the nut, and the greater the force on the grapes.

SLOPING RAMPS

How can an inclined plane, or ramp, be a machine? It is a type of machine because it makes going uphill, or moving an object uphill against the force of gravity, much easier. Think about a moving van and people trying to lift a heavy box inside it. It might take two people working together to lift the box up high enough to reach into the van. One person could push the box up a gently sloping ramp on his or her own.

Ramps are useful in many different situations. You often see ramps on building sites, and stairs are ramps, too. The shallower (less steep) the slope, the easier it is to move an object up it, but the further the object must move to gain the same amount of height. For example, when you are walking uphill on a zig-zag path you are using ramps. Walking along the gently sloping sections of the path is easier than walking straight up the steep hillside, but you have to walk much further to reach the top. Railways have to use winding routes to go up hills because trains cannot get up very steep hills without sliding backward.

Mud-brick ramp
These are the remains of a ramp made of mud bricks. The ramp was built by the Ancient Egyptians about 3,000 years ago. Egyptian pyramid and temple builders had no cranes. They used ramps to move building materials up to where they were needed.

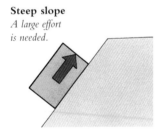

Steep slope
A large effort is needed.

Shallow slope
A small effort is needed.

On a steep slope, all the work is done in a short distance and needs a large effort. On a gentle slope, the work is done over a much longer distance, making it easier.

Ramps for building
A ramp is being used to construct a building in this picture, which was copied from an ancient Egyptian tomb painting. Without construction machines such as cranes, the Egyptians had to build huge sloping ramps to pull stone blocks to the upper levels of the building.

Ramps for loading

A car is driven up a ramp on to the back of a delivery truck. Long, gently sloping ramps are easier to drive up than short, steep ones. Loading and unloading cars from a transporter truck is easy using ramps because the cars can be driven on and off the truck. No winches or cranes are needed.

Access ramps

A disabled man is using a ramp to get down to the beach. Ramps make it much easier for vehicles with wheels to travel from one level to another. Many public buildings, such as libraries, sports centers and hospitals, often have ramps leading up to their doors as well as steps. Without ramps, people with wheelchairs find it very difficult to get in and out of buildings.

Fast track

When engineers plan roads such as highways, they try to avoid steep carriageways. Cuttings and embankments are built into hillsides to provide gentle slopes. Vehicles are able to climb the slopes without having to slow down too much.

Zigzag roads

Mountain roads, such as this one in South Africa, zigzag upward in a series of gentle slopes. A road straight up the side of the valley would be much too steep for most vehicles to drive up.

FACT BOX

• Most canals have flights of locks to move boats up and down hill, but a few use inclined planes, or ramps. In a 1-mile-long inclined plane in Belgium, the boats float inside huge 5,000-ton tanks of water. The tanks are hauled up the inclined plane on rails.

• The railroad running from Lima to Galera, in Peru, climbs 14,340 feet. In some places the track zigzags backward and forward across the very steep hillsides.

WEDGES AND SCREWS

A pair of scissors and your front teeth have something in common. They are simple machines called wedges that use inclined planes (ramps) to work. A wedge is a type of ramp, or two ramps back-to-back. Pushing the thin end of a wedge into a narrow gap with a small effort makes the wedge press hard on the edges of the gap, forcing the gap apart. Chisels, axes and plows all work with wedges. If you look closely at their blades you will see that they widen from the cutting edge.

Screw threads are also a type of inclined plane. Imagine a long, narrow ramp wrapped around a pole. This is what a screw thread is. Screw threads make screws, nuts and bolts and car jacks work. It only takes a small effort to turn a screw thread to make it move in or out with great force. Screw threads provide a very secure way of attaching something together, or of raising a heavy load.

Wedging a door
A door wedge stops a door from opening or closing. Pulling on the door pulls the bottom of the door further up the wedge's ramp. This makes the wedge press even harder against the bottom of the door and the floor.

Wedges as cutters
An axe is used to cut down a tree. The axe head is wedge-shaped. When it hits the wood, its sharp edge sinks in, forcing the wood apart and splitting it. The handle allows the person operating the axe to swing it with great speed and lever out pieces of wood.

Wedges for woodworking
Wedges are useful for shaping materials. The axe in the foreground uses a wedge to split wood. The woodworker in the background is using a small wedge-shaped tool to remove small amounts of material from the wood, which is spun at high speed by a foot pedal.

Digging with screws
The screw-shaped tool in this picture is called an auger. It is used to dig deep holes for fence posts, or for filling with concrete, to make secure foundations for buildings. The auger is operated by a mechanical digger. The auger both loosens soil from the bottom of the hole and transports the soil to the surface.

screw thread

Screws

A screw uses a screw thread to attach itself firmly into wood or metal. A screw thread is a ramp wrapped around a pole. Turning the thread is like moving up or down the slope.

bolt

nut

Nuts and bolts

A nut and bolt are used to join objects together. The screw threads on the nut and bolt interlock so that turning the nut makes it move down the bolt.

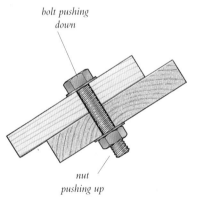

bolt pushing down

nut pushing up

When the nut is screwed onto the bolt the combined force of the nut and bolt squeezes the two pieces of wood tightly together.

Spiraling slope

A corkscrew has a screw thread that makes it wind into a cork as the handle is turned. The screw only moves a small way into the cork for each turn of the handle. This makes winding the corkscrew quite easy.

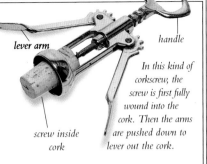

lever arm

handle

In this kind of corkscrew, the screw is first fully wound into the cork. Then the arms are pushed down to lever out the cork.

screw inside cork

Uncorking a bottle

A corkscrew such as this one combines three simple machines: the wheel and axle, the wedge and the lever. The handle of the corkscrew acts as a capstan to make turning in the screw easier. One end then folds down to rest on top the bottle's neck, and the other end forms a lever for pulling out the cork.

The point of a wood screw helps it to sink into the wood. The thread makes the point go in deeper as the screw is turned.

Driving force

Using a screwdriver increases the force with which you can turn a screw. As it turns, the screw thread bites into the wood. The screw is also wedge-shaped to help it force its way into the wood. Using screws is a strong and secure way of attaching all kinds of materials together.

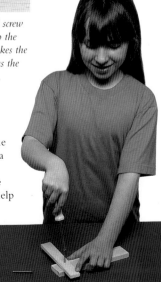

PLANES AT WORK

Although screw threads are most commonly used for joining things together, they can also be used to lift a weight upward. In a screw jack, the force made by turning the screw thread is used to lift a weight upward. With a screw jack, a huge weight, such as a car, can be lifted easily, but slowly. One turn on the handle of the jack using a small effort raises the heavy load a tiny bit.

The first project on these pages shows you how to make a simple type of screw jack. The second project shows you how to make a device to measure force, or the effort needed to raise an object. Use it to compare how a gentler slope makes lifting an object easier.

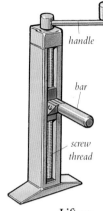

handle

bar

screw thread

MAKE A SCREW JACK

You will need: *piece of wooden board or thick cardboard, long bolt with two nuts and washers to fit, strong glue, popsicle stick or short piece of wood, cardboard tube, cardboard, a weight to lift.*

Squashing with screws
The apple press uses a screw to squeeze the juice from apples. Turning the screw is quite easy, but it makes a huge force for crushing the apples.

Lift up
If a tire gets punctured, the driver can lift the car with a screw jack before changing the tire. The driver places the jack on the ground with the bar underneath the car. As the driver turns the handle, the bar moves up the screw thread and lifts the car.

3 Stick the tube to a cardboard rectangle. Place the tube over the bolt so it rests on top of the washer. Move a weight up and down by turning the handle on

1 Put a nut on one end of the bolt. Glue the bolt to the middle of a square piece of wooden board or thick cardboard so that the thread is pointing upward. Let dry.

2 Glue the end of the popsicle stick to the side of a nut (the nut must fit the bolt) to make a handle. When the glue is dry, wind the nut onto the bolt and put the washer on top.

MAKE A FORCE MEASURER

You will need: piece of wood or thick cardboard, rubber band, paper fastener, string, pencil or felt-tipped pen, ruler, model vehicle, materials to make a slope (such as a plank and books).

1 Measure and cut a piece of wood or cardboard about 6 x 2 in. Attach the rubber band near one end with a paper fastener. Tie a piece of string to the other end of the band.

2 Mark inches along one edge of the wood, for recording how far the rubber band stretches when it is pulled by the weight. You have now made your force measurer.

3 Use your force measurer to find the weight of the model vehicle. Hang the model from your measurer and note where the band stretches to. Write down the measurement.

On a level

The ancient Egyptians used ramps to lift huge stone blocks to build their pyramids. As the building progressed, more ramps were added so that they were always level with the top of the building.

4 Make a slope—try using a plank propped up on books. How much force is needed to pull the vehicle up the slope? Is it more or less than the model's weight? Try again with a shallower slope. Does the force needed change? You should see that it needs less force to pull the model vehicle up the shallower slope.

LIFTING WITH PULLEYS

Using a pulley is often the easiest way to lift a heavy load high up. The pulley is a simple machine. The most basic pulley system is a wheel with a groove in its rim in which a rope is placed. The wheel rotates around an axle. The rope hangs down on either side of the wheel, with one end attached to a load. Pulling down on the rope lifts the load hanging on the other end. It does not reduce the amount of force needed to lift an object, so there is no mechanical advantage. It does, however, make lifting the load easier, because it is easier to pull down than it is to pull up. A pulley's special advantage is that it changes the direction of the force.

Using several pulleys together makes lifting even easier, and many pulley systems have more than one wheel that operate together. A pulley system such as this is called a block and tackle. Pulleys are useful for lifting loads on building sites and dockyards, and for moving heavy parts and machinery in factories.

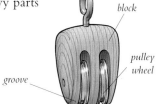

block

pulley wheel

groove

A block and tackle has two blocks like the one shown above, arranged one above the other. The pulley wheels are designed to turn easily as the rope runs around them, through the groove.

Pulling down
The simplest pulley system is a single pulley wheel with a rope running over it. It changes the direction of the pull (the effort) needed to lift an object (the load) off the ground. Instead of pulling up on the object, the boy is pulling down on the rope. He can use his weight to help.

Winching with pulleys
An air-sea rescue helicopter uses an electric winch to lift sailors from the sea on the end of a wire. The wire runs from the winch over a pulleywheel on the side of the helicopter.

Pulleys for building
Workmen use a pulley to lift building materials to construct the walls of a great city in the 1500s. The workman at the bottom turns a handle to haul up the bucket. The pulley was probably devised by ancient Greeks about 2,500 years ago and has been in use ever since.

Half the effort

This pulley system has two pulley wheels. Pulling the rope raises the lower wheel and the load. With two wheels, the effort needed to lift the load is halved. This makes it easier, but the rope has to be pulled twice as far.

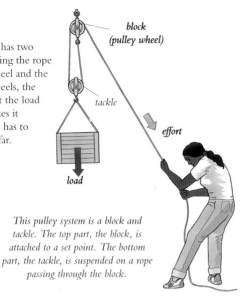

block (pulley wheel)

tackle

effort

load

This pulley system is a block and tackle. The top part, the block, is attached to a set point. The bottom part, the tackle, is suspended on a rope passing through the block.

Up and away

A light pull on the loop of chain lifts a very heavy boat engine. This pulley system has a very high mechanical advantage—it takes little effort to pull a massive weight.

Dockyard block and tackle

The lower end of the block and tackle on a dockyard crane can be seen in this picture. The crane is lifting heavy pallets of cargo from the deep hold of a ship.

Boats away!

A ship's lifeboats hang on pulley systems ready to be lowered quickly into the sea if the ship has to be abandoned. The pulley systems allow the heavy boats to be lowered by one person standing inside the boat itself.

Higher and higher

A dockyard crane uses pulley systems to lift very heavy loads. The cable from the pulley is winched in and out by an engine to make the lifting hook rise and fall. Other engines move the crane's arm up and down.

PULLEYS AT WORK

The two projects on these pages illustrate how pulley systems work. In the first project, a simple double pulley system is constructed. It does not have pulley wheels. Instead, the string passes over smooth metal hoops. This would be no good for a real system because friction between the rope and metal would be too great, but it does show how a pulley system is connected together.

The second project investigates how adding more turns on a block and tackle reduces the effort needed to move a load. You may notice, however, that the more turns you make, the greater the friction becomes. Using wheels in a block and tackle cuts down on this friction.

Lifting materials
A pulley is useful for lifting materials up to a new building's upper floors. It does not increase the lifting power here, but works because it is easier to pull down on a rope than up.

Linking up
Heavy-duty block and tackle systems, like this one in a dockyard, are used for lifting the heavy cargo. They have metal chain links, which are much stronger than a rope would be. The chain links interlock with the shaped pulley wheels.

MAKE A SIMPLE PULLEY

You will need:
lengths of string,
two large paperclips,
a weight.

1 Take a short length of string. Use the string to tie a large paperclip to a door handle, or coat hook on a wall. Make sure the paperclip is tied securely to its support.

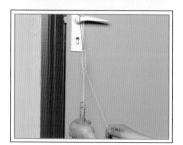

2 Cut a long piece of string and feed it through the paperclip's inner hoop. Now feed it through the top of a second paperclip and tie it to the outer hoop of the top clip.

3 Tie a weight, using another piece of string, to the bottom paperclip. Pull the end of the long string to lift the bottom paperclip, which will lift the weight.

MAKE A BLOCK AND TACKLE

You will need:
two broom handles or lengths of thick dowel, strong string or thin rope, two friends.

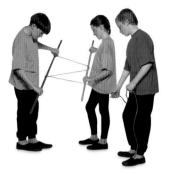

1 Ask each of your friends to hold a broom handle, or length of dowel, between outstretched hands. Tie the end of a long piece of string, or rope, to one handle.

2 Wrap the string around each handle once, keeping the loops fairly close together on the handles. Now pull on the string. How easy was it to pull your friends together?

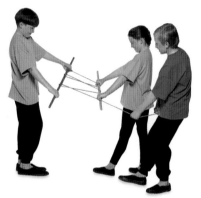

3 Now wrap the string twice around each handle, making sure you keep the turns close together. Now pull on the end of the string again. What differences do you notice this time? Is it any easier?

FACT BOX

• Using a block-and-tackle system with a mechanical advantage of 20 (with ten wheels at each end), you could lift an elephant easily by hand!

• One of the first people to make use of block and tackle systems was the famous Greek scientist Archimedes. He is said to have pulled ships ashore with them, in the third century B.C.

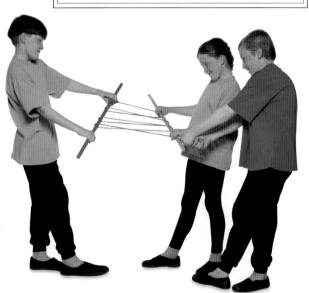

4 Make more turns around the handles and try pulling again. Do more turns make the effort you need to make smaller? Do you have to pull the rope farther than before?

GEAR WHEELS

A gear is a wheel with teeth around its edge. When two gear wheels are put next to each other, their teeth can be made to interlock. Then when one wheel turns, the other one turns, too. Gears are used to transmit movement from one wheel to another. If both wheels are the same size, the wheels turn at the same speed. If one wheel is bigger than the other, the gears can be used to speed up or slow down movement, or to increase or decrease a force. Many machines, from kitchen whisks to trucks, have gears that help them to work.

Belt drives and chain drives are similar to gears. In these, two wheels are linked together by a belt or a chain instead of teeth. This is another way of transferring power and movement from one wheel to another. Speed can also be varied by changing the size of the wheels.

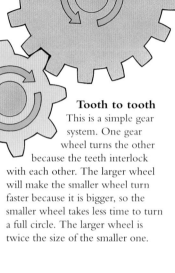

Tooth to tooth
This is a simple gear system. One gear wheel turns the other because the teeth interlock with each other. The larger wheel will make the smaller wheel turn faster because it is bigger, so the smaller wheel takes less time to turn a full circle. The larger wheel is twice the size of the smaller one.

Mining with gears
Huge gear wheels are part of an old lift mechanism from a mine. The teeth on the interlocking gear wheels press very hard against each other. They need to be very wide and thick so that they don't snap off.

Transmitting a force
In the center of this kitchen whisk is a set of gears. They are used to transmit the turning movement of the handle to the blades of the whisk. The gears speed up the movement, making the blades spin faster than the turning handle. The gears turn the movement through a right angle, too. These sort of gears are called beveled gears.

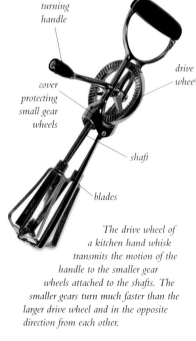

turning handle

cover protecting small gear wheels

drive wheel

shaft

blades

The drive wheel of a kitchen hand whisk transmits the motion of the handle to the smaller gear wheels attached to the shafts. The smaller gears turn much faster than the larger drive wheel and in the opposite direction from each other.

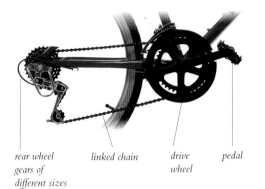

All geared up

Bicycle gears use wheels and a chain to transmit the drive from the pedals to the bicycle's rear wheel. As a rider turns the pedals, the drive wheel is moved around. This moves a linked chain, which turns a set of gear wheels of different sizes attached to the rear wheel. With the chain on the largest of these gears (in low gear), pedaling is easy but the bicycle travels slowly. With the chain on the smallest gear (in high gear), pedaling is harder but the bicycle moves faster.

rear wheel gears of different sizes   *linked chain*   *drive wheel*   *pedal*

interlocking gears

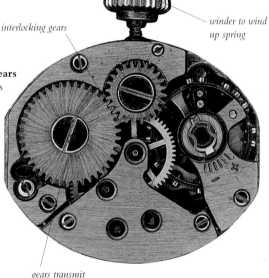

winder to wind up spring

Wind-up watch gears

The back has been removed from this wind-up watch so you can see the tiny gear wheels inside. Different-sized gear wheels are arranged so that they move the hands of the watch at different speeds. The clock is powered by a spring, wound up by hand. The spring makes a gear wheel turn, which moves the minute hand. Another gear slows down this movement to turn the hour hand.

gears transmit energy from spring

Swinging time keeper

This pendulum clock uses gear wheels to control its speed. A spring drives one gear around, which drives other gears that show time. The speed that gears turn at is controlled by a swinging pendulum that interlocks with the teeth on a gear wheel called the escape wheel. The escape wheel gives the pendulum a small push on each swing to keep the pendulum moving.

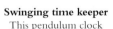

Belt drives

Wide belts, called belt drives, stretch between wheels in the roof and the machines of a factory. The photograph was taken in about 1905. The wheels in the roof are turned by an engine, and the belts transmit this movement to drive the machines.

MAKING GEARS WORK

Before engineers used metals, they made gear wheels from wood. One way of making gear-wheel teeth was to attach short poles to the edge of a thick disc. The poles on different gear wheels interlocked to transmit movement. Gears like this were being used 2,000 years ago. If you visit an old mill, you might still see similar wooden gears today. The first project shows you how to make a simple gear wheel system. What do you notice about how the wheels turn? They turn in different directions and the smaller wheel (with fewer teeth) turns one and a half times for every one rotation of the larger wheel. The second project shows you how to make a simple belt drive and how it can turn an axle at different speeds.

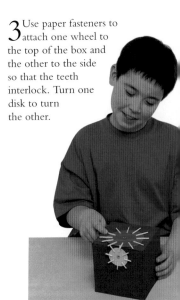

Slow pedal power
Old sewing machines, such as this one, were powered by a foot pedal that turned a large pulley wheel. This wheel was linked by a drive belt to a small pulley wheel on the machine. So pedaling slowly made the small wheel turn quickly.

MAKE A SET OF GEAR WHEELS

You will need: compass and pencil, protractor, thick cardboard, scissors, used matchsticks or thin dowel, glue, paper fasteners, small cardboard box.

Spiral gears
A computer graphic image shows part of a car gear box. These gears are helical (spiral) gears, which are more efficient than gears with straight teeth.

3 Use paper fasteners to attach one wheel to the top of the box and the other to the side so that the teeth interlock. Turn one disk to turn the other.

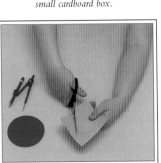

1 Using a pencil and a compass, mark out two disks on cardboard and cut them out. Make the diameter of one disk twice the diameter of the other, for example 3 in. and 1½ in.

2 Glue eight matches around the edge of the small disk. First glue four matches in a cross shape, then add four more half-way. In a similar way, glue 12 matches to the large disk.

MAKE A BELT DRIVE

You will need: *cardboard box, dowel, scissors, strips of thin card stock, glue, thick rubber band, felt-tipped pen.*

1 Cut two pieces of dowel each about 2 in. longer than the width of the box. Cut two holes in both sides of the box. Slide the rods through to make two axles.

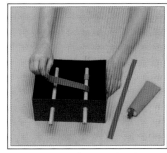

2 Cut a strip of card stock. Glue it to one of the axles. Wrap it round and glue the end down to make a wheel. Make a bigger wheel with a strip of card stock three times longer than the first.

3 Put a wide rubber band around both axles. The band should be slightly stretched when it is in place. Make a mark at the end of each axle so you can see how fast they turn.

Printing gear

Computer printers use gears driven by electric motors to move sheets of paper past the print head (where the ink is fired onto the paper) bit by bit at the correct speed. More gears move the print head from side to side, making up lines of the image.

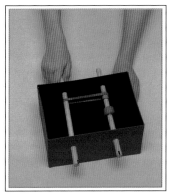

4 To test your belt drive, put the rubber band onto the smaller wheel and start turning the plain axle. Does the wheeled axle turn more or fewer times than the plain?

5 Now move the rubber band onto the larger wheel and start turning the plain axle again. What difference does it make to the speed of the wheeled axle? Use the pen marks to compare the speeds.

POWER FOR MACHINES

Early machines, such as axes and ramps, relied on human muscle power to make them work. Then people started using animals to work many simple machines. Animals, such as oxen, can carry, pull and lift much heavier loads than people can. Eventually people realized they could capture the energy of the wind or flowing water by using windmills and water-wheels. These became the first machines to create power that in turn was used to make other machines work. This energy was used to do such things as grinding grain to make flour or pumping up water from underground.

Today, wind and water energy are still captured to generate electricity, which we use to light and power our homes, schools, offices and factories.

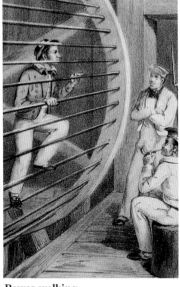

Wind for milling

A windmill uses the power of the wind to turn heavy mill stones that grind grain to make flour. The whole building can be turned around so that the sails are facing into the wind. The speed of the mill is controlled by opening and closing slots in the sails.

Power walking

A man is operating a treadmill in Australia in the 1840s. He is walking up the rungs so that his weight turns the wheel. The movement of the wheel is used to operate machinery. Human treadmills are no longer used.

Overshot water-wheel

There are two different types of water-wheel. This one is called an overshot wheel because the water flows over the top of the wheel and falls into buckets on the wheel. The water's weight pulls the wheel around.

Undershot water-wheel

The second type of water-wheel is called an undershot wheel because rushing water in a stream or river flows under the wheel and catches in the buckets at the bottom of the wheel. The force of the water spins the wheel.

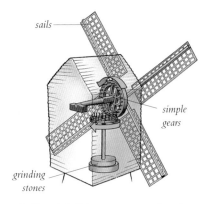

Inside a windmill is an arrangement of wooden gear wheels, which transfers power from the sails to the grinding stones. Mills like this have been in use for centuries.

Grinding stones

Many windmills and watermills generate power to turn millstones. The grinding stones in this picture are used to squeeze oil from olives. Only the top millstone turns while the bottom stone stays still.

Modern mills

Wind turbines, like these shown on a wind farm, are a modern type of windmill. The wind spins the huge propellers, which turn an electricity generator inside the top of each turbine.

Power from water

A hydroelectric station generates electricity from the water of a fast-flowing river. The water is stored behind a huge dam. As it flows out, it spins a turbine, which is like a very efficient water-wheel. The turbine turns a generator, which makes electricity.

Underground power

In the underground turbine hall of a hydroelectric power station, each of the generators can produce about a gigawatt of electricity—enough electricity to work about 10 million light bulbs.

WIND AND WATER POWER

M odern windmills are called wind turbines and are used to generate electricity. The most efficient wind turbines only have two or three blades, as in the propeller of an aircraft. Hundreds of wind turbines can be grouped together to make a wind farm. Sometimes one or two large turbines generate enough electricity to power a small community. There are several shapes of wind turbine. One of the most efficient is the vertical-axis type. This has an axle standing vertical to the ground. It is very efficient because it works no matter which way the wind is blowing.

The first project shows you how to make a vertical-axis turbine. The second project shows you how to make an overshot water-wheel. This captures the energy of falling water to lift a small weight. Try pouring the water onto the wheel from different heights to see if it makes a difference to the wheel's speed.

MAKE A WINDMILL

You will need:
plastic bottle, scissors, tape, thin dowel, tacks.

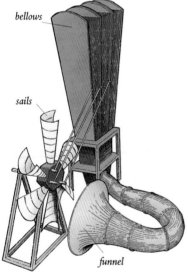

bellows

sails

funnel

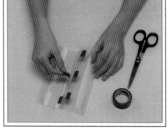

1 Cut the top and bottom off the bottle to leave a tube. Cut the tube in half lengthwise, then stick the two halves together in an S shape, so the edges overlap by 1 in.

2 The piece of dowel should be about 1½ in. longer than the vanes. Slide it into the slot between the vanes. Press a tack gently into each end of the dowel.

Round and round again
This machine was devised in the 1500s by an Italian inventor. He believed that as the sails turned, they would operate a set of bellows. The bellows in turn would provide enough wind to drive the sails to set up a continuous cycle of movement. It cannot work because the sails do not provide enough energy to squeeze the bellows.

3 To make the windmill spin, hold it vertically with your fingers on the tacks at each end of the dowel. Blow on the vanes. The windmill will spin easily.

MAKE A WATER-WHEEL

You will need: *large plastic bottle, scissors, wire (ask an adult to cut the bottom out of a coat hanger), cork, craft knife, tape, string, weight, pitcher of water, large plate.*

1 Cut the top third off the plastic bottle. Cut a small hole in the bottom piece near the base (this is to let the water out). Cut a V-shape on each side of the rim.

2 Ask an adult to push the wire through the center of the cork to make an axle. From the top third of the plastic bottle, cut six small curved vanes as shown.

3 Ask an adult to cut six slots in the cork with a craft knife. (This might be easier without the wire.) Push the plastic vanes into the slots to make the water-wheel.

4 Rest the wheel's axle in the V-shaped slots. Tape a length of string toward one end of the axle and tie a small weight to the end of the string. Fill a pitcher with water.

FACT BOX

• In a strong breeze, the world's largest wind turbine, in Hawaii, would be capable of operating more than 4,000 microwave ovens.

• China's Three Gorges Dam will generate 18 gigawatts of electricity—enough to power 24 million microwave ovens!

5 Put the water-wheel on a large plate or in the sink. Pour water onto the wheel so that it hits the upward-curving vanes. The weight should be lifted.

Animal power

A water-raising wheel such as this one would be operated by an animal or a person walking in a circle, pulling the horizontal pole on the right. Buckets attached to a chain driven by the wheel go down into the well, scoop up water, lift it, and empty it into a chute.

ENGINES AND MOTORS

Many modern machines are powered by engines and motors, which are complicated machines themselves. An engine is a machine that makes movement energy from heat. The heat is made by burning a fuel, such as gas. The first engines were driven by steam.

Most engines today, such as the ones used in cars, are internal combustion engines. This means that the fuel is burned inside the engine. In a car engine, as the gas explodes, it produces hot gases that push pistons inside cylinders up and down. The pistons turn a crankshaft, which carries the movement energy from the engine to the wheels of the car. An electric motor is a machine that makes movement energy from electricity rather than from burning fuel. Most of the electricity we use is made in power stations or from the chemicals inside batteries.

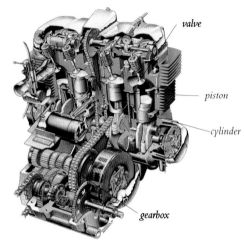

valve

piston

cylinder

gearbox

Burning inside
This diagram shows the pistons inside the internal combustion engine of a car. At the top are valves that let fuel and air into the pistons and let exhaust gases out. At the bottom is the gearbox that sends the power from the engine to the wheels.

Early steam power
An atmospheric engine was one of the first types of steam engines. Steam was fed to a cylinder, where it was cooled and turned back to water, forming a vacuum. The atmospheric pressure outside the cylinder pushed the piston in.

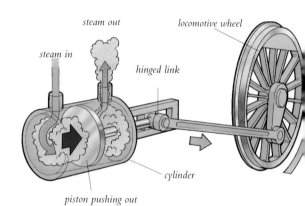

steam out

steam in

locomotive wheel

hinged link

cylinder

piston pushing out

Piston power
In a steam engine, steam made by heating water in a boiler is forced along a pipe into a cylinder. The pressure of the steam pushes a piston in the cylinder outward. The moving piston then turns a wheel that is used to drive a locomotive or power a machine.

Engines for cars

A car's internal combustion engine is usually fitted under the hood. The engine's cylinders are inside the large black engine block. You can see the exhaust pipes that carry waste gases away from the cylinders.

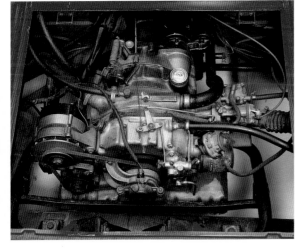

Under the hood

The top of an internal combustion engine in a small truck. On the left are the starter motor (an electric motor that makes the engine turn to start it up) and the alternator, that makes electricity for the electrical parts, such as the lights, of the truck.

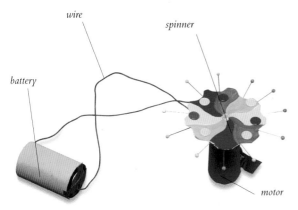

wire

spinner

battery

motor

An electric motor with a colorful spinner on top is connected to a battery by two wires. This makes an electric circuit.

Electric motors

Electricity is turned into movement by an electric motor. When the motor is connected to a battery, its shaft spins around. Electric motors are small and clean, which makes them useful for household gadgets.

HYDRAULICS AND PNEUMATICS

Did you know that a machine can be powered by a liquid or a gas? Machines that have parts moved by a liquid are called hydraulic machines. Those that have parts moved by a gas are called pneumatic machines. A simple hydraulic system has a pipe filled with oil and a piston (a cylinder that moves back and forth) at each end. Pushing one piston into the pipe forces the piston at the other end outward, transmitting power from one end of the pipe to the other. In a simple pneumatic system, compressed air is used to force a piston to move.

Hydraulic and pneumatic machines can be very powerful. They are also quite simple and very robust. Machines that work in dirty and rough conditions, such as diggers, drills and dump trucks, often have hydraulic or pneumatic systems instead of motors. Most dental drills are also worked by a pneumatic system. Air, pumped to the drill, makes a tiny turbine inside the drill spin very fast.

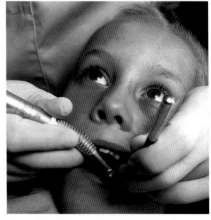

Dental drilling
The high-pitched whine of a dental drill is made by the air that powers it. Inside is an air turbine that spins an amazing 10,000 times a second as air is pumped through it.

Pump it up
Using an air pump is a simple way to blow up a balloon. A valve in the pump's outlet allows air to be pumped into the balloon as the piston is pushed in. It prevents the air from being sucked out again when the piston is pulled out.

Lift it up
Pneumatic power can lift a book. The girl blows air into the inflated balloon and pushes the book upward. Less effort is needed to lift the book like this than is needed to lift it by hand.

air outlet

cylinder

piston

Sucking in air
All pneumatic machines need a device to suck in air from the outside and push it into the machine. This is called an air pump, or a compressor. The simple air pump above sucks in air as the piston is pulled back, and forces air out as the piston is pushed in.

Hydraulic lift

Lifting and moving a heavy load is made easy with a hydraulically-powered machine such as a fork-lift truck. The forks are lifted by hydraulic rams. Each ram consists of a cylinder and a piston that moves inside it. Pumping special oil, called hydraulic fluid, into the cylinder makes the piston move in or out, depending on which end of the cylinder the oil is pumped into.

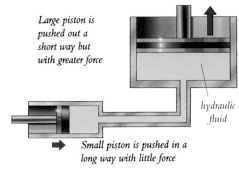

Large piston is pushed out a short way but with greater force

hydraulic fluid

Small piston is pushed in a long way with little force

Pushing in, pushing out

A simple hydraulic system has two pistons connected by a cylinder filled with hydraulic fluid. Using different-sized pistons creates a mechanical advantage. Pushing the small piston creates a greater force at the large one.

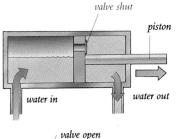

valve shut

piston

water in

water out

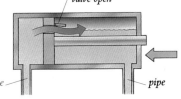

valve open

pipe

pipe

Pumping water

Moving a water pump's piston in and out moves water from the pipe on the left to the pipe on the right. The valve opens to let water through as the piston moves in. The valve shuts automatically as the piston moves out because the water presses the valve closed.

Hydraulic digging

The sections of the arm of a digger are moved by powerful hydraulic rams, each with a cylinder and piston. Hydraulic fluid is pumped to the cylinders by a pump powered by the digger's diesel engine. The fluid flows along very strong pipes called hydraulic lines, which you can see on the upper part of the arm.

Breaking through

A pneumatic drill is an air-powered drill used to break up road surfaces and concrete. The air forces the drill's heavy blade to jump up and down very quickly. The drill needs a supply of compressed air to make it work, which comes along a strong, rubber pipe from a machine called a compressor.

LIQUID AND AIR AT WORK

MAKE AN HYDRAULIC LIFTER

You will need: large plastic bottle, scissors, airtight plastic bag, plastic tubing, tape, plastic funnel, spray can lid, heavy weight, pitcher of water.

Hydraulic machinery uses a liquid to transmit power, while pneumatic machinery uses compressed air. The first project shows you how to make a simple hydraulic machine that uses water pressure to lift an object upward. A central reservoir (a pitcher of water) is poured into a pipe. The water fills up a plastic bag, which is forced to expand in a narrow cylinder. This forces up a platform, which in turn raises a heavy object. Many cranes, excavators and trucks use this principle to lift heavy loads, using hydraulic rams.

The second project shows you how to make a simple air pump. An air pump works by sucking air in one hole and pushing it out of another. A valve stops the air from being sucked in and pushed out of the wrong holes. When the air tries to flow through one way, the valve opens, but when the air tries to flow through the other way the valve stays shut.

1 Cut the top off the large plastic bottle. Make sure the plastic bag is airtight and wrap its neck over the end of a length of plastic tubing. Seal the bag to the tube with tape.

Firing water
Fire-fighters spray water on to fires through hoses so that they can stand back from the flames. The water is pumped along the hoses by a powerful pump on the fire engine.

2 Attach a funnel to the other end of the tube. Make a hole at the base of the bottle and feed the bag and tubing through. The bag should sit in the bottom of the bottle.

3 Put the spray can lid on top of the bag and rest a book, or another heavy object, on top of the bottle. Lift the funnel end of the tubing up, and slowly pour in water. What happens to the can lid and the book?

MAKE AN AIR PUMP

***You will need**: large plastic bottle, scissors, hammer, small nails, wooden stick or dowel, cardboard, tape, ping-pong ball.*

1 Cut around the large plastic bottle, about one-third up from the bottom. Cut a slit down the side of the bottom part of the bottle so that it will slide inside the top part.

2 Ask an adult to help you nail the bottom of the bottle to the end of a wooden stick or piece of dowel. You have now made a piston for your air pump.

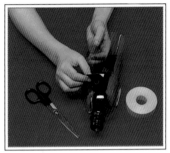

3 Cut a hole about ½-in. across near the neck of the bottle. Cut a piece of cardboard about 1 x 1 in. Tape one edge of the cardboard to the bottle to form a flap over the hole.

4 Drop a ping-pong ball into the top part of the bottle so that it rests in the neck. Push the bottom part of the bottle (the piston) into the top part (the cylinder).

FACT BOX

• A fire-engine pump can pump 1,000 quarts of water a minute—enough to fill eight large soda bottles a second.

• Fire-fighters free people trapped in crashed cars with hydraulically powered cutting and spreading machines.

Dumpster truck
A dumpster truck has hydraulic rams to lift a full dumpster. The rams are controlled by levers, and powered by a pump operated by the engine.

5 Move the piston in and out to suck air into the bottle and out of the hole. Can you see how both the valves work? The flap should automatically close when you pull the piston out.

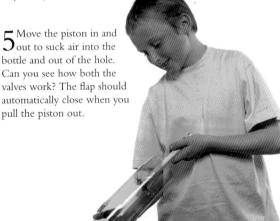

MACHINES AT HOME

zipper

Your home is full of machines. Look in the kitchen, the bathroom, the living room and bedroom. In your kitchen you should find several simple gadgets, such as can-openers, taps, scissors and bottle openers. There might also be more complicated machines, such as a washing machine or a dishwasher. Other machines you might find include a vacuum cleaner and a refrigerator. In other rooms there may be a hairdryer, a shower and a television. Even the zippers on your clothes are machines. Think about how each one saves you time and effort. What would life be like without them?

Most machines not only save you work, but also improve the results—a modern washing machine cleans clothes better than an old-fashioned tub, and a vacuum cleaner is more efficient than a broom. Many machines save time, too. For example, it is much quicker to heat food in a microwave oven than over an open fire. Many of these machines need electricity to work and are powered from the mains supply.

Zip it up
One of the simplest machines is the zipper. If you look carefully at a zipper fastener, you will see a wedge shape in the middle. This forces the two edges of the zipper together to do it up, and apart again to undo it. Before there were zippers, people had to fasten their clothes with buttons or hooks and eyes, which took longer.

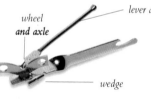

wheel and axle — *lever arm* — *wedge*

Can-opener
Can you see four different types of machine in a can opener? You should be able to find levers, a wedge, a wheel and axle and a gear wheel. Together, they make it simple to open a can.

FACT BOX

• The zipper was invented in 1893. The first zippers were unreliable, until tiny bumps and hollows were added to the end of each tooth, to help the teeth interlock.

• Electrically powered domestic machines were only possible once mains electricity was developed in the 1880s.

• One of the earliest vacuum cleaners was built in England, in 1901. It was so large that it had to be pulled by a horse and powered by a gas engine!

• The spin dryer was conceived of by a French engineer in 1865, but it was not developed until the 1920s.

How a refrigerator works

Inside a refrigerator is a pump that squeezes a special liquid called a refrigerant. As the refrigerant expands again, it uses up heat, making the compartment cold.

What, no bag?

This clever bagless cleaner spins the dusty air at high speed, which throws the dust to the sides of the dust-collecting container. Most vacuum cleaners have a bag that lets air through but traps dust, and the bag has to be replaced regularly. The bagless cleaner's container lasts for much longer.

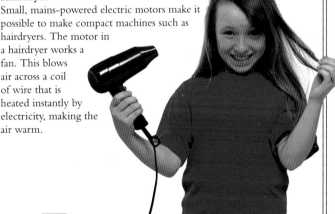

Washing by machine

A modern washing machine is a combination of several machines. It has electric motors (to turn the drum), pumps (to pump water in and out of the machine) and valves (that let water in or out). All these machines are controlled by an automatic program timer.

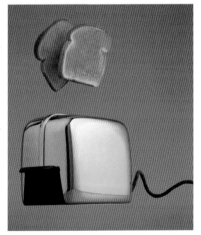

Perfect toast

A toaster is a machine that heats bread using electric heating elements until it detects that the surface of the bread is hot enough. Then it ejects the toast and turns off the elements.

Hairdryer

Small, mains-powered electric motors make it possible to make compact machines such as hairdryers. The motor in a hairdryer works a fan. This blows air across a coil of wire that is heated instantly by electricity, making the air warm.

DOMESTIC HELP

MAKE A CAN CRUSHER

You will need:
*two short planks of wood about
20 x 4 in. and ½–1-in. thick,
hinge, screws, screwdriver,
two coffee-jar lids, glue.*

Household machines are designed to make life easier. Here
you can make a really useful can crusher and a hand-
operated vacuum cleaner. The can crusher can be used to flatten
empty soda cans before you take them for recycling or to the
dump. Crushed cans take up much less space than empty, full-
sized ones. This makes them easier to store and to carry.

The crusher is a simple machine that uses a lever action to press
on the ends of the can. It is much easier to crush a can with the
machine than it is with your hands. The vacuum cleaner is based
on the air pump that you have already made. It uses the same
principles to pick up scraps of paper as a more sophisticated
vacuum cleaner does to pick up household dust. Tissue paper is
used for the collection bag because it allows air to pass through it
and filters out the scraps of paper. Securing the ping-pong ball to
the neck of the pump makes the cleaner more efficient, as it
prevents the ball from falling too far out of place.

1 Lay the two planks end to end.
Ask an adult to help you screw
them together with a hinge, using
screws and a screwdriver. Make sure
the hinge is secure.

Shredded in seconds
A blender has high-speed chopping
blades at the bottom that will cut
vegetables and other foods to shreds in
seconds. The blades are based on a
simple machine: the wedge. Many
kitchens are full of gadgets to help
make food preparation faster.

2 Glue a jar lid to each plank of
wood with the top of the lid face
down. The lids should be about
halfway along each plank and the
same distance from the hinge.

3 To crush a can, put the can
in between the lids so that
it is held in place. Press down
hard on the top piece of wood.

MAKE A VACUUM CLEANER

You will need: *large plastic bottle, scissors, hammer, small nails, wooden stick or dowel, ping-pong ball, string, tape, tissue paper, glue.*

1 Do the air pump project but don't add the valve. Tape string to the ball. Feed the string through the bottle's neck. Tape string to the neck so that the ball falls out a little way.

2 Make a tissue paper bag and glue it over the hole in the bottle. Air from the pump will go through the bag, and anything the vacuum picks up should be trapped.

FACT BOX

• One of the first vacuum cleaners used small pumps like bellows that were attached to the bottom of shoes. The user had to run around to suck up dust!

3 Try picking up tiny scraps of paper with the vacuum. Pull the piston out sharply to suck the scraps of paper into the bottle. Push the piston back in gently to pump the paper into the tissue bag. How much can you pick up with your homemade cleaner? Can you pick anything else up, such as grains of salt?

Up the tube
Modern vacuum cleaners have an air pump operated by an electric motor. The pump creates a vacuum inside the cleaner, and dusty air rushes in from the outside to fill the vacuum. A bag at the end of the pipe lets air through but traps dust.

BUILDING MACHINES

Constructing houses, office parks, bridges, roads and railroads involves digging into the ground, moving rock and earth, and transporting and lifting steel, concrete and other heavy building materials. There are specialized construction machines, such as diggers, bulldozers, concrete mixers and cranes, to carry out all these jobs. Many of them use the principles of simple machines to work. For example, cranes use pulleys and balanced levers to help them lift. Most construction machines have large diesel engines to provide the power they need, and some have hydraulic or pneumatic systems to move their parts.

Machinery of old
The Flemish artist Pieter Brueghel painted the mythical Tower of Babel in 1563. It shows the sort of construction machines that were in use in the 1500s, such as chisels, levers, pulleys and simple cranes, operated by large treadmills. The huge cathedrals found in many European cities were built with simple machines like these.

FACT BOX

• The height of a tower crane's tower can be increased. A new section of tower is hauled up and positioned on top of the existing tower.

• Tunnels that go through soft rock, such as chalk, are dug with tunnel boring machines. The machine bores its way through the rock with a rotating cutting head.

• Around 2,000 years ago the Romans used cranes for building. The cranes were powered by slaves walking around in a giant treadmill.

Earth mover
A bulldozer is used to push away rock, soil and rubble to clear a building site ready for work to start. Its wide tracks, called caterpillar tracks, stop it from sinking into muddy ground.

Digging out
A mechanical excavator is used to dig up rock and soil. It makes trenches for pipes, and holes for foundations. Its powerful digging arm is operated by hydraulic rams.

Loading machine

A machine called a loader has a wide bucket that skims along the ground scooping up waste soil. When the bucket is full, hydraulic rams lift it into the air so that the loader can carry it to a waiting dump truck.

Mix it up

A concrete mixer carries concrete to the building site from the factory. Inside the drum a blade, like a screw thread, mixes the concrete. The blade stays still while the drum rotates.

Hammering in

A pile driver hammers piles, or metal posts, into the ground. It repeatedly lifts a large weight with its crane and drops it onto the top of the pile. The piles form the foundation of a new building.

Dumping out

Dump trucks are used to deliver hardcore (crushed up stones used for foundations) and to take away unwanted soil. To empty the load on to the ground, the back of the dump truck is lifted by hydraulic rams. The load slides to the ground.

Towering crane

These tower cranes look flimsy, but they do not topple over even when they are lifting heavy weights. This is because of a concrete counterweight behind the cab.

ON THE FARM

Some of the oldest types of machines in the world are used for agriculture. Farmers use machines to prepare the soil, to sow and harvest their crops, and to feed and milk their animals. One of the first, and still one of the most important farm machines, was the plow. Archaeologists have found evidence of plows from about 9,000 years ago. They began as simple, sharpened sticks that were used to turn up the soil. Today, a seven-furrow plow hauled behind a modern tractor can cover 40 hectares of land—as much as 80 soccer fields—in a day.

Modern farming uses many specialized machines to make cultivated land more productive. In some parts of the world, powered machinery, usually operated by a tractor, does all the work. But in many countries, plows are pulled by animals, and crops are harvested using simple hand tools.

Tractor and plow
Modern, tractor-pulled plows have several individual plows in a row to break up the soil into furrows. This makes it much quicker to plow a field than with a single plow. At the rear end of the tractor is a rotating shaft called a take-off shaft. It provides the power for the plow.

FACT BOX

• On many farms in arid areas, the pumps used to raise water from wells or streams for irrigation, and for animals to drink, are powered by small windmills.

• One of the most important agricultural inventions was the seed drill, which planted seeds in neat rows and at the correct depth. It was invented more than 5,000 years ago.

Steam power
Steam-driven traction engines were the first type of tractor. This one was built in 1880. It replaced the farm's horses and powered other machines, such as the thresher shown here.

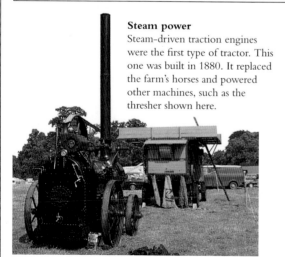

Animal power
A water buffalo pulls a plow through the soil. Animals, especially oxen, are still widely used by farmers who cannot afford machinery or who live in hilly or mountainous areas.

Pneumatic milking

In a milking parlor, milk is sucked from cows' udders by pneumatic milking machines. A large parlor can milk dozens of cows at the same time. The milk pours into tanks, where it is measured and then pumped to a refrigerated tank to wait for collection by a milk tanker.

Hay wrapper

A baling machine automatically makes hay into bales and wraps them in plastic to keep them dry. Here, the machine is spinning the bale one way as it wraps plastic sheeting around it the other way.

Combine harvester

A combine harvester cuts and collects crops. A reel sweeps the crop into a cutter bar that slices the stalks off at ground level. The stalks are pushed into the machine and the grain is stripped from them. Special screws, called impeller screws or augers, are often used to move the grain around inside the harvester.

A close shave

A sheep farmer uses electrically operated shears to cut the fleece from a sheep. The shears work like a pair of scissors. The electric motor moves the blades together and apart at high speeds.

MAKING FARM MACHINES

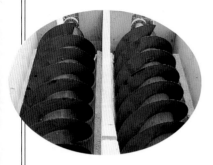

The two projects on these pages will show you how to make two simple machines like those used on farms. The first is an Archimedean screw. In parts of the world where water pumps are expensive to buy and run, Archimedean screws are used to move water uphill in order to irrigate crops. The machine is made up of a large screw inside a pipe. One end of the machine is placed in the water and, as a handle is turned, the screw inside revolves, carrying water upward. This water-lifting device has been in use for centuries, and it is named after the ancient Greek scientist, Archimedes.

The second project is to make a simple plow. By pushing the plow through a tray of damp sand you will be able to see how the special, curved, wedge shape of a real plow lifts and turns the soil to make a furrow. A furrow is a trench in which the farmer plants the seeds.

Screwed-up water
Inside an Archimedean screw is a wide screw thread. Water is trapped in the thread and is forced to move upward as the screw is turned. A screw thread like this is also called an auger.

MAKE AN ARCHIMEDEAN SCREW

You will need:
small plastic bottle, scissors, plastic tubing, waterproof tape, two bowls.

1 Cut the top and bottom off the bottle. Wrap a length of plastic tubing around the bottle to make a screw thread shape. Tape the tubing in place with waterproof tape.

2 Put one end of the bottle in a bowl of water and rest it on the bowl's edge. Place the other bowl at the end of the tubing. Slowly turn the bottle. After a few turns, the water will pour out of the top of the tubing.

FACT BOX

• Every year Australian farmers have to shear tens of millions of sheep. As an experiment in 1986, Australian engineers built a robot that could shear a sheep in about 90 seconds.

• The first plows were made from wood or from stag antlers. They were invented in Egypt and India about 5,500 years ago.

MAKE A SIMPLE PLOW

You will need:
*small plastic bottle,
scissors, strip of wood or
dowel, tack,
tray of damp sand.*

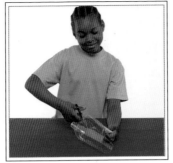

1 Start by cutting a triangle of plastic from one side of the small plastic soda bottle. This triangle will form the blade of your plow.

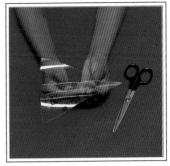

2 Cut a slot in the triangle, as shown above. Fold the triangle in half along the line of the slot against the curve of the plastic.

3 Holding the two sides of the blade together, attach it to the length of wood or dowel with a tack. Make sure the blade is securely attached to the handle.

Soil-turning wedges
Each metal blade on this plow works as a wedge. The front point slices easily through the soil, splitting it up. As the soil slides along the blade's side, the curved shape lifts and turns it over. The plow buries weeds and brings fresh soil to the surface for new crops to grow in. This is called tilling.

Guided plow
The wheels on a plow from the 1400s stop it from sinking too far into the ground. The farmer guides the plow to make a neat furrow, while a helper urges on oxen and horses.

4 Fill up the tray with damp sand and push the plow through the sand in lines. Does your plow lift and turn the soil to make a furrow?

MACHINES IN INDUSTRY

In a spin
A steam-powered circular saw is used to cut large logs into shape. The saw has a razor-sharp blade with teeth that cut into the material as it spins. The object that is being cut is moved backward or forward across the blade.

Machine tools are machines used in factories to manufacture objects. The operations they are used for are cutting, drilling, grinding, turning and milling. Each of these operations is done by a special machine. For example, the operation of turning (forming a curve in the material) is done on a lathe, and cutting is done with a saw. All machine tools have a cutting blade or edge, which is normally made of metal, but may include diamond or other tough materials. The blade moves against the object being cut, called the workpiece, shaving off unwanted material.

Machine tools are used to make engine parts and other complex machines in which the parts have to fit together perfectly. Industrial robots are versatile machines that can be programmed to do many jobs, such as moving workpieces or drilling very accurately.

A perfect fit
Under computer control, this miniature milling machine is shaping a piece of ceramic material so that it will fit perfectly into a cavity in a dental patient's tooth. A milling machine cuts out areas of a piece of material. The cutting tool has rotating teeth, similar to a gear wheel.

Pedal power
A pole lathe is powered by a foot-operated pedal. The lathe spins the workpiece around very fast. The operator presses cutting tools against the spinning wood, shaving off a layer each time. How accurately the workpiece is finished depends on the skill of the lathe operator.

Pressed panels
A machine called a die press flattens sheets of steel into shaped panels, such as those used for car hoods. The top part of the machine moves down to press the panel into shape. Each sheet of steel is pressed into exactly the same shape every time.

Digital control

An engineer makes a heating element from a graphite rod using a computer-controlled milling machine. Data describing the shape and size of the heating element is fed into the machine's computer, normally from another computer on which it has been designed. The computer then determines the cutting movements required to make the heating element from the rod and operates the milling machine very precisely.

Keeping cool

The milky liquid pouring onto this drill is, in fact, colored water. As the drill bit cuts into the metal workpiece, it gets very hot. The water keeps the drill cool, stopping the tool from melting and washing away waste metal.

Industrial robots

Robots are used for welding car components together. The robot is shown how to do the job once and can then do it over and over again, much faster than a human worker.

FACT BOX

• In some industries, high-energy lasers are used for cutting and shaping materials instead of traditional machine tools. The most powerful lasers can cut through 2 ½ inches of steel.

• In some car-making factories, parts for the cars are delivered by robot vehicles that are programmed to drive themselves around the floor of the factory.

MACHINES OF THE FUTURE

Machines that do complicated jobs need controls. Some of these machines need a human operator who controls the machine manually. For example, a car needs a driver to control its speed and direction. Other machines control themselves—once they are turned on, they do their job automatically. For example, an automatic washing machine washes and spins your clothes at the press of a button. One of the first machines to use a form of automatic control was the Jacquard loom. Punched paper cards were fed into the loom and told it which threads were to be used. Today, many machines are controlled by computer to perform a set task whenever it is required. The most advanced machines are even able to check their own work and change it if necessary.

Flying by wires
Airliners and fighter aircraft may have a "fly-by-wire" control system, where a computer, rather than the pilot, actually flies the plane. The pilot monitors how the plane is working by watching a computer screen instead of dials.

Journey through space
Shuttle-like space planes, such as the experimental X-33, will eventually be used to transport passengers via space. Space planes could reduce the usual flight time from New York to Tokyo from nearly 14 hours to just a couple of hours.

Robotic rover
A toy robot dog has built-in artificial intelligence. It knows nothing at first, but it gradually figures out the layout of its new home and learns to respond to its new owner's commands.

Tiny machine
The rotor in this photograph is actually only about ½ millimeter across. It is part of a meter that measures liquid flow. It is made of silicon and was manufactured using similar methods to those used to make microchips. Tiny machines such as this are called micromachines.

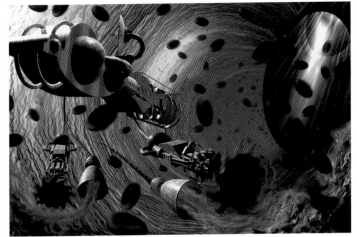

Robotic surgeon

In the future, it is possible that microscopic machines will be used in surgery. In this futuristic painting a microscopic robot is repairing a human body. The robot, just 1/10 millimeter long, has been injected into a blood vessel through the needle on the right. Around the robot are red blood cells. With its rotating blades, the robot is cutting away a blockage made of debris (shown in gray). The robot sucks up the debris for removal.

Invisible gears

These gear wheels look quite ordinary, but they were made using microscopic experimental technology called nanotechnology. The width of the wheels is less than the width of a human hair. A hundred of these gear wheels piled up would be only as tall as the thickness of a sheet of paper!

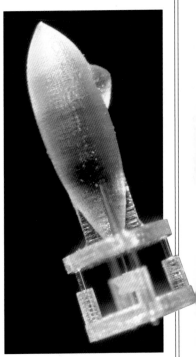

Handy android

An android (a human-like robot) uses electronic eyes and ears to figure out where objects are and its hand to pick them up. With its artificial intelligence, it can decide what kind of object it is holding. Androids help scientists to research how robots can be made to act like humans.

Car control

Many of this car's systems are controlled by a microchip called a microprocessor. It continually checks signals from sensors and sends a control signal back again. It calculates the speed, distance and fuel consumption of the car and displays them on the dashboard.

Mini submarine

A miniature submarine that measures just 3/16 inch from top to bottom was made using an experimental technique for creating microscopic machine parts. The technique uses tiny laser beams to solidify selected parts of a pool of liquid plastic to form the submarine's shape.

AUTOMATIC CONTROL

CONTROLLING A ROBOT

You will need:
blindfold, egg and egg-cup.

1 Ask a friend to put on the blindfold. Use the list of commands opposite to direct your friend to where the egg is located.

2 Your friend should not know where the egg is or what to do with it. Instruct your friend to carefully pick the egg up. Only use commands in the list.

Machines that perform very difficult, complicated tasks need to be controlled with precision. Robots are machines that are programmed with instructions for different situations. They can respond to each situation in an "intelligent" way, rather like human beings. However, although robots seem to be very clever, they can only do what they are told to do. The project below will show you how tricky it is to program a robot to do even the simplest job. Using only the words that are from the list of commands, see if a friend can carry out the task successfully.

The second project shows you how to make a simple control disc. This is the sort of device used to control some washing machines. The metal track on the disc is part of an electric circuit. As the disk turns, the track completes or breaks the circuit, turning parts of the machine, such as lights and motors, on and off.

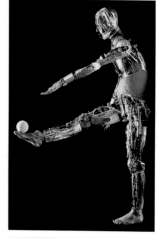

Robot commands
FORWARD
STOP
TURN LEFT
TURN RIGHT
ARM UP
ARM DOWN
CLOSE FINGERS
OPEN FINGERS

3 Now ask your friend to accurately place the egg on another surface. See if your friend can put it in the egg-cup. How quickly was your friend able to complete the task? The faster your friend completes the task, the better you are at programming.

MAKE A CONTROL DISK

You will need: compass and pencil, ruler, cardboard, scissors, aluminum pie pan, glue, tape, paper fastener, wire, three plastic-coated wires, battery, flashlight bulb and holder.

1 Use a compass to mark out a 4-in. disc of cardboard and cut it out. Also cut a 2½-in. ring from the foil dish and glue it onto the cardboard.

2 Put pieces of tape across the foil track. The bare foil will complete the circuit. The pieces of tape will break the circuit.

3 Push a paper fastener through the middle of the disk and mount it onto a piece of cardboard. Using the wire, make two contacts with a bend in the middle, as shown.

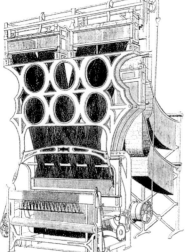

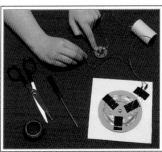

4 Stick the contacts to the cardboard so they press on the foil. Connect a battery to a bulb with plastic-coated wire. Attach a second piece of plastic-coated wire to the bulb, and a third to the battery.

Loom control

The Jacquard loom, invented in 1801, was one of the first machines with automatic control. Cards with patterns of holes in them, called punched cards, controlled how threads were woven together to create patterns in the fabric that the loom made. The pattern created could be changed simply by changing to another set of cards with a different pattern of holes.

5 Attach the two loose wires to the two contacts on the cardboard. You have now made a circuit. Turn the disk slowly. The light bulb goes on and off as the disk turns. As the contacts go over a piece of tape, the circuit is broken and the light goes out. When they touch the foil again, the circuit is completed and the light comes back on.

CANON VIDEO LENS 16×

OPTICAL
IMAGE
STABILIZER

16x/320x
DIGITAL ZOOM

MIC

Canon

R PCM STEREO L

DIGITAL
EFFECTS

PART THREE

CAMERAS

When you understand how different cameras work, it will make a huge difference to how well or badly your photographs turn out. Learning about lenses, apertures, shutter speeds and film speeds gives you the knowledge and confidence to take photographs in different lighting and weather situations. It is even possible to pick up some tips used by professional photographers and to print your own photographs. It is important to keep up with new developments too, for digital and video photography offer exciting new opportunities for those interested in taking and using pictures.

AUTHORS
Chris Oxlade • Al Morrison
CONSULTANT
John Freeman

YOU AND YOUR CAMERA

What is the one vital piece of equipment you must not forget if you are on vacation or having a birthday party? Your camera! To most people, a camera is simply a device for taking snapshots of their favorite places and people. Cameras are really sophisticated machines that make use of the latest breakthroughs in science and technology. A camera is designed to do a specific job. It makes a copy of a scene on film by collecting light from that scene and turning it into a picture. It works in a very similar way to your eyes, but it makes a permanent record of the scene instead of simply looking at it.

As simple as blinking
Using a camera is like looking through a special window. Blink your eyes. This is how a camera records light from a scene. A shutter opens to let light pass through a glass lens and fall onto the film.

With your camera, you can record all kinds of events, such as parties and holidays. A simple point-and-shoot compact camera is all you need.

Early cameras
The first practical cameras with film were developed in the 1830s. Today, cameras do the same job but are much easier to use. In the early days, it could take half an hour to take a photo. Modern cameras have much shorter exposure time. Scenes can be recorded in a fraction of a second.

Producing prints

A camera is useless without film inside to record the images the lens makes. If you want prints, then the film is developed, or processed to produce negatives. Prints are then made from the negatives and can be enlarged to a variety of different sizes. Frame numbers and details of the type of film used appear on the edge of the strip. The notches are for the use of the processing mini-lab. You can see which of the negatives on this strip produced the print next to it.

negative

print

The winning picture

If professional photographers are shooting a sports or news event, they must get a clear image. Their pictures appear in magazines and newspapers and help us to understand the story.

Professionals at work

These professional photographers are using telephoto lenses to get a closer picture of the event they are recording. Professionals need to use sophisticated equipment and usually carry two or three cameras, a selection of lenses, a tripod, a flash and rolls of film of different speeds.

WHAT IS A CAMERA?

All cameras, from disposable to professional models, have the same basic parts. The camera body is really just a light-proof box. This keeps the light-sensitive film in complete darkness. A section of film is held flat in the back of the body. At the front of the body is the lens, which collects light from the scene and shines it onto the film. Between the lens and the film is a shutter. When you take a photograph, the shutter opens to let light come through the lens onto the film.

Many cameras have additional features that help you to take better photographs. In some cameras, the shutter timing and lens position are automatically adjusted to suit different conditions.

Disposable cameras come with the film already inside. You take the whole camera to the film processor when the film is finished.

Compact camera

A compact camera is a small camera that will fit in your pocket. With many models, all you have to do is aim at the scene and press the shutter release button. Simple compacts are also called point-and-shoot cameras.

shutter release button

viewfinder

flash unit, to light up dark scenes

115

lens protected by plastic flap when camera is not in use

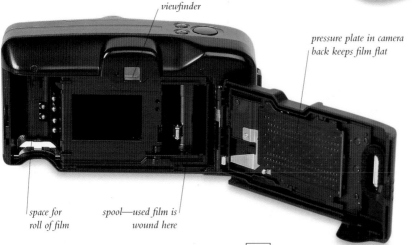

viewfinder

pressure plate in camera back keeps film flat

space for roll of film

spool—used film is wound here

Inside the camera

You open the back of the camera to load and unload the film. There is space for the film cassette and a spool where the used film is stored. The film is advanced, or wound, either by an electric motor or by hand.

Close-up care

The view that you see in the viewfinder of a compact camera is not quite the same as the view that the lens sees. This is because the viewfinder is higher up than the lens. Remember to leave some space around close-up objects in the viewfinder.

lens view

viewfinder view

You look through a viewfinder to see what will be in your photo. The guidelines you see in many viewfinders (seen in red here) show you what area of the scene will be included in your picture. If the photographer takes this picture, the boy's hat will be cut off.

Instant photos
Polaroid cameras use special film that produces prints almost instantly.

SLR camera

Focusing on an image

Most modern 35-mm cameras (those needing 35-mm format film) use a single-lens reflex (SLR) design. When you look into the viewfinder, you see exactly what the lens sees. You can change the lens of an SLR camera to achieve different effects.

HOW A LENS WORKS

Making your own simple viewer will show you just how a camera lens collects light from a scene and makes a small copy of it on the film. The copy is called an image. Just like a real camera, the viewer has a light-proof box. At the front of the box is a pin-hole, which works like a tiny lens. The screen at the back of the box is where the film would be in a real camera. This kind of viewer is sometimes called a camera obscura (which just means a dark box used to capture images of outside objects). In the past, artists used these to make images of scenes that they could paint.

MAKE YOUR OWN VIEWER

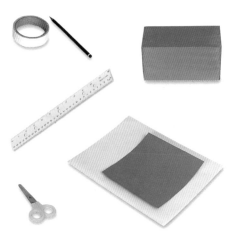

You will need: ruler, scissors, small cardboard box, card stock, sharp pencil, tape, tracing paper.

Light rays
Light travels in straight rays. You can see this when you shine a flashlight. When you look at a scene, your eyes collect rays of light that are coming from every part of it. This is just what a camera does.

1 Using scissors, cut a small hole, about ½ x ½ in., in one end of the cardboard box.

2 Now cut a much larger square hole in the other end of your cardboard box.

3 Cut a square of card stock 1½ x 1½ in. Pierce a tiny hole in the center with a sharp pencil.

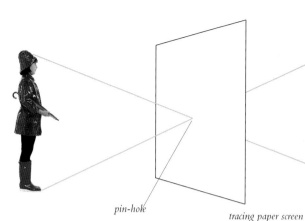

If you look at a person through your viewer, light rays from their head hit the bottom of the viewer's screen. Rays from their feet hit the top of the screen. So the screen image is upside down. Left and right are swapped, too.

pin-hole

tracing paper screen

Making an image with light

When you use your viewer, the pin-hole lets in just a few light rays from each part of the scene. The rays keep going in straight lines and hit the tracing paper screen, making an image of the scene.

A camera obscura

Some camera obscuras are more like rooms than boxes, but they work in the same way. Light from a small hole or simple lens creates a reversed and upside down image on a flat surface. This can be seen in the darkened interior of the room.

6 Now look out of a window, through the screen of tracing paper. Try tracing the image you see onto the paper.

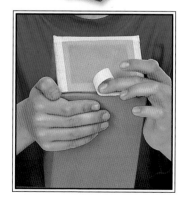

4 Place the card stock over the box's smaller hole. Make sure that the pin-hole is centered over the hole. Now tape it into place.

5 Cut a square of tracing paper slightly bigger than the larger hole. Tape it securely over that hole. Your viewer is ready to use.

EXPERIMENT WITH LIGHT

HAVING FUN WITH BEAMS

You will need: *ruler, two pieces of card stock, scissors, flashlight, glass of water, magnifying glass, mirror.*

Light is refracted and reflected inside cameras by lenses and mirrors. The best way to see how this happens is to send some light beams through lenses and then bounce them off mirrors yourself. You can make narrow light beams by shining a flashlight through slots in a sheet of card stock. Try these experiments and then see if you have any ideas of your own. Vary the size of the slots to see how the light beams change.
Carry out the experiments in a room with the lights off and the blinds or curtains closed.

Converging light rays
The lens of a magnifying glass makes light rays from objects converge, or bend inward, toward each other. So, when the rays enter the eye, they seem to have come from a bigger object.

1 Cut a slot about ⅛ in. wide and 2 in. long in two pieces of card stock. Bend the bottom edges so they stand up. Shine the light beam of a flashlight through both.

2 To see how the beam can be refracted put a glass of water in its path. Move the glass from side to side to see how the beam widens and narrows.

3 Replace the second piece of card stock with one with three slots in it. Put a magnifying glass in the path of the three beams to make them converge, or bend inward.

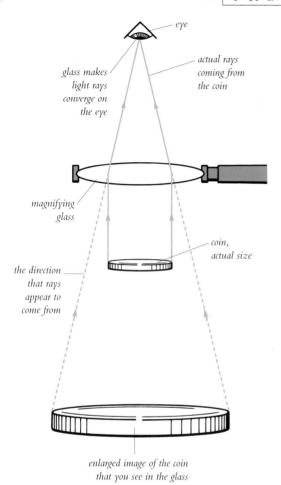

eye

actual rays coming from the coin

glass makes light rays converge on the eye

magnifying glass

coin, actual size

the direction that rays appear to come from

enlarged image of the coin that you see in the glass

Water mirror

Unlike other cameras, single-lens reflex cameras (SLRs) give crisp, clean images. To see why, try this simple experiment. Hold a glass of water up so that you can see the bottom surface of the water clearly. Now poke your finger into the water from above. You should see a clear, single reflection of your finger in the surface. This is because the surface acts just like a mirror *(now see box below)*.

4 Now try each of the experiments, but put a mirror in the way of the different beams. Can you see how the pattern of rays stays the same?

MIRRORS AND PRISMS

Stopping reflections

If you look carefully at a reflection in a normal mirror, you will see a "ghostly" second image. The water mirror above does not make a "ghostly" image. To keep from getting "ghostly" images on your pictures, the SLR has a glass block called a pentaprism (a five-angled prism), which treats reflections in the same way as the water mirror.

The same view

The pentaprism in an SLR camera also makes sure that the image you see in the viewfinder is exactly the same as the image on your developed photo.

COMING INTO FOCUS

Before taking a photograph, you need to make sure that your subject is in focus. When it is, all the rays of light that leave a point on the subject are bent by the lens so that they hit the same place on the film. This makes a clear, sharp image on the film. Parts of the scene in front or behind the subject will not be in focus. On some cameras you have to choose the part of the scene that you want to be in focus yourself. Autofocus cameras focus the lens by automatically choosing the object at the center of the focal plane.

In this photograph (above), the subject is in sharp focus. You can see all the fine detail. When the same shot is out of focus (below), it makes the subject look blurred.

focal plane

The focal plane
When the image of a subject is in focus, the light rays meet on the film focal plane. The camera's film is held flat in the focal plane by a pressure plate, visible if you open the back of your (empty) camera.

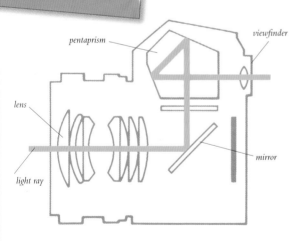

pentaprism

viewfinder

lens

light ray

mirror

Focusing SLRs
With an SLR camera, you see exactly what the image looks like through the viewfinder. On a manual-focus SLR, you turn a ring around the lens to get your subject in focus.

Getting closer
Use a magnifying glass and lamp to make an image of an object on a sheet of paper. Move the magnifying glass closer to and farther away from the paper, to bring different parts of the scene into focus.

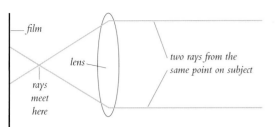

The lens, here, is too far away from the film. Rays from the subject meet in front of the film, so it is out of focus.

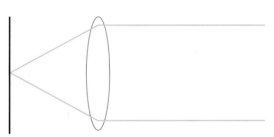

To focus, the lens is moved backward, toward the film. The rays now meet on the film.

In and out of focus

A camera focuses on a subject by moving the lens backward and forward so it gets closer to, or farther away from the film. This brings parts of the scene that are at different distances from the camera into focus. When the lens is set closest to the film, objects from the distance are in sharper focus.

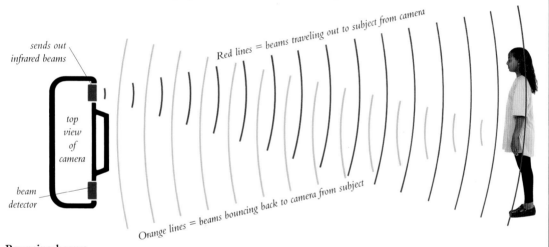

sends out infrared beams

top view of camera

beam detector

Red lines = beams traveling out to subject from camera

Orange lines = beams bouncing back to camera from subject

Bouncing beams

With the type of autofocus system shown here, the camera emits a wide beam of invisible infrared light. It figures out how long the infrared light takes to bounce back, and so knows how far away the subject is. A small electric motor then moves the lens.

Autofocus errors

Most autofocus cameras focus on objects that are in the center of the scene in the viewfinder. If your subject is off to one side, the camera focuses on the background, and your subject will be blurred *(left)*. If you have a focus lock, you can prevent this by aiming at the subject first, and then using your focus lock before recomposing the shot and shooting *(right)*.

MAKE YOUR OWN CAMERA

MAKING A PIN-HOLE CAMERA

You will need: pin-hole box viewer, aluminum foil, scissors, tape, pencil, black paper, thin card stock, thick cloth or plastic, photographic paper, rubber band.

You can make your very own simple camera with just a few basic pieces of equipment. This project combines all the main principles of photography. For simplicity, this camera uses photographic paper (paper with a light-sensitive coating on one side) instead of film and a pin-hole instead of a lens. When the "film" (paper) is processed, you will have a negative. Then turn to the "Printing and Projecting" project to find out how you can make a print from the negative. Find out about the equipment you need in the "Recording an Image" project.

1 Make the pin-hole viewer from the "How a Lens Works" project, but remove the tracing-paper screen. Replace the 1½-in. card stock square with aluminum foil. Pierce a hole, about ⅛ in. across, in the center of the foil using a sharp pencil.

2 Open the back of the box and line the inside with black paper. Alternatively, color the inside with a black felt-tip pen.

3 Cut a square of card stock large enough to cover the aluminum foil. Tape just the top edge to the box, so that it will act as a shutter.

4 Cut a square of card stock to fit right across the other end of the box. Tape it to one edge so that it closes over the hole like a door or flap.

5 Find some heavy, black, light-proof cloth or a plastic sheet. Cut a piece large enough to fold around the end of the box.

6 In a completely dark room, feeling with your fingers, put a piece of photographic paper under the flap at the end of the box.

7 Close the flap, then wrap the cloth or plastic sheet tightly over it. Next, put rubber band tightly around the box to secure it.

8 Now you can turn the light on. Point the camera at a well-lit object and open the shutter. Leave the camera still for about five minutes and then close the shutter.

Disposable camera
Single use cameras have the film already loaded and ready to use. You send the whole camera when you want the film to be developed.

Opening the shutter allows light to strike the piece of light-sensitive paper. The paper is coated to turn dark where light strikes it. This gives you a negative, on paper instead of on film. Next, you need to develop the image on the paper with developing fluid (see the "Printing and Projecting" project). This will give you the negative image on the sheet of paper as it appears here.

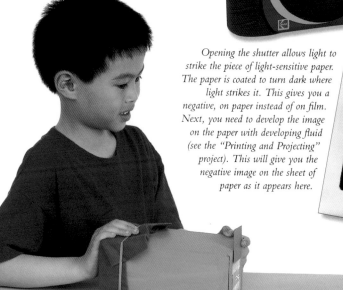

USING FILM

The camera's job is to create a focused image of a scene, but this would be no use without a way of recording the image. This is the job of the film. Film is coated with a type of silver that is affected by light. So when an image strikes the film, the silver records the patterns of light, dark and color. You cannot look at film right away. It must be developed first with chemicals that turn the silver black or gray where light has struck it. Until then, it must be kept in complete darkness. If undeveloped film is exposed to direct light, it turns completely black.

Always load and unload film in dim light or in shadow, to prevent light from leaking into the film canister.

film   lens

The film is exposed by the camera when you photograph something, such as this bird against a light background (left).

latent image   crystals in this sky area are exposed to light

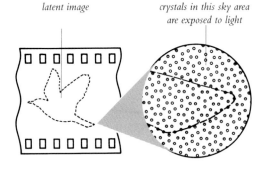

Crystals in the light area of the image change. Crystals in the dark area do not. The image has been recorded chemically. Nothing shows up on the film, and the image is called the latent (hidden) image.

Types of film

There are several different types of film. The one most people use is film for color prints. This is called color negative film. Other common types are black-and-white negative film for making black-and-white positive prints and color reversal film for making slides.

Exposing a film

Black-and-white film contains millions of microscopic light-sensitive crystals that contain silver. When a photograph is taken, some of the crystals that are exposed to light begin to break down, leaving silver metal. In the areas where more light falls, more crystals begin to change.

Processing film

Amateur photographers develop black-and-white film at home, in a small developing tank. In the dark, the film is wound carefully onto a plastic spiral. The spiral is then placed in the tank and a lid is put on. A chemical called developer is poured into the tank and left for a few minutes before being poured out. Then chemical fixer is poured in. Finally, the film is washed.

Film drying

After washing, film is carefully dried. They are usually hung up to dry in a dust-free area, sometimes in a special drying cabinet. Once the film is dry, the photographer can cut it into manageable strips and choose which ones to print.

black background with white bird

changed crystals

unchanged crystals

During developing (above), all the crystals that had begun to break down change completely to silver. They look black. The unchanged crystals stay as they are.

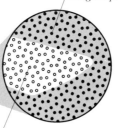

black background with clear bird

changed crystals

no crystals

Fixing gets rid of all the unchanged crystals, leaving clear film. The result is a negative, where dark areas on the original subject are light, and light areas are dark.

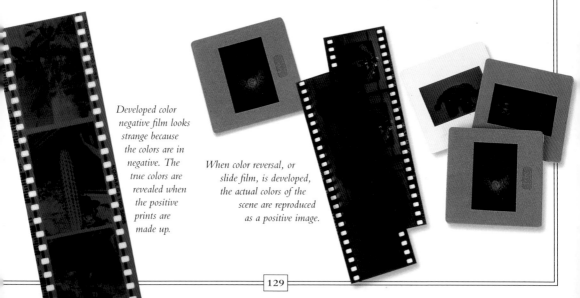

Developed color negative film looks strange because the colors are in negative. The true colors are revealed when the positive prints are made up.

When color reversal, or slide film, is developed, the actual colors of the scene are reproduced as a positive image.

THE RIGHT FILM

There are three basic types of film. They are color negative film, color-reversal film and black-and-white film. Film comes in different sizes (called formats). Most cameras use 35-mm film, which comes in a preloaded container called a cassette. Film also comes in different lengths. The lengths are measured by the number of exposures, or photographs, that will fit on the film. The usual lengths are 24 and 36 exposures. You also have to decide which speed of film to use. Fast film reacts to light more quickly than slow film. Film speed is referred to by its ISO (International Standards Organization) rating. The most common speeds are ISO 100 and ISO 200, which are medium-speed films.

All the details of a film (format, speed and length) are printed on the film carton and the film cassette. The carton also has an expiration date.

Automatic coding
On one side of a film cassette is a pattern of black and silver squares. This is called a DX code and it indicates the film's ISO rating and length. Modern cameras have sensors that can read the code and display it in the viewfinder. On older cameras, you have to set the ISO rating manually on a dial.

Which film speed?
The difference between films of different speeds is the size of their crystals (or grains). Fast film (ISO 400 and above) is perfect for shooting in dim light and for action shots (or when the subject won't sit still). They have larger grains than slow films. This is because larger grains can react to much less light than small ones. These large grains often show up in the final picture *(above right)*. Slow films (ISO 50 and below) are perfect for fine, crisp detail *(above left)*.

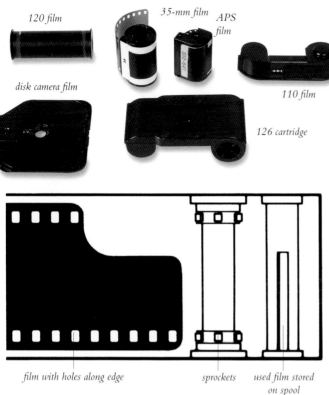

120 film

35-mm film

APS film

disk camera film

110 film

126 cartridge

Film and photo formats

Format is the size of the film and the size and shape of each image recorded on the film. Large-format films give much more detail. Smaller formats are more convenient. Some cameras can take photographs of different formats on the same film using adapters or masks.

film with holes along edge

sprockets

used film stored on spool

Winding on

35-mm and APS (Advanced Photographic System) film have small holes along each side. The holes fit over sprockets in the camera that turn to wind on the film. This brings a fresh part of unexposed film behind the lens. Roll films have backing paper that shields the film from stray light. This film is wound from one spool to another as it is exposed.

Indoor film

Most color film is designed for use in daylight. If you use it indoors, with light from lightbulbs, the photos come out yellowy. You can buy indoor film called tungsten film, which gives the right colors, or use a conversion filter that compensates for indoor light.

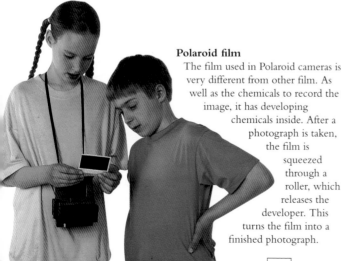

Polaroid film

The film used in Polaroid cameras is very different from other film. As well as the chemicals to record the image, it has developing chemicals inside. After a photograph is taken, the film is squeezed through a roller, which releases the developer. This turns the film into a finished photograph.

FACT BOX

- Infrared film is coated with chemicals that react to heat, rather than to the visible light rays, coming from a scene.

- The largest negative that has ever been used measured 21 by 1 ft. This massive negative was made for a huge panoramic picture of 3,500 people, photographed in the United States in 1992.

- 35-mm format film was originally developed for movie cameras. It is still the most common format for movie camera film.

RECORDING AN IMAGE

MAKE A PHOTOGRAM

You will need: lamp, photographic paper, different-shaped objects such as keys, disks and scissors, rubber gloves, protective goggles, plastic tongs, plastic dishes, chemicals (see below).

Photographic chemicals
You will need two photographic chemicals: developer for paper (not film) and fixer. Buy them at a photographic supplier. Ask an adult to help you follow the instructions on the bottles to dilute (mix with water) the chemicals, and make sure you protect your eyes and hands when handling them. Store the diluted chemicals in plastic bottles. Seal the bottles and label them clearly.

Y ou do not need a camera to see how film works. In fact, you do not need film either! You can use black-and-white photographic paper instead. Photographic paper is the paper that prints are made on. It works in the same way as film. Here, you can see how to make a picture called a photogram. It is made by covering some parts of a sheet of photographic paper with objects and then shining light on the sheet. When the paper is developed, the areas that were hit by the light turn black, leaving you an image of the objects.

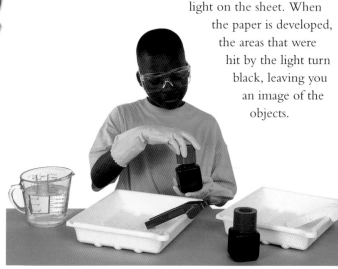

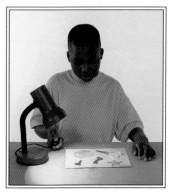

1 Turn off the light. Lay a sheet of photographic paper down, shiny-side up. Put objects on it. Turn the light on again for a few seconds.

2 Pick up the paper with the tongs and put it into the dish of developer. Push it down so that the paper is under the liquid.

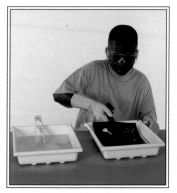

3 After a minute, use the tongs to move the paper into the fixer. Leave it under the liquid for a minute, until the image is set.

This symbol, on photographic chemical bottles, means that they can be dangerous if not used with care. Always wear gloves and goggles.

Photographic paper

For black-and-white prints, you need paper called monochrome paper. Buy the smallest size you can, and choose grade 2 if possible, with a gloss finish. The paper comes in a light-proof envelope or box. Only open the envelope in complete darkness. The paper is in a second, black plastic envelope.

The finished photogram should show the objects in white on a black background. Try experimenting with other ideas. How about cutting out letters and making your name, or crumple up transparent materials to create more exciting effects?

4 Now you can turn the light back on. Using the tongs, lift the paper out of the fixer and wash it with running water for a few minutes. Then lay the paper on a flat surface to dry. This technique is an excellent way of producing unique invitations or greeting cards quickly and effectively.

THE CAMERA SHUTTER

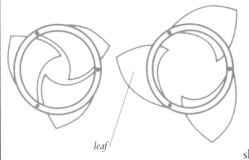

leaf

A leaf shutter has thin metal plates called leaves. These overlap each other to close the shutter (left) and swivel back to open it (right).

All cameras have a shutter between the lens at the front and the film at the back. The shutter is much like a door. It is closed most of the time, so that no light gets to the film. When you press the button to take a photo, the shutter opens briefly and then closes again, to let light from your subject reach the film. The time for which the shutter is open is called the shutter speed. Compact cameras have a leaf shutter close to the lens. SLR cameras, which have interchangeable lenses, have a focal-plane shutter, which is located just in front of the film. You should be careful not to touch the shutter when loading film in this type of camera.

first curtain

Focal-plane shutter
This has two curtains. When the camera takes a photograph, the first curtain opens to let light hit the film. The second curtain follows closely behind, covering up the film again. The smaller the gap between the curtains, the faster the shutter speed.

second curtain

Shutter speeds
Most photographs are taken with a shutter speed of between 1/60 and 1/250 of a second. On some SLR cameras, you have to set the shutter speed by turning a dial *(below)*. Each setting gives a shutter speed about twice as fast as the one before.

Camera shake
When the shutter is open, even tiny camera movements make the image move across the film, causing a slightly blurred picture. This is called camera shake. It can happen if the shutter speed is below about 1/60 of a second.

A tripod forms a steady base for a camera. It is very useful if you are taking photographs with slow shutter speeds because there is no chance of camera shake. Using a tripod will also help you to compose your pictures really well, because you do not have to worry about holding the camera. You can also vary the height of your viewpoint.

Panning

This shows the famous sprinter and long jumper Carl Lewis in action. The photographer has panned the camera (moved it to follow the athlete), which has blurred the background, enhancing the impression of speed.

Panning, or moving your camera to follow a moving subject, helps to stop the area that is traveling across the frame from being blurred. The stationary elements (background) of the photo will still appear fuzzy.

When you photograph action, such as people running, a fast shutter speed will freeze the action and prevent a blurred shot. Panning will also help, especially if your subject is moving across the scene. To pan, aim at your subject and swing the camera to follow it, squeezing the shutter release button when the subject is where you want it.

There are several ways of keeping your camera steady as you take a photograph, even if you do not have a tripod. For example, stand with your legs slightly apart, or crouch down with one knee on the ground. Squeeze the shutter release button slowly. For extra steadiness, lean against a tree, or try resting your camera on a wall. A friend's shoulder or a chair are also good ideas.

WHAT AN APERTURE DOES

The aperture ring on an SLR lens. Aperture size is measured in f-numbers (such as f/8).

The aperture is basically a hole, situated behind the camera lens, that can be made larger or smaller. When the aperture is small, some of the light rays that pass through the lens are cut off so that they do not reach the film. This does not cut off any of the image on the film, but it does reduce the amount of light that hits the film, making the image darker. Changing the size of the aperture also affects how much of the scene is in focus. Some cameras, such as the disposable variety, have a pre-set aperture.

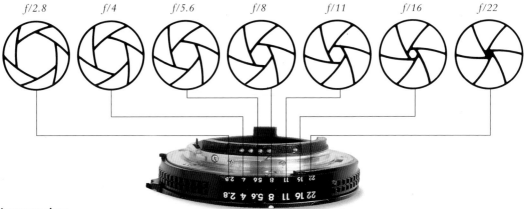

Aperture sizes
The mechanism that changes aperture size has interlocking metal leaves. These fold in to make the aperture smaller. The f-number is a fraction—f/4 means a quarter of the focal length of the lens. (Focal length is the distance from the lens to the focal point, where light rays from an object come together.) So an aperture of f/8 is half the width of one of f/4, and lets in one-quarter of the amount of light.

Changing depth of field
Depth of field is the distance between the nearest part of the scene that is in focus and the farthest part of the scene that is in focus. As f-numbers get bigger, the aperture gets smaller and the depth of field increases. Shooting on a sunny day will let you use a small aperture. This makes it easier to get a large depth of field. The depth of field can be set on some cameras.

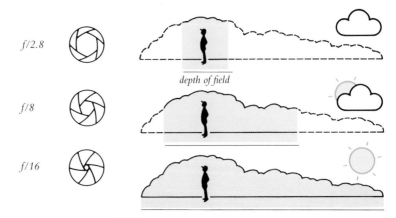

This photograph was taken with a much smaller aperture than the photograph on the far left, making the depth of field much deeper. Almost everything in the scene is in focus. Greater depth of field is useful for photographs of scenery or architecture where you want to show clear detail. It is also useful if you have people in the foreground and want both the people and the background to be in focus.

In this photograph, the subject (the children) is in focus, and the background is totally out of focus. This is called a shallow depth of field because only the objects that are a certain distance from the camera are in focus. Using shallow depth of field is ideal if you want to make parts of the scene that might confuse your picture disappear into a blur.

FACT BOX

• A lens always has its maximum aperture written on it. For example, a lens described as 300 f/4 has a focal length of 300 mm (12 inches) and a maximum aperture of f/4.

• Large maximum apertures tend to be very expensive because the lenses have to be much bigger. For example, an f/1.4 lens can cost several times as much as an f/4 lens.

• A pin-hole camera the size of a shoe-box has an aperture of about f/500 (1/500th of the focal length).

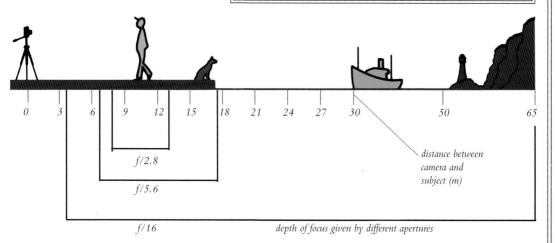

| 0 | 3 | 6 | 9 | 12 | 15 | 18 | 21 | 24 | 27 | 30 | 50 | 65 |

distance between camera and subject (m)

f/2.8

f/5.6

f/16   *depth of focus given by different apertures*

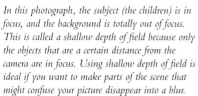

Try focusing your camera at a certain object and then changing the aperture. You will see how different areas of the picture come into focus.

Lens focused at 9 ft
Aperture at f/2.8
Depth of field=5 ft

Lens focused at 9 ft
Aperture at f/5.6
Depth of field=11½ ft

Lens focused at 9 ft
Aperture at f/16
Depth of field=65 ft

THE RIGHT EXPOSURE

E xposure is the word for the amount of light that reaches the film in your camera when you take a photograph. Exposure depends on the shutter speed (slower shutter speeds give more time and allow more light through) and the aperture (larger apertures also allow more light through). You might see exposure stated on your camera as a combination of shutter speed and aperture—for example, f/16 at 1/60 sec. All but the simplest cameras measure the amount of light coming from the scene and figure out what exposure is needed for the speed of the film in the camera. They do this with an electronic light sensor called a metering system.

In this picture, too little light has reached the film, and the chemicals have not reacted enough. This is called underexposure. The finished photo looks too dark and usually has a grainy quality. Nothing can really be done to improve it in processing.

Here, too much light has reached the film, and the chemicals in the film have reacted too much. This is called overexposure. The final photo is washed out. It can be corrected in printing, unlike underexposure.

When this photograph was taken, the exposure was correct and exactly the right amount of light reached the film. The finished picture is well-balanced—neither too light, nor too dark.

Shutter speed and aperture

Try using different combinations of shutter speed and aperture, each of which lets in the same amount of light *(see right),* and see what a difference it makes. For example, f/8 at 1/125 second gives the same amount of light as f/4 at 1/500 second. But a narrower aperture (f/8) gives a greater depth of field. You might use the wider aperture (f/4) for a fast, action shot and the narrower aperture (f/8) for a landscape shot where you want greater depth of field.

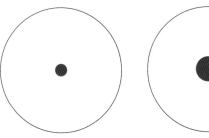

f/16 at 1/30 sec

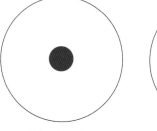

f/8 at 1/125 sec

f/4 at 1/500 sec

FACT BOX

• Some cameras can measure the changes in brightness across a scene automatically and then take an average reading for the whole scene.

• There are certain advanced APS (Advanced Photographic System) cameras that can remember the exposure settings for each picture on a roll of film.

• It is more important to get the exposure right if you are using slide (color reversal) film, rather than print film (color negative). This is partly because it is possible to correct mistakes when making prints, but not when making slides.

In the picture on the left, the light shining through the window is brighter than the main subject— the girl. This means that the camera measures more of the light coming from the brighter area. As a result, the background is correctly exposed, but the girl is underexposed and looks too dark.

In this picture, the background was still by far the brightest part of the picture. The problem was solved, however, by using a much larger exposure, and the balance is just right. Bright lighting coming from the background is called backlighting.

LETTING IN THE LIGHT

Changing a camera's aperture affects both the brightness of an image and the depth of field. You can see how it works with a few simple experiments. First, look at your own eyes. Like an aperture, your pupils automatically narrow in bright light to protect your retinas, and open wide to let you see in dim light. To see a shutter at work, open the back of your camera (when there is no film in it). Now look for a leaf shutter near the lens or a focal-plane shutter just behind where the film would be.

INVESTIGATING APERTURES

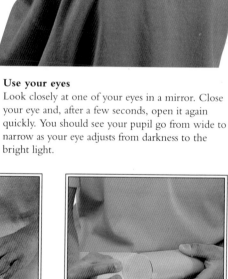

You will need: *magnifying glass, cardboard tube, tape, scissors, thin card stock, tracing paper, table lamp, pencil.*

Use your eyes
Look closely at one of your eyes in a mirror. Close your eye and, after a few seconds, open it again quickly. You should see your pupil go from wide to narrow as your eye adjusts from darkness to the bright light.

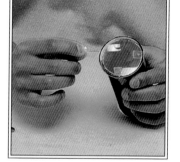

1 Carefully attach the magnifying glass to one end of your cardboard tube using small pieces of tape.

2 Roll a piece of thin card stock around the other end of the tube. Tape the top edge down to make another tube that slides in and out.

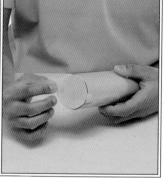

3 With tape, attach a circle of tracing paper across the end of the sliding cardboard tube. This will form your viewing screen.

See a shutter at work

To see just how a shutter works, open the back of your camera (when there is no film inside) and carefully place a small strip of tracing paper where your film usually goes. Now aim the camera at a subject, preferably one that is brightly lit, and press the shutter release button. You should see a brief flash of the image on your tracing paper—although there will be no lasting picture! Be very careful not to put your fingers on the shutter blades in the focal-plane cameras.

4 With the screen nearest to you, aim your tube at a table lamp that is turned on. Can you see an image of the bulb on the screen?

5 Slide the tubes together until the image of the bulb is clear. Now adjust them again so that the image is slightly out of focus.

6 Mark then cut a small hole (about ¼ in. wide) in a piece of card stock, to make a small aperture. Look at the light bulb again and put the card stock in front of the lens. The smaller aperture will bring the light bulb into focus. Is it clearer? Can you read the writing on the bulb?

PRINTING

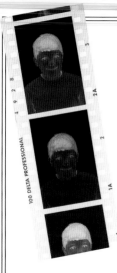

When film is developed, the images on the film are usually too small to look at. You can view slide films with a projector, which makes a large copy of the image on a screen. But before you can look at photographs taken with negative film, you have to make prints. The paper used for prints is light-sensitive, just like film. To make a print, the negative image is projected onto the paper. When the paper is developed, you get a positive image, so that the scene appears as you saw it originally.

Negatives
When black-and-white film is processed, light areas of the scene appear dark and dark areas appear light. This is a negative.

If you are using black-and-white film, bear in mind that bright areas of the image change the chemicals in the film more than dark areas.

Developing and fixing
The paper is processed in the dark, using chemicals. The three trays hold the developer, water or stop bath (to stop the developer) and fixer. Areas where light has hit the paper come out dark. So light areas of the negative come out dark, as in the original scene.

Enlarging
This is the first stage in making a print. An enlarger projects the negative onto paper placed below it. This must be done in the dark, so that no stray light ruins the paper. Lighter areas of the negative allow more light to reach the paper than darker areas.

The final print
After processing, the final print must be dried carefully, to prevent it from getting scratched or curling at the edges. Once developed, take care of your prints by mounting them on card stock using a glue such as photo spray mount. You can then frame your favorite pictures, or keep them in a photograph album.

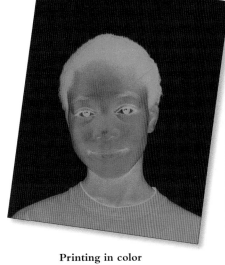

Printing in color

Color prints are produced in the same way as black–and–white prints. The negative *(above)* is projected onto color photographic paper. When the paper is developed, the colors are reversed once again, so that they come out looking natural.

Color photos

When you take a photo with color negative film, the film records the patterns of color in a scene. When the film is developed, the colors on the film look very strange, but the prints come out correctly. Color film has three layers, one on top of the other. These react to three primary colors, yellow, magenta (blue-red) and cyan (blue-green), which together can produce all of the different colors in the light spectrum.

FACT BOX

• The negative/positive method of photography was invented in 1839 by an Englishman named William Fox Talbot.

• High-contrast printing paper makes blacks look blacker and whites look whiter. Low-contrast paper creates less of a difference between the blacks and the whites.

• Professionals can make parts of a print look lighter or darker by using special techniques on the enlarger. For example, they can "burn" certain areas, which means making more light get to them.

Processing and printing

Most people send their film to be processed and printed *(above)* by a special photographic laboratory. Some stores, however, have their own automatic processing and printing machines, often called mini-labs. These can produce prints on the spot in a very short period of time.

PRINTING AND PROJECTING

QUICK AND EASY PRINTS

You will need: *photographic paper and chemicals, negative from pin-hole camera, flashlight or table lamp, safety goggles, rubber gloves, plastic dishes, plastic tongs or tweezers.*

If you have just taken a photograph with your own pin-hole camera, you can find out how to turn it into a print below. There is also a simple projector for you to make. A projector lets you look at slide film. On this type of film the colors of the image on the developed film are the same as the colors in the original scene. Projecting a slide is much like the reverse of taking a photograph. First, light is shone through the slide. The light then passes through the lens of the projector and is focused on a flat surface such as a wall, where an enlarged version of the slide appears.

A slide viewer is a special magnifying glass with an opalescent (milky-color) screen used for looking at slides. It is an alternative to a projector. You can also use a light box (a glass box with a light inside) to look at your slides before viewing in a projector.

1 In a totally dark room, lay a fresh sheet of photographic paper on a flat surface, shiny-side up. Lay the negative from your pin-hole camera face-down on top.

2 Shine a flashlight or a table lamp on the top of the two papers for a few seconds. Turn the flashlight off and remove your paper negative. Put on the goggles and gloves.

3 Put the fresh paper into a tray of developing fluid, then fix and wash the fresh paper (see the pages on "Printing"). You should end up with a print of the original image.

DO-IT-YOURSELF PROJECTOR

Old projector

This device *(left)* from around 1900 provided a way of looking at color slides. Instead of three layers of color on the film, three separate negatives were taken. Blue, green and red light were projected simultaneously at the same place as the black-and-white slides. The three colors combined to produce the range of colors in the slide scene.

You will need: *cardboard tube, scissors, developed color negative film, thin card stock, tape, magnifying glass, tracing paper, flashlight.*

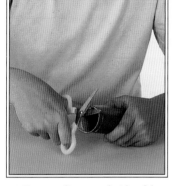

1 Cut two slits on each side of the cardboard tube at one end. They must be wide enough for a strip of negatives to slide through. Only use old negatives that you do not want.

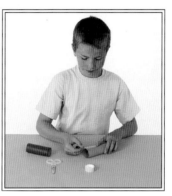

2 Wrap a piece of card stock around the other end of the tube. Tape down the edge to make another tube that slides over the first tube.

3 Tape the magnifying glass to the end of the adjustable tube. Now tape a disk of tracing paper over the slotted end of the main tube.

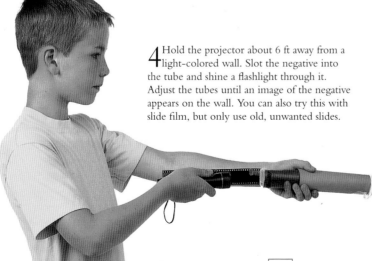

4 Hold the projector about 6 ft away from a light-colored wall. Slot the negative into the tube and shine a flashlight through it. Adjust the tubes until an image of the negative appears on the wall. You can also try this with slide film, but only use old, unwanted slides.

the image as projected on the wall or screen

WIDE AND NARROW

All camera lenses have their own focal length, which is written somewhere on the lens. The focal length is the distance between the center of the lens and the focal plane inside the camera where the light coming through the lens creates an image of the object being photographed. Lenses of different focal lengths produce images on the film that contain more or less of a scene. If you use a 50-mm lens, you see the same scene as you do with your eyes. Lenses with shorter focal lengths take in more of the scene, and longer lenses take in less than you would normally see.

What the lens sees
Put your hands on each side of your face. Your view is similar to what a 50-mm lens can see. Keeping your hands the same distance apart, move your hands steadily away from your face. The view between your hands will show you what a telephoto lens sees.

Only light rays that pass through the very center remain straight.

A wide angle lens has a wider angle of view (about 50% more) than the human eye.

Ultra-wide angle
The widest type of lens collects light from a complete half-circle (180 degrees). It makes straight lines appear curved, and the center of the scene seems to bulge outward. It is called a fish-eye lens because fish have eyes that gather light from wide angles.

Long-lens wobble
With telephoto lenses, which have very long focal lengths (300-mm or more), the tiniest bit of camera shake blurs the image. Professionals always use a tripod or monopod with these lenses to keep the camera steady. This is also important because the amount of light that reaches the lens is quite small, and so slow shutter speeds are often needed.

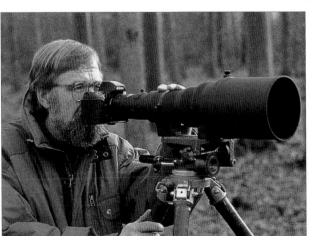

View from a compact camera

The simplest compact cameras usually have a 35-mm lens. This gives a slightly wider view *(left)* than you see with your own eyes. Many compacts now come with a built-in zoom lens enabling you to get a closer shot of your subject while you are still far away from it. These are especially useful for taking portraits (see "Close-up Shots" to find out more).

compact camera with variable lens

the view through a telephoto lens

Telephoto lens view

Any lens that gives you a magnified view of a scene is called a telephoto lens. A telephoto lens is a little like a telescope, because it homes in on just one part of the scene. Telephoto lenses are often used to photograph portraits and distant wildlife, and for coming in close on the small details in a scene.

a wide-angle lens view

Wide-angle lenses

Any camera lens that gives a wider view than we usually see with our eyes is called a wide-angle lens. Extremely wide-angle lenses (of 28 mm and less) allow you to get a huge amount of a scene into your photograph. A really wide-angle lens is perfect to use for panoramic photographs of scenery—such as cityscapes.

CLOSE-UP SHOTS

To keep from having to carry several lenses with different focal lengths, many photographers use one lens, called a zoom lens. These can change their focal length. A zoom lens usually consists of three separate lenses, with adjustable distances between them. They let you change how much of a scene will be in a shot without having to move your body.

The built-in lens on many compact cameras, and the lens that comes with most SLRs, is a zoom. A common zoom is 35–70, which means the lens can have focal lengths between 35 mm and 70 mm. It goes from wide angle to short telephoto (which brings objects closer). Macro, or close-up, lenses can focus on things that are very close to the lens. They are ideal for shots of flowers and insects.

A compact camera with a built-in zoom lens. Pressing a button on the camera makes the zoom get longer or shorter.

Super-zooms
A super-zoom lens has a very large range of focal lengths. For example, a 28–200 zoom goes from very wide angle to long telephoto.

A photograph taken at the 28-mm setting on a 28–200 zoom lens.

SLR zooms
With an SLR and two interchangeable zoom lenses, such as 28–70 and 75–300, you can have a huge range of focal lengths. The focal length is changed by turning or sliding a wide ring on the lens. Because zoom lenses are so complicated, they can make straight lines in a scene look slightly bent, especially at the picture's edges. A special streaked effect can be produced if you zoom in on a subject during a long exposure.

Zooming in for detail with a 200-mm setting.

Close-up equipment
Special high-powered microscope cameras, such as the one on the right, are used for some very close-up shots, such as the close-up of an insect on the left. SLR camera lenses can be removed and replaced with a microscope adapter.

Extension tubes
Extension tubes fit between the camera body and the lens. They move the lens farther from the film. This means that the lens can bend light rays into focus from objects that would usually be too close. A set of extension tubes has three tubes of different lengths for different magnifications.

extension tube

FACT BOX
- A telephoto doubler fits between an SLR and its lens. It doubles the focal length of the lens.
- A 500-mm telephoto lens with a maximum aperture of f/8 weighs several pounds.
- The longest lenses you can buy have a focal length of 1000 to 1200 mm.
- A standard 50-mm lens might be made up of five glass lenses. Most zoom lenses contain at least twelve lenses.

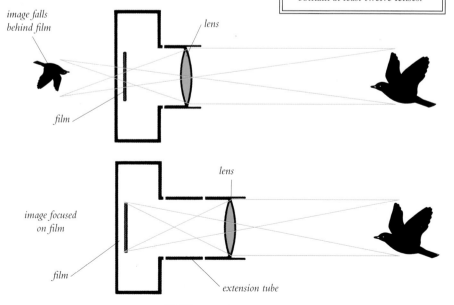

Usually, the light rays from a close-up object are not bent enough to form a focused image.

image falls behind film

lens

film

With an extension tube, the lens moves forward, making room for the rays to become focused.

image focused on film

lens

film

extension tube

FOCAL LENGTHS

If you have either an SLR camera or a compact camera with a zoom lens, then you will probably have taken photographs at different focal lengths. The simple experiments shown on these two pages will help to explain how different focal lengths make more or less of a scene appear on the film. These will help you to give more impact to your pictures. In the mini experiment on the left, try to find as many convex lenses as you can to experiment with. You will find that weaker lenses, which have longer focal lengths, make larger images. This is the opposite to what happens if you use them as a magnifying glass.

Working with lenses
Standing by a window, use a magnifying glass to form an image of the window on a piece of paper. See what happens when you use different convex lenses.

ZOOMING IN AND OUT

You will need: cardboard tube, thin card stock, tape, scissors, sharp pencil, tracing paper.

Camera lenses
Some camera lenses consist of several lenses, or elements. As rays of light pass through a lens, they are refracted (bent) at different angles. These rays can distort, resulting in multi-colored edges on your print. Multiple-element lenses, like the ones seen here, help to prevent the light rays from distorting.

1 Cover one end of a cardboard tube with thin card stock and tape it down. Pierce a small hole in the center with a sharp pencil.

2 Wrap a large square of card stock around the other end of the tube. Tape the edge down to form another tube that slides over the first.

3 Cut a circle of tracing paper big enough to stick over the end of your sliding tube. Tape it firmly in place. This is your focal plane.

Record what you see through your zoom lens. Slide the tubes in and out to make the image bigger (left) or smaller (below)

4 Aim the tube at a window or bright light (with the tracing paper end at your eye). Hold it right up to your eye to get it level with your line of sight, and then hold it at least 4–6 in. away from your eye. You should now see an image on the tracing paper screen.

Flat and curved mirrors

Some cameras have one or more mirrors instead of a lens. All the rays that hit a mirror are reflected. A flat mirror *(right)* reflects all rays in the same way, so your image looks unchanged (although left and right seem reversed).

A convex mirror reflects and bends light *(left)*. It works like a mirror and a lens together to distort the image.

Simple close-ups

Put a small object, such as a coin, on a flat surface. Hold a magnifying glass (the larger, the better) in front of the viewfinder and move the camera until the coin fills about a quarter of the frame. Put the magnifying glass in front of the camera lens and take the photograph. Take a few more shots with the camera a little closer and then try moving the camera a little farther away. A macro lens can be attached to a camera to take close-ups, and some have a mini-macro lens attached permanently.

LIGHTING AND FLASH

Lighting is one of the most important parts of photography. The kind of light you take your picture in, how that light hits the subject, and where you take the picture from, all affect the results. Outdoors, most photos are taken with natural light. Artificial light is needed indoors, or outdoors when there is not enough natural light. Photographs can be taken in dim natural light without additional artificial light, but only with very long exposures. Lighting can also create dramatic effects. Flash lighting makes a very bright light for a fraction of a second. Most small cameras have a small, built-in flash unit.

Lights and reflectors

Photographic studios have lots of strong lights. They allow the photographer to create many different lighting effects, without worrying about natural light. Some lights make light over a wide area, others make narrow beams. Using umbrellas and sheets of reflecting material can direct the light, too. These can be used to help reduce the contrast on bright sunny days.

With frontlighting, light is coming to the subject from the same direction as the camera position or slightly above. It lights the subject evenly, but gives a flat look because there are no strong shadows or highlights.

Backlighting means that the subject is between the light and the camera. It can make your subject look darker. The light does not have to be directly behind. Here, two lights have been set at a 45-degree angle behind the subject, one on either side.

If a picture is side-lit from the back, then the light is coming across your subject. Sidelighting will often give the most interesting or dramatic photographs, because it creates shadows that give more shape and depth to the subject.

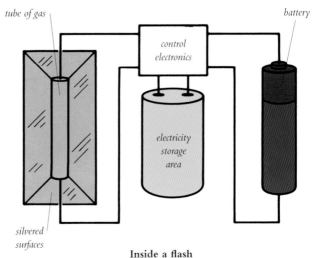

tube of gas

battery

control electronics

electricity storage area

silvered surfaces

Light in a flash

Light from a flash unit only lasts for a fraction of a second. It is carefully timed to flash when the camera's shutter is open. Many cameras have a built-in flash unit. A more powerful flash gun can be added to an SLR camera *(above)*. Most cameras have a signal that tells you when you need to use the flash.

Inside a flash

Flash *(above)* is made by sending a very large electric current through a narrow tube of gas. This makes a lightning-like flash. The flash's batteries gradually build up a storage area of electric charge, which is released very quickly. It is like filling a pitcher from a dripping tap and then pouring all the water out at once, or blowing up a balloon and then bursting it.

Bouncing and diffusing

Direct flash from the camera to the subject can cause harsh shadows and red-eye (where the flash creates red reflections in a person's eyes). Bounce flash means aiming the flash at the ceiling, so that the light spreads out. Some photographers diffuse flash with a sheet of material attached to the top of the flash, as on the right.

These people are sitting at different distances from the flash. This means that some of them are overexposed (have too much light), while others are underexposed.

Arrange people so that they are all about the same distance from the camera. This should ensure that everyone is properly exposed.

WORKING WITH LIGHT

Red-eye is caused by light from a flash unit near the camera lens bouncing off the retina (at the back of the eye) and back into the lens. With SLR cameras, the flash can be moved to one side to avoid red-eye.

Y ou can improve many of your photographs by giving thought to the lighting before you shoot. For pictures of people, try some of the simple suggestions here. If you're taking pictures outside, move around your subject to study the effects of light as it falls at different angles. You can also ask people you are photographing to tilt their heads at different angles, so that the sunlight lights up their faces. If there isn't enough light, some cameras have a backlight button that lengthens the exposure time for dark subjects. You could also use flash to light up the darker areas. This is known as using fill-in flash.

CREATING LIGHTING EFFECTS

You will need: a camera, large sheets of white and colored paper or card stock, aluminum foil, desk lamp, flashlight, colored tissue paper.

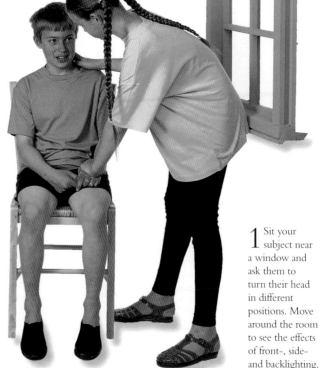

1 Sit your subject near a window and ask them to turn their head in different positions. Move around the room to see the effects of front-, side- and backlighting.

2 Hold a sheet of white paper or card stock near your subject to reflect some light from the window back onto their face. The reflected light fills in the shadows caused by the sidelighting. Do the same with colored paper. This will add color to your subject's face.

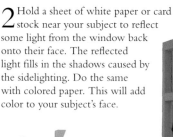

3 Try the same with aluminum foil or a piece of shiny card stock. See how this gives a much brighter reflected light. Crushing the foil and then smoothing it out again will diffuse the light in interesting and creative ways.

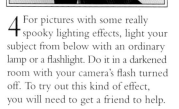

4 For pictures with some really spooky lighting effects, light your subject from below with an ordinary lamp or a flashlight. Do it in a darkened room with your camera's flash turned off. To try out this kind of effect, you will need to get a friend to help.

5 To take this approach even further, experiment with putting your hand in front of the light. As with the previous step, turn off your camera's flash if you can, and hold the camera very still. If you have a tripod, use that to free your hands.

6 For less harsh lighting, put a sheet of tissue paper in front of the lamp or flashlight. Try this with colored tissue paper to see what effects you can achieve. You can also take flash photos with a small piece of tissue paper over the flash unit.

USING FILTERS

A photographic filter changes the light as it enters the camera's lens. There are hundreds of different filters, and each one creates its own effect. The most common filter is called a skylight filter. It lets all visible light through the lens but stops invisible ultraviolet light from getting in, as ultraviolet light can make photographs look unnaturally blue. Filters called graduate filters make some parts of the scene darker. They are often used to darken very bright skies. Colored filters, such as red or yellow, can make black-and-white photographs look very dramatic. There are other special-effect filters that you can buy for adding different effects to your photographs. Smearing petroleum jelly on the edges of a clear filter can give a photograph a soft effect.

Normally filters are only used on SLR cameras. Some filters are circular, and screw onto the end of the camera's lens. Others are designed to slot into a filter holder at the front of the lens.

Bright lights
You will not always want strong reflections and bright light in a picture *(right)*.

Polarizing filter
Here *(left)*, putting a polarizing filter in front of the lens has made the reflections and strong light disappear. These filters cut out certain light rays from a scene, but let others through. They can also have a dramatic effect on skies, making them a much darker blue. If you want to take pictures through a window, a polarizing filter will reduce reflections in the glass.

Creating a sunset
With a sunset filter, you can turn a daytime sky *(left)* into a beautiful sunset *(below)*. Half the filter is clear and the other half has a slight orange tint. Position the tint at the top of your shot and the sky appears reddish.

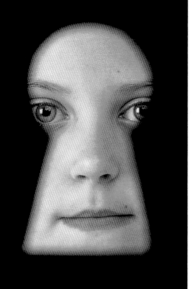

Making your own
You can make filters from transparent, colored candy wrappers. Put clean wrappers in front of the viewfinder to see what effect they have. Then attach them to the front of the lens with small pieces of tape.

Interesting shapes
A frame filter is a black mask with a shape cut in it. This makes the scene you are shooting come out in that shape. The other parts of the scene will be black. Frame filters come in simple shapes, such as squares and ovals, and more complex shapes, such as keyholes. Shooting through holes in walls or old trees can give you the same creative effects.

USEFUL TIPS

Here are a few simple tips that should help you to improve your photographic technique and avoid some common mistakes. Good technique is made up of technical skill and an eye for an interesting subject. Remember that a complicated SLR camera does not necessarily take the best photographs, and that great shots are perfectly possible with a simple point-and-shoot camera. The first thing to decide is the type of film you want to use (color print, color slide or black-and-white). Always load and unload your film in dim lighting. Once it has all been exposed, place it in its container and get it processed as soon as possible.

Hold a camera steady with both hands. Be careful not to put your fingers over the lens, flash or autofocus sensor. Keep your elbows close to your body and squeeze the shutter release button slowly. Do not jab at it.

Check the background
When you are taking portraits, or photographs of groups of people, always look at the background as well as at your subject. If necessary, recompose your picture to avoid the sort of accident that has happened in this shot. Many cameras have a portrait setting that gives a shallow depth of field. This automatically makes the background go out of focus.

Fill the frame
Do not be afraid to get close to your subject. For example, if you are taking a portrait, make sure the person's head and shoulders fill the frame *(right)*. But be careful not to get too close, because the camera may not be able to focus *(far right)*. If you get too close with an autofocus camera, it will not let you take a picture.

Natural frames

Try adding some interest to photos by shooting through archways or doors to frame the subject. With photos of groups or scenery, you can include overhanging branches in the foreground.

The rule of thirds

Try using the rule of thirds: place the subject a third of the way across or up or down the frame. This makes the shot more interesting. With autofocus cameras, you often have to use your focus lock to point at the subject first and then recompose the picture before shooting. Try this with landscapes—for example, having a mountain range in the top third of the frame.

A different viewpoint

Photographs taken from a standing position have the same viewpoint as your eyes usually do. Changing the camera's viewpoint can give more interesting results. Try kneeling, or even lying down.

Bad weather photographs

You do not always need to wait for good weather before taking photos. In fact, overhead sunshine tends to give flat, dull pictures. Stormy clouds can be much more interesting than cloudless skies. Remember to protect your camera in extreme weather conditions to make sure it stays dry.

SPECIAL PHOTOGRAPHY

Most cameras and lenses are designed for general photography. However, there are some types of camera that take photographs in unusual formats or in special conditions. For example, you can use certain cameras to take really wide panoramic views, or to shoot scenes entirely underwater. It is also possible to take pictures inside the human body with an attachment called an endoscope. There are also some unusual types of film. Some produce odd colors or shades in your photographs. Another type of film records technical information about each shot, while self-processing film does not have to be developed.

Disposable underwater cameras can take photographs while completely submerged. The camera's body is recycled after the film is processed.

Underwater SLRs

Divers take photographs underwater with special SLR cameras that are waterproof even when they are many feet down. They can also withstand the high pressure of being in deep water. Special housings are available for many cameras to enable land cameras to be used underwater or in adverse conditions such as during a cave diving or pot-holing expedition.

If you want to photograph anything deep down in the sea, you need to use extremely bright lights.

Spacious photographs

Panoramic cameras can take very wide photographs, which are good for shots of large groups of people or landscapes. Many compact cameras take pictures that are called panoramic, but they actually only appear to be so. They are no wider than a standard frame, just shorter, to help you compose your shot.

Laser photographs

A hologram is a three-dimensional (3-D) picture that looks 3-D no matter what angle you look at it from. The picture changes as you move your head from side to side. However, holograms are not taken with a camera. Another kind of equipment is used to record how laser light bounces off the subject from different directions.

Advanced systems

Many new compact cameras (and some SLRs) work according to the APS, or the Advanced Photographic System. They allow you to set the frame size for each shot individually and even to change film rolls midway without damage.

AMAZING EFFECTS

Discover how to take stereo photos and how to get an amazing three-dimensional effect from them. It is easier than you might think, and you can do it with the most basic compact camera. Simply take two photos of the same scene from different angles. When they have been developed, place them side by side to see the three-dimensional effect for yourself. The effect works because, like many animals, humans have binocular vision. This means that the two different views from our two eyes overlap. In the overlapping area, our eyes see slightly different views, which makes things appear in three dimensions. Once you have tried this experiment, you can to find out how to construct a grand panoramic picture by taking a series of photos of the same scene.

Place your pair of stereo photographs side by side to view them.

The diagram on the right shows how the stereo effect is created—because our two eyes see slightly different views.

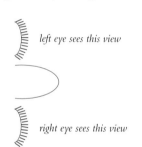

left eye sees this view

right eye sees this view

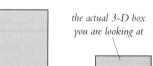

the actual 3-D box you are looking at

MAKE YOUR MODEL COME ALIVE

You will need: *camera, model.*

1 Choose a simple object such as this model of a toy. Holding the camera very steady, take a picture. Try to include a little space around your subject.

2 Take a step about 8 in. to your left, and take another photo. Try taking more pairs of photographs, using different distances between the two photographs.

3 Put your pictures down side by side on a flat surface. Stand over them and place your index finger between the two. With your eyes directly above the photos, look down at the finger and slowly raise it toward your nose, keeping it in focus. The two images you see below should merge into one 3-D image.

Make a panorama

Choose a good general landscape scene, with no close-up objects in it. Now, using a camera lens set at 35 or 50 mm, take a series of photographs that overlap slightly. Start by looking toward your left and move your head slightly around to the right for each of the following shots. When your prints are developed, lay them out in the right order to recreate your scene. When you are happy with the arrangement, tape them together carefully.

This completed panorama (above) works well because it is a simple, open scene. If it had been filled with small objects, then the effect might not have been as good. If you want people in your scene, try to keep them away from areas that will overlap in the finished panorama. On the other hand, you could ask a friend to move into different parts of the scene for each different shot and produce a picture with multiple images of him or her.

MOVING PICTURES

A movie camera is used to take moving pictures. It takes a whole series of photographs in quick succession (usually about 25 every second), on a very long roll of film. Any moving object appears in a slightly different position in each frame. When the photographs are displayed quickly, one after the other, the movement in the original scene appears to be recreated. The films are usually transparency, or positive rather than negative. The films are put into a projector to be shown. Today, movie cameras are used mainly for professional movie-making. Home movie cameras used to be very popular, but today they have been replaced by video cameras.

Moving pictures rely on the fact that we have persistence of vision. This means our eyes remember a picture for a split second. To see how this works, look at a scene and close your eyes quickly.

Recording motion
The first movie cameras grew out of experiments to record and study animal motion rather than for entertainment. This sequence *(left)* was taken by British photographer Eadweard Muybridge (1830–1904). He had first come up with the idea of moving pictures in 1877 after taking a series of photographs of a horse running, using 24 different cameras. Muybridge produced hundreds of images recording the complex movements of animals and humans that were too quick for the unaided human eye to follow. Artists used his pictures as reference for their paintings.

Movie film
This is just like the rolls of film you put in a stills, or ordinary, camera. In fact, 35-mm film was originally made for movie cameras. The image in each frame of the film is slightly different than the one before.

Electronic images
Unlike the film used in movie and ordinary cameras, video cameras use tape with a magnetic coating. It does not record the amount of light in a scene; instead, pictures are recorded by an electronic signal that distorts the tape. The video player reads this signal and reproduces the image.

Inside a movie camera

A movie camera has similar parts to an ordinary camera—a lens, shutter and aperture. It also has some extra parts for taking photos in quick succession. The film is wound on, ready for the next frame, while the shutter is closed. The shutter speed is always the same and the exposure is controlled just by the aperture.

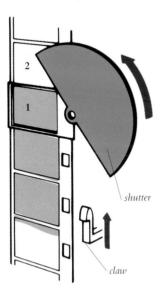
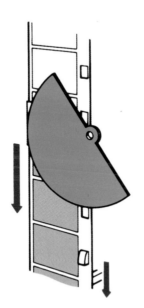
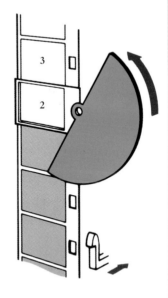

shutter open, first frame exposed

shutter closed, claw pulls film down

shutter open, second frame exposed

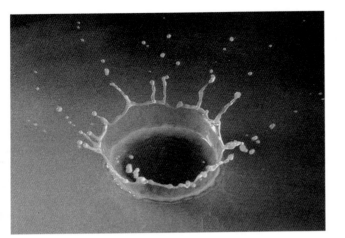

High-speed photos
This is a frame from a high-speed film. Some movie cameras can take hundreds, or even thousands, of photographs every second. When they are played back at normal speed, the action is slowed right down.

FACT BOX

• The world's fastest movie cameras are used by scientists. They can take 600 million frames every second.

• If you used a movie camera like this to film a bullet fired from a gun, the bullet would take 1,000 frames to move just one millimeter.

• Like normal camera film, movie camera film comes in different formats. Professionals on location shoots tend to use 16-mm format.

• In an IMAX cinema, the screen is as high as seven elephants sitting on top of each other.

• On IMAX film, the frames are four times larger than 35-mm film.

ANIMATION

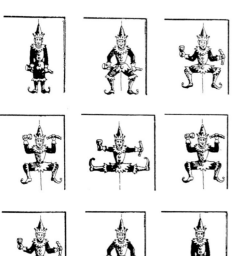

Animation is making inanimate objects, or objects that cannot move by themselves, appear to move. Frames of the film are photographed one at a time with a special movie camera, although you can create animation using video cameras. Between each frame, the objects are moved slightly. Sometimes this is combined with camera movement or zoom effects. When the finished film is viewed, the objects seem to move. Some animated objects are models, which are photographed to make animated movies. Others are drawings, which are photographed to make cartoons. Modern cartoon animation is often done by computer, so the photography stage is not needed. Quite often only the main drawings are made by an artist, and a computer plans the movements and frames using animation software.

Photo flick-book

The simplest way of making moving pictures is to put all the frames into a book and flip through the pages. In the early 1800s, flick-books of photographs (called filoscopes) were used to entertain children as movies had not yet been invented. You can see some of the pages from an old filoscope above.

Turning marvel

A thaumotrope is a double-sided disk, often made of cardboard, which has partial pictures on either side. When you spin the disk, the pictures appear to merge. So, if you had a bird on one side and a cage on the other, when the disk was spun you would see the bird in the cage. The name "thaumotrope" comes from the Greek words for marvel and turning.

This picture shows a scene from one of the popular Wallace and Gromit films, made by Aardman Animations Ltd. Model animation is a highly skillful and time-consuming job. The models must be moved very, very slightly between each frame. There are about 25 frames for every second of film.

This picture appears in the top right-hand corner of every other page in this book. Flip all the pages of the book quickly and watch the pictures. What can you see happening?

Enjoying animation

Producing animated children's films is big business. Many cartoons are made with the aid of computers. Some computer packages do all the time-consuming drawing and painting. They can also produce complex, three-dimensional characters, or add cartoon elements to film of real actors. In special effects scenes, real actors may be replaced by computer-generated images of themselves.

Cartoon cels

Until the 1980s, cartoons were made by photographing a series of drawings. The drawings were done on transparent plastic sheets called cels. Moving characters were drawn on one cel and the still background on another, to prevent having to draw the background again and again for each frame. Once the cels were completed, they were photographed with a movie camera. When these were shown in rapid succession, a moving film appeared.

background cels

character cels (notice how each one is different either in expression or the clothing)

EASY ANIMATION

During the 1800s, there was a craze for optical toys, such as flick–books. Many of them created an illusion of movement by displaying a sequence of pictures in quick succession. At first, the pictures were hand-drawn. Later, photos taken by early movie cameras were used as well. Here, you can find out how to make a toy called a phenakistoscope, and how to use it to turn a series of pictures into animation. Our toy is slightly different from the Victorian one on the right, as it has slots cut around the edges, rather than in the center.

A phenakistoscope (above) was an early device used to view moving pictures in a mirror. It held a set of images that were all slightly different. When you spun the disk, you saw an action sequence through the slots.

A series of simple drawings works best. This strip of images is for a zoetrope.

MAKE YOUR OWN PHENAKISTOSCOPE

***You will need**: thick, dark-colored card stock, sharp pencil, ruler, scissors, paper, dark felt-tip marker, tape, camera, models.*

1 On a piece of thick card stock, draw a circle measuring 10 in. across. Divide it into eight equal segments. At the end of each segment line, draw slots 2 in. long and ¼ in. wide.

2 Now cut out your disk, and the evenly spaced slots around the outside of it. Make sure that the slots are no wider than ¼ in. These will be your viewing holes.

3 On pieces of light-colored paper, draw a series of eight pictures. These should form a sequence of movements. Make sure that your drawings are fairly simple and clear, and that they are drawn with clean, strong lines.

4 Attach the little drawings to the disk by taping them just under the slots. You may need to cut them to fit, but make sure the picture is centered below the slot. Push a pencil through the center of the card stock disk to make a handle.

5 Stand in front of a mirror. Hold the disk vertically, with the pictures toward the mirror. Spin the disk and look through the slots. You should see an animated loop of action in the mirror.

Once you have mastered the technique of making a photo phenakistoscope, you can get more adventurous with your subjects and story lines. Try adding more models or props—for example, putting hats on the models.

PHOTO PHENAKISTOSCOPE

1 Now try a model animation. Take eight photographs of a model from the same position (use a tripod if you can). Move the model(s) slightly each time. The models should take up the middle third of the photograph frame.

2 Cut your photos to size and stick them to the phenakistoscope, one under each slot. Your phenakistoscope will work better if the photos have a dark frame, or you can just cover the edges roughly with a black felt-tip marker pen.

A zoetrope
This zoetrope from the 1860s was used to display long strips of drawings showing simple action sequences. They were placed inside a cylinder that could be rotated by hand. The moving pictures were then viewed through the vertical slots cut in the cylinder.

CAMERAS IN SCIENCE

Most of us use our cameras for recording special occasions, and when traveling, or for taking pictures of our friends. Photography is also extremely important in science and technology. For example, it is used for recording images that have been made by scientific instruments, so that they can be studied later. It is also used to record experiments that happen too fast for the human eye to see, and for analyzing experimental results. In many modern scientific instruments, electronic cameras have taken the place of film cameras. Their images can be transferred easily to computers for analysis.

Some advanced microscopes (above) can take very detailed close-up photos. You can also do the same thing with a normal microscope, by fitting an SLR camera to it. You remove the SLR's lens, and the microscope acts as a close-up lens for the camera.

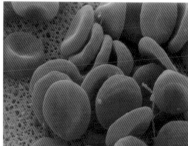

Microscope photographs
A photograph that is taken with a microscope is called a photomicrograph. This one is a close-up of the red blood cells in our blood.

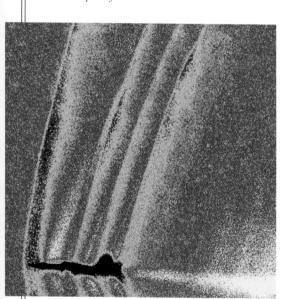

Recording speed on camera
This type of photograph is known as a schlieren photograph. It shows the shock waves around a T-38 aircraft flying at great speed—1.1 times the speed of sound, or Mach 1.1. The waves appear as red and green diagonal lines in the photograph. It enables scientists to see that the main shock waves come from the nose and tail of the plane. Smaller shock waves come from the engine inlets and wings. The yellow stream behind the aircraft is caused by the exhaust of the jet engine.

Photographing heat
All objects give off heat rays called infrared rays. Hotter objects give off stronger rays. A special type of film called infrared film is sensitive to heat rays rather than light rays. Hot and cold objects show up in different colors or shades.

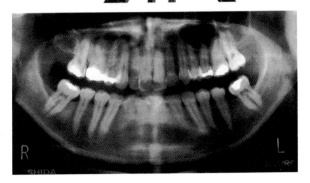

When you are taking photos of the sky with a telescope using long exposures, the telescope often has to move slowly across the sky. This is to prevent the stars from becoming streaks on your prints. This happens because the Earth and stars are slowly moving. It is like taking a picture of a traffic light from a moving car. The lights would appear streaked.

Capturing the stars

Just as a camera can be added to a microscope to take close-up pictures, one can also be added to a telescope. The telescope acts like a very powerful telephoto lens for the camera. (A telephoto lens makes distant objects seem much closer.) Light from the stars is very weak, and so long exposures are needed.

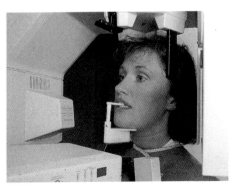

Where more X-rays reach the film, through soft parts of the body, the film turns a darker tone when it is developed. Bones and teeth show up white.

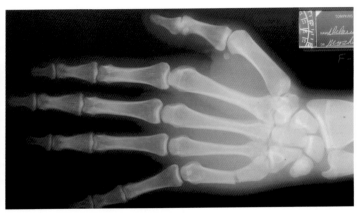

Taking X-ray pictures

X-rays are used to photograph inside bodies. Unlike light rays, X-rays can pass though the soft parts of your body—skin and muscle. X-ray film is simply processed to produce negatives not prints. X-rays help dentists or doctors to find out all kinds of things about the body. The picture on the left shows the hand of a boxer with a fractured finger caused through punching. Other kinds of X-ray technology are used to scan for faults in the structure of buildings or aircraft, enabling repairs to take place before a part fails or causes an accident.

CAMERAS AND COMPUTERS

Just like ordinary cameras, digital cameras come as compacts and SLRs. They have a lens and shutter, but, in the space where the film would normally be, they have a light-sensitive microchip. This means that the photographs are stored in the camera's memory.

Photographs are often used in computer applications. For example, a multimedia CD-ROM about nature might contain thousands of photographs of animals and plants. Photographs stored and displayed by computer are called digital images because they consist of a long series of numbers as opposed to being a physical print on paper. Digital images are either prints that have been scanned into a computer to turn them into digital form, or images that have been photographed with a digital, filmless, camera. Digital images can be copied over and over again, without any loss in quality. This means that they can be sent easily from one computer to another—over the Internet, for example.

Video phone
The digital video camera on top of this computer *(above)* takes pictures that are sent down the telephone line and appear on another computer's screen. This lets the people at both computers see each other.

Floppy disk camera
The digital camera on the right uses a normal floppy disk that can be placed directly into a computer. The pictures can then be worked on using computer software.

Pixel pictures

A digital image is made up of pixels, or dots. A number represents the color of each tiny dot. High-resolution (sharper) images divide the picture into a greater number of smaller dots than low-resolution ones, but they take up more computer memory.

Retouching

Once a photo is digitized, it can be altered in any way by the computer. For example, colors can be changed or another photo can be added in. A polar bear could be put in a desert! It is much easier than trying the same thing with normal photography.

Morphing

Many films and television programs make use of computer-manipulated photographs and film images to create stunning special effects. Morphing, for example, is where a person or object changes into something or someone else slowly, on screen. To achieve this, the computer software gradually merges two totally different images together.

This shows a digitized picture on a computer screen before it has been manipulated.

Here is the same picture after it has been manipulated by computer. Can you see how it has changed?

PART FOUR

COMPUTERS

The explosion of computer technology toward
the end of the 1900s transformed people's lives.
Complex, repetitive tasks that previously took
hours or days could suddenly be accomplished in
minutes, or even seconds. Early computers took
up entire rooms, while today's computers, with
far more power, fit on a person's lap. At home and
at work, the worlds of e-mail and the Internet have
opened ways of communicating ideas and of
buying goods of every kind at a speed that would
have been thought impossible only fifty years ago.

AUTHOR
Stephen Bennington
CONSULTANT
Paul Fisher

COMPUTER BASICS

THOUSANDS of everyday tasks are now much easier to do thanks to the development of computers. Many activities, such as writing, drawing, playing music, sending messages, playing games, looking up information and even shopping are regularly done using these powerful machines. Living in today's computer age means that almost everyone has access to the technology—in offices, schools, stores and at home. Indeed, computers are such an integral part of modern society that it is hard to imagine how humans once coped without them.

monitor

Some people believe that computers can think like people. In fact, they can only use information that is put into them. The most important job computers do is to process such information much more quickly and accurately than a person could. Performing complex calculations, checking for spelling mistakes in a story or copying pictures from one place to another, for example, are done much faster using a computer. Essentially, computers are just tools like washing machines and cars. They are used in many different ways to do an enormous range of interesting and useful tasks.

Disks and data
Data (information) can be stored on disks outside the main part of the computer. The disk can be in the form of a CD (compact disc), DVD (digital video disc), Zip disk or floppy disk. These are placed in different slots, called drives, in the computer to allow new data to be put in and recorded data to be taken out.

Processing power
The computer's brain, where data is handled and rearranged, is called the processor. This is a complicated electronic circuit board, which contains smaller electronic circuits called silicon chips. These chips are the powerhouses of all computers. They contain other electronic circuits that are so small that they can only be seen under a microscope.

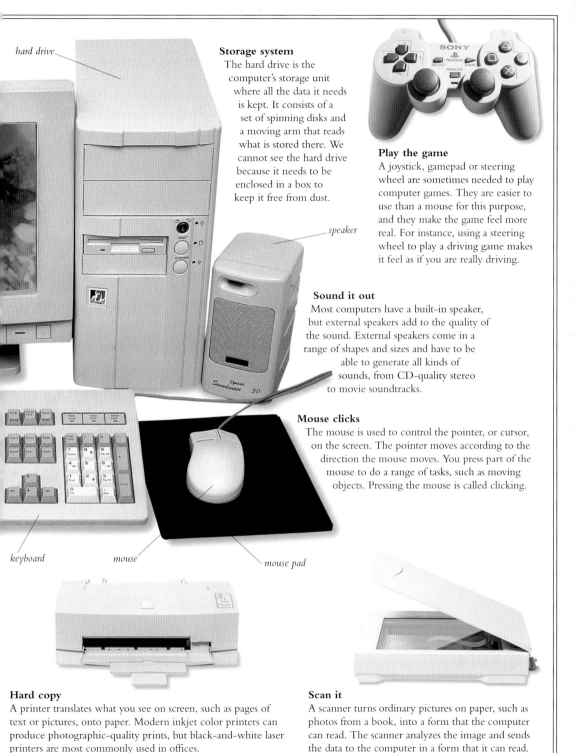

Storage system

The hard drive is the computer's storage unit where all the data it needs is kept. It consists of a set of spinning disks and a moving arm that reads what is stored there. We cannot see the hard drive because it needs to be enclosed in a box to keep it free from dust.

hard drive

speaker

Play the game

A joystick, gamepad or steering wheel are sometimes needed to play computer games. They are easier to use than a mouse for this purpose, and they make the game feel more real. For instance, using a steering wheel to play a driving game makes it feel as if you are really driving.

Sound it out

Most computers have a built-in speaker, but external speakers add to the quality of the sound. External speakers come in a range of shapes and sizes and have to be able to generate all kinds of sounds, from CD-quality stereo to movie soundtracks.

Mouse clicks

The mouse is used to control the pointer, or cursor, on the screen. The pointer moves according to the direction the mouse moves. You press part of the mouse to do a range of tasks, such as moving objects. Pressing the mouse is called clicking.

keyboard   *mouse*   *mouse pad*

Hard copy

A printer translates what you see on screen, such as pages of text or pictures, onto paper. Modern inkjet color printers can produce photographic-quality prints, but black-and-white laser printers are most commonly used in offices.

Scan it

A scanner turns ordinary pictures on paper, such as photos from a book, into a form that the computer can read. The scanner analyzes the image and sends the data to the computer in a form that it can read.

ALL TALK

EVERY subject uses a set of words and phrases, called jargon, to describe things that have not existed before. This is certainly true when you start exploring the world of computers. Computer jargon is usually made up of either new scientific terms, such as "computer," or existing words that have been given a new meaning, such as "mouse." They can also be words made from the first letters of phrases, such as "RAM," which stands for Random Access Memory. These are called acronyms. One of the main reasons people have difficulty with learning a new subject, and even give the subject up, is because they come across a lot of new and confusing words that they do not fully understand. If you are not sure what a word means then you will probably find it in the Glossary at the end of this book. If not, then you are bound to find it in an up-to-date dictionary. Knowing what computer jargon means when you see and hear it is very important. Remember that everyone is in the same position when they learn about a new subject. You will gradually pick up what each new word means as you read and learn more about it. The boxes on the opposite page will start you off with some essential computer jargon.

HARDWARE WWW NETIQUETTE INTERNET SOFTWARE ICON

What does it mean?
Sometimes people find themselves feeling puzzled, confused or even bored when they try to learn about computers. These feelings often come from not fully understanding the many new and sometimes strange words that are associated with the subject.

Speaking the language
Lots of unusual words and phrases are used to describe computers. For example, the piece of equipment above is called a monitor, and it displays computer data on a screen much like a television. The monitor above shows a CD-ROM. Do you know what CD-ROM stands for?

SOME FIRST JARGON WORDS

- **Hardware** Equipment, such as the processor, monitor, keyboard, scanner, and mouse, that makes up your computer system.

- **Home page** An introductory page on a web site, that contains links to other pages.

- **Icon** A small picture that you can click on with the mouse to make the computer do something.

- **Internet** A worldwide computer network, through which computers can communicate with each other.

- **Netiquette** A code of good conduct and manners, developed by Internet users, that suggests acceptable and unacceptable ways of behaving on the Internet.

- **Software** A set of coded instructions, called an application, that tells your computer what to do.

- **Web site** A computer document written in HTML (see right), that is linked to other computer documents.

INTERNET
A worldwide computer network, through which computers communicate with each other.

A helping hand
There are many ways to find out about computers and the jargon that comes with using them. Your family and friends may be able to help, or you could join a computer club and meet lots of other people who are trying to find out about computers. You could even use the Internet to try and answer your questions.

COMPUTER JARGON

Here are some common terms that you will come across regularly.

- **CD-ROM** (**C**ompact **D**isc **R**ead-**O**nly **M**emory) A disk similar to an audio CD, that contains information that can only be read by the computer.

- **CPU** (**C**entral **P**rocessing **U**nit) The brain of the computer, that contains the processing chips and circuit boards.

- **HTML** (**H**yper**T**ext **M**ark-up **L**anguage) A computer code that is added to word-processed documents to turn them into web pages.

- **ISP** (**I**nternet **S**ervice **P**rovider) The companies through which Internet connection is made.

- **Modem** (**MO**dulator/ **DEM**odulator) A device that allows computer information to be sent through a telephone line.

- **RAM** (**R**andom **A**ccess **M**emory) Computer memory that holds information temporarily until the computer is switched off.

- **URL** (**U**niform **R**esource **L**ocator) The address of a site on the Internet that is specific to one web page.

- **WWW** (**W**orld **W**ide **W**eb) A huge collection of information that is available on the Internet. The information comprises web sites, that are made up of many web pages.

HISTORY OF COMPUTERS

Blaise Pascal's calculator
In 1642, French mathematician Blaise Pascal invented the first automatic calculator. The device added and subtracted by means of a set of wheels linked by gears. The first wheel represented the numbers 0 to 9, the second wheel represented 10s, the third stood for 100s, and so on. When the first wheel was turned ten notches, a gear moved the second wheel forward a notch and so on.

THE idea of using machines to do automated tasks and calculations is not a new one. The first calculating machine was developed in the 1600s and used moving parts such as wheels, cogs and gears to do mathematical tasks. The first big step towards developing an automatic computing machine came about in 1801. Joseph-Marie Jacquard, a French weaver, invented a weaving machine that was controlled by a series of punched cards. Where there were holes, the needles rose and met the thread, but where there were no holes, the needles were blocked. This was the first time that stored information had been used to work a machine.

Early in the 1900s, electronic devices began to replace mechanical (hand-operated) machines. These computers filled an entire room, yet they could only perform simple calculations. In later years, two main inventions—the transistor in the 1950s and the silicon chip in the 1970s—allowed the modern computer to be developed. Both of these devices control tiny electrical currents that give computers instructions. Today, computers can be made to fit in the palm of your hand.

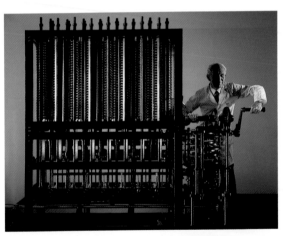

Mechanical mathematics
In 1835, British mathematician Charles Babbage invented a mechanical calculating machine called the Analytical Engine. When performing calculations, the machine stored completed sets of punched cards that were reusable. The Analytical Engine had all the elements of a modern computer—storage, memory, a system for moving between the two and an input device. The people who used his machines were called "computers."

The first programmer
Ada, Countess of Lovelace, was the daughter of English poet Lord Byron and probably the world's first computer programmer. Between 1833 and 1843, she became interested in the work of fellow mathematician Charles Babbage. She created a punchcard program that was used to record the data for Babbage's Analytical Engine.

Controlling the current
Today, computers work by electrical currents that flow through circuits. The current is controlled by devices called transistors. These are found on a wafer-thin piece of silicon called a chip. Some chips are no larger than a fingernail and contain millions of transistors. These are known as integrated circuits (ICs).

Code cracker

During World War II, British mathematician Alan Mathison Turing developed the first fully electronic calculating device. It was called Colossus because of its huge size. This machine was equipped with over 1,500 vacuum tubes that were used to control thousands of electrical currents. Colossus was designed to decipher a German communications code called Enigma. The machine was successful and helped Britain and its Allies win World War II (1939–1945). Colossus can still be seen at the Bletchley Park Museum in the United Kingdom, the site where the code-cracking operation took place.

Two-room calculator

In 1943, ENIAC (Electronic Numerical Integrator and Computer) was constructed by Presper Eckert, John Atansoff, and John Mauchly at the University of Pennsylvania. This early computer was enormous, filling two rooms and using as much electricity as ten family houses. It contained about 18,000 vacuum tubes, that acted as electronic switches and could perform hundreds of calculations every second. ENIAC was slow to program, however, because thousands of wires and connections had to be changed by hand.

COMPUTER DEVELOPMENTS

Television link
British inventor Sir Clive Sinclair developed many personal computers, including the ZX80 in 1980. This used a normal television as a monitor.

All in one

The Commodore 8032-SK was launched in 1980 and was the first computer to have a built-in monitor to display information.

BBC Model B
The BBC Model B was launched in 1981 by British computer firm Acorn to accompany the British Broadcasting Company (BBC) computer literacy program.

Laptop
International Business Machines Corporation (IBM) was instrumental in the development of a portable computer, called a laptop, in the early 1990s.

iMac
The iMac, developed by Apple Computers, revolutionized the design of desktop computers when it appeared on the market in the late 1990s.

iBook
Apple introduced the iBook in 1999. As powerful as a desktop iMac, this portable model also comes in a variety of bright, attractive colors.

Palm Pilot
A hand-held, pocket-size computer appeared in the late 90s. Not only does it feature an electronic pen for writing directly on the screen, it can also connect to the Internet.

BREAKING THE CODE

COMPUTERS are digital machines, which means they work by using a sequence of alternating numbers. The word "digit" actually means a counting finger, but it is used in computing to mean every single number between 0 and 9.

The number code that computers use is called binary code, which means it is made up of just two digits—0 and 1 (binary means two). Combinations of 0 and 1 can be used to represent any kind of information, for example, the letters of the alphabet. The theory behind this binary code is essentially the same as the one that Joseph-Marie Jacquard used for the punched cards that worked his weaving looms. Jacquard's punched cards were used to represent two kinds of information—a hole (1 in binary code) or no hole (0 in binary code).

Coded messages
This device, called the Enigma machine, was used by German forces during World War II (1939–1945). Uncoded messages were typed into the keyboard, and the machine then converted the message into a complex coded form. So complex was Enigma that a single letter could be represented by several different coded characters.

BINARY CODE

A	01000001	N	01001110	0	00110000
B	01000010	O	01001111	1	00110001
C	01000011	P	01010000	2	00110010
D	01000100	Q	01010001	3	00110011
E	01000101	R	01010010	4	00110100
F	01000110	S	01010011	5	00110101
G	01000111	T	01010100	6	00110110
H	01001000	U	01010101	7	00110111
I	01001001	V	01010110	8	00111000
J	01001010	W	01010111	9	00111001
K	01001011	X	01011000	10	00111010
L	01001100	Y	01011001		
M	01001101	Z	01011010		

Zeros and ones
Binary code is the language that all computers use in their calculations. Computers understand the code in terms of an electrical current (flow of electricity). An electrical current being on or off is represented by 0 and 1. In computing, zeros are used to mean off and ones are used to mean on. In this way, binary code can be used to represent all kinds of different information on a computer. For example, it can be used to represent decimal numbers or the letters of the alphabet, as shown in the chart on the left. Computers recognize each number or letter as a group of eight binary digits. Combinations of binary digits represent different numbers or letters.

A STRING OF BITS

*You will need: 16 small
pieces of colored paper, black marker,
stencil, two 3-ft lengths of string,
16 clothes pegs.*

1 Look at the binary code version
of the alphabet on the opposite
page. See how many 0s and 1s you
need to represent the initials of your
name. Use a black marker and a
stencil to draw them on the paper.

2 Arrange the 0s and 1s in two
rows, one for each initial of your
name. Each piece of paper represents
a bit. This is the smallest amount of
digital information in a computer.

3 When you have finished, double-
check with the chart opposite to
make sure you have got the 0s and 1s
in the right place. The group of eight
bits that represents each letter of
the alphabet is called a byte.

4 Take the two pieces of string
and the clothes pegs. Peg each bit
to the string in the correct order,
putting your first initial letter on one
piece of string and your second initial
on the other piece. The example in
the picture shows the binary code
version of the letters P and C.

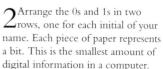

THROUGH THE LOGIC GATE

INFORMATION flowing inside a computer is called data. It is in the form of electrical pulses. Data changes as it passes through part of the computer called the central processing unit (CPU). The CPU has thousands of separate high-speed switches called logic gates. These logic gates are microscopic transistors cut into a silicon chip. They can flick on and off up to 300 million times a second. Data flows into the input side of each gate. It only flows out again if the gate is switched on. The computer program sets up how the gates switch on and off and so controls the data flow through the computer.

There are three main types of gates, called AND, NOT and OR gates. Working together, they act as counters or memory circuits to store data. Logic gates are also used to control things, such as washing machines. In this project, you can make a model AND gate to show how the output depends on the settings of the two input connections.

AND gate	A—⊐D—c B	
Input A	Input B	Output C
OFF	OFF	OFF
OFF	ON	OFF
OFF	ON	OFF
ON	ON	ON

OR gate	A—⊐D—c B	
Input A	Input B	Output C
OFF	OFF	OFF
OFF	ON	ON
ON	OFF	ON
ON	ON	ON

On or off?
AND and OR gates both have two inputs (A and B) and one output connection (C). The tables show how the ON/OFF states of the inputs affect the ON/OFF state of the output. These tables are called "truth tables."

MAKE A LOGIC GATE
You will need: felt-tipped pen, ruler, stiff card stock in 3 colors, scissors, stapler, pencil, red and green circle stickers.

1 Mark and cut out three pieces of card stock. Referring to the colors shown here, the sizes are: dark blue 6 x 4 in., light blue 4 x 3½ in. and yellow 1½ x 8 in.

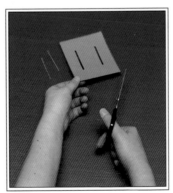

2 On the 4 x 3½-in. card stock, draw two slots that are slightly more than 1½ in. wide and 1½ in. apart. Cut each slot so that it is about ⅙–⅛ in. wide.

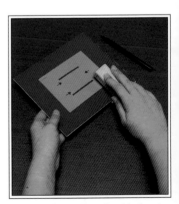

3 Place the card stock with slots in the center of the dark blue card stock. Staple them together with one staple at each corner of the top card stock. Draw the three arrows as shown.

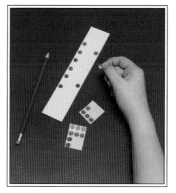

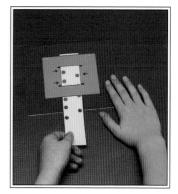

4 At ¾-in. intervals, stick colored circles in the order shown onto the left side of the long card stock strip. This is the input side.

5 Add colored stickers to the right (output side) at 1½-in. intervals in this order: green, red, red, red. Notice that each sticker is midway between the two on the left.

6 Push the strip between the two stapled pieces of card stock and feed it through the lower slot. Keep pushing the strip and feed it through the top slot and out between the stapled strips.

7 Move the strip until there is a green dot at the top of the input side. There should be a green dot on the output side, showing that both inputs must be ON for the output to be ON.

8 When the input shows red at the top with a green dot below, then a green dot appears on the output side. Your model is showing that the output is OFF when only one input is ON.

9 Here is your completed model AND gate. Now make a similar model with the stickers in the right places to show how an OR gate works. You will find that AND gates and OR gates are very different.

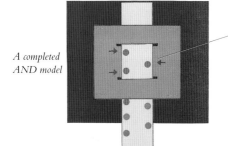

A completed AND model

Red dots indicate both inputs on model AND are OFF.

10 When both inputs on your model AND gate show red, then a red dot appears opposite the output. As you might expect, the output of an AND gate is OFF when both inputs are OFF.

GETTING STUFF IN AND OUT

COMPUTERS can only work with the information that you put into them. The main way that you put information into a computer is by using a keyboard and a mouse. The mouse controls the cursor (a movable visible point) on the monitor and allows you to select different options. The keys on a keyboard have one or more characters printed on them, such as a letter or a number. When you press a key, the main character on the key will appear on the screen. Other keys on the keyboard are used to give the computer specific instructions. There are two main types of home computer—a PC (personal computer) and a Mac (Apple Macintosh—named after the company that developed it). Their keyboards are slightly different, but they do the same jobs.

You can see the work you have created as words, numbers or pictures on the computer's monitor. You can print it on paper, save it on the hard disk or save it to a removable disk at any time.

It is a good idea to save your work every few minutes so that it is firmly recorded. If anything should go wrong with the computer, the data that you have not saved will be lost and you will have to redo all the work you have done.

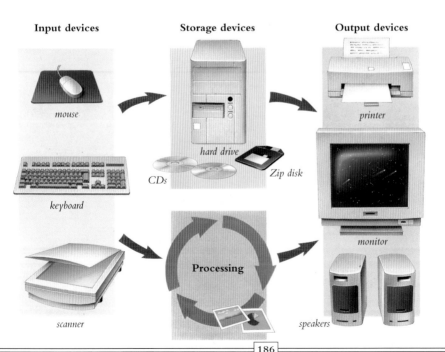

Input devices

mouse

keyboard

scanner

Storage devices

hard drive

CDs

Zip disk

Processing

Output devices

printer

monitor

speakers

Using computers
When people use a computer, they are doing four different things:

1. Inputting data (information) using an input device.

2. Storing the data so that it can be reused (often called data storage).

3. Working with the data they put in (often called processing).

4. Retrieving and looking at the data using an output device.

The **Shift** key is used in combination with
a letter key to type a capital letter. It is
also used in some keyboard shortcuts to
tell a computer to do a specific task.

The **Back Space** key is
used to remove selected words
or images in an application.

The keyboard

All keyboards
do the same jobs,
although some
are designed
differently from
others. The one
shown here is
a Mac keyboard.
You can also
buy ergonomic
keyboards, that
are designed to
suit the human
body. The keys
fit the natural
positions and
movements
of the user's
hands, avoiding
muscle strain.

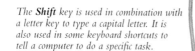

The **Control**
key is used with
different letter
keys to tell the
computer to do
different tasks.

The **Apple** key is
a special key that
can be found on the
keyboards of Macs.
It is used together
with letter keys to do
specific tasks. On a
PC, the **Windows**
key does the same job.

Pressing the **Enter**
key on a keyboard
is like saying OK
to the computer.
This key is also
used in typing for
taking words over
to the next line.

Monitors

As you input information to the computer, the results of
your actions appear on the screen of a monitor. The
picture on the screen is made up of small dots of light called
pixels. Some monitors can display more pixels than others,
producing a better-quality picture on screen. These monitors
are said to have a high resolution.

Pictures from pixels

This picture shows a close-up
of a red, blue and green
picture element, or pixel for
short. Pixels are dots of light
out of which the pictures on
a computer screen are
made. The pictures on a
computer monitor are
made up of millions of
red, blue and green pixels.

STORING AND FINDING

The first computer program
The punched cards that Joseph-Marie Jacquard used in 1801 to operate his weaving machine worked in exactly the same way as the electrical impulses in binary code. The needles could pass through a hole in the card to meet the thread and make a stitch (equivalent to the binary digit 1, or on), but they were blocked if there was no hole (equivalent to the binary digit 0, or off). In this way, different patterns of holes on the punched cards represented different patterns of woven cloth.

Ticker tape
Ticker tape was first used in the 1930s by German scientist Konrad Zuse. Holes were punched in the tape in the same way as Jacquard's cards, but the tape was fed into the computer as a continuous strip. A hole was read as the binary digit 1. No hole was read as the binary digit 0. The smaller holes held the tape in the machine.

THE part of the computer that does all the calculations is called the microprocessor. It consists of millions of electronic switches, called transistors, and other electronic devices that are all built into a wafer-thin slice of a chemical element called silicon. Electricity passes through tiny lines of metal on the silicon chip. The transistors switch the electricity on and off. These on-and-off pulses of electricity represent the 0s and 1s of binary code, which the computer interprets to do different tasks.

Microprocessors control a number of other devices besides computers, including telephones, car engines and thermostats (heat-control devices) on washing machines.

Silicon chips control other devices in a computer such as memory chips. These store information that is needed by the microprocessor to run software such as a word-processing application. Other data is stored on various kinds of disks, including hard disks, floppy disks, Zip disks and CDs.

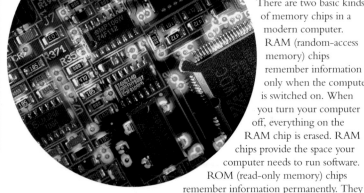

Memory chips
There are two basic kinds of memory chips in a modern computer. RAM (random-access memory) chips remember information only when the computer is switched on. When you turn your computer off, everything on the RAM chip is erased. RAM chips provide the space your computer needs to run software. ROM (read-only memory) chips remember information permanently. They store essential data, such as the program that enables your computer to start up.

land — *pit*

CD (Compact Disc)

Data is recorded on to a compact disc by a laser beam cutting into a thin metal layer under the plastic coating of the disk. The disk becomes covered with microscopic indentations (pits) and flat areas (lands). These are read by another laser in the computer. The pits are read as binary 1 and the lands as binary 0. Most CD-ROMs can store around 750MB of information.

Storing data

Magnetic disks, such as the computer's hard disk, floppy disks and Zip disks, store data arranged in a circular track. This is divided into sections, like pieces of pie, to make compartments. A device in the computer, called the read/write head, moves from one section to another to read or change the data. Hard disks have the largest storage capacity, and they are the most popular way of storing information.

Floppy disk

These disks are made of thin magnetic plastic encased in a stiff plastic shell. The plastic inside the disk stores a pattern of 1s and 0s in the form of magnetic particles. Floppy disks can store up to 1.4MB of data, which is the same as three paperback books. Floppy disks are becoming less popular as a way of saving and sending information due to their small capacity.

Zip disk

Like floppy disks, Zip disks use magnetism to store data, but are able to hold about 80 times as much information. Although about the same size as a floppy disk, they hold between 100 and 250MB of data (about the same as 80 floppy disks). Zip disks are a very useful way of storing large computer files, and many people use these disks to back up all the files on their computer's hard disk.

HARD DISK STORAGE

THE hard disk of a computer consists of a number of flat, circular plates. Each one of these plates is coated with microscopic magnetic particles. The hard disk also contains a controlling mechanism, called the read/write head, which is positioned slightly above the magnetic disks.

When storing information, a series of electrical pulses representing the data are sent through the read/write head onto the magnetic disks, which are spinning at very high speeds. The electricity magnetizes the magnetic particles on the disks, which then align to produce a record of the signal.

When reading information, the hard disk works in the opposite way. The magnetic particles create a small current, which is recognized by the read/write head, converted into an electrical current and then into binary code.

When you load new information onto the computer, it is stored in a section of one of the plates, depending on where there is free space. The computer then keeps a record of what is stored in each section. This project shows you how the magnetic disks in your computer's hard drive work.

STORING DATA ON A DISK

You will need: *piece of white card stock, compass, pencil, scissors, ruler, red marker, plastic cup, reusable adhesive, paper clips, magnet, tack.*

1 Draw a circle with a diameter of 4in. on the piece of white card stock. Draw three circles inside, each with a diameter 1½in. smaller than the last. Cut out the largest circle.

Inside the drive

A typical hard drive consists of a stack of thin disks, called a platter. The upper surface of each disk is coated with tiny magnetic particles, and each disk has its own read/write head on a movable arm. When storing and reading information, the disks spin at very high speeds (up to 100 revolutions a second).

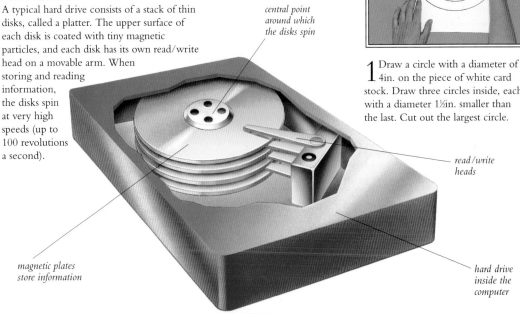

central point around which the disks spin

read/write heads

magnetic plates store information

hard drive inside the computer

2 Position a ruler at the center of the circle where the compass point has made a hole. Draw four lines through the middle to divide the circle into eight equal parts.

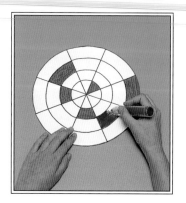

3 Use a red marker to color in six or seven sections as shown above. Leave the remaining sections white. The white areas represent full disk space. Red areas are empty disk space.

4 Attach some reusable adhesive to the rim of a plastic cup. Then turn it upside down on a smooth surface. Press it down gently to make sure it is secure.

5 Push the tack through the middle of the colored disk and into the bottom of the cup, making sure that the disk can move around the pin. Scatter some paper clips on the surface. Hold the magnet under the disk. Move it around the disk.

6 The paper clips will move around the disk surface of the disk, too, and will all line up in a section of the disk. This is what happens to the magnetic particles on a hard disk when an electric current is passed through them by the read/write head. In a computer, the way the magnetic particles line up is a record of the data stored on the hard disk.

7 Remove the paper clips from the disk. Spin the disk clockwise with one hand and with a finger of the other touch areas of the disk. If you stop the disk on a white part you have found data. If you stop on a red section you have found empty disk space.

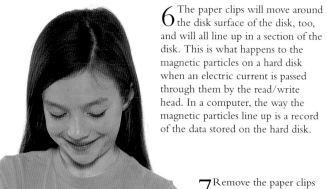

COMPUTER SOFTWARE

Linux

If you see this picture of a penguin when you are using a computer, then you know the computer is running an operating system called Linux.

S OFTWARE is a means of carrying a series of instructions that controls what computers do. There are two different types—systems software and applications software.

The basic systems software that controls the computer and makes it possible for us to use it is called the OS, or operating system. It includes instructions that manage the computer's memory, organize files and control devices such as scanners, printers and external storage drives. The operating system you have will depend on the type of computer you have. The most common is Microsoft Windows, which is used to operate most PCs. Apple Macintosh computers work using the Mac OS. Linux is another operating system that will run on both Macs and PCs. The operating system runs in the background all the time that the computer is on.

The Mac start-up screen

If you see this picture when you start up a computer, then you know it is an Apple Macintosh computer running a version of the Mac operating system.

Applications software includes programs that allow the computer to perform specific tasks. It runs on top of the operating system. Common applications software includes word-processing packages such as Microsoft Word, graphics applications such as Adobe Photoshop, and also games such as Tomb Raider.

Applications software

When you click on the Microsoft Word icon on your computer, a start-up screen appears on the monitor. Microsoft Word comes in many different languages so that people all over the world can use the application. The ones pictured are: Arabic (top left), German (bottom left), French (top right) and Spanish (bottom right). The start-up screen lets you interact with the computer. You can tell the computer what you want to do by clicking on various parts of the screen. Microsoft Word is an example of applications software, which is a set of instructions that allows you to carry out different tasks on your computer. Microsoft Word allows you to perform word-processing tasks such as writing a letter or a story.

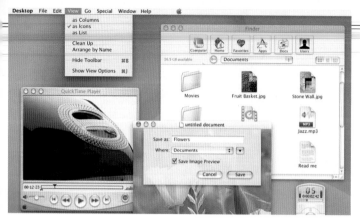

The Mac desktop
When an Apple Macintosh computer is switched on, the Mac operating system will automatically boot up. The desktop then appears on the monitor. The desktop is the starting point for doing tasks on the computer, and there are a number of different options you can choose from. The white bar at the top of the desktop is called the Menu Bar. If you hold down the mouse button on one of the words in the Menu Bar, a drop-down menu appears. If you highlight View, for example, you can change the way your desktop appears on the screen.

Using icons
Simple pictures, called icons, appear on the desktop to represent different jobs that the computer can do. You click on them to access files or to perform tasks. Icons are easy to recognize and help you to work easily. For example, Folder icons are where you keep your work. You can name the different folders so that you can find different files easily. The Hard Disk icon represents the main disk drive built into the computer. It stores the Operating System software, applications software and your work.
The Recycle Bin on a PC and the Wastebasket on a Mac are where you put the files you do not want any more before you delete them for good. As long as they stay in the Wastebasket, you can take them out again if you change your mind.

Signpost icons
Each application software has a unique icon. When you double click on the icon with a mouse, the application opens so that you can use it. There are many different kinds of applications software. Word-processing software allows you to type and arrange text. Graphics software allows you to create images or manipulate old ones to improve them or turn them into a new picture. Internet browsers and e-mail software are essential if you want to use either facility. The icons above represent a range of different software.

Drop-downs and pop-ups
Most software works using drop-down and pop-up menus. When you click with your mouse on a word on

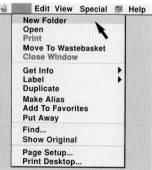

the monitor screen, you often find that a menu either drops down or pops up on screen and offers you a number of choices. Move the cursor to the one you want to select and click on it to perform the task you want.

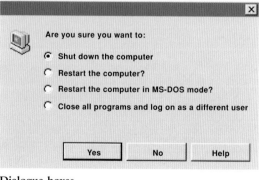

Dialogue boxes
When the computer needs to ask you a question, a window appears on the screen. If you are not sure what to do, there is a Help option, where you can look up information.

MOUSE CARE AND MOUSE PAD

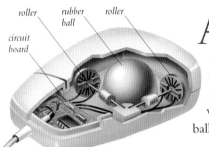

roller *rubber ball* *roller*

circuit board

A MOUSE is a device that allows you to interact with your computer. It moves the cursor on the screen, so that you can select different options. A rubber ball inside the mouse rolls like a wheel so the mouse can move over a special mouse pad. The ball then pushes against electrical contact points, which send signals to your computer. Unfortunately, the rubber ball picks up dust and dirt from the mouse pad, which then sticks to the contact points. As more dirt accumulates, it becomes more difficult to move the cursor where you want it to go. The project on this page shows you how to clean your mouse.

Inside the mouse
Tiny circuits inside the mouse convert the movement of the rubber ball into electrical signals. The contact points are set on rollers in front of the mouse and to one side.

HOW TO CLEAN YOUR MOUSE

You will need:
rubbing alcohol, cotton swabs.

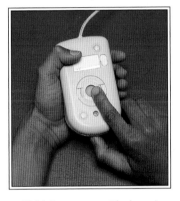

1 Hold the mouse upside down in one hand. Use the other hand to remove the cover around the ball. There are usually arrows on the mouse to show you how.

Mouse pads are made from a spongy material that provides a good surface for the mouse to move around on. There are lots of fun designs, but you can make your own one if you like. The project on the opposite page shows you how.

4 You can wipe the ball clean as well if you like. When it is clean, place the ball back inside the mouse. Reposition the cover. Now your mouse should work better.

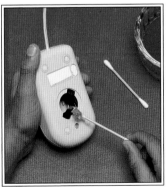

2 When the cover is loose, place the palm of your hand over the bottom of the mouse and turn it back the right way. The ball will fall out into your hand.

3 Moisten a cotton swab with rubbing alcohol and use it to clean the inside of the mouse. Most dirt sticks to the contact points, so be sure to clean these thoroughly.

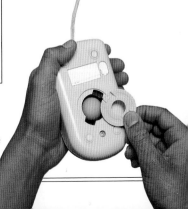

MAKE A MOUSE PAD

You will need:
*computer and printer, heat-transfer
printing paper (available from a computer store),
plain mouse pad, pencil, ruler, scissors, iron.*

1 Open up a colorful picture file from the clip-art folder. Measure the mouse pad and adjust the height and width of the picture (using the Measurements tool bar) so that it will fit on the pad. The image will be reversed when it is on the mouse pad, so don't choose a picture that has any writing on it.

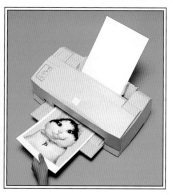

2 Put a piece of heat-transfer paper into the paper tray of your printer. Print the picture onto the coated side of the paper.

3 Place the pad over the printed picture and draw around the edge of the pad with a pencil. Carefully cut around the pencil marks.

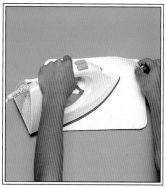

4 Look at the instructions given with the heat-transfer paper and set the iron to the right temperature. Put the print face side down on the top side of the pad and iron over it.

5 While the transfer paper is still warm, carefully peel off the backing paper to reveal your image. Let the mouse pad cool down for a few minutes.

6 It will take about 30 minutes for the mouse pad to cool before you can use it. The surface of mouse pads is designed to let the mouse run smoothly over them, but also to provide enough grip for the rubber ball to move. You could make a whole selection of mouse pads with different pictures on them—one for every day of the week.

WORKING WITH WORDS

WORD-PROCESSING applications are designed for working with text, such as a letter, and are widely used in offices and at home. They allow you to edit (change) the words you write at any time and even add pictures, too. If you want, you can stop your work for a while, store it on the computer's hard disk and return to finish it later. The final document can be printed on paper.

Word-processing applications can do some amazing things. You can move words around, copy words from one document to another and change the size and style of the letters very easily. It is even possible to check your spelling and grammar. Before word-processing applications were invented, people could write letters and documents on a typewriter. However, the time and trouble saved by using word-processing applications means that typewriters are rarely used today.

Typewriter trouble
An old-fashioned typewriter from the late 1800s could produce quicker and neater text than handwriting. However, mistakes had to be erased or painted over. The typist also had only one choice of type size and style.

News reporters
It would be hard to find a modern office that does not use computers in some way. Most of the workers in this CNN newsroom use a computer to do their work. The reporters use a word-processing application to type their reports, which makes it very easy to change any mistakes, add extra text or check the spelling and grammar. The most common word-processing applications are Microsoft Word for PCs and AppleWorks for Macs.

Fun with fonts

A typeface, or font, is a style of lettering. There are hundreds of fonts, and each one has a name that was thought up by the person who designed it. Some are installed on your computer when you buy it. These are called the system fonts. Others can be bought on a disk and loaded onto the computer's hard drive. You can put different fonts in the same document by choosing from the menu bar.

Helvetica

Times

Weiss

Chicago

Styling the type

Styling means changing the appearance of a font. Most fonts come in a set that contains a plain font and its alternatives. The alternatives are **bold**, which is a heavy type, *italic*, which is sloping, and ***bold italic***, which is both heavy and sloping. However, you can change the format of any font by checking a box in the tool bar. Here, you can underline fonts, outline them and even put shadows on them. You can also make the typeface a different color if you want, although you will only be able to print this if you have a color printer.

plain

bold

italic

<u>underline</u>

outline

Font size

You can choose how big your type appears by changing its point size. Points are measurement units that are smaller than ⅙ of an inch. This is 11.5 point, but you can see some different sizes on the right.

14 point

24 point

44 point

64 point

selected text

Selecting text

To delete words, copy them, align them or style them to change their appearance, you first have to select the text. To do this, move your cursor to the beginning of the words you want to change. Click with your mouse. You will see the insertion point appear. Drag your mouse across the words. They will become highlighted with a color. You can now edit them as you wish.

Text alignment

Words need to start and end somewhere specific to look neat on the page. Alignment makes words line up to the left or right margin or line up with the center of the page. You can change the alignment of a selected paragraph or sentence by checking one of three boxes (right, left or center) in the main tool bar.

You can also make the text spread out evenly between the left and the right margins, which is called justification. This paragraph is justified.

Alignment is making words line up to the left, center or right of the page.

This text is aligned or ranged LEFT.

Alignment is making words line up to the left, center or right.

This text is aligned CENTER.

Alignment is making words line up to the left, center or right.

This text is aligned or ranged RIGHT.

MY LETTERHEAD

Y OU can design a personal letterhead to use whenever you write a letter. As well as including your name and address, you can also add pictures. To design your letterhead, you will need word-processing application software such as AppleWorks or Microsoft Word, but any kind of word-processing software will do. You will also need a printer to print the finished design.

To illustrate the letterhead, you can use a photograph or an existing picture from a clip-art collection on disk. You can even draw and paint your own, using a graphics application if you have one. You will be amazed at the professional-looking results that can be achieved in a short amount of time.

STEPHANIE

Your personal logo

Companies and organizations all over the world have their own logo (badge), which identifies them. The logo might include a picture, a name designed in a certain typeface, and a color. You could design your own logo for your letterhead, using some of these ideas.

Clip art

Collections of images that come on disks are known as clip art. The different language versions shown in this picture of Microsoft Word clip art are: Hebrew (top left), German (bottom left), French (top right) and Spanish (bottom right). You can buy clip-art disks but some come free with computer magazines. Most office software includes clip-art collections. You can also download images from Internet sites to build up your own collection. Images are usually arranged into categories, such as animals or sports. To illustrate a word-processing document, you need to import the picture file from where it is stored, such as your computer's hard disk or a CD-ROM.

MAKE YOUR OWN LETTERHEAD

You will need:
computer with a word-processing application, printer, paper.

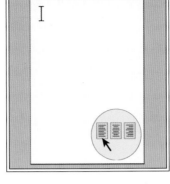

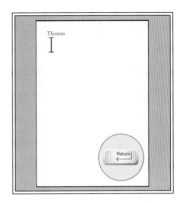

1 Open a new document. Set the size of your paper to 8½ × 11 in. Click on the page and look for the insertion point. This is where your writing will go when you start to type.

2 Type in your name. Press the Return key when you want to go to a new line. You can choose a different font and change its size and color if you like.

3 When you have finished typing your address, place the insertion point where you want the picture to be. Drop in the picture file using the appropriate command on your computer.

4 Try arranging the words and pictures in different ways. When you are happy with your design, save the document as "My letterhead" in your documents folder.

5 When you have finished writing your first letter, save it under a different name, such as "Letter 1." This means you can keep the original version of your letterhead to use again. Finally print a copy of your letter from your printer.

HOME OFFICE

Organizing your life
Some computers have an appointments diary, or personal organizer, as part of the office software. Some organizers can even remind you that you have an appointment by sounding an alarm.

MANY people keep records of useful information on their computer. They might list people's names and telephone numbers or record what needs to be done each day, just like a computerized diary. Office software, such as Microsoft Office, can be used for this purpose. As its name suggests, office software is mostly used by businesses, but it can be used by anyone.

For instance, you may want to store the names and addresses of all your closest friends. You would use a database program to do this. Databases allow you to store lots of information, which can be easily accessed and updated. Libraries use databases to store information about all the books they have. Information about your allowance can be recorded by using a spreadsheet program, which can perform all kinds of automatic calculations. Spreadsheets can add and subtract, converting dollars to pounds, for example, with the data they contain. You can also plot graphs and charts to show the information in a visual way.

Address book
Databases are used to keep records of data such as names, addresses, telephone numbers and e-mail addresses. They help you find and use the stored information easily. Databases can sort the information in different ways, such as in alphabetical or numerical order. Most office software contains a database application.

NAME	ADDRESS	PHONE	E-MAIL
Lucy	4 Big Street	555 1234	lucy@
James	23 Long Road	555 4567	james@
Poppy	14 Short Way	555 7890	poppy@

CANTEEN FOOD				Total of types
Pizzas	220	360	209	789
Pasta	170	238	273	681
Burgers	186	92	156	434
Fish	26	15	29	70
Total meals a month	602	705	667	

Counting and calculating
A spreadsheet is a display of numerical information that does automatic calculations. A spreadsheet is made up of lots of little boxes called cells. The size of the cells can be changed to fit the information—either words or numbers—entered. Spreadsheet software can work out calculations on numbers contained in the spreadsheet. For example, each column can be added up. If you change one number, the total appears automatically at the bottom of the column. In this way, people can easily keep up-to-date records of their finances.

Comparing information

Sometimes it is useful to show numerical information visually to help you understand it more easily. Many spreadsheet applications can automatically draw pie charts or graphs to represent information in an accessible way. The pie chart on the right shows how much of each kind of food is being eaten during school mealtimes. The total number of meals is represented by the circle. Each section, or pie, represents the different sorts of meals that are being eaten. From the chart, it is possible to see in an instant that pizzas are the most popular food by far and that fish is chosen the least. You can also see that about a quarter of the total number of meals eaten are burgers.

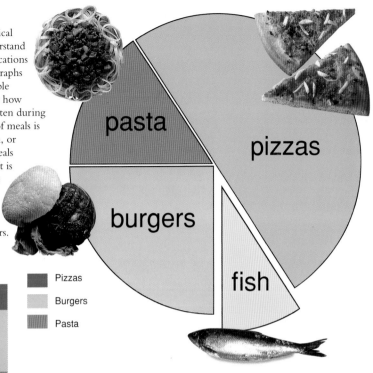

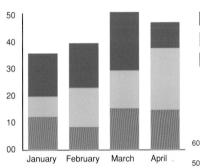

Column graphs

Spreadsheet packages can draw graphs to show how two different things, called variables, are related to one another. A common variable is time (days, weeks or months), which is always plotted horizontally, from left to right. Other variables, such as the type of food being eaten, can be plotted vertically from bottom to top. By reading the two sets of information on the graph above, you can see exactly how much of each kind of food was eaten in four given months of the year. There are two main types of graph—a column graph (above) and a line graph (above right). These graphs are two different ways of representing the same information.

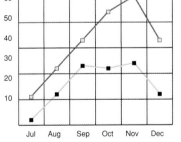

Line graphs

As in the column graph, time is shown horizontally, and another variable, such as food being eaten, is show vertically. Each line represents one type of information, in this case pizzas or pasta. It is easy to see that more pizzas are being eaten than pasta in every month.

timetable	9:00	10:00	11:00	12:00	1:00	2:00	3:00
MONDAY	math	gym	science	lunch	computing	english	art
TUESDAY	music	english	math	lunch	science	history	geography
WEDNESDAY	history	english	geography	lunch	english	gym	gym
THURSDAY	english	music	art	lunch	math	geography	history
FRIDAY	science	computing	math	lunch	music	art	english

Make a timetable

You could make your own chart to remind you of your daily schedule or important events. Using a spreadsheet program, make a chart for your school timetable. Type in the days in a vertical column on the left and the hours along the top line. Then fill in the corresponding activities.

DESKTOP PUBLISHING

DESKTOP publishing (DTP) is the term given to computer applications that allow words and images to be arranged together on a page. Most books and magazines are designed using desktop publishing software, because writing, typesetting (arranging words on a page) and illustration can all be done in one place and sometimes even by the same person. This has made the publishing process easier than ever before.

Today, anyone with a computer and the necessary software can create his or her own magazine or newspaper. Each different part of the publication—the words, photographs and illustrations—is prepared separately. Then the software brings all the elements together. Desktop publishing software is fairly easy to use. Changes to the layout of a page, such as moving an illustration or inserting an extra paragraph into a story, can be done at any point during the process. Today, millions of books and magazines are created in such a way that they can even be published on the Internet.

From words to a page
Journalists and authors may make written notes or tape record their work and then type it up using a word-processing application such as Microsoft Word. They can e-mail their work to the newspaper or publishing office where it can be worked on and made into pages.

Instant pictures
Digital cameras capture still images electronically and do not use photographic film. The photographs are stored on a disk and can be loaded directly on to a computer, missing out the expensive and time-consuming film-processing stage. The images can then be imported straight into the pages of the document.

Making the layout
All pages in newspapers, books and magazines are arranged on a basic grid like the one on the right, because it makes the pages neat and easy to read. The first stage in making a page is to design a blank grid or to use one that already exists. A grid shows the size of the page and the area in which the text and the pictures will fit. It might also show where the text and the pictures line up. Then the designer can start to work on each individual page. He or she will import (place) the pictures into boxes on the page where they look best.

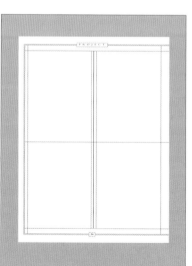

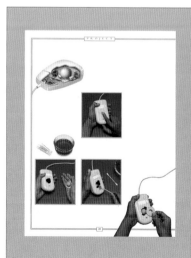

The publishing process

A book designer works on the illustrations before importing them into the pages. Before computers were invented, it took many different processes and many more people to arrive at a stage where a book or newspaper was finished. Today, the process is more straightforward and involves fewer people. This is especially important for newspapers, because they have to get the latest news to their readers as quickly as possible.

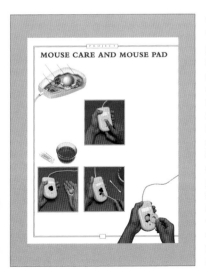

The finished page

The designer imports the text that goes with the pictures. He or she tries out different layouts until a good design has been found. The editor then checks the text and makes sure it matches the pictures, and that the blocks of text are not too long or too short. When the designer and the editor are both happy that the page is correct, it can go off to be printed and published. Desktop publishing applications make it easy to write, design and print your own pages, with a professional look. You can create posters, invitations or newsletters—any document that combines words and pictures.

DAILY NEWS

A LOT of thought goes into designing the pages of a book or newspaper. First, the contents of the page are carefully planned on paper. Then, the layout designer arranges the words and pictures using a professional page-layout application such as QuarkXPress. The good thing about using a computer to do this kind of work is that it can be changed with little effort. This project shows you how to make a magazine page using your own computer. If you do not have a page-layout program, word-processing applications, such as Microsoft Word or AppleWorks, can be used instead.

Type an article
The first step in making any publication is to decide what you want to write about. You could gather together some stories and poems from your friends, or you could type some articles about news and events. Arrange them into an order that would make sense if someone was reading them all together on a page.

Scan some pictures
You will also need some pictures for your publication. If you have a scanner, scan in all the pictures and save them in a separate folder. If you do not have one of your own, use the scanner at school. When you have scanned all the images, copy them onto a removable disk, take the disk home and copy all the files onto your hard drive.

EDITOR FOR A DAY

You will need: computer with a desktop publishing application or a word-processing application such as Microsoft Word, printer, paper.

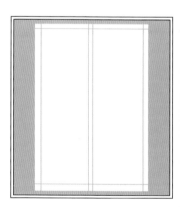

1 Collect all the items you want to put on your page. This will enable you to work out how much space you will need to fit all the words and pictures onto your page.

2 Open a document and set the document size to 8½ × 11 in. Set a 1½-in. margin around the edge of your page. Position two guide lines in the center of the page, about ¾ in. apart.

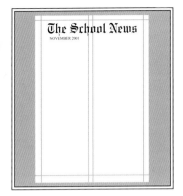

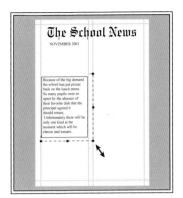

3 Make a text box at the top of the page. Type in a title. Increase the point size to make the words bigger. Make a smaller text box to add other header information.

4 Make another text box in the first column. Set the point size to 12 and type your story. You can resize the text box by dragging the corner points with the cursor.

5 Make a picture box and import your picture. You can resize the box by dragging the corner points to fit the column. Position the picture near the text box.

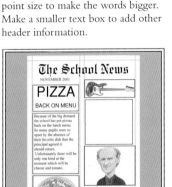

6 Add more pictures and words until the page is full. The boxes can be moved around or resized to fit everything on the page. If you have too many things to fit on one page, make another page.

7 Once you are happy with the layout, print out as many copies as you need and give them to your family and friends.

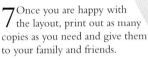

Pictures on screen
A layout designer in a newspaper office scans some images onto his computer. He will then use them to make up part of the article he is laying out on the page.

A SPLASH OF COLOR

Angular Selection	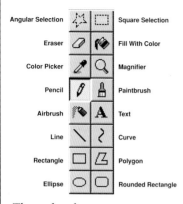		Square Selection
Eraser			Fill With Color
Color Picker			Magnifier
Pencil			Paintbrush
Airbrush			Text
Line			Curve
Rectangle			Polygon
Ellipse			Rounded Rectangle

MANY special visual effects are possible with computers that would be very difficult to do by hand. Graphics applications have the advantage that if mistakes are made, it is very easy to correct them. For example, all graphics applications have an Eraser tool, which can instantly remove something you don't like. As well as the normal drawing and painting tools, other tools can be used to create special effects. The Airbrush tool creates a fine spray effect to paint colors on your picture. There is a variety of backgrounds to give the final picture a different appearance. Most computers come with basic painting and drawing software. For a wide range of special finishing touches, such as gradient fills and airbrush effects, advanced software such as Painter and Microsoft Paint is available.

The tools palette
The Toolbar contains digital versions of real art tools such as a pencil, an airbrush and an eraser. Clicking on these icons will activate them. The Toolbar also gives you the option of drawing specific shapes, such as circles, and styles of lines. You can use a combination of all these effects on one illustration.

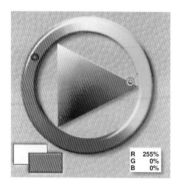

R	255%
G	0%
B	0%

Choosing color
Painting software contains palettes of different colors from which you can select and mix. Each color has a number equivalent on the Red–Green–Blue (RGB) scale. By typing in varying percentages of red, green and blue, you can mix different colors. You can save these numbers on the color palette and use the same shade again.

Multiple techniques
Most painting software enables you to create many different effects. Some give brush strokes of varied thickness, and others create airbrush effects to add to your work. Try all the different tools. The four segments of this apple were drawn using (clockwise from top left): a colored pencil, an airbrush, different brush strokes, chalk and wax crayon textures.

Brush strokes

Most applications provide a selection of different tools, such as brushes, pens, crayons and pencils, to choose from. You can experiment with crayon and chalk textures for graffiti styles, soft pencils and airbrushes for shading, washes for backgrounds and even watercolors and oil paint effects to recreate more classic works of art. You do not have to be a brilliant artist to draw and paint pictures on a computer, because the software is designed to be easy to use. Most of the effects can be created in just one click of a mouse.

Basic shapes

Basic shapes, such as circles and squares, can be made by selecting them from the Toolbar. Another tool, called the Polygon tool, lets you draw your own shapes. You can fill the shapes with color.

Looking closer

When an image is magnified, you can see that it is made up of individual blocks of color that, in turn, consist of thousands of tiny dots of light called pixels (short for picture elements). Just like words, pictures are stored in the computer as binary code.

Gradient fills

A gradient fill is a graduated blend between two or more colors or tints of the same color. You can achieve smooth color and tonal transitions when filling images with the Gradient tool.

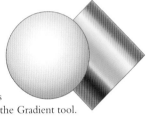

Photo painting

Painting software allows you to work with photographs you may have already scanned and saved on your computer's hard disk. Draw in a hat, some glasses and a moustache to a picture of your face to make a fun picture.

COMPUTER GRAPHICS

ARTWORKS that are created using computer technology are called computer graphics. Graphics applications can be used to create new pictures or to change existing pictures, such as photographs, that are already stored as a picture file on a computer. Pictures are displayed on the screen as small dots of color called pixels. The computer registers these tiny bits of information as binary code. Whenever you change a picture by moving it, cutting parts out or adding new parts, the computer makes a note of how the pixels have been changed and revises the binary code to record what you have done. Once people used to say that a camera never lies. Today, however, nearly all the photographs used in advertisements have been altered by computers in some way.

Computer graphics can range from simple photographic images to the complex and extremely realistic drawings used in virtual reality, the process by which a computer is used to create an artificial place that appears real, such as in a flight simulator.

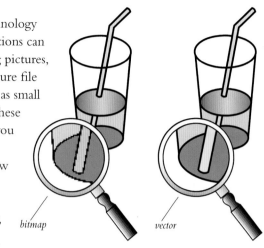

bitmap   *vector*

The make-up of an image

Computer graphics are either bitmap images or vector graphics. Photographs and painted effects are bitmaps. Each pixel that makes up a bitmap is given a specific color and location by the computer. Vector graphics are used a lot for line drawings. In these, the computer records each shape and color as a code. The difference is most apparent when the images are enlarged. Bitmaps develop jagged edges, but vector graphics stay smooth at any size.

Funny faces

Some weird and wonderful effects can be created by applying different filters to a photograph. A filter is a mathematical formula that the computer uses to distort a picture. Most computer graphics applications have filters built into them. Different filters move pixels around in different ways. Some filters do simple things such as sharpening or blurring an image. Others can distort a picture to add an unusual texture or make color changes.

Coming to life

Animation is the process by which pictures are made to move around. Animation is done by putting together hundreds of pictures, each one showing a small change in movement. The pictures that make up an animation can either be flat (two-dimensional) or three-dimensional (appear to have depth). Before computers, animations were done by hand. Computers can fill in the gaps between movements and reduce the number of pictures that need to be drawn.

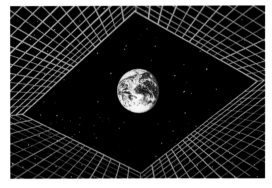

Clear or fuzzy?

The number of pixels that make up an image is known as the resolution, which is usually measured as the total number of pixels in a square inch. The more pixels, the clearer the image. For example, the two pictures above are the same, but the one on the left has a higher resolution.

Creating the image

Three-dimensional graphics have to be modeled in the same way as sculptures. Firstly, a simple shape, called the wireframe, is made of lines. The wireframe above forms a tunnel looking down at Earth. It will be covered with texture and color to give it a realistic appearance.

Altered images

Graphics software, such as Adobe Photoshop and Microsoft Paint, allow you to do amazing things with images. For example, you can copy parts of one photograph and put them on another to create an unusual or unreal image. In the picture on the left, the fish have been copied from one photograph and then positioned on the picture of Concorde flying in the sky. Using graphics software, you can also clean marks or scratches on a photographic image, change its size, brightness, resolution and color and then print it out. Some graphics software allows you to select and remove areas of a picture or paint over them with other parts of the same image. So you could create a photograph of yourself in a famous city where you have never been.

CREATE A PHOTO POSTER

CHANGING photographs is easy on a computer. You can erase parts that you do not want, paint in new areas, such as a background, or copy and move parts of the picture around. This project uses an application, such as Adobe Photoshop or Paint Shop Pro, that enables you to open picture files and then change them. Collect some photographs you find around the house, such as pictures of your family and friends. Even passport-size photographs will do. All the changes you make are done on a picture file on the computer, so you can be as experimental as you like without worrying about ruining the original photograph. You will need to use a scanner unless you have your photos on a disk or stored in the computer already. A scanner transfers the photograph on to your computer as a picture file.

Caricatures
A caricature of the British pop group the Spice Girls has been drawn using computer graphics software. You could get together with some of your friends, take photos of each other and then scan them on to your computer's hard disk. Alter the photos using a graphics application such as Painter.

MAKING YOUR OWN PHOTO POSTER

You will need: photographs, computer with a scanner, printer and a computer-graphics application.

1 Collect some pictures of your friends. Use the scanner to transfer them on to your computer. Save each picture file in a new folder named "Photos of my friends."

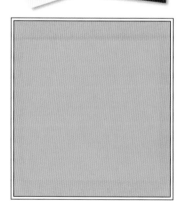

2 Start your graphics application. Open a new document and make a page 8in. wide and 8in. high. Fill it with a colored background. Save the document as "My friends."

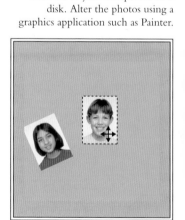

3 Open a picture file. Click on the picture and copy it. Click on your new document and paste the picture, dragging it into place with your mouse. Do the same with all the picture files.

4 Select the background color from the color palette. Select a brush and paint out the background behind the faces. Use a smaller brush around the edges of the picture.

5 Select the Text tool from the tools palette. Click where you want the words to start and type them in. Choose a bold typeface and a color that shows up well on the background.

Computer art
There are lots of ways that people create art using computer technology. One of the most amazing effects can be produced by using fractals (short for fractal dimension). Fractals are complex shapes often found in nature. Computer programs create fractal images using complex mathematical formulas. By manipulating the formulas, artists can generate stunning and intricate patterns, such as this one on the right.

6 Once you are happy with your design, save the document onto your computer's hard disk. You can then print it out poster-size. Select the Print menu from the menu bar, adjust the printer setting to fit your poster on the paper and press Print.

GAME FOR A LAUGH

COMPUTER games are the second biggest use of computers after word-processing. The computers people use to play games come in different forms. The largest are arcade machines that have big screens, loud sound effects and special controls such as steering wheels and guns. However, you can play games at home on computers such as GameBoy, PlayStation, Xbox, GameCube, or even on your desktop computer.

The most popular computer games are probably the interactive games, in which the player can control what happens on screen.

Some games can be played using the mouse and keyboard. Other games use special devices, such as a joystick or gamepad, to control parts of the game. These allow easy and fast control of the graphics in action games, when you need to react quickly to what you see on screen. Today's computer games feature high-speed, colorful, three-dimensional graphics, as well as realistic visual and sound effects.

GameBoy
One of the most popular game computers is the hand-held GameBoy. The games are supplied on cartridges, which slot into the back of the GameBoy. There are hundreds of different games to choose from.

Sport for all
Today, you can play just about every type of sport on a computer. There are football, car racing and snowboarding games, to name a few. Some sports games are called simulations, because they re-create the sport in lifelike way. In this skiing simulation, the player holds poles and stands on moving platforms, which simulate skis. The movements of his arms and legs are interpreted by sensors on the computer and then re-created on the computer screen.

Console computers
The PlayStation and Xbox are called console computers, which means they need to be connected to a television to display pictures. The game is controlled using a gamepad, which consists of two joysticks and lots of buttons. Console computers can now connect to the Internet so people from all over the world can play against each other.

Be a pilot

Simulation games let you imitate real-life situations that you control through the computer. In the flight simulator shown on the left, you can get an idea of what it is like to fly a civil aircraft to destinations all over the world. Others involve battles with military aircraft.

Rule the world

In strategy games, the player takes on the role of a government or ruler and must follow a set of objectives to create a successful city or civilization. Examples of strategy games include Alpha Centauri, Civilization, Settlers, Sim City and Tiberian Sun. In Sim City, the player becomes the mayor of a futuristic city. The people who live there want it all—industry and clean air, convenient housing and open space, low taxes and low crime rates. Can you strike a balance and turn your city into a thriving metropolis? Other strategy games allow you to create people with different personalities. You can put them in houses and make them act out real-life situations.

Spin and play

People watch while a girl spins around and upside down in an R-360 video game. The player is strapped into a small cockpit. She uses a joystick to control a jet fighter during a virtual dog-fight (fight between two planes). The cockpit is enclosed in a gyroscope, which allows the cockpit to spin around in any direction, simulating the movement of a real jet fighter.

Role playing

Forget what it is like to be human and become a fantasy character in a role-playing game such as Diablo II. You can immerse yourself in a world of intrigue and adventure set in a forgotten land. Role-playing games such as Diablo have attractive graphics and are very easy to use.

DESIGNING GAMES

Many people are involved in designing a computer game, and it is a very time-consuming process. Graphic designers come up with lifelike pictures of characters, and computer animators make characters and objects move in a realistic way. When all the parts of a game are finished, people called computer programmers write a list of instructions, called a program, which the computer uses to make all the different parts of the game work together so you can play it. It is very difficult to learn how to program modern computers to play games.

If you like playing games, here is a spot-the-difference game that you can make using your computer and play anywhere. It can be created just by using photographs or by painting and drawing your own picture.

Central character
Many games have a central character for the players to identify with. This is one of the characters from the game Crash Team Racing.

GAMING AROUND

You will need: photographs, computer with a scanner, printer and a computer-graphics application.

Playtime
A boy plays games on his computer. At the side of the keyboard, there is a selection of floppy disks from which he can download different games. More and more people have their own computers at home. Although computers are useful tools and are fun to play with, it is important not to spend all your spare time using your computer. You should do other things as well, such as playing outdoor sports and talking or listening to music with your friends.

1 Choose some images to make into a picture. Before you begin, sketch out your picture as a guide. Scan each photograph and save them all on your computer's hard disk.

Computer chess

Chessmaster 7000 is a computerized version of the traditional board game, chess. Instead of playing with another person, however, the computer is your opponent. Before you start, you select the level of difficulty to match the standard of your play.

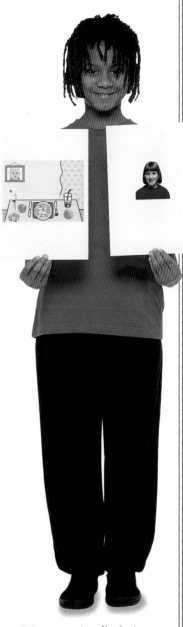

2 Open your graphics application. Then open a new document and save it as "Picture 1." Choose a background color and draw in the main areas of your picture.

3 Open one of the photograph files you scanned. Copy and paste it onto the main picture. Do the same for all the photograph files. You can draw and paint images if you like.

4 When you have completed your picture, save it as "Picture 1" again. Then select Save As from the File menu. Type "Picture 2" and save a second copy of the same picture.

5 Now you can change things on Picture 2. Change the color of something, change its size, move it to another place and remove or add things. Make about six changes.

6 Print out copies of both pictures, and ask a friend to spot the differences between the two. The more subtle you make the changes, the harder it will be for the person playing the game to spot them all. The person who spots all the differences the quickest is the winner.

MULTIMEDIA

M ULTIMEDIA means bringing together different kinds of communication (media) such as text, photographs, moving pictures and sounds. Encyclopedias, especially, can be a lot of fun when they can let you hear the sound a bird makes or show you how a machine moves. Multimedia is used for teaching, games, giving information in public places, advertising, and accessing reference material. The multimedia user is given control over the information, which means he or she can make choices about how they move through the work and can select what is presented to them. This way of working with the information is called interaction. Click with a mouse on a picture or highlighted words to jump to other pages or bring special effects into play such as animations, sound or a video clip. Multimedia is commonly found on the Internet and reference CD-ROMs such as Microsoft's *Encarta* encyclopedia.

Home library
Reference books, such as encyclopedias and atlases, work well when translated into multimedia because they can show much more than flat, still, visual information. Video clips can show how machines or animals move or what people and places look like. Added sounds can reproduce people's voices or allow the music of a singer or composer to be heard. Multimedia reference publications can also link similar articles together.

Showing the way
Museums, airports, and other public places often have multimedia kiosks to give information to the public. They often use a technology called touch screen where viewers point to the item they want to know about with their finger instead of a mouse. Sensors detect changes in the electrical current on the screen, work out what area of the screen is being touched and then provide information related to the area of interest.

Learn a language
This boy is learning how to speak French on his home computer using a multimedia language package. Foreign language students can hear the language being spoken as well as having their own voice recorded and checked for the correct pronunciation. Interactive games and puzzles can test the student's understanding of a particular topic they have learned. Multimedia is an extremely useful tool in the classroom, because the students can work through the topic at their own speed. They can replay any information they are unsure about and can quickly cross-reference related areas by adding bookmarks and their own personal notes. Many school subjects are now being taught using multimedia CD packages.

video clips

photographs and illustrations

sounds

written information

Making multimedia

There are many stages involved in making a multimedia product. First, how the product is going to look, what it will contain and how the parts will link together have to be worked out. When this has been decided, a team of researchers must find all the material, such as video clips, images, sounds and written information.

The final result

Once all the information has been gathered, the various media are linked using a special computer language. This is an electronic connection between media in the product, allowing the user to cross-reference between similar topics, pictures, animations or videos. At the same time, a team of software engineers will develop the "run-time engine," a computer application that coordinates and runs all the elements of the product. Once everything is in place, the product is tested extensively to identify any problems that may have cropped up during the production process.

control panel for the video clip and sound

subject areas within the encyclopedia

subject heading

menu bar to help you find your way around the encyclopedia

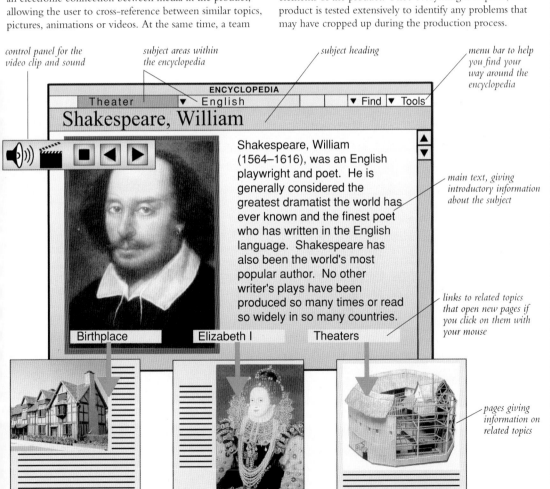

ENCYCLOPEDIA

Theater ▼ English ▼ Find ▼ Tools

Shakespeare, William

Shakespeare, William (1564–1616), was an English playwright and poet. He is generally considered the greatest dramatist the world has ever known and the finest poet who has written in the English language. Shakespeare has also been the world's most popular author. No other writer's plays have been produced so many times or read so widely in so many countries.

main text, giving introductory information about the subject

links to related topics that open new pages if you click on them with your mouse

Birthplace   Elizabeth I   Theaters

pages giving information on related topics

VIRTUAL REALITY

COMPUTERS can create an artificial place and situation that looks very real indeed. The virtual world is actually made up of many different three-dimensional graphics, which together imitate the real world or create a very convincing one. The viewer can move around the virtual environment by using an input device such as a control pad, mouse or keyboard. As the viewer changes view or moves somewhere, the graphic on the screen changes to respond to the action of the viewer. There are two types of virtual reality (VR)—immersive and desktop. Immersive VR is extremely realistic and is most often used for arcade games and for scientific and business research. Desktop VR is less sophisticated and can be experienced on a home computer.

In another world
Immersive VR is so realistic that it makes viewers believe they are actually inside a different world. The user may have to wear a head-mounted display unit on his or her head. This is a helmet that has a computer screen inside. The screen displays the virtual environment. As the user's head turns, the display on the computer screen changes, just as in real life. The viewer can interact with the environment using a glove with sensors to detect hand movements.

Squash for one
A boy plays squash on a virtual reality court. As the ball comes towards him, he swings the racket. The computer senses his movements and plays the ball back to him. Virtual squash might be fun, but you would get more healthy exercise playing a real game of squash.

Drive safely
In this version of virtual reality, the image is projected on to a screen in front of the user. The screen fills the field of vision, so that the player actually feels as if he or she is driving along the road. Sensors attached to the car and to the driver's helmet detect the eye, arm and leg movements. This virtual reality situation is designed for developing a computerized warning system in cars that will alert the driver if he or she is about to do anything dangerous. Applications of this type are increasingly popular ways of training people in situations that would otherwise be too dangerous.

Virtual visitor

VR has been used to recreate the tomb of Nefertari, the wife of Pharaoh Ramses II of Egypt. The virtual visitor can walk through the burial chambers, which are decorated with murals and hieroglyphic writing. The viewer uses a trackball mouse to move around the burial chambers. This mouse has a rolling ball on top, which makes navigation smoother. Some even have an up and down facility so that the viewer can observe high and low viewpoints of his or her surroundings. This virtual reality is called desktop VR, because you can use a home computer to explore the environment. Although the effect is convincing, it is not as lifelike as immersive virtual reality. The controls available are less sophisticated, although headsets are now becoming available.

Fun and games

These people are playing a virtual reality game in an amusement park. The players are using their headsets to collect clues needed to solve a mystery in a virtual world. Games such as these allow players to interact with one another as they move around their environment.

Practice makes perfect

The cockpit of a flight simulator imitates all aspects of flight, including weather conditions and details of all the airports in the world. By imitating real flight, the pilot can make mistakes without putting real passengers in danger.

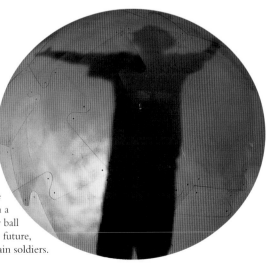

The future of virtual reality

The cybersphere is the next step in virtual reality technology. It allows the user to be totally immersed in a simulated world, not just via a headset. It is a large see-through ball made of interlocking plates and mounted on a cushion of air. Users can walk, run or jump, and a smaller ball connected to the large one detects these movements. In the future, this technology could be used in the military to train soldiers.

THE SOUND OF MUSIC

RECORDING and playing sounds and music is another task that a computer can do. You can play audio CDs or write, record and mix your own music. The sound that we hear—for example, from a musical instrument—travels to our ears through the air in waves, called sound waves. Computers can convert sound waves to electrical signals. These are subsequently converted into binary code, so that the computer can recognize them. When a microphone picks up sound waves, it passes them to an analogue-to-digital converter. This device converts sound waves to digital signs. The opposite conversion takes place when the computer plays music.

Sound files take up a lot of the computer's memory, but new technology, such as the MP3 system, can reduce the size of the files while keeping the quality of the sound. There are hundreds of web sites on the Internet where you can download MP3 files of your favorite music and store it on your own CDs. In the future, most of our music may come from the Internet in this way. In this project, you can find out how to make your own CD covers for music that you download.

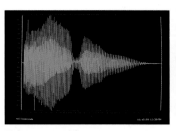

Voice recognition
Talking to a computer is not as strange as it might seem. Software can now analyze a person's voice patterns, making it possible to give a computer instructions without ever touching it. This software is very useful for people with disabilities.

MAKE A CD COVER

You will need: *a selection of images, computer with a computer-graphics application, printer, scissors, CD case.*

Sound studio
Digital sound recording has practically replaced analogue (tape) recording because the sound quality is so much better. Computers have made the job a whole lot easier, too. Applications called sequencers record tracks (different parts of a piece of music, such as guitar or drums). The sequencer records short sequences of the sound the instruments are producing at regular intervals. These are then translated into binary code so they can be stored in the computer.

1 Choose all the images you would like to use on your CD cover. Place them all in their own folder on your computer so that you will be able to find them easily.

2 Using your graphics application, draw a box that measures 5 × 5 in. Use the ruler guides to help you get the right size. Start to create a design using the painting tools.

3 Bring in photographic images if you want to use them. Open the photo first, select it, and then use Copy and Paste to transfer it to your design. Add some text for the title.

4 When you are happy with your design save it on your computer's hard disk. Print the final design out at 100 percent. Carefully cut out your print.

5 Slide the print into the CD case lid. You can also take out the removable plastic disc holder and make another design for the back and spine of the CD case.

Composer

HAPPY BIRTHDAY TO YOU.   HAPPY BIRTHDAY TO YOU.   HAPPY BIRTHDAY DEAR

Music maker

Some music software can actually make the sounds of musical instruments. They also write out the music as the notes are being played. The computer then records the sound and stores it so it can be played again.

6 If you have a CD writer and regularly download music from the Internet, you will not have a cover to make your CD stand out. It is easy to make your own covers using existing pictures and photos. Look in your clip-art folder to see if there are any images you can use. You can even draw and paint your own designs.

THE INTERNET AND E-MAIL

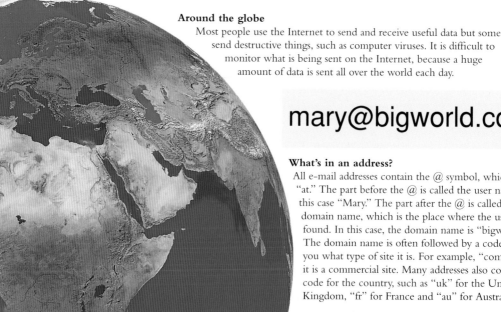

THE Internet is a global network that allows computers to exchange information. The first computer networks were developed in the 1960s, but the rapid explosion of the 1990s resulted from the rapid growth of personal computing and the improvement of the modem (modulator/demodulator). The Internet has many applications. Perhaps the most popular is electronic mail, or e-mail for short. Using e-mail, messages can be delivered to a computer user on the other side of the world in a matter of minutes. However, the most impressive application of the Internet is the World Wide Web (www). This allows a user to set up a computer document called a web page, look up other web pages, search for data using a search engine and download the latest software.

Sky high
Communications satellites are just one part of a vast system that enables data to be transmitted all over the world by the Internet.

Traffic jams
A computer graphic represents Internet traffic throughout the world. Each colored line represents the Internet traffic from a different country. For example, the United States is pink and the United Kingdom is dark blue. Internet traffic is set to increase as more and more people connect to the Internet.

Around the globe
Most people use the Internet to send and receive useful data but some send destructive things, such as computer viruses. It is difficult to monitor what is being sent on the Internet, because a huge amount of data is sent all over the world each day.

mary@bigworld.com

What's in an address?
All e-mail addresses contain the @ symbol, which means "at." The part before the @ is called the user name, in this case "Mary." The part after the @ is called the domain name, which is the place where the user can be found. In this case, the domain name is "bigworld." The domain name is often followed by a code that tells you what type of site it is. For example, "com" means it is a commercial site. Many addresses also contain a code for the country, such as "uk" for the United Kingdom, "fr" for France and "au" for Australia.

Mailing electronic messages

E-mail software allows you to send and receive e-mails, write and edit messages, and store e-mail addresses in a contacts folder. To use e-mail on your own computer, you must be connected to the Internet, and a company known as an Internet Service Provider (ISP) allows you to do this. You also have to install a browser (software that lets you look at the Internet) on your computer. Alternatively, you can use a service provided by an e-mail portal company, such as Hotmail and Yahoo! This service allows you to send and access your mail from any computer connected to the Internet.

Internet browsers

Two well-known browsers are Internet Explorer and Netscape Navigator. Both have an e-mail facility built into them. When you start up your e-mail software, which is called logging on, messages that have been sent to you show up automatically on the screen.

Smileys

These little pictures are made up from combinations of keyboard punctuation marks, such as semi-colons, colons, dashes and parenthesis. Smileys are used by people in their e-mails to describe an expression or emotion that they want to communicate to the reader. They are used to represent faces. Look at them sideways to see the face. Here are some well-known smileys. Maybe you can think of some new ones.

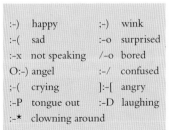

:-)	happy	;-)	wink
:-(	sad	:-o	surprised
:-x	not speaking	/-o	bored
O:-)	angel	:-/	confused
;-(	crying	]:-[	angry
:-P	tongue out	:-D	laughing
:-*	clowning around		

Coffee and Internet

Internet cafes, or cybercafes, allow people who do not have a computer of their own to access the Internet. You can surf the Internet and look at different web sites while you have a cup of coffee or some lunch. Cybercafes are also ideal for people who travel a lot or are on holiday. However, they may become less popular when pocket-size personal computers that can connect to the Internet become available.

SEND AN E-POSTCARD

Have you ever missed an important birthday and found yourself rushing to catch the mail? This will never happen again if you use an e-postcard. You can choose, write and send a card at any time of the day and all without leaving your comfort of your home. Electronic postcards, or e-postcards, are picture postcards that can be sent over the Internet from your computer in minutes. To receive an e-postcard, you must have an e-mail address. You can even send one to yourself. There are many web sites on the Internet that offer this as a free service. A good one can be found at www.apple.com/icards, which is part of the Apple Computer web site. Other e-postcard web sites include www.greetings.yahoo.com and www.egreetings.com.

Snail mail
Traditional mail sent across great distances is normally transported by plane. Even so, it can take a week for letters to reach Europe from North America. Traditional mail is nicknamed snail mail by Internet users, because it is so slow compared to e-mail.

POST AN E-CARD

You will need: computer connected to the Internet, your friend's e-mail address.

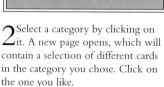

1 Open your Internet browser and connect to the Internet. Type in one of the addresses shown above to access the e-postcard web site. A page then shows you all the different cards.

2 Select a category by clicking on it. A new page opens, which will contain a selection of different cards in the category you chose. Click on the one you like.

3 Another page opens, which displays a larger version of the picture to let you see it better. If you are happy with it, click on the icon that says "Edit This Card."

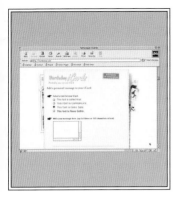

4 Choose a typeface that will suit your greeting card. When you have chosen a suitable typeface, type your message in the box at the bottom of the screen.

5 Fill in your name and e-mail address and your friend's name and e-mail address in the spaces provided so that the computer will know where to send the card.

6 The computer then combines your message with the e-postcard and sends it to your friend. The computer will tell you if there has been a problem with the system and the card hasn't been delivered.

7 If you like, you can print any e-postcards that you receive and keep them just like birthday cards and Christmas cards. Collect as many different e-postcards as you can.

An e-journey
Whenever you send an e-mail, it travels down a telephone line to your ISP. Here, e-mails are sorted according to their destination and then sent by satellite to the recipient's ISP. It is then sent back down a telephone wire to the recipient of the e-mail. E-mails can arrive in minutes, but sometimes they are sent in batches and can take a few hours to reach their destination.

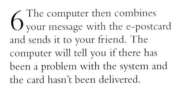

THE WORLD WIDE WEB

THE World Wide Web (www) has created huge interest in the Internet, because it makes it possible to access information from all over the world. The Internet and the www are not the same thing. The www is just a way of finding information on the Internet. The www is made up of millions of web sites about almost anything you can think of. Many organizations, colleges and schools have web sites, and there are a million others made by people just like you. You need an Internet browser to display web pages for you.

Web sites are much like a magazine. There is always a first page, similar to a magazine cover, which is called the home page. This displays a list of the web site's contents and allows you to explore your way around the web site.

Worldwide success
In 1990, an Englishman named Tim Berners-Lee developed the World Wide Web at the European Laboratory for Particle Physics in Switzerland (also known as CERN). He wrote the original HTML (Hypertext Mark-up Language) code. This enables web pages to be viewed on a computer. Today, the www is the most popular way of accessing information on the Internet, and it is used by millions of people throughout the world.

Web site addresses
Web addresses always start with http:// (hypertext transfer protocol), which is the way your computer reads web pages. Then comes www, followed by the domain name, which tells you where the web site can be found.

http://www.apple.com

YAHOOLIGANS!®

the Web Guide for Kids

Arts & Entertainment

Around the World

Computers & Games

Web sites
When you open a web site, the first page you will see is the home page. A home page such as Yahooligans! has a list of the site's contents, which will to help you to navigate your way around the web site. Yahooligans! is a site that acts as an Internet guide for young people. You can find all kinds of subjects, varying from information on arts and entertainment to computers and games. With a home computer and Internet access it is possible to answer such questions as "What is the capital of Peru?" or "Who was the first person in space?" in just a few minutes. There are web sites devoted to information on any subject you can think of, as well as commercial sites, which seem destined to change forever the way we do business.

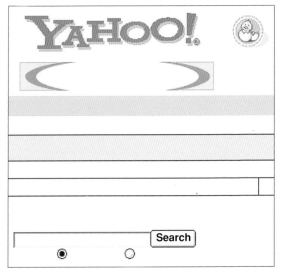

Search engines

Many people find that the Internet is one of the best ways to find out information. Unfortunately, searching the Internet for specific information can be difficult, because there are so many web sites that you might have to search through. In this situation, a search engine may be a handy tool. Yahoo! is just one of many search engines on the Internet. Simply type in your question in the text box on screen, and let Yahoo! do the work for you. Yahoo! also presents information in organized categories, such as science and sports, to make searching for information even easier. Just click on the category link and pick one of the sites. Despite their name, search engines are not really engines at all. They are a piece of automated software that search web sites, making a note of the essential information such as the site title, address and often the first line of text on the web site. This information is stored on a huge database, which can be accessed by the Internet user.

Servers

All the web pages on the www are stored on large, powerful computers known as servers. The picture to the right shows the main server room for the www in Geneva, Switzerland. Servers belong to the many different Internet Service Providers (ISPs). When a user types in the unique address of a web site using an Internet browser, the browser links to the server where the web site is stored and sends a GET command. It then tells the server to send all of the information needed to reconstruct the web pages on your own computer.

Web games

There are many Net game web sites, and some allow you to download games on to your computer and play with people from all around the world. Some games need special software called a plug-in, which may make the graphics of the game look much more realistic. You can download plug-ins free from games web sites.

WEB CULTURE

Mᴜsᴇᴜᴍs house some of the world's finest collections of antiquities and art, but their one disadvantage is that they are spread out all over the world, so it is difficult to get to all of them. Thanks to the World Wide Web, however, you can see museums such as the Metropolitan Museum of Art in New York on your computer screen. Most museums have their own web sites, which include pictures of the galleries and the exhibits they contain. Some web sites allow you to take a "virtual tour" of the galleries, and you can zoom in to take a closer look at the exhibits. One of the most popular web sites of this type is that of the Louvre Museum in Paris, France (www.louvre.fr).

See Paris

When you visit the Louvre's web site, this is the image that you see. It is just as if you are visiting for real. In the 1990s, large parts of the Louvre were reconstructed to make the museum more accessible to visitors. The ground level entrance to the museum was relocated to the central courtyard, called the Cour Napoléon, and was crowned by a steel-and-glass pyramid designed by American architect I. M. Pei.

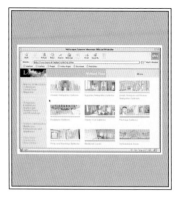

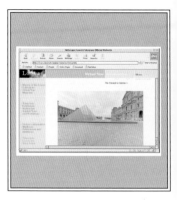

1 Open your Internet browser and connect to the Internet. Type in the web site address of the Louvre (www.louvre.fr). Click on the words "Discover Our Virtual Tour."

2 A new page offers you choices of different areas of the museum that you might want to visit. Choose "Architectural Views" to see the huge glass pyramid.

3 You need to download Quick-Time to view the pictures. Type www.quicktime.com. Follow the instructions. Then click on the icon next to "Pyramid at daytime 1."

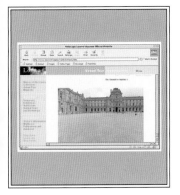

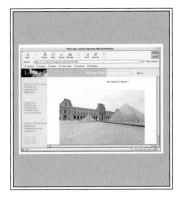

4 When the picture appears, look at the buildings by holding the mouse button down and dragging it over the picture. The picture moves to show you different views.

5 You can see the courtyard and the pyramid from different sides, as if you were walking round it. If you can't go to Paris to see it for yourself, this is the next best thing.

6 Return to the main menu and click on "Paintings Galleries." See the *Mona Lisa* by Leonardo da Vinci in the *Salle des Etats*. Move around and zoom in and out using the mouse.

7 The Egyptian Antiquities Galleries are also good to look at. Again, use your mouse to move around the gallery and look at the exhibits up close.

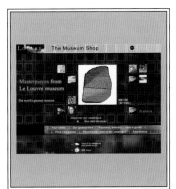

8 You can also browse in a "virtual shop," which sells cards, posters, and books about some of the things you have seen in the museum.

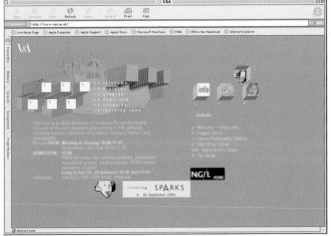

London museums online

The Victoria and Albert Museum in London in the United Kingdom is the world's largest museum of decorative arts, containing over 140 galleries of photography, sculpture, fashion, furniture, and painting. Many of the works of art can be viewed online, through the museum's web site. Access the web site by typing in www.vam.ac.uk. This takes you to the museum's home page. You can then choose to explore one of the galleries by pressing your mouse on the "Explorer" box. Not only will you be able to look at the works of art on the web site, but you can also find more information about them. Other web pages contain pictures of the museum's galleries, and you can also access the museum shop and buy reproductions of some of the pieces of art.

COMPUTERS IN EVERYDAY LIFE

COMPUTERS are used in all areas of our lives. They are found in shops, libraries, offices and in our homes. Most simple electronic machines, such as washing machines, microwave ovens and telephones, contain some kind of computer technology. Even a digital watch contains microchips. Some people worry that we are becoming too dependent on computer technology. Most, though, admit that computers make many things a lot easier and faster. It is amazing to think that computers were almost unheard of only 50 years ago. Today, almost everyone's lives are affected by computers in some form or another.

Bar codes
Many libraries use bar-code scanners that electronically scan bar codes printed on all their books. Bar codes consist of a number of parallel lines and spaces, which the reader scans and feeds back to the library's main computer. The bar code represents lots of data about the book, for example, its author, publisher and when it was published. This computer keeps a record of all this data. The computer also records who has borrowed the book and when they borrowed it, so the library staff will know when the books are due to be returned.

Computer-aided clothing
A clothing production designer uses computer-aided design (CAD) software to transfer the paper patterns seen at the lower left of the picture on to the computer screen. The shapes, or "nest," of patterns together form a single garment. CAD helps the production designer to check the different sizes and shapes of clothing before they are manufactured. CAD is used in many areas of industry. Systems generally consist of a computer with one or more work stations, featuring video monitors and interactive graphics-input devices.

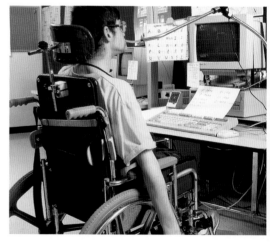

Computers and disabled people
This man is unable to use his arms, but he can still operate a computer by using a mouthpiece. Computers have made the lives of disabled people much easier than before. For example, the houses of people who have difficulty moving around can be set up so that many tasks, such as turning on a light switch, can be done using their computer.

Tracking flights

The air traffic control tower at Los Angeles Airport uses an array of computerized equipment to keep track of the positions of hundreds of aircraft. Air traffic is increasing every day. The technology used by air traffic controllers and pilots to avoid collisions and bad weather has had to become more sophisticated.

Medicine

A doctor uses a digital camera to photograph a man's eye for keeping with his medical records. The resulting image is displayed on the computer screen and is kept for analysis by other doctors. Medical specialists who may live far away can be consulted. This enables instant response and saves on travel costs.

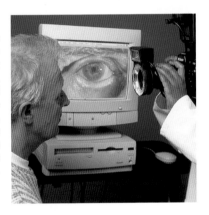

Computer banking

Plastic bank cards are used to obtain cash from ATMs (automated teller machines or cash machines). Credit and debit cards, often called electronic money or plastic money, are also used to pay for goods without using real money. People can even access their bank accounts on the Internet to transfer money between accounts and pay bills.

Growth of the Internet

Today, over 50 million people around the world own a personal computer. Soon, using the Internet will become as common as using the telephone. Even those people who do not have their own computer, or who are traveling, can find one to use. Many libraries have computers that can be used for free. Internet cafes, where you pay to connect to the Internet, are opening up all over the world. Today, you do not even have to own a computer to use the World Wide Web. Televisions and telephones have already been developed that connect to the Internet.

HEALTH AND ORGANIZATION

I T is essential to organize the space around your computer so you can use it properly. Keep all your papers in files and make sure your desk is tidy so you can use your keyboard easily and see the screen clearly to prevent muscle and eye strain. The project on the opposite page shows you how to make some files to help keep your work tidy.

Store your floppy disks and CDs in their covers when you are not using them to keep them clean and safe from scratches. The disks can also be affected by magnets, so do not put them on objects such as speakers, which have magnets in them. Positioning your computer is also important. If there is too much light shining on the screen, the glare will make it hard to see what you are doing.

Sitting positi
You must
comfortably wh
using a compu
Adjust the hei
of your seat
look dowr
the screen, a
keep your ba
straight. Alw
take regular bre
if you are using
computer fo
long tir

Eye strain

Staring at a computer screen for long periods of time is not good for you, because it will cause you to strain your eyes. Here are some eye exercises you can do to help prevent eye strain.

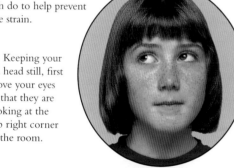
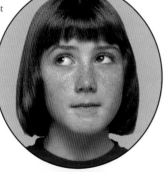

1 Keeping your head still, first move your eyes so that they are looking at the top right corner of the room.

2 Relax them for a moment. Then move your eyes to look at the top left corner of the room.

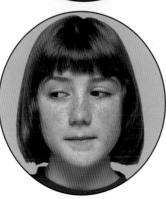
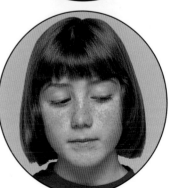

3 Relax again. Now move your eyes to look at the bottom right corner of the room.

4 Relax once more. Finally, move your eyes to look at the bottom left corner of the room.

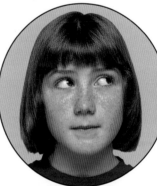

MAKING YOUR OWN FOLDERS

You will need:
one large piece and some small pieces of colored paper, black marker.

1 Take the large piece of paper. Fold it in half and flatten the crease. Make sure the corners meet. Fold the other pieces of colored paper in the same way.

2 You will end up with one large folder and four smaller ones. Draw a symbol on each folder to show what will be kept in it. You could either copy the ones above, or design your own.

3 For instance, you could draw an envelope on your letters folder, a paint palette for your paintings and drawings, a CD for your music homework, or a book for your essays.

4 Collect your papers together and sort them out into categories. Put each category into a different folder, so that you can find them easily.

5 Now put each small folder in the large one. This system of keeping things in folders is the one used by most computers. The large folder represents your computer's hard disk. The smaller folders represent the individual folders for different subjects.

6 To make a new folder on your computer, go to File in the menu bar and select New Folder if you are using a Mac or Folder if you are using a PC. A new folder will be created with the name bar highlighted ready for you to type in its name. Your work will be organized, so that you can find it easily.

CHANGING LIFESTYLES

OMPUTERS are becoming smaller, faster and more powerful all the time. Microprocessors have developed very rapidly in the last ten years, and it looks as if they will continue to do so. Data storage is improving all the time. In a few years, huge amounts of data will be stored on tiny pocket-size computers. Computers will become so small that they will be incorporated into the clothes that we wear. In fact, they have changed human life so much in recent years that it is difficult to imagine how they will be used in the future.

Growth of the Internet
Televisions and telephones that connect to the Internet are already in production. This is a WAP (wireless application protocol) phone, which means the user can access the Internet without connecting to a normal telephone line.

Computer glasses
This man is wearing an i-glass. It is a head-mounted display unit that links up to a tiny personal computer. Information is displayed as three-dimensional images on a color monitor in front of the man's eyes. Sound is heard through earphones. Data is inputted into the computer using a hand-held keyboard, a microphone or cameras attached to the man's clothing. This is truly mobile computing.

Computerized clothing
These futuristic outfits were designed by a team of fashion designers and computer scientists. The red outfit has a solar panel in the hat, which powers a mobile telephone. The chest brooch contains a device to stop the woman from getting lost, while the kneepads light up so that she can see where she is walking in the dark. The silver outfit can receive e-mail, which is played through earphones or projected on to the glasses.

Wrist camera

The world's first mini digital wrist camera, the Casio WQV-1, was launched in January 2000. The camera can store up to 100 images, which can be viewed on the watch's screen. The images can then be stored, deleted or downloaded on to a PC for editing and archiving using the latest infrared technology.

FOODSTORE.COM

SEARCH

bananas

DEPARTMENTS

bread and cakes

breakfast cereals

canned goods

dairy

delicatessen

fruits & vegetables

jams and preserves

pasta and grains

ADD TO BASKET?

apples, cooking

bananas

grapes, seedless

oranges

pineapple

Internet shopping

Foodstore.com, shown above, is a fictional web site, but from the picture you can imagine just how easy it is to shop online. Just type in what you want to buy, and add it to your shopping basket. When paying for products on the Internet, you type your credit card details in to a secure form. This is checked by the Internet retailer, who will then arrange for the goods to be delivered to your door.

New working lifestyles

Once it was thought that people who worked together had to be in the same place. Today, the Internet allows people from all over the world to work together. By using video conferencing, they can see each other on their computer monitors, and they can also have a live conversation.

Movies on a disk

Sony's new Digital Video Disc (DVD) player allows you to watch the latest feature films on a disk the size of a conventional CD. DVDs may contain a combination of video, audio, and computer data, but the advantage lies in the fact that they can hold up to seven times as much data as a typical CD.

PART FIVE

SHIPS

For centuries, those who were masters of sea travel were masters of the world. Countries with fast and reliable ships were the most successful traders, explorers and conquerors. The story of water-borne vessels starts several thousands of years ago and has, in many ways, shaped the course of civilization. Most of the basic design principles of keeping a vessel afloat have remained the same from the days of the dug-out canoe and the first sailing boats. What you will discover here, though, is the enormous variety of ships that has evolved through the ages. You will find out about all sorts of ships, past and present, from simple rafts, small leisure craft and rescue boats to streamlined racing yachts, hovercraft and supertankers.

AUTHOR
Chris Oxlade
CONSULTANT
Trevor Blakeley

WHAT IS A SHIP?

PEOPLE have used rafts, boats and ships to travel across water for many thousands of years. At its simplest, a ship is any craft that travels on water, but ships have developed from simple log rafts into vast oil tankers. This development has affected life on land, in shipbuilding yards and at ports where hundreds of people work loading and unloading cargo. The difference between a ship and a boat is not very clear. Generally, ships are larger and travel across seas and oceans. Boats are smaller and usually travel on rivers, lakes and coastal waters. Ships and boats come in a huge variety of shapes and sizes and have a wide range of uses from simple rowboats to massive cruise liners. The selection of ships and boats shown here illustrates the wide range of jobs they do, and their importance for transport, commerce, leisure, exploration and combat. Simple projects will help you understand the technical side of ships—how they float and how they are powered and controlled.

Boats on inland waters
Two types of boat common on rivers and canals are shown here. In the foreground is a very simple rowboat. It has many uses—transport, fishing and ferrying from ship to shore. It is usually propelled by oars, but it can be fitted with sails or an outboard motor. Behind is a narrow, flat-bottomed canal boat. It is used for transporting cargo.

Parts of a ship
This fishing trawler looks similar to many other ships and boats. The body of the boat is called the hull. The backbone of the hull is the keel. The bow (front) is sharply pointed to cut easily through the water. A deck provides a watertight covering for the crew to work on. An engine-driven propeller pushes the ship along. The rudder at the stern (back) is used for steering.

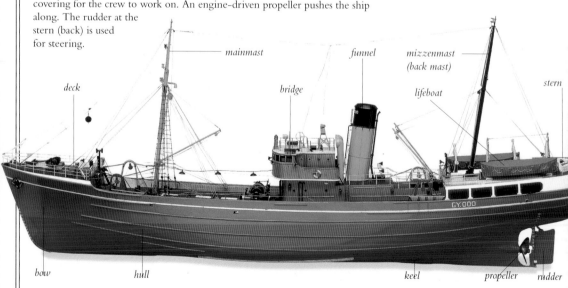

deck   mainmast   funnel   mizzenmast (back mast)   stern   bridge   lifeboat

CY.000

bow   hull   keel   propeller   rudder

Fishing boats

One of the earliest uses of boats was fishing. Today there are fishing boats designed to catch different fish in all sorts of conditions—from calm lakes to the deepest oceans. Fishing trawlers drag nets through the water behind them.

Cargo carriers

The largest moving machines ever built are big cargo ships. There are several types designed to carry different types of cargoes. The one pictured here is a container ship, that carries different cargoes packed in large metal boxes.

Fast and fun

The fastest boats are racing powerboats. They are just one of many different types of boat used for having fun on the water. Their hulls are designed to rise out of the water and skim the surface at high speed. The deep V-shape of the hull helps the bow lift out of the water and slice through the waves.

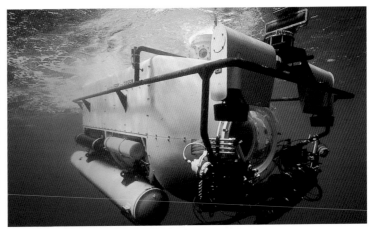

Underwater

Submersibles and submarines are the only types of boat designed to travel underwater as well as on top. The submersible shown here is just breaking the surface of the water. Submersibles are small craft used for underwater research, exploration and repairs to seabed pipes and cables. Submarines are usually larger, and most are for military purposes. They are used to launch missiles and sink ships. Most submersibles can dive much deeper than a military submarine.

HOW DO SHIPS FLOAT?

Ships and all other objects that float can do so because the water they are floating in pushes upward against them. This pushing force is called upthrust. An object will float if the upthrust of the water is great enough to overcome the downward push of the object's weight. The size of the upthrust depends on how much water the object pushes out of the way. When you put an object in water and let it go, it settles into the water, pushing liquid out of the way. The farther it goes in, the more water it pushes away and the more upthrust acts on it. When the upthrust becomes the same as the object's weight, the object floats. However, if, when the object is fully underwater, its weight is bigger than the upthrust, it will sink. The simplest boats, such as rafts, float because the material they are made of is less dense (lighter) than water. Heavy metal ships float because they are specially designed to displace (push aside) a large weight of water. Not all water has the same density. Salt water is denser than fresh water and gives a stronger upthrust. Ships float higher in salty seawater than in fresh lake water.

Fresh water

Salt water

Measuring density

The density of water is measured with a hydrometer. Make a simple hydrometer by putting a lump of modeling clay on the end of a straw. Put it in a glass of water and mark the water level with tape. Now put the straw in an equal amount of salty water. What happens?

TESTING UPTHRUST

You will need: *two styrofoam blocks (one twice the size of the other), wooden block, marble.*

1 Put the two styrofoam blocks into a tank of water. They will float well, because their material, styrofoam, is so light. Only a small amount of upthrust is needed.

2 Try pushing the blocks under the water. Now you are pushing lots of water aside. Can you feel upthrust pushing back? The bigger block will experience more upthrust.

3 A wooden block floats deeper in the water, because wood is more dense (heavier) than styrofoam. A marble sinks because the upthrust on it is not as great as its weight.

HOLLOW HULLS

You will need: *scissors, aluminum foil, ruler, marbles.*

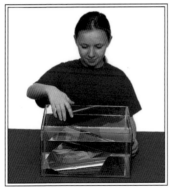

1 Put a piece of aluminum foil about 8 in. by 6 in. into a tank of water. It will sink. This is because it does not displace much water, so there is very little upthrust.

2 Lift the sheet of foil out of the water. Now mold it into a simple boat shape with your fingers. Take care not to tear the foil.

3 Put your foil boat back into the tank of water. It should now float. Its shape pushes aside much more water than it did when it was flat, so the upthrust is greater.

4 Try filling your foil boat with small objects such as marbles, for cargo. As you put more marbles in it will float lower and lower. How many marbles can your boat hold before it sinks?

The boat shape traps air inside it and pushes aside more water.

Foil float

This simple foil boat works like a real ship's hull. Even though it is made of metal, it is filled with air. This gives the hull shape a much lower overall density.

THE FIRST BOATS

NOBODY knows exactly when people first started using craft to travel on water, but it must have been tens of thousands of years ago. The first craft were probably extremely simple—perhaps just a log, an inflated animal skin, or a bundle of reeds tied together. People discovered that craft like these, made from what was available close by, could help them cross a stretch of water more easily. These craft probably developed into early simple boats, such as dug-out canoes and skin-covered boats, in which a person could sit while fishing or traveling along a river. The basic designs are still in use in many areas of the world today and have many advantages over modern boats. They are simple to make from cheap local materials. Although they are not very long-lasting, there are no high-tech materials to mend or engine parts to replace. The simplest boats do not use expensive fuel or hard-to-find equipment such as batteries.

Simple raft
A raft like this one from Australia can be built with very basic tools. It is used in shallow water and propelled along with a long stick pushed into the riverbed. Rafts are probably the oldest form of water transport. Aboriginals may have used sea-going rafts to first reach Australia around 55,000 years ago.

FACT BOX

• In 1970, Norwegian Thor Heyerdahl built a large Egyptian-style reed boat called *Ra II*. He sailed it from Africa to the Caribbean. This proved the Egyptians could have been able to reach America more than 4,000 years ago.

• One of the greatest sea battles of all time took place at Salamis, off Greece, in 480 B.C. In the battle, 380 Greek triremes defeated an invading fleet of around 1,000 Persian ships.

Dug-out canoe
A dug-out canoe is made by hollowing out a thick tree trunk to leave a thin wooden hull. The hull is smoothed and shaped so that it moves easily through the water. Dug-out canoes are fairly heavy boats and sit low in the water.

Yak-skin boat
This strange-looking boat was photographed on a river in Tibet, now part of China. It is made by stretching yak hide (a type of ox skin) over a wooden framework. The hide is then treated to make it waterproof.

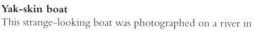

Inuit kayak
The kayak was developed by the Inuit people of the Arctic. It is also a hide boat, made from sealskin stretched over a driftwood frame. Kayaks were used as fast hunting craft for harpooning seals, fish and walruses. Boats like this work well in rough seas. A skilled paddler can turn the kayak upright if it capsizes (rolls over).

Nile boat
A model boat from an ancient Egyptian tomb shows the type of craft used on the river Nile about 5,000 years ago. Boats like these were the first to use a simple sail. The boat was propelled with oars when there was no wind or the wind was in the wrong direction. It was steered using a long oar hanging over the stern.

square sail

A tiller (handle) was used to move the steering oar.

steering oar

rigging (ropes and poles)

The helmsman steered the boat.

A crew raised and lowered the mast, or rowed the boat.

shallow-scooped, wooden hull

oar

passenger

Greek warship
This is a full-scale replica of an ancient Greek trireme. A trireme was a warship with three banks of oars operated by about 170 men. Triremes attacked other ships by ramming them. Soldiers were also transported on deck.

Roman galley
A Roman mosaic from Tunisia, made around A.D. 200, shows that Roman warships were very similar to earlier Greek ships. In the stern they often had wooden towers painted to look like stone. Underneath the high bow was a ram.

MAKE SIMPLE BOATS

Yᴏᴜ can build your own models of ancient types of boat that are still in use today. Instructions for making a model reed boat are given in the first project. Reed boats are made by tying thousands of river reeds together into huge bundles. The bundles themselves are then tied together to make hull shapes. Small reed boats are still built in southern Iraq and on Lake Titicaca in South America. In ancient Egypt, quite large boats were made like this from papyrus reeds. Some historians believe that Egyptians may have made long ocean crossings in papyrus craft. The model in the second project is of a craft called a coracle. This is a round boat made by covering a light wooden frame with animal hides. Like reed boats, coracles are still made today, builders use a covering of canvas treated with tar instead of hide. Sometimes, today, the frames are made of wicker. They were small enough for one person to paddle along a river and were used for fishing.

Chariots, boats and bladders
A stone carving from 860 B.C. shows Assyrian soldiers crossing the river Tigris. They are transporting a war chariot in their coracle-like boat. Assyrian soldiers also used inflated pig's bladders as buoyancy aids to help them swim across wide rivers.

MAKE A REED CRAFT

You will need: large bunch of raffia, scissors, ruler.

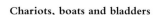

1 Make bundles of raffia by tying a few dozen strands together with a short length of raffia. You will need two bundles about 8 in. long and two more about 10 in. long.

2 Tie the two long bundles and the two short bundles together. Tie the short bundles on top of the long ones. Place a strand between each end to make the ends bend up.

3 Gently lower the reed boat onto the surface of a tank of water. How well does it float? Does it stay upright? Try leaving it in the water to see if it becomes waterlogged.

MAKE A CORACLE

You will need: scissors, craft cane, string, dark cotton cloth, white glue, paintbrush.

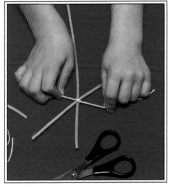

1 Cut one long and three short pieces of cane. Using short lengths of string, tie all three short pieces to the long piece to make a triple-armed cross.

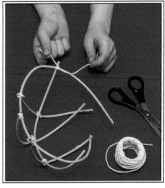

2 Cut a much longer piece of cane. Form it into a loop and tie it to all the ends of the triple cross shape. Bend the ends of the cross up as you tie them to form a dish shape.

— *waterproof covering*

lightweight frame

Model of an ancient craft
The design of the coracle has not changed in thousands of years. Early Britons used them 9,000 years ago. They are light to carry, easy to maneuver and stable enough to fish from.

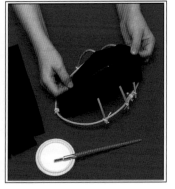

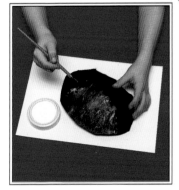

3 Cut pieces of cotton cloth about 6 in. by 2 in. Apply glue to the outside of the frame and put the pieces over it. Glue the pieces to each other where they overlap.

4 Glue down the cloth where it folds over the top of the frame. Put two coats of glue on the outside of the cloth to waterproof it. Let the glue dry completely.

5 When dry, put the finished coracle into a tank of water. How well does it float? Try making a person from modeling clay to sit in your model coracle.

THE AGE OF SAIL

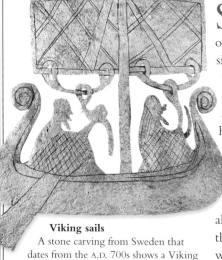

AILS capture the wind and use it to push ships and boats along. As far as experts can tell, sails first appeared on ships on the river Nile in about 3500 B.C. These ships had just one simple square sail on a single mast. They were only useful when the wind was blowing in the same direction that the crew of the ship wanted to go. If the wind was blowing in another direction, such as from their destination, the crew had to row there instead. Viking boats in the A.D. 600s used square sails to sail the coasts of Scandinavia. Later, large coastal Viking ships crossed the Atlantic to reach North America. In the Middle Ages, the lateen (triangular) sail was invented by the Chinese and Arabs. The lateen sail allowed ships to be sailed with the wind from the side. From the 1100s, European sailors began building fully-rigged ships with a combination of square and lateen sails. This allowed them to make maximum use of the wind. Their boats also had sturdy, seaworthy hulls. In ships like these, European sailors began long voyages of exploration.

Viking sails

A stone carving from Sweden that dates from the A.D. 700s shows a Viking merchant boat with a simple square sail. The sail was made from cloth reinforced with diagonal strips of leather. Sails like this helped the crew sail downwind.

Triangular sails

This fishing boat on the river Nile is called a felucca. Its design has been in use for 1,000 years and is most often seen on Arab trading vessels called dhows. The single triangular sail is an example of a lateen sail.

Chinese way ahead

The Chinese developed multi-masted ships called junks. These used triangular sails several centuries before they were introduced to Europe. This modern junk has sails that hang from poles that are hauled up the mast. The sails can swivel around the mast to take advantage of wind from behind or the side. They are made with cloth stiffened by bamboo poles. The poles keep the sails flat, make it easy to fold up the sails and provide a handy ladder for the crew.

A mixture of sails

This painting shows ships off the coast of
Portugal in the 1520s. The large ships are
heavily-armed carracks, a design that used
both square and triangular sails. Smaller
carracks were used as merchant vessels.
The flagship *Santa Maria*, which took
Columbus to America in 1492, was
probably a small carrack.

Men-of-war

These French
ships are typical
of the men-of-
war (warships)
that developed by
1700. They had
many rows of
cannons and
hulls that were
richly carved
and gilded.

Life on board

A cartoon shows sailors celebrating victory in battle
with Admiral Nelson in 1798. Hundreds of men
were needed to sail a man-of-war. They lived in
cramped conditions on the gun decks. Tables and
hammocks were suspended between the guns.

The golden age of sail

By the 1850s, sleek, fast and efficient ships called clippers carried
cargo such as tea and wool around the world. They represented
the peak of sailing ship design and were the largest wooden vessels
ever built. Larger merchant ships with iron hulls and up to seven
masts were built up to the 1930s.

STEAM POWER

THE first steam engines were developed in the early 1700s for pumping water out of mines. By the end of the century they had become small and more efficient, and engineers began to use them in trains and ships. Steam power meant that a ship could keep going even if the wind was in the wrong direction or not blowing at all. The first craft to use steam power was a small river boat called the *Charlotte Dundas*, launched in 1802. At sea, steamships carried sails to save fuel when the wind was blowing in the right direction. Early steamships used paddles, but propellers gradually proved to be more efficient. After the 1850s, shipbuilders began to use iron instead of wood. The superior strength of iron meant that much larger ships could be built, which could also be fitted with more powerful steam engines.

Stoking the boilers
To create steam, stokers constantly fed the fire boxes under a ship's boilers with coal. It was hot, unpleasant work in the stokehole.

Crossing the Atlantic
The huge *Great Eastern* was built in 1858. Steamships arrived at a time when crossing the Atlantic Ocean was becoming more popular. Steam power allowed faster and more reliable crossings, which people were willing to pay for. The *Great Eastern* could carry 4,000 passengers. It was the only ship to have both paddles and a propeller. But passengers did not quite trust steam, so it was also fitted with sails.

An iron monster
This print shows the construction of the *Great Eastern's* central compartment. At 689 feet long and 32,000 tons, it was by far the largest ship in the world at its launch in 1858. It was the last of three revolutionary ships designed by British engineer Isambard Kingdom Brunel. The *Great Eastern's* design was copied on other steamships for several decades. The hull was divided into ten watertight compartments, with double iron plating from the keel to the waterline. It took three months and seven attempts to finally launch the *Great Eastern*. Unfortunately, it had a pronounced roll in heavy seas, which passengers did not like. The ship was sold for scrap in 1888.

Steam-powered riverboats on the Mississippi

On the shallow rivers of the southern United States, steam-powered riverboats with huge paddles were developed. Here, two steamboats are racing each other on the Mississippi River in about 1850. Riverboats had flat, shallow hulls and no keel. Paddlewheels were mounted on each side or at the stern.

Steaming to war

Steam power and iron construction gave warships much greater speed, maneuverability and strength. *Dreadnought,* built in 1906, was the fastest battleship of its day and became the model for the period.

Tramp steamer

A typical cargo ship was known as a three-island steamer. This was because it had three raised decks, or islands. They were also called tramp steamers if they sailed from port to port with no set route.

Luxury travel

As transatlantic travel grew, shipping companies built large, luxurious ships called liners. This 1920s poster is from the golden age of the liner. Rival companies competed to provide the quickest crossing.

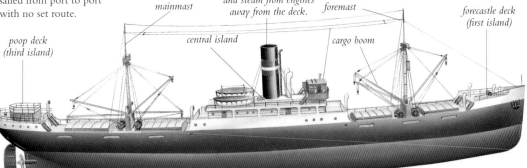

poop deck
(third island)

mainmast

central island

A funnel carries smoke and steam from engines away from the deck.

foremast

cargo boom

forecastle deck
(first island)

SHIPBUILDING

SHIPS are constructed in a shipbuilding yard. Large ships are usually made from steel. Generally, the hull is built first by welding pieces of steel together. Often the hull is built in large sections that are then welded together. When the hull is finished, the ship is launched onto the water, where the rest of the ship is completed. Dozens of different tradespeople, such as welders, crane drivers, painters, electricians and carpenters, work in shipyards. Boatbuilding takes place in smaller boatyards. Boats are usually made from wood or glass-reinforced plastic (GRP).

Shipbuilding methods have changed as new materials have become available. Originally all ships were made from wood. A skeleton hull was made, then covered with planks. Steel ships are built with the metal skin forming part of the structure. New ships are designed on computer, and models of them are tested before the ships are built.

Viking boatbuilders
This is part of the Bayeux Tapestry. It shows Norman shipwrights building the fleet that invaded England in 1066. The Normans were descended from the Vikings and shared many of the same boatbuilding techniques. They used special tools, such as axes and augers (hole borers), to shape the hull of a ship. Slender, Viking war boats were called longships.

FACT BOX

- The size of a ship is given in gross registered tonnage (g.r.t.). This is not a measure of its weight, but of the space inside it. One ton is equal to 100 cubic feet.

- The displacement of a ship is equal to the weight of the water that it pushes out of the way when it floats. This is usually equal to the weight of the ship and everything on it.

- The deadweight of a ship is the difference between the ship's displacement when empty and when it is full. It measures the weight of the cargo and passengers.

Wooden ribs
Here, the ribs of a wooden boat are being attached to the central keel. The timbers form a skeleton frame to which the planks of the hull and deck will be attached.

Covering the hull
Planks are attached edge to edge to the ribs of a wooden boat to make a smooth hull. The tight-fitting planks will be given several coats of paint or varnish to make a watertight finish.

Naval architects

Just as there are architects who design buildings, there are naval architects who design ships. These architects are planning the deck layouts of the cruise liner *Oriana*.

Shipbuilding shed

This picture shows the bow section of the cruise liner *Oriana* under construction. You can see the steel decks, bulkheads (watertight walls and doors) and skin. The ship is being built in a huge construction shed, where its progress is unaffected by the weather.

Float out

Once the hull has been completed, the floor of the construction shed is flooded so that the entire hull can be floated out. Here *Oriana* is being floated out at its launch. Smaller ships are built on slipways before being launched by sliding them down into the water.

Fitting out

Work on electrical equipment, lighting, pipes and other fixtures and fittings is completed after the ship is launched. This process is called fitting out. After fitting out, the ship will undergo sea trials.

HULLS

The main part of a ship is the hull, which sits in the water. The hull does four things. It provides the strong, rigid shape that makes the structure of the ship. It is a waterproof skin that stops water from getting in. It supports all the equipment in the ship, such as the engines, and it provides space for the cargo. The shape of the hull also lets the ship slide easily through the water. The hull shape of a ship or boat depends on what that ship or boat is designed to do. Long, thin hulls are designed for traveling at speed, while broad hulls are designed to carry as much cargo as possible. Wide, shallow hulls float high in the water and are good for traveling on shallow lakes, rivers and canals. The hull shape also dictates the stability of the ship, or how easily it tips from side to side. Inside the hull, solid walls called bulkheads make the hull stiffer and divide it into a number of watertight compartments.

Hulls for floating
Try pushing a light ball underwater. It will spring back up. Upthrust from the water makes a hollow hull float in the same way.

Multihulls
This canoe will not tip over because it has outriggers. The outriggers work like small hulls on each side of the canoe, making it a very stable vessel. Catamarans (boats with two hulls) and trimarans (three hulls) work in the same way. Boats with only one hull are called monohulls.

Plastic hulls
A white-water kayak has a one-piece hull made of tough, rigid plastic. Its materials are strong enough to resist bumping against rocks and the riverbed. The hull's long, thin shape is designed for speed, slicing through the rough water. The canoeist sits in a sealed cockpit, which prevents water from getting in. This not only keeps the canoeist dry but means that the kayak remains buoyant (afloat).

Hulls in halves

Here, two halves of a yacht hull are made from GRP (glass-reinforced plastic). GRP is made by filling molds with layers of glass fiber and glue. It is light but strong and has a smooth finish.

Points and bulbs

While a fishing boat is in dry dock it enables us to see the parts of the hull usually underwater. The bulb shape at the bottom of the bow helps the boat slip more easily through the water.

Changing shape

If you could cut through a ship and look at the cut ends, you would see a cross-section of its hull. Here you can see how the cross-section of a container ship's hull changes along its length.

Overlapping planks

This is a head-on view of the bow of a 1,000-year-old Viking ship. The hull is made from a shell of overlapping planks, hammered together with nails and strengthened by internal ribs. Hulls constructed of overlapping planks are called clinker built.

stempost

ocean-going high bow

wide, stable hull shape

16 overlapping oak planks

keel

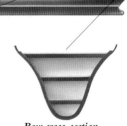

Stern cross-section
The sides curve inward to make the bottom narrower than the deck.

Central cross-section
The hull is almost square. This allows the maximum space for cargo.

Bow cross-section
Just behind the sharp bow the bottom is very narrow and the sides are high.

FAST AND SLOW

W HENEVER an object such as a ship moves through the water, the water tries to slow it down. The push that the water makes against the object is called water resistance, or drag. The faster the object moves, the bigger the water resistance gets. If you look around a busy harbor, you will see dozens of different hull designs. Sleek, narrow hulls with sharp bows cause less resistance than wide hulls with square bows, so they can move through the water faster. You can test how the shape of a bow affects the speed of a ship in the project below. The deeper a hull sits in the water, the more resistance there is. Some hulls are designed to just touch the water. For example, a small speedboat has a flaring, V-shaped hull designed to skim across the surface. A cargo ship, however, has a more square-shaped hull that sits lower in the water. Speed is not as important for the cargo ship as it is for the speedboat. Instead, the cargo ship is designed for stability and to carry the maximum amount of cargo.

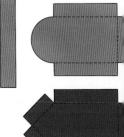

TESTING HULL SHAPES

You will need: *colored thick card stock, pen or pencil, ruler, scissors, tape, aluminum foil, paper clips, modeling clay, scale, string, watering can, plastic tub, three wooden blocks.*

Templates
Use these three templates to help you cut out and make the three boat shapes in this project. Their dimensions are roughly 6 inches long, by 4 inches wide. Make the sides of each boat shape about 1¼ inches deep.

1 Use a ruler to carefully draw the three templates shown above on sheets of thick card stock. Make sure the corners are square and the edges straight. Cut out the shapes.

2 Using scissors, score along the lines inside the base of each shape (shown as broken lines above). Bend up the sides and tape the corners together.

3 Make the round-ended and pointed boats in the same way as the first boat. Use a separate piece of card stock to make the round bow, and tape to the base in several places.

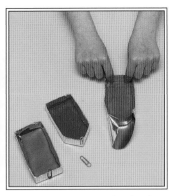

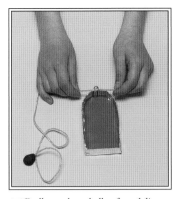

4 Now cover the outside of each shape with foil, neatly folding the foil over the sides. This will make the shapes more waterproof. Attach a paper clip to the bow of each boat.

5 Roll out three balls of modeling clay about the size of a walnut. Weigh the balls to make sure they are the same weight. Attach a ball to the bow of each boat with string.

6 Put a large plastic tub on a table or a strong box. Fill the tub with water to about ½ in. from the top of the tub.

Try timing the boats with a stopwatch. You could find the difference between the fastest and slowest.

8 Release the boats all at the same time. The weighted strings will pull them along the length of the tub. Which one wins the race to the other end of the tub?

7 Line up the boats at one end of the tub. Hang the strings and modeling clay balls over the other end of the tub. Put a small wooden block inside each boat.

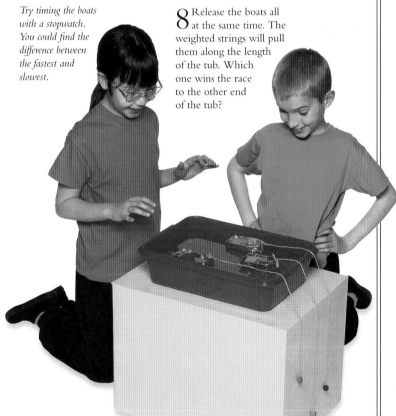

The shapes on test
Boats' hulls are usually pointed to help them cut through the water. Energy is wasted pushing a flat end through the water, which makes a boat slower.

SHIP POWER

THERE are many different ways of propelling boats and ships through the water. The most basic, such as rowing and paddling, are human-powered. Oars and paddles work by pushing against the water. Today, they are only used in small vessels. Sails harness the natural power of the wind to propel a boat or ship. Engines convert the energy stored in fuel into the movement of a propeller. As the propeller spins, its blades force water to rush backward, which thrusts the boat or ship forward. Most engines used in boats and ships are diesel engines. Other types of marine engine are gasoline engines, gas turbine engines and steam turbine engines. Some short-distance ferries move by pulling themselves along a wire or chain attached to the bank on the other side of a lake or river. Other craft, such as hovercraft, have aircraft-like propellers. These are useful in very shallow or plant-filled water where an underwater propeller could be easily damaged.

Punting
In a punt, a person stands on the back of the boat to push down on a long pole against the bottom of the river. Each push propels the boat forward. The pole is also used to steer the punt and keep it straight.

FACT BOX

• In 1845, two ships, one with a propeller and one with paddlewheels, fought a tug-of-war. The battle was to find the most efficient. The propeller easily won.

• In the future, boats may lift up out of the water altogether. Wingships use air pressure to skim above the water's surface. They can fly along about 6 feet above the waves.

• In the swamps in the South, people travel in swamp skimmers pushed along by a huge fan at the back.

Rowing with oars
An oar is a long pole with a flattened blade at one end. It is attached to a pivot on the edge of the rowboat, called a rowlock. The rower faces backward and propels the boat forward with a continuous cycle of strokes. Rowing a boat using a pair of oars is called sculling.

Paddles
A dragon boat from Hong Kong is propelled along by a team of paddlers. A paddle is a short pole with a flat blade at one end used to propel a canoe. Paddles are easier to maneuver than oars, but they are not as efficient.

Propeller power

A propeller is made up of several angled blades (usually between two and six) attached to a central hub. The enormous propeller being checked here will be one of a pair used on a large cruise liner. Its blades are specially curved to cut down on turbulence as water is drawn past the hull. Each propeller will be driven by an electric motor.

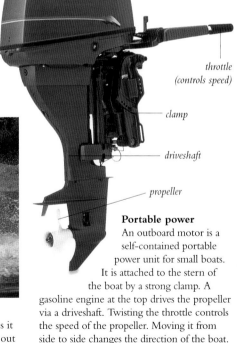

Pits on the surface of the blades help with water flow.

Capturing the wind

Sails catch the wind and push a boat along. The sailors adjust the position of their sails to make the best use of the wind. These yachts have the wind blowing from behind and are using large sails called spinnakers for extra speed.

housing for gasoline engine

throttle (controls speed)

clamp

driveshaft

propeller

Jet propulsion

A jet ski has no propeller. Instead, its engine sucks in water and pumps it out of the back of the ski in a powerful jet. The jet of water shooting out backward pushes the ski forward. Boats powered by waterjets can reach much higher speeds with less wear on the boat than those with propellers.

Portable power

An outboard motor is a self-contained portable power unit for small boats. It is attached to the stern of the boat by a strong clamp. A gasoline engine at the top drives the propeller via a driveshaft. Twisting the throttle controls the speed of the propeller. Moving it from side to side changes the direction of the boat. When not in use, the whole engine can be unclamped and taken away.

CONTROLLING A SHIP

ALL ships and boats have simple controls for steering. Usually this is a rudder at the stern. The rudder is controlled by a tiller (handle) or wheel. The rudder only works when the boat or ship is moving through the water. Powered craft also have engine controls for adjusting speed. Many boats have twin propellers and can also be steered by running the engines at different speeds or in different directions (forward or reverse). Large ships may also have bow and stern thrusters, which are used in port to push the ship sideways or rotate it on the spot. On modern cruise liners, which often have to enter a different dock every night of the cruise, the ship can be moved by means of a small joystick on the bridge. Large modern ships have a computerized autopilot like that on an aircraft. This automatically adjusts the rudder and engine speed to follow a set course.

Simple rudder
The rudder on a Norman ship from the Bayeux Tapestry is a single oar. The long oar is set on the right side of the ship at the stern. Many early boats were steered with simple side rudders like this.

flow of water *boat goes straight*

rudder

flow of water is deflected left

rudder is turned to left

boat turns to the left

boat travels ahead

rudder straight

How a rudder works
The rudder works by cutting into the flow of water. With the rudder in the center, water flows past each side and the boat goes in a straight line.

When the rudder is turned to the side, the flow of water is deflected away to that side.

The water pushes hard against the blade of the rudder. This makes the stern go to the right, swinging the bow left.

When enough turn has been made, the rudder is brought back to the center. The boat straightens out and travels ahead on its new course.

Under the stern
Here, the propeller and rudder of a cargo ship are being cleaned of barnacles in dry dock. In almost all ships and boats, the rudder is attached behind the propeller under the stern. The rudder is turned by machinery in the stern that is controlled from the bridge. The propeller pushes water past the rudder, which makes the ship easier to turn from side to side at slow speed.

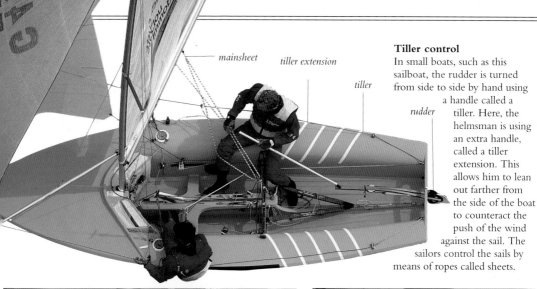

Tiller control

In small boats, such as this sailboat, the rudder is turned from side to side by hand using a handle called a tiller. Here, the helmsman is using an extra handle, called a tiller extension. This allows him to lean out farther from the side of the boat to counteract the push of the wind against the sail. The sailors control the sails by means of ropes called sheets.

mainsheet   *tiller extension*   *tiller*   *rudder*

On the bridge

The bridge (also sometimes called the wheelhouse) is the control center of a ship. There are rudder and engine controls and navigation equipment, such as a compass and radar. The bridge is high up on the ship to give good, all-around visibility.

Steering wheel

On larger yachts a tiller would be too cumbersome to use. Instead, the rudder is operated by a large wheel linked to the rudder by a system of pulleys. The helmsman steers the yacht from the cockpit.

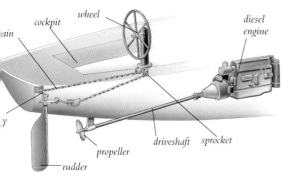

ain   *cockpit*   *wheel*   *diesel engine*

y   *rudder*   *propeller*   *driveshaft*   *sprocket*

Connecting up the wheel and the propeller

In this large cruise yacht, the rudder is moved by wires linked to the wheel in the cockpit. The wheel drives a sprocket, which moves a chain. Wires attached to the chain move the rudder via a set of pulleys. The yacht is also equipped with a diesel engine that is connected to a single propeller via a driveshaft. A soundproof engine room insulates the hull from noise and vibration made by the engine.

POWER AND STEERING

THE project below will show you how to build a simple boat driven by a propeller and controlled by a rudder. The propeller is powered by the energy stored in a wound-up rubber band. The two blades of the propeller are set at different angles and push the water backward as the propeller spins. In turn, this makes the boat move forward. When you have built your model, you could try making other designs of propeller (for example, more blades set at different angles) and testing them to see which works best. After making the propeller you can add a rudder. The rudder can be moved to different positions to make your model boat turn to the left or right, but it will only work when the boat is moving. Without the rudder, the boat does not go in a straight line very well. So, as well as making the boat turn from side to side, the rudder also helps your model (as it does a full-size boat) travel straight ahead.

Simple propeller
The simplest propeller has two blades that twist in opposite directions. This is the propeller of a small pleasure boat. Three- and four-bladed propellers are more powerful. The hole in the center is where the driveshaft from the engine fits into the propeller.

MAKE A POWERED BOAT

You will need: *cork, awl, scissors, small plastic bottle, large plastic bottle, large paper clip, ruler, pliers, bead, long rubber bands, small pencil, thin garden cane.*

1 Make a hole through the middle of the cork using an awl. Cut a diagonal slot in either side of the cork. Push two strips of plastic cut from a small bottle into the slots.

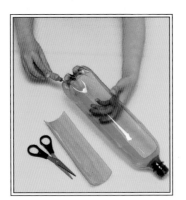

2 Cut a rectangular strip from one side of the large plastic bottle. This slot is the top of your boat. With the awl, make a small hole at the back of your bottle in the bottom.

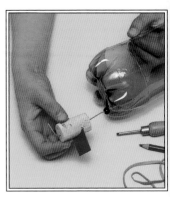

3 Straighten a large paper clip (you may need pliers). Bend the last ½ in. of wire at right angles. Push the wire through the cork and thread it through the bead and small hole.

The model will go in circles.

4 Bend over the end of the wire inside the bottle. Hook a rubber band over the wire and stretch it up through the neck of the bottle. Secure in place with a pencil.

5 To wind up the band, turn the pencil as you hold on to the propeller. Keep holding the propeller until you put the boat into the water and release it. What happens?

6 Now make a rudder for your boat. Cut a piece of plastic about 1½ in. by 1½ in. and pierce two holes near one edge. Push thin cane through the two holes.

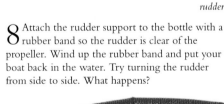

Straight and turning
This is the finished model of the boat. To test the controls, start with the rudder centered to make the boat go straight. How tight a circle can you make your boat turn in?

rubber band engine

propeller

rudder

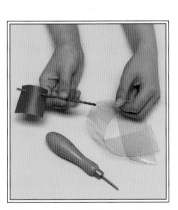

8 Attach the rudder support to the bottle with a rubber band so the rudder is clear of the propeller. Wind up the rubber band and put your boat back in the water. Try turning the rudder from side to side. What happens?

7 Use the strip of plastic cut from the large bottle to support your rudder. Pierce two holes about ¼ in. apart in the center of the strip and push the cane through them.

CARGO SHIPS

CARRYING cargo has always been the main job of ships. Even today, in the age of air travel, it is still the cheapest way of transporting goods. In fact, more that 95 percent of goods are transported around the world in the holds of cargo ships. A cargo ship is basically a long, box-shaped vessel, providing the maximum amount of room inside for cargo. The first cargo ships carried their cargo in barrels or jars in the hold. Modern cargo ships have been developed to carry specific cargoes, such as oil and cars. There are still many general cargo ships, including container ships. Different types of cargo ship have also been developed for use in rivers, in coastal waters and for long-distance ocean travel. Ocean-going ships are huge and expensive to build, so they are designed to spend as little time as possible in port.

Canal-sized
The Panama Canal in Central America provides an important short-cut for ships traveling between the Atlantic and Pacific oceans. Many cargo ships are built to dimensions called panamax—the largest size that can fit through the canal.

Parts of a container ship
A container is a standard-sized, steel box that can be filled with any sort of cargo. On a container ship, the prepacked containers are stacked in piles in the hold and on the deck. Some of the containers on deck may be refrigerated. The ship is driven by a giant diesel engine.

River barge
A slow, wide barge carries cargo along the river Rhine in Germany. The river reaches from the North Sea deep into the industrial heartland of Germany. Coal, grain and timber are often carried by barges like this one.

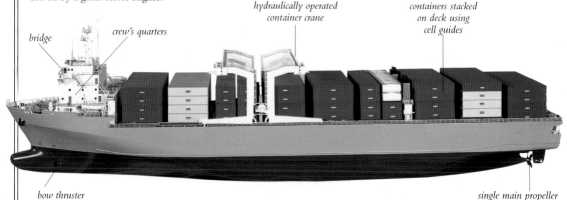

hydraulically operated container crane

containers stacked on deck using cell guides

bridge

crew's quarters

bow thruster

single main propeller

Unloading containers

In port, giant cranes transfer the containers from the ship. The standard-size containers are lowered onto specialized trucks, which carry them to huge dockside parking lots where they are stacked in rows. The containers are then loaded onto lorries or railroad cars and taken to their final destination.

FACT BOX

• The oil tanker *Jahre Viking* is the world's largest ship. It has a deadweight of 564,763 tons and is about 1,503 feet long.

• The world's largest container ship can carry 6,000 19 foot-long containers.

• A lighter aboard ship (LASH) carries river barges stacked like containers on its deck. A reefer ship carries fruit and vegetables in its refrigerated holds.

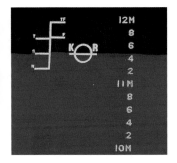

Not too deep

Load lines (also called Plimsoll lines) show how low a ship is safely allowed to float in the water when it is fully loaded. The load lines on the left of the picture are for different types of water. TF means tropical fresh water, F is fresh water, T is tropical salt water, S is salt water in summer and W is salt water in winter. The scale on the right shows the distance to the keel of the ship in meters.

Return to sail

A few cargo ships have experimental computer-controlled sails. The rigid sails are used to save fuel. When set, they move automatically. They are rotated by electric motors guided by computer. Sails like these are very efficient at achieving the best angle to the wind.

Specialty carriers

This ship is specially designed to carry just one kind of cargo—liquefied petroleum gas (LPG), such as methane or butane. The gas must be cooled to a very low temperature to keep it liquid. The pipes on the deck control the gas.

SHIP STABILITY

M ANY ships look as though they are top heavy, so how do they manage to stay upright and not capsize? These projects will help you find out what makes a ship stable. The shape of the hull's cross-section is important—some hull shapes are more stable than others. When a ship tips over, the hull on that side sinks into the water. On the other side it rises up out of the water. The water creates more upthrust on the side that sinks in, pushing the ship upright again. The more one side of the hull sinks in, the bigger the push and the more stable the hull. The position of the cargo in the hull is important, too. Heavy cargo high up on deck makes the ship top heavy and more likely to tip over. Heavy cargo or equipment low down in the hull makes the ship more stable. Cargo that can move is dangerous, because it could slip to one side of the ship, making it more likely that the ship will tip over. The first project looks at the stability of a multihulled boat called a catamaran.

Pile it high
Containers are piled high on the deck of a container ship. The containers are loaded evenly to prevent the ship from becoming unstable.

Two hulls
The two hulls of a catamaran are joined together by a strong bridge. This double-hulled shape makes the boat very stable.

MAKE A CATAMARAN

You will need*: small plastic bottle, scissors, thin garden cane, rubber bands, some small wooden blocks or other cargo.*

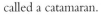

1 Remove the top from a small plastic bottle and carefully cut the bottle in half lengthwise. This will leave you with two identical shapes to form the catamaran hulls.

2 Place the two halves of the bottle side by side. Lay two medium-length pieces of garden cane on top. Securely fasten the canes to the bottle halves using rubber bands.

3 Put your completed catamaran into a tank or bowl of water. Load the hulls with cargo such as wooden bricks. Can you make your boat capsize?

LOADING CARGO

You will need: *plastic bottle and square tub of about the same size, scissors, wooden blocks, modeling clay.*

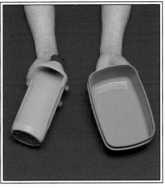

1 For this project you need one container with a round hull shape and another about the same size with a square hull shape. Cut a strip from the round container to make a hold.

2 Put both containers in a tank or bowl of water. Gradually load one side of each hull with wooden blocks. Which hull capsizes first? Which hull is more stable?

3 Now load the square hull evenly with wooden blocks. You should be able to get a lot more in. Press down on one side of the hull. Can you feel the hull trying to right itself?

Unstable round hull
When a round hull tips to one side, there is little change to the amount of hull underwater. This makes the shape unstable.

Stable square hull
When a square hull tips to one side, there is a great change in the amount of hull underwater on that side. This makes it stable.

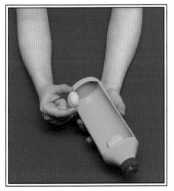

4 To stabilize the round hull, press some lumps of modeling clay into the bottom of the rounded hull. The clay adds weight called ballast to the bottom of the hull.

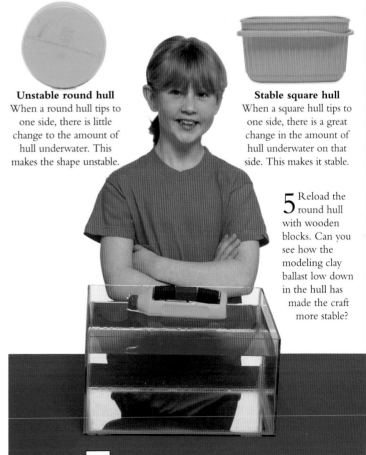

5 Reload the round hull with wooden blocks. Can you see how the modeling clay ballast low down in the hull has made the craft more stable?

FERRIES

FERRIES are ships and boats designed to carry passengers, cars, coaches, trucks and sometimes even trains across water. There are several different types of ferry. Each one is designed for a different type of crossing, such as small, raft-like ferries for short river crossings of a few minutes, or larger cruise-liner ferries for long sea crossings of several days. Most vehicle-carrying ferries have wide doors and ramps at the bow and stern. These allow cars and lorries to quickly drive on and off the ship. They are known as a roll-on roll-off (or ro-ro) ferry. In a typical large ferry, the lower decks are like a big parking garage. The passengers travel on the upper decks, where there are lounges, restaurants and stores. Ferries like this work day and night, all year round. Some ferries, such as catamarans, hydrofoils and hovercraft, are designed for short sea and lake crossings and are much faster.

Cable-drawn ferry
This ferry travels along a chain stretched between the two river banks. Its engine pulls on the chain instead of working a propeller.

Loading and unloading
Cars drive along a ramp to reach the car deck of a small ro-ro ferry. The ferry's bow slots into a special dock for the loading process. The ferry will be unloaded through doors at the stern. Larger ferries have separate ramps for loading cars and trucks.

FACT BOX

• The largest superferries have three huge decks to carry up to 850 cars and trucks. There is room for up to 1,250 passengers in the cabins above.

• Train ferries carry railroad cars. They have railroad tracks on deck that the cars roll onto at the docks.

• The world's fastest car ferry is called the *Finnjet* and it operates on the Baltic Sea. It is capable of over 30 knots (33 mph).

Superferry
The huge ferries that travel on long sea routes are called superferries. They can carry hundreds of cars and trucks and thousands of passengers. There are cabins for passengers to sleep in on overnight sailings, and stores, restaurants and cinemas to keep people entertained.

Speedy catamaran

Catamarans like the SeaCat are some of the fastest vehicle-carrying ferries. Having two hulls instead of one and super-powerful, gas turbine engines makes this ferry much faster than a traditional passenger ferry.

Flying in water

A hydrofoil is the fastest type of ferry. Under its hull there are wing-like foils. These lift the hull out of the water as it speeds along. Lifting the hull out of the water reduces water resistance (drag), allowing the hydrofoil to travel much faster.

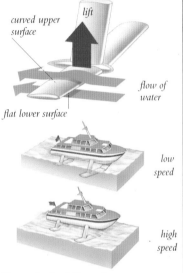

curved upper surface

lift

flow of water

flat lower surface

low speed

high speed

How a hydrofoil works

Water flows faster over the foil's curved upper surface than it does over the flat lower surface, so creating lift. Foils only work when traveling at high speed. At low speed the boat's hull sits in the water.

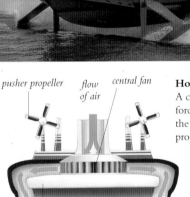

pusher propeller *flow of air* *central fan*

buoyancy tank *air cushion*

How a hovercraft works

A central fan draws in air and forces it between the hull and the skirt. Two large pusher propellers drive the craft along.

Hovering on air

A hovercraft skims across water supported on a cushion of air. The air is held in place by a rubber skirt. A hovercraft can also travel on flat ground, so it can leave the water to load and unload. Buoyancy tanks stop the hovercraft from sinking if the air cushion fails.

FISHING BOATS

There are millions of fishing boats in the world. Most of them are small traditional boats sailed by a single person or a small crew. Others are larger, commercial fishing boats. The very largest, called factory ships, are able to stay at sea for up to a month. Fishing was one of the earliest uses of boats, and dozens of different styles of fishing boat have been developed all over the world. Some fish are caught with hooks and lines or traps, such as crates, left in the sea and attached to the seabed by an anchor. Most fishing, however, is done with nets that trap schools of fish. Different types of net are used to catch different schools of fish. Commercial fishing boats have special equipment for handling the nets and storing the fish they have caught. Many also have sonar equipment for tracking schools of fish under the water. In the 1970s many countries' fishing industries collapsed due to over-fishing. International regulations now limit the number and size of fish caught in order to preserve fish stocks.

Fishing fleets
Coastal towns and villages all over the world have their own fishing fleets based in small harbors. This one is on the island of Skye in Scotland. Most people in the town are involved in the fishing industry. Laws to reduce catches and conserve fish stocks have hit many small ports.

Inshore fishing boat
This is a typical wooden fishing boat used for fishing in inshore (coastal) waters. It is used up to 60 miles from port and catches surface-living fish such as herring, mackerel and anchovies.

Deep-sea trawler
Ships designed for fishing hundreds of miles off shore have high bows for breaking through waves. Trawlers like this catch fish such as cod, hake and flounder.

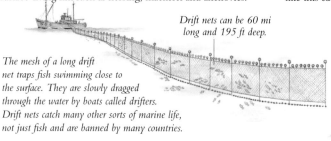

Drift nets can be 60 mi long and 195 ft deep.

The mesh of a long drift net traps fish swimming close to the surface. They are slowly dragged through the water by boats called drifters. Drift nets catch many other sorts of marine life, not just fish and are banned by many countries.

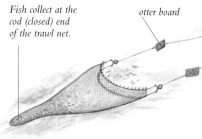

Fish collect at the cod (closed) end of the trawl net.

otter board

Bringing in the catch

A net bursting with cod and other fish is hauled on board. Fishing nets are pulled in after they have been in the sea for a few hours. A mechanical hoist lifts the full net out of the water. The net's closed end is released and its catch emptied out on deck.

Processing the catch

A catch is sorted as soon as it is on board. The fish may be cleaned and gutted before being frozen. Larger trawlers have equipment on board to process the fish—cutting off heads and tails and removing the bones.

A dip net is used to scoop up fish over the side of the boat.

dip net

Traditional fishing

Off the coast of Tanzania, in Africa, many fishermen use outrigger sailboats and dhows. Small fishing boats like these have not changed for many centuries. Nets, lines and spears are used to bring in the catch. Small scale fishing like this does not deplete fish stocks as large commercial vessels can.

A stern trawler drags a large trawl net behind it. Ships like this were developed to catch huge shoals of cod living at depths below 50 ft.

Floats keep the top of the net on the surface.

A school near the surface of the sea is quickly encircled by a purse seine net. The net is closed by gathering the bottom edges like a purse.

Fishing boats and nets

The type of net a boat carries depends on the fish it is going to catch. Some boats fish for species that live near the surface of the sea, while others trawl the waters deeper down. Floats and weights are attached to the net to keep it in shape underwater. For example, otter boards are used to force open the mouth of a trawl. There are regulations restricting the size of the holes in the net so that young fish can escape.

ANCHORS

A N anchor is a device for stopping a ship or boat from drifting in the wind or current. It is used when the engines are turned off or the sails taken down. The anchor is attached to the ship by a strong chain and its particular shape makes it embed firmly in the seabed. There are several reasons for using an anchor. The most common is for stopping close to shore when there is no harbor or the ship is too big for the harbor (such as an oil tanker). In an emergency, such as an engine failure in bad weather, an anchor can keep a ship from drifting onto the shore and being wrecked. Different designs of anchor are suitable for different sizes of ships and for different types of seabed, such as sandy or rocky. The projects on these pages will show you how to make two different types of anchor that are used in very different conditions.

Ship's anchor
This type of anchor is called a stockless anchor and is used on most metal ships. The points of the anchor dig into the seabed, securing the ship.

MAKE A ROCK ANCHOR

You will need: *large paper clip, pliers, ruler, short pencil, rubber bands, thin garden cane, scissors, string, tray of pebbles (about 2 to 4 in. in size).*

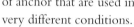

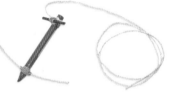

Catching the rocks
Your model is similar to an anchor used on a traditional fishing boat. The spikes catch hold of the crevices on a rock-strewn seabed.

1 Unbend a large paper clip using pliers. Cut about 4 in. of wire off and bend it slightly. Attach the wire to a short pencil with a rubber band wound tightly around the joint.

2 Cut a piece of thin garden cane also about 4 in. long. Attach this to the other end of the pencil, but at right angles to the wire. Use an rubber band to secure the cane.

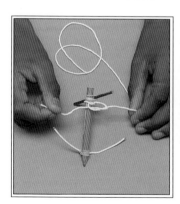

3 Cut a long piece of string for an anchor chain. Tie one end of it to the pencil, below the garden cane. Fill a tray with pebbles to test your anchor (see opposite).

MAKE A SAND ANCHOR

You will need: *large paper clips, pliers, tape, plastic straw, scissors, sheet of plastic, coins, string, tray of sand.*

1 Bend a paper clip into a T-shape with a foot. Use pliers to cut another piece of wire to fit across the top of the T. Attach with tape and two lengths of plastic straw.

2 Cut two blades from a sheet of plastic. Make sure they will fit inside your T-shape. Tape the blades securely to the leg of the T and the two straws.

3 Find two medium-size coins. Tape one to each blade. The coins add weight to make the anchor dig into the sand better.

Blade

Digging into sand
This is a model of a Danforth anchor. The wide, flat blades dig deep into either a muddy or a sandy seabed.

Testing your anchors
To test out your anchors, lay them on top of the sand or pebbles in the tray. Now pull the anchors along the length of the tray with the string. How well do they work? Try the anchors in the other trays. Do they still work as well now?

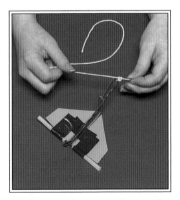

4 Shape another paper clip to make a straight arm with a hook at each end. Hook one end to the anchor and rest the arm in the upright foot. Tie a length of string to the other end. Use a tray of sand to test your anchor.

SAILING

SAILS catch the power of the wind to propel the boat or ship along. Today, sail power is mainly used by leisure craft, for racing and cruising. In some parts of the world, sail power is still common for fishing boats. Sails were originally made of strong cloth called canvas, but are now usually made of synthetic fabrics. Sails are supported by masts and ropes or wires called rigging. Ropes used to trim (adjust) sails are called sheets. Large yachts have different sets of sails for different wind conditions, including small storm sails. There are many different arrangements of masts, sails and rigging. Most modern sailboats and yachts have two triangular sails called a mainsail and jib supported by a single mast. The keel on a yacht and the centerboard on a sailboat stop the boat from drifting sideways in the wind. A heavy keel also makes a yacht more stable.

mainsail — mainmast

batten (sail stiffener)

jib

boom

mainsheet

tiller

jibsheet — hull

rudder — centerboard

Parts of a sailboat
The main parts of a typical sailboat are shown above. A sailboat like this would usually have a crew of two people—a helmsman who operates the tiller and the mainsail and a crew who works the jib and centerboard. The jib is a small triangular sail in front of the mainmast. Sailboats also use spinnakers (three-cornered sails used in racing) for extra speed.

Racing sailboat
In very windy conditions, the helmsman and crew lean out over the side of the boat. They do this to keep the boat balanced and upright. The crew uses a harness called a trapeze attached to a wire running to the top of the mast. They lean out to the windward side of the boat.

Racing yacht
Large racing yachts have enormous sails and need a large crew to change them quickly. Sails are raised and lowered using winding wheels called winches. Yachts like this are designed to be sailed across oceans.

Cruising yacht

A cruising yacht has comfortable cabins, a galley and bathroom. It has smaller sails than a racing yacht and is easier to sail. This type of yacht, rigged with one mast, is known as a sloop. It has two jib sails, so it is called cutter rigged.

Fastest of all

A trimaran has a main hull and two outriggers. The outriggers make the yacht very stable, which means it can use enormous sails for its size. Although multi-hulled vessels have been in use for centuries, offshore racing trimarans have only been developed since the 1960s. Since then, they have set records for the fastest transatlantic crossing.

Old designs

These big, two-masted yachts are called schooners. A schooner has a foremast ahead of the mainmast. Here, their sails are gaff rigged (supporting poles at an angle to the masts).

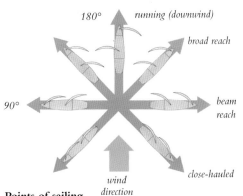

Points of sailing

A boat can use the wind to sail in every direction, except straight into the wind. The crew adjust the sails to go in different directions called the points of sailing. To head upwind a boat must follow a zigzag course. This is called tacking. If a boat turns when the wind is behind it, it is known as jibing. Running (sailing downwind) is not the fastest direction. Reaching (sailing across the wind) is faster.

FACT BOX

• The first person to sail solo around the world was an American named Joshua Slocum. The voyage took three years, from 1895 to 1898 on a vessel called *Spray*.

• The record time for sailing around the world is 64 days, 8 hours and 37 minutes. It was set in 2002 by the catamaran *Orange*.

• In the galley (kitchen) of a yacht, the stove is mounted on hinges. This keeps it level when the boat keels in the wind.

SAILS FOR POWER

THE project on these pages will show you how to make a model of a simple sailboat. Once you have made your model, use it to find out how a sailing boat works and how sailors use the wind. To sail in the direction the sailor wants to go, he or she must look at the direction that the wind is blowing from and adjust the position of the sails to make the most use of the wind. A boat can sail in every direction except straight into the wind. When a boat faces directly into the wind, its sails flap uselessly and the boat is in the no-go zone. To sail toward a place where the wind is blowing from, the sailors must sail a zigzag course. This means first sailing across the wind one way, then sailing across it the other. This is called tacking. Making the most of the wind is the art of sailing, and it takes lots of practice. Sailors have to learn to control many different parts of the boat at the same time.

Finished boat
Once you have finished your boat, you could try adding a centerboard. Does it make any difference to the boat's handling?

MAKE A SAILBOAT

You will need: pencil, ruler, thick card stock, scissors, tape, sheet of plastic, stapler, awl, modeling clay, thin garden canes, colored paper, plastic straws, small plastic bottle, string, paper clip.

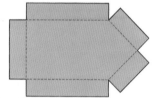

Template
Use this template to make your model. The dimensions are 10 inches by 4 inches with sides about 1½ inches deep.

1 Cut out your hull shape from thick card stock, using the template above as a guide. Score along the broken lines with the scissors. Use tape to attach the sides.

2 Lay the hull on a sheet of plastic. Cut around it leaving a 2 in. gap around it to overlap the sides. Fold the plastic over the sides of the hull and staple it in place.

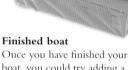

3 Pierce a hole in the middle of a strip of card stock a little wider than the hull. Staple in place. Put modeling clay under the hole. Push a 12 in. cane through the hole into the clay.

4 Cut a sail from paper. Attach a straw along the side and a garden cane along the bottom with tape. Slip the straw over the mast.

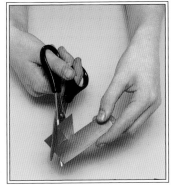

5 Cut an L-shape (about 3 in. long, 1½ in. wide at base and ¾ in. wide at top) from the small plastic bottle. Cut the base of the L in half to make two tabs, as shown.

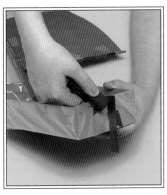

6 Fold back the L-shape's two tabs in opposite directions and staple them to the stern (back) of the boat. This is the boat's rudder.

Finding out about the points of sailing

When you test your boat out, try setting the sails in these different positions. Alter the position of the sail by using the string taped to the boom (cane). Follow the arrows shown here to see which way the wind should be blowing from in each case. Why not try blowing from other directions to see if this makes a difference to your boat?

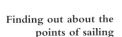

direction of wind

8 To test out how your sail boat works, make a breeze by waving a large sheet of paper near to the boat. Adjust the string to move the sail in to the right position.

7 Cut a piece of string about 8 in. long. Tape one end to the back of the boom (the cane) and feed the other end through a paper clip attached to the back of the boat.

WARSHIPS

THE first true warships were the many-oared galleys of ancient Greece and Rome. By the 1400s, heavily-armed galleons with many cannons were developed. In the early 1900s, steam-driven, iron battleships were the forerunners of modern warships. Today's warships carry a huge amount of special equipment. They have weapons for attacking other ships and submarines and for defending themselves against air attack, and electronic equipment for tracking ships and aircraft and controlling their weapons. The largest warships are aircraft carriers, which act as air bases at sea. Smaller warships, such as frigates and destroyers, are designed for speed and have powerful gas turbine engines. The smallest ships are minesweepers and patrol boats. A country's navy defends its waters, transports and supports fighting troops and helps in emergencies around the world. A navy needs many ships to keep its warships supplied with fuel, food and ammunition.

Operations room
At the heart of a warship is the operations room. From here the crew monitors what other ships and aircraft are doing and make decisions about what actions to take.

Frigate
A frigate is a small, fast-moving ship used to escort convoys of larger ships. It carries anti-submarine and anti-aircraft weapons. Small frigates are sometimes called corvettes.

FACT BOX

• Aircraft carriers are the largest warships. They have displacements of more than 90,000 tons and crews of 5,000 sailors and air crew.

• During World War I (1914–18) huge battleships fought at sea. Their weapons were enormous guns. Hulls were protected by 16 inches of thick armor.

• The world's largest submarines are Russian Typhoon class. They have displacements of 26,500 tons and are about 558 feet long.

Destroyer
A destroyer is generally larger than a frigate and is an all-purpose warship. This guided-missile destroyer has several radar dishes for weapons control as well as navigation. It also has a helicopter deck at the stern.

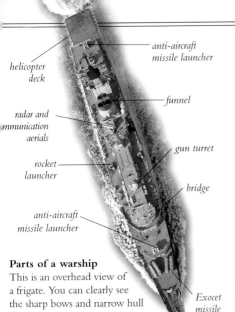

helicopter deck

anti-aircraft missile launcher

funnel

radar and communication aerials

gun turret

rocket launcher

bridge

anti-aircraft missile launcher

Exocet missile launcher

Parts of a warship

This is an overhead view of a frigate. You can clearly see the sharp bows and narrow hull that help to give it speed. It has a range of guns and missiles aboard ship as well as armed helicopters.

Naval guns

Modern naval guns, such as this 114mm single gun, are aimed automatically. A fire-control radar keeps track of the target and moves the gun from side to side and up and down. Missiles are also used to bring down enemy aircraft. Some have on-board sensors that home in on their target.

Airfield at sea

An aircraft carrier's deck is a runway where aircraft take off and land. The runway is short so a steam catapult is used to help launch the aircraft at takeoff. Underneath the deck is a hangar where aircraft are stored and serviced. The aircrafts' wings fold up to save storage space below deck.

Support ships

This ship is a specialized support ship used in landing troops. In the stern is a dock for landing craft to be loaded. The landing craft ferry troops and equipment to the shore.

Inflatables

Special forces, such as commandos, use a small, inflatable craft for transferring from ship to shore. This boat can be used above the water or underwater as a diving craft. It can even be submerged and hidden on the seabed until it is needed. You can see the electrically powered propeller for underwater use.

This inflatable dinghy (small boat) is powered by two outboard motors.

SUBMARINES

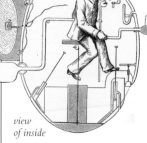

view of outside

view of inside

A submarine is a vessel that can travel submerged underwater as well as on the water's surface. Most submarines are naval ships. There are two main types—hunter-killer, or patrol submarines, which search for and try to sink enemy shipping, and ballistic missile submarines, which carry nuclear missiles. Naval submarines use two different types of power—conventional and nuclear. When a conventional submarine is on the surface its diesel engine makes electricity. The electricity is used to run the electric motors that work the propeller and also to recharge the batteries. When the submarine is submerged, the diesel engine is turned off and the electric motor is powered by the batteries. In a nuclear submarine, the power comes from a nuclear reactor. The main weapon of a hunter-killer submarine is the torpedo—a sort of underwater missile. Another type of underwater vessel is the submersible. Submersibles are small diving craft used for ocean research, exploration and the repair of undersea pipes and cables.

The Turtle
American engineer David Bushnell built the first working combat submarine in 1775. It was called the *Turtle* and made of wood. It was moved by two screw-shaped, hand-operated propellers.

Nuclear submarine
A nuclear submarine, such as this Trident, can stay submerged for months on end. Its reactor can run for this long without refueling. An air conditioning plant recycles the air on board to make fresh air.

U-boat
The potential of the submarine as a weapon was realized during World War II (1939–45). The German U-boats (*Unterseeboot*) had greatly increased range and speed. They sank thousands of Allied ships with their torpedoes.

Parts of a submarine

A modern submarine, such as this nuclear ballistic missile submarine, is nearly as long as a soccer field—around 100 yards. It has a crew of around 140 who work in shifts. Like other ships, it has an engine, propeller and rudder at the stern. Heat from the nuclear reactor generates steam. This drives the turbines that turn the submarine's propeller. Like all submarines, its hull is strong, but very few submarines can go below 1,640 feet. Buoyancy tanks fill with water to submerge the submarine. To resurface, compressed air pushes the water out of the tanks. Small movable wings, called hydroplanes, control the submarine's direction.

Towers and periscopes

The conning tower stands clear of the water when a submarine surfaces. Communication masts and periscopes top the tower. Periscopes are a device that lets the crew see above water when the submarine is submerged. There are usually two periscopes—a large one for general observation and a smaller one for attack.

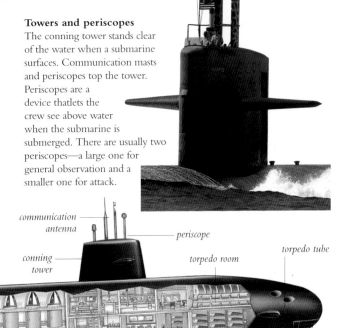

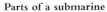

communication antenna — periscope

stabilizer fin — turbine — conning tower — torpedo room — torpedo tube

hydroplane — electric motor — nuclear reactor — missile tube — control room — crew's living quarters — forward hydroplane — sonar array

Mini-submersible

Small submersibles, carrying one or two people, are used to work at depths that would be too dangerous for a free-swimming diver. They are equipped with cameras, floodlights and robot arms. Highly accurate navigation systems let the crew find their way in the pitch black of the seabed. A mini-submersible runs on batteries and can stay under only for a short time—less than a day.

Research submersible

Teams of people dive to the ocean floor in submersibles. They have extremely strong hulls for diving very deep, up to about 5 miles. Submersibles dive and return to a support ship waiting on the surface. Special, deep-diving vessels called bathyscaphes can dive even farther—up to 7 miles.

DIVING AND SURFACING

A submarine dives by making itself heavier so that it sinks. It surfaces again by making itself lighter. To do this, it uses large tanks called buoyancy tanks. When the submarine is on the surface, the buoyancy tanks are full of air. To make the submarine dive, the tanks are flooded with seawater, making the submarine heavy enough to sink. To make the submarine surface again, compressed air is pumped into the tanks, forcing the water out. This makes the submarine lighter, and it floats to the surface. In this project, you can make a model submarine that can dive and surface using buoyancy tanks. When it is underwater, a full-scale submarine moves up and down using hydroplanes. These are like tiny wings and work like rudders as the submarine moves along. Submarines need very strong hulls to prevent them from being crushed by the huge pressure under the water. As submarines dive down, the weight of the water pressing down on them becomes greater and greater. The tremendous pressure from the water builds up quickly.

tanks are full of air and valves are closed

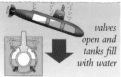

valves open and tanks fill with water

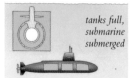

tanks full, submarine submerged

air is forced in, so water is forced out

MAKE A SUBMARINE

You will need: *large plastic bottle, sand, plastic funnel, two small plastic bottles, awl, scissors, ruler, two plastic straws, rubber bands, modeling clay, two small bulldog clips.*

Diving and surfacing
Water is let into buoyancy tanks by opening valves to let the air out. Water is expelled by pumping in air stored in tanks of compressed air.

1 Fill the large plastic bottle with sand using a funnel. Fill it until it just sinks in a tank of water. Test the bottle (cap firmly screwed on) to find the right amount of sand.

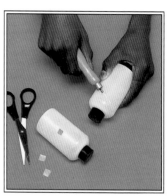

2 Make a large hole (about ½ in. across) in one side of two small plastic bottles. On the other side make a small hole, big enough for a plastic straw to fit into.

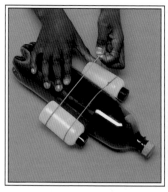

3 Attach the two small bottles to either side of the large bottle using rubber bands. Twist the small bottles so that the small hole on each one points upward.

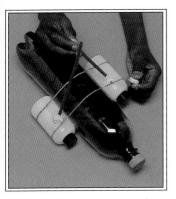

4 Push a plastic straw into each small hole so that a bit pokes through. Seal around the base of the straws with modeling clay to make a watertight seam.

5 Put a small bulldog clip about halfway down each straw. The clips need to be strong enough to squash the straw and stop air from being forced out by the water.

6 Put your model submarine in a tank of water. With the clips on it should float. Remove the clips, and water will flood the buoyancy tanks. The submarine will sink.

Final adjustments
This is the finished model submarine. You might find your model sinks bow first, or stern first. If this is the case, level it by shaking the sand evenly inside the bottle.

8 When your model submarine has resurfaced, keep blowing slowly into the tanks. Replace each bulldog clip, and your model submarine will remain floating on the surface.

7 To make the submarine surface again, blow slowly into both straws at once. The air will force the water out of the buoyancy tanks, and the submarine will rise to the surface.

PLEASURE CRAFT

THERE are many boats and ships designed for relaxation and sport. Boats offer a huge range of activities; people can rent a rowboat and cruise the oceans in a luxury yacht. Many people enjoy cruising and touring vacations afloat. Some vacationers operate the boat themselves, while others take the opportunity to relax with a crew to do the sailing. The ocean liners that regularly sailed across the world's seas have long gone, but their place has been taken by cruise liners. These ships are like floating hotels and are specifically designed for vacationers. On a trip, a cruise ship usually calls at a number of different ports. Some enthusiasts even sail around the world. Watersports such as rowing, canoeing, sailing and windsurfing are very popular. Spectacular tricks and stunts can be executed on windsurfers, surfboards and body boards. Canoes and kayaks offer the excitement of shooting down white-water rapids. Other people enjoy racing in sailboats, yachts, rowboats and powerboats.

Wind and waves
In strong winds a windsurfer can perform amazing flying leaps using a board. The board is steered by a sail. Experienced surfers take part in competitions, such as course racing and wave performance.

White-water racing
A kayak has a closed cockpit so that no water can get into the hull, even in very rough water. This makes it excellent for white-water racing. There are two types of racing. In wildwater racing, racers are timed over a course of obstacles such as rocks and rapids. In slalom, racers negotiate a course of gates.

Touring canoe
The canoe is an open boat, as opposed to the closed cockpit of a kayak. The canoeist sits or kneels and can use either single or double-bladed paddles. Canadian canoes are used for slalom races over a set course. Open canoes are a good way of seeing the natural world, because they move quietly through the water, not disturbing the peace.

Rafting

Traveling down the turbulent waters of a mountain river in an inflatable raft is a popular adventure sport. Rafters use single-bladed paddles. Everybody wears a lifejacket because there is a danger of falling out of the raft.

Sailing cruiser

Many people enjoy days out and longer vacations on sailing cruisers. This yacht, the *Wind Spirit*, is a cross between a sailing yacht and a cruise liner.

Luxury cruiser

A few people are lucky enough to be able to afford a large luxury motor yacht, or cruiser, like this. These yachts are equipped with every sort of luxury as well as the latest in satellite navigation equipment and cruise control.

Powerboat racing

A ride in a powerboat is incredibly fast, but very bumpy. Their hulls are specially shaped to skim across the surface. There are two types of powerboat racing—inshore and offshore. Boats are put into different classes, depending on their size and engine. Fast Formula 1 powerboats race all over the world.

Cruise liner

Many people spend their vacations on cruise liners. The liners travel around scenic parts of the world, stopping at interesting ports. A large cruise liner is part resort and part luxury hotel. It may be equipped with swimming pools, whirlpools, sundecks, tennis courts, gyms, theaters and even a golf course.

SERVICE BOATS

SERVICE vessels do special jobs in rivers or at sea, usually to help other boats and ships. The most common service boat is the tug. The tug's main job is to move other ships, sometimes to maneuver them into harbor, other times because their engines have failed. The largest tugs, called salvage tugs, can tow even the biggest cargo ships, and also help in emergency situations. Tugs have high bows to break through large waves, a high bridge to give a good view, a large deck to carry cargo and onboard winches. They also have extremely powerful engines and are highly maneuverable. A selection of service vessels is shown here. There are many more, however, such as cable-laying ships, oil drilling vessels and light ships. Lifeboats are also service boats.

Towing to sea
These tugs are towing part of an oil rig. They will tow it all the way from where is was built to its station at sea. Each tug has a strong towing hook where two steel ropes are attached.

Dredger
A dredger digs silt (mud and particles carried by water) from the bottom of rivers and canals. It does this to stop them from becoming too shallow. A bucket dredger is shown below. It uses a long line of buckets to scoop silt into a barge.

Research ship
An ocean research ship is a floating science laboratory. This ship has a bathymetry system for surveying the seabed. It also has onboard computer systems and equipment for lowering instruments and submersibles into the sea. It can carry 18 marine and technical staff on voyages of over 40 days. The engines have been specially modified to reduce engine noise, which might affect sensitive recordings. Research vessels like this help biologists to explore life on the seabed. They also help oceanographers (scientists who study the oceans) to examine undersea mountains and trenches.

two tugs
maneuver
the bow

supertanker

two tugs
push the
stern

tugs push on opposite
sides to turn the ship
around

Pushing around

These tugs are maneuvering a huge supertanker
into port. The tanker is so big it has difficulty steering
in enclosed waters. Tugs using towlines and pushing
with their bows can turn the ship around. They gently
nudge it into its berth or to an offshore mooring buoy.

Fire fighting

Every major port has a fire-fighting tug on stand-by all the
time. It sprays foam or water, which is sucked from the sea by
powerful pumps. The water is fired from guns on the upper
deck onto burning ships or port buildings. Foam is used to
smother oil and chemical fires from tankers.

Floating crane

A salvage barge is like a floating crane. It is used to
recover sunken or capsized vessels. Huge cranes like
this can lift large cargo ships from the seabed.

Breaking the ice

An icebreaker has a very strong hull. It is
designed to ride up on the ice so that
the ship's weight breaks through the
thick ice. Most icebreakers have
propellers in the bow to draw the
smashed ice back behind the ship.
Some also have special tanks on
board to allow the ship to tilt if
necessary to free it from the
surrounding ice. Icebreakers are used
to keep shipping lanes in northern waters
traversed during winter. They are used in
countries such as Canada, Denmark, Russia,
Sweden and the United States.

NAVIGATION AND SIGNALING

one

two

three

C (yes)

N (no)

O (man overboard)

G (I require a pilot)

Aᴛ sea, navigation includes many different jobs. It involves planning a safe route, checking the ship's position regularly to see how it is progressing, avoiding collisions with other vessels, and keeping an eye on the weather. The basic tools of navigation are a chart (map) of the sea and a magnetic compass. The chart shows coastlines, the depth of the water, landmarks on shore, hazards such as wrecks, the strength of tides and so on. Modern navigating tools, such as satellite-controlled Global Positioning System (GPS), mean that boats and ships with the correct equipment always know their position. Lighthouses and buoys help with navigation by indicating safe shipping channels and hazards. Signals are a way of sending messages to the shore or another vessel without using radio. Ways of signaling include signal flags and lamps.

Signal flags
An international system of signal flags has been used for centuries. Each flag stands for a number, a letter or a complete message. A flag's basic meaning can be changed by hoisting it on a different mast or in a certain combination with other flags. A selection of flags, with their meanings, is shown here.

lantern

A light at sea
A lighthouse warns of dangerous islands, rocks and headlands. It sends out a bright beam of light that sweeps around in a circle. At sea, it appears as a flashing light. Anchored light ships are also used to mark treacherous spots.

When lighthouses needed people to run them, the crew's quarters were in the tower. Today, most are automatic.

Signal lamp
Morse code (a code of long and short pulses) is another way of sending messages. An Aldis lamp has a trigger that the operator uses to turn the light on and off.

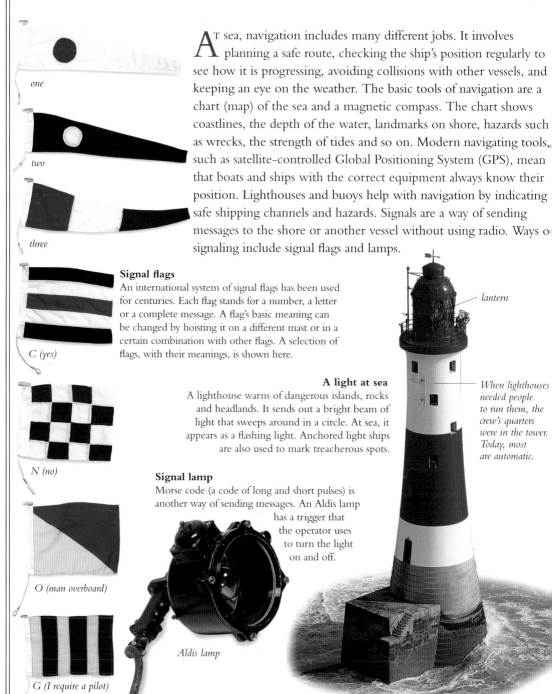

Aldis lamp

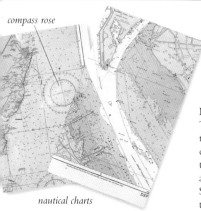
compass rose

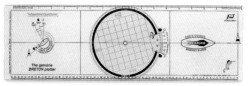
dividers

Navigation tools

The simple equipment here can be used to plot a course on a chart. Plotting a course involves drawing a series of lines on the chart that the ship will follow. The pilot also checks the boat's position from landmarks. Shown on the chart is the compass rose used for taking bearings (directions).

magnetic compass

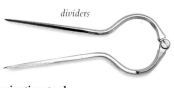
nautical charts

parallel ruler

Breton plotter

Navigation buoys

The shape and color of a buoy give it its meaning. Most buoys are red or green and indicate the sides of a safe channel. All buoys have flashing lights as well.

A red port buoy marks the lefthand side of a channel.

A green starboard buoy marks the righthand side of a channel.

Yellow and black cardinal buoys mark hazards or points of interest.

Electronic navigation

The navigation equipment on a modern ship includes radar, sonar and satellite receivers. Radar shows the position of the coast and other ships. Sonar shows the depth of water under the ship. Satellite GPS gives the ship's exact position to within a few yards.

Computers in navigation

At the chart table of this yacht are several computers. One receives images directly from a weather satellite. Another displays the ship's position on an electronic chart.

NAVIGATION LIGHTS

THERE are no street lights at sea, so all vessels have to display lights to warn other vessels that they are there. The types of light and number of them depend on the size of the vessel and what it is doing. For example, a sailboat must carry a white light at the top of its mast. A small powered boat that is underway must carry a red/green light and a white light above it. A red light is always hung on the port side (the lefthand side as you face the bow) of a boat or ship, while a green light is hung on the starboard (right). The project on these pages will show you how to make a simple red/green light. Larger ships that are underway carry a red/green light and several white lights. From these lights, the crew of one ship can tell what size another ship is, whether it is moving and which direction it is going in. This is especially important at night or in fog when visibility is poor. Fishing boats also display extra colored lights when they are fishing so that other ships can avoid their nets.

moving to starboard (right)

moving to port (left)

heading straight ahead

Which way?
The color of the light you can see shows which way the ship is moving.

MAKE A NAVIGATION LIGHT

You will need: pencil, ruler, thick card stock, scissors, four insulated wires, screwdriver, two bulb holders and bulbs, modeling clay, tape, clear plastic bottle, red and green colored plastic, battery.

1 Draw a simple boat shape about 12 in. long and 8 in. wide on a sheet of thick card stock. Give the shape a pointed bow and a flat stern. Cut out your shape.

2 Attach two wires to a bulb holder, one on either side. Screw in a bulb. Attach the holder to the center of your boat shape with a piece of modeling clay.

3 Cut three rectangles of card stock, about 4 in. by 2⅔ in. Trim one corner of each piece of card stock to fit around the bulb and holder. When secure they will divide up the light.

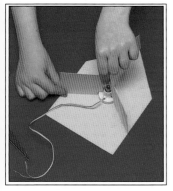

4 Attach the trimmed ends of the three pieces of card stock together. Place over the bulb and stick to the boat base.

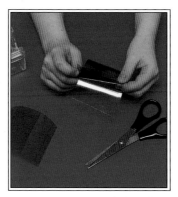

5 Cut two rectangles of plastic from a bottle. Tape green transparent plastic to one and red to the other.

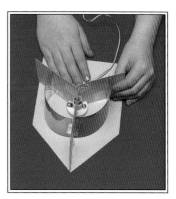

6 Tape the red plastic to the left (port) side of the boat. Tape the green to the right (starboard) side.

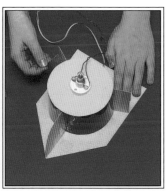

7 Cut a circle of card stock and tape it over the bulb and colored windows to make a lid. Attach another bulb and bulb holder with wires attached to the top of the boat.

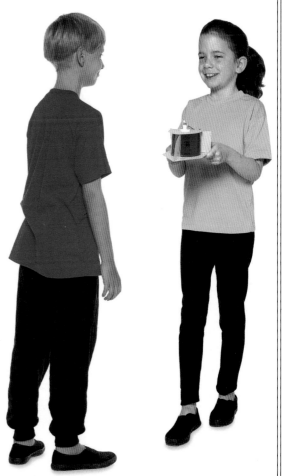

8 Now attach a battery. Tape a wire from each bulb to one end of the battery. Tape the other two wires to the other end of the battery. Both bulbs should light up.

9 Try testing out your red/green light in a darkened room. Ask a friend to observe while you walk toward him or her. Can they tell which way the boat is moving? Is it coming toward them, away from them, to their left, or to their right?

SHIPPING DISASTERS

THE seas and oceans can be very dangerous places. Every year, hundreds of ships are lost and many of their crews drown. The worst hazard is the weather. Strong winds blowing across a wide expanse of water create huge waves as tall as a house. The waves can swamp a small boat or cause a ship to capsize. Long, high waves can break the back of a ship if they lift its bow and stern, leaving its center unsupported. Another main cause of accidents is human error. Mistakes in communication or navigation cause collisions between vessels, sometimes sinking one of them. Ships also run aground due to errors in navigation. Other accidents are caused by engine failures, fires or explosions. These can have very serious consequences if a ship is carrying a dangerous cargo that may cause long-lasting damage to the environment.

Running aground
Once a ship has run aground it is hard to refloat. If it runs aground on rocks it may even be holed. Eventually a wreck like this will break up in the waves.

Fire on board
Despite being surrounded by water, fire is one of the worst hazards at sea. This ship is lucky that there is a fire boat in range. Usually the crew has to fight the fire themselves.

FACT BOX

• At sea, distances are measured in nautical miles. One nautical mile equals approximately 6,076 feet. Speed is measured in knots. One knot equals one nautical mile per hour.

• Depth was once measured in fathoms. One fathom was 6 feet, which equals 2 yards.

• The biggest collision at sea was between two oil tankers. Their combined deadweight was 660,000 tons. Around 300,000 tons of oil was spilt into the Caribbean Sea.

Tanker disaster
The oil tanker *MV Braer* ran aground in the Shetland Islands, Scotland in 1993. The hull was holed and 80,000 tons of oil leaked into the sea, creating a huge oil slick. Spills like this result in major ecological damage.

Deadly oil

Seabirds caught in an oil slick are most at risk. They try to clean their feathers and swallow the harmful oil. If birds are caught in time, they can be cleaned with detergents.

Beach clean up

If an oil slick reaches the shore, it coats the rocks with oily sludge. Clearing up a large spill with suction pumps takes months and is very expensive. The coastline takes years to recover.

Capsize

Once a boat has capsized it is almost impossible to right again. The crew may survive by climbing inside the hull or sitting on top of it. Even the largest ships can capsize if they are hit by a very large, powerful wave.

The sinking of the *Titanic*

The most famous boating disaster of all was the sinking of the ocean liner *Titanic* on April 15, 1912. With more than 1,500 lives lost, it remains one of the worst peacetime disasters. This painting of the event is exaggerated—the ship's hull was holed by ice under the water. The disaster was made worse because there were not enough lifeboats.

IN AN EMERGENCY

Lifeboat stations
In an emergency, passengers on this cruise liner would get in the lifeboats shown here. The lifeboats would be lowered down the side of the ship, into the sea.

WHEN an accident does happen, the crew immediately begins to follow an emergency procedure. If they have a radio, they will send a Mayday call to the emergency services. Other vessels in the area will go to help, a lifeboat may be launched, or a helicopter sent to search. To help rescuers locate their stricken vessel, flares are fired and emergency horns sounded. Larger boats and ships have an automatic radio beacon that sends out a distress call when it falls into the sea. The emergency services can hone in on the beacon. If the crew has to abandon ship, they put on life jackets, perhaps survival suits, and launch lifeboats or life rafts. All but the smallest vessels have fire-fighting equipment on board. Cruise liners have a computerized warning and sprinkler system.

FACT BOX

• Ships on which there is a risk of explosion, such as drilling and gas-carrying ships, have lifeboats next to the crew compartments. These drop into the sea for quick evacuation.

• If a submarine cannot surface, its crew escapes in buoyant personal escape suits. These act as life rafts on the surface.

• The crew of an offshore lifeboat wears helmets and is harnessed to their seats to stop them from flying about as waves crash into the boat.

Inshore lifeboats
Small lifeboats, such as this Australian surfboat, help rescue people near the coast. Swimmers, surfers and sailboat users are rescued quickly by boats like this. It is specially designed to ride over the high surf.

Lifeboat launch
Offshore lifeboats can be swiftly launched down a slipway. When the emergency call comes through, the crew jumps into the boat, starts the engine and releases a holding wire. The boat hits the water at speed. This is a much faster way to launch a boat than setting off from a harbor.

Life rafts

Inflatable life rafts are stored in a container on the deck of a ship or yacht. When the container is thrown into the sea, the raft inflates automatically. It is designed to maintain body heat and not capsize. Inside the raft are medical and food supplies.

Lifeboat at sea

Offshore lifeboats are designed to operate in the worst weather at sea. They have very powerful engines for reaching an emergency quickly. Lifeboats are self-righting and quickly right themselves if a wave knocks them flat.

Helicopter rescue

A helicopter winchman is lowered onto a lifeboat. He carries a cradle to pick up a casualty from the boat. Air-sea rescue helicopters take part in searches, winch crew from stricken ships and carry casualties quickly to hospitals on shore.

foghorn

flares

The coastguard

Some countries have coastal patrol boats. This Canadian patrol boat is operated by the coastguard service. It acts as a police boat as well as a lifeboat.

Flares and horns

Sailors in trouble fire flares and sound foghorns to show their position. Flares are like large fireworks. Some simply burn brightly. Others fire a burning light into the sky. The foghorn uses compressed air to make an ear-piercing noise.

KEEPING AFLOAT

MAKE A SELF-RIGHTING BOAT

You will need: *pencil, ruler, sheet of styrofoam, scissors, modeling clay, rubber bands, small plastic tub.*

A crew's first reaction in a collision or grounding is to try to keep their ship afloat if possible. For a start, all ships have bilge pumps. These are used to pump water out of the bottom of the boat's hull and into the sea. Small boats, such as sailboats and canoes, have bags of air or blocks of styrofoam inside to keep them afloat. Most lifeboats are self-righting, which means that they bob back upright if they capsize. Lifeboats are built of tough, lightweight materials such as plastic and foam. They are completely watertight—even their air inlets have seals to keep out the water. Their heavy engines are set low down, while the hull and high-up cabins are full of air. This arrangement ensures that the lifeboat flips upright without needing help. You can find out how to make a simple self-righting boat in the first project.

The hull of a large ship below the waterline is divided into watertight sections by strong metal walls called bulkheads. The doors in the bulkheads are also watertight when they are closed. These are designed so that if one section floods, the water cannot fill the whole hull. Even if a ship is sinking, bulkheads stop it from capsizing due to water rushing to one side. In the second project you will see how a hull with bulkheads works much better than one without bulkheads.

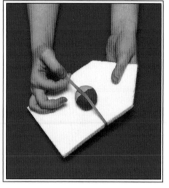

1 Cut a boat-shape about 6 in. by 4 in. from styrofoam. Attach a golf-ball sized lump of modeling clay to one side with a rubber band.

2 Put your boat into a tank or bowl of water. Have the modeling clay, which represents the crew and equipment, on top. If you capsize the boat it will stay capsized.

3 Add another lump of modeling clay underneath the boat to represent heavy engines or ballast. Add an upturned plastic tub on top to represent a watertight cabin.

4 Now try to capsize it again, and it will flip back upright. This is because air trapped underwater by the tub and a heavy weight on top forces the boat upright again.

INSTALLING BULKHEADS

You will need: plastic container and lid, awl, marbles, scissors, modeling clay, wooden blocks or other "cargo."

1 Pierce a hole in one corner of a plastic container using an awl. This represents the holed hull of a cargo ship.

2 Add some marbles (cargo) and lower the container into a tank of water. It will fill up with water and slowly sink.

3 Cut three rectangles from the lid of the container. Make sure they fit across the tub. Round off the bottom corners if you need to.

5 Put some cargo in each section of the hull and put the whole thing back into the water. This time the container will stay afloat because only one section floods. The bulkheads prevent the water from filling the whole hull.

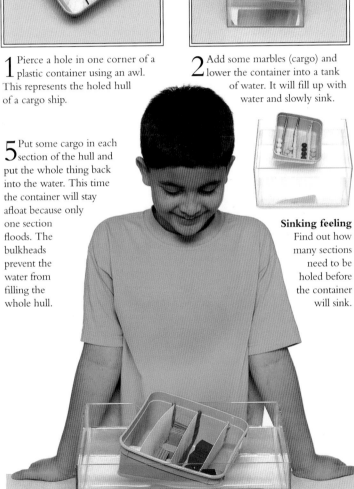

Sinking feeling
Find out how many sections need to be holed before the container will sink.

4 Position the plastic walls inside the container so that they divide it into four compartments. Press modeling clay around the edges to make a watertight seal.

IN PORT

SHIPS and boats move cargo and people from place to place, so they need ports where they can load and unload. Every port has areas called docks where ships tie up along the quayside. The docks are often inside an area of water called a harbor, which is protected from the sea by a massive stone wall or natural cliffs. On the dock are huge cranes for unloading the ships and warehouses for storing cargo. In the port area there may be ship repair yards, parts shops and customs offices. Until recently, large numbers of people were employed as dockers, and many major coastal towns and cities have grown up around ports. But the increased use of containers has dramatically reduced the number of workers. Huge merchant ships now dock at purpose-built ports or terminals, which are specially designed for handling cargoes, such as containers, oil and gas.

Tying up
Berthing ropes hooked over bollards are used to tie ships to the quayside. Quays may also be known as wharves.

Container port
An aerial view shows part of Hong Kong's vast container terminal. Special loading cranes, called straddle carriers, are used to fetch and carry the containers.

The pilot
The entrance to a harbor is often narrow and busy. It may also have treacherous shallow areas such as sandbanks outside it. A pilot is a person who knows the harbor well. He or she always takes control of large ships to guide them as they enter and leave the port.

Marina

A marina is a small harbor area where leisure craft, such as motorboats and sailing yachts tie up. Marinas are usually separate from the normal harbor. They are also common on coasts where there are few natural harbors for small boats to shelter in. Each bay, called a berth, in a marina has water and electricity supplies.

High and dry

Repair and maintenance facilities in port may include a dry dock. This submarine is being repaired in dry dock. The submarine entered the dock when it was flooded with water. The gates were then closed and the water pumped out. Scaffolding is erected to keep the submarine upright.

Unloading in port

A dockside crane unloads a Japanese ship in the port of Vladivostock, Russia. The crane can be moved along the dockside on railway tracks. This ship's decks, as well as its hold, are piled with freight packed in boxes called tea chests.

Old harbors

The old harbor in Sydney, Australia is a popular tourist attraction. Many old docks are too small for modern merchant ships. After years of neglect, their harbors are being renovated to provide leisure facilities.

PART SIX

TRAINS

The ancient Greeks recognized the value of railed tracks along which wheeled vehicles could run smoothly. But it was not until the early 1800s that rails were combined with steam power to launch one of the greatest transport revolutions in history. The social and economic impact of trains was enormous. Goods that had been too heavy, or which degraded too quickly to travel long distances, could now be transported speedily and efficiently. This insight into the railroad story explores trains inside and out, explains how different types of locomotive work, takes a look at stations from around the world and the people who keep them running, and takes a glimpse into the future.

CONSULTANT

Michael Harris

RUNNING ON RAILS

THROUGHOUT HISTORY, people have looked for ways to move themselves and their possessions faster and more efficiently. Wheels were invented about 5,500 years ago. As wheels are round, they turn well on smooth surfaces and reduce the rubbing, slowing force called friction. However, it soon became clear that wheels do not work well on rough, soft or muddy ground.

To solve this problem, tracks of wood or stone were cut into or laid onto the ground to provide a smooth surface on which wheels could turn. This kept friction to a minimum, so that vehicles could move more easily and shift heavier loads.

The ancient Greeks made the first railed tracks in about 400BC by cutting grooved rails into rock. They hauled ships overland by setting them on wheeled cars that ran along the tracks. Iron rails came into use in Europe by the mid-1700s. They were laid, mainly in mines, to transport cars loaded with coal or metal ores. Steam-powered locomotives were developed in the early 1800s. Before then, cars in mines were pulled by horses or by the miners themselves, which was slow and only possible for short distances.

Pulling power
A horse pulls a freight car along rails. Modern railroads developed from ones first laid in European mines in the mid-1500s. Heavy loads, such as coal and metal ore, were carried in cars with wheels that ran along wooden planks. The cars were guided by a peg under the car, which slotted into a gap between the planks. Horses and sometimes even human laborers were used to haul the cars long before steam locomotives were invented.

Riding rails
It is just possible to make out the grooves where iron rails were laid at the Penydarran Ironworks in South Wales in the early 1800s. The world's first steam-powered train ran along these rails on February 13, 1804. The locomotive was designed by British engineer Richard Trevithick and hauled cars loaded with 11 tons of iron and 70 passengers at a speed of 5mph.

1769–1810	1811–1830	1831–1860	1861–1880
1769 FRENCHMAN NICHOLAS CUGNOT builds the first steam-powered vehicle.	**1825** THE STOCKTON AND DARLINGTON Railway opens in Britain—the first public railroad to use steam-powered locomotives.	**1833** GEORGE STEPHENSON devises the steam brake cylinder to operate brake blocks on the driving wheels of steam locomotives.	**1863** LONDON UNDERGROUND'S Metropolitan Line opens and is the world's first underground passenger railroad.
	1827 THE BALTIMORE AND OHIO Railroad is chartered to run from Baltimore to the River Ohio, Virginia, in the USA.		**1864** AMERICAN GEORGE PULLMAN builds the first sleeping car, the *Pioneer*.
			1868 PULLMAN builds the first dining car.
1804 BRITISH ENGINEER RICHARD TREVITHICK tests the first steam locomotive for the Penydarran Ironworks in Wales.	**1829** ROBERT AND GEORGE STEPHENSON'S *Rocket* wins the Rainhill Trials. It becomes the locomotive used for the Liverpool and Manchester Railway.		**1869** THE CENTRAL PACIFIC and Union Pacific railroads meet at Promontory Summit, linking the east and west coasts of the USA.
1808 TREVITHICK BUILDS a circular railroad in London, Britain, and exhibits the *Catch Me Who Can* locomotive.		**1840s** SEMAPHORE SIGNALING is introduced. First tickets for train journeys are issued.	**1872** AMERICAN GEORGE WESTINGHOUSE patents an automatic air-braking system.

Trackless trains

The world's longest trackless train runs at Lake County Museum in Columbia, South Carolina, in the USA. Trackless trains are common in theme parks. They carry passengers in carts or wagons running on rubber-tired wheels. The trains are pulled by a tractor that is made to look like a railroad locomotive.

Puffing Billy

The locomotive in this painting was nicknamed *Puffing Billy* because it was one of the earliest to have a smokestack. It was designed by British mine engineer William Hedley and built in 1813. The first steam engines were built in the early 1700s. They were used to pump water from mineshafts, not to power vehicles. *Puffing Billy* can be seen today in the Science Museum in London, Britain. It is the world's oldest surviving steam locomotive.

Modern rail networks

Today, nearly all countries in the world have their own railroad network. Thousands of miles of track crisscross the continents. Steam power has now given way to newer inventions. Most modern trains are hauled by locomotives powered by diesel engines, by electricity drawn from overhead cables, or from an electrified third rail on the track.

1881–1900	1901–1950	1951–1980	1981–present
1883 THE LUXURIOUS *ORIENT-EXPRESS* first runs on June 5 from Paris, France, to Bucharest in Romania.	**1901** THE FIRST COMMERCIAL monorail opens in Wuppertal, northwestern Germany.	**1955** THE WORLD'S MOST POWERFUL single-unit diesel-electric locomotives, the Deltics, first run between London and Liverpool.	**1981** TGV (*TRAIN À GRANDE VITESSE*) first runs between Paris and Lyon in France.
1893 THE NEW YORK CENTRAL AND HUDSON RIVER Railroad claims that its steam locomotive No. 999 travels faster than 100mph.	**1904** THE NEW YORK CITY SUBWAY opens.	**1957** TRANS-EUROP EXPRESS (TEE) fleet of trains operates an international rail service across western Europe.	
1895 BALTIMORE AND OHIO No. 1 is the first electric locomotive to run on the mainline Baltimore and Ohio Railroad.	**1938** *MALLARD* SETS the world speed record for a steam-powered locomotive (126mph). **1940s** UNION PACIFIC BIG BOYS are built by the American Locomotive Company.	**1964** THE BULLET TRAIN first runs on the Tokaido Shinkansen between Tokyo and Osaka in Japan.	**1994** CHANNEL TUNNEL completed, linking rail networks in Britain and the Continent.
1900 THE PARIS *METRO* opens.		**1980** THE FIRST MAGLEV service opens at Birmingham Airport in Britain.	**1996** MAGLEV TRAIN ON THE Yamanashi test line in Japan reaches a staggering 350mph.

RAILROAD TRACK

A FULLY LADEN freight or passenger train is heavy, so the track it runs on has to be tough. Today, rails are made from steel, which is a much stronger material than the cast iron used for the first railroads. The shape of the rail also helps to make it tough. If you sliced through a rail from top to bottom you would see it has an "I"-shaped cross section. The broad, flat bottom narrows into the "waist" of the I and widens again into a curved head. Most countries use a rail shaped like this.

Tracks are made up of lengths of rail, which are laid on wooden or concrete crossbeams called ties. Train wheels are a set distance apart, so rails must be a set distance apart, too. The distance between rails is called the gauge. In Britain, the gauge was fixed at 4 feet 8½ inches in the mid-1800s. Before then, the width of trains and gauges varied from one rail network to the next. So a train from one rail network could not run over the lines of another rail network.

Hard labor

Laying rail track is backbreaking work. Up until the mid-1900s, it was always done by hand. The ground is leveled first. Then crushed rock is laid to form a solid base before the ties are put into position. The rails rest on metal baseplates to hold them firm. The baseplates are secured to the ties either by spikes (big nails), track bolts or large metal spring-clips. Today, machines are used to lay track in most countries, although some countries still use manual labor.

MAKING TRACKS

You will need: *two sheets of stiff card measuring 10¼ x 4¼ in., pencil, ruler, scissors, glue and glue brush, silver and brown paint, paintbrush, water pot, one sheet of foam board measuring 8 x 5 in., one sheet of paper (11 x 8½ in.), masking tape, one sheet of thin card measuring 4 x 2 in.*

1 Place one 10¼ x 4¼-in. piece of card lengthwise. Draw a line ½ in. in from each of the outside edges. Draw two more lines, each 1⅜ in. from the outside edges. This is side A.

2 Turn the card over (side B) and place it lengthwise. Measure and draw lines 1½ in. and 1¾ in. in from each edge. Repeat steps 1 and 2 with the second piece of 10½ x 4¼-in. card.

3 Hold the ruler firmly against one of the lines you have drawn. Use the tip of a pair of scissors to score along the line. Repeat for all lines on both sides of both pieces of card.

4 Place the cards A side up. For each one in turn, fold firmly along the two pairs of outer lines. Fold up from the scored side. Turn the card over. Repeat for inner lines.

5 With the A side up, press the folds into the I-shape of the rail. Open out again. Glue the B side of the ¾-in.-wide middle section as shown. Repeat for the second rail.

6 Give your two rails a metallic look by painting the upper (A) sides silver. Leave the paint to dry, then apply a second coat. Leave the second coat to dry.

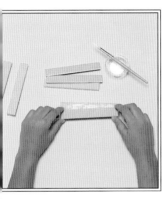

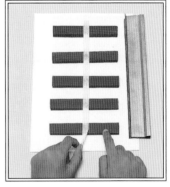

7 Use a pencil and ruler to mark out ten 5 x ¾-in. strips on the foam board. Cut them out. Glue two strips together to make five thick railroad ties. Leave them to dry.

8 Paint the ties brown on their tops and sides to make them look like wood. Leave them to dry, then apply a second coat of paint. Leave the second coat to dry, too.

9 Lay the ties on a piece of paper, 1³⁄₁₆ in. apart. Run a strip of masking tape down the middle to hold them in place.

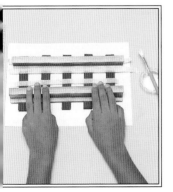

10 Glue the base of one rail and press it into place along the line of ties. The outside edge of the rail should be ⅜ in. in from the edge of the tie. Glue the other track into position in the same way. Secure the rails in place with masking tape until the glue is dry. Then gently remove all the masking tape.

11 Make at least two sets of rails. These will be able to carry the *Toy Train* and *Brake Van* described in later projects. To join the rails together, roll up the 4 x 2-in. length of thin card. Insert one end into the top of the I-shape in one rail. Gently push the second rail on to the other end.

STEAMING AHEAD

Horses, oxen or people provided the pulling power for cars on rails and roads for thousands of years. In the 1800s, inventors came up with an alternative. They worked out how to use steam power for pulling wheeled vehicles. In 1825, the world's first public steam railway, the 25-mile-long Stockton and Darlington line, opened in England. On its opening day, the train hauled both freight and passenger cars. Later, it was used mainly for carrying coal. Five years later, the Liverpool and Manchester line opened with its new, steam-driven passenger trains. The company had run a competition called the Rainhill Trials to find the best locomotive for its railway. Both horse-drawn and steam locomotives took part. The steam-driven *Rocket* won.

The success of the *Rocket* convinced investors to back the development of steam-powered locomotives. The brains behind the *Rocket* and the Stockton and Darlington and Liverpool and Manchester railways were George Stephenson and his son Robert. In 1823, they set up the world's first locomotive factory. Other British engineers began to experiment with steam power, and locomotives were made for use in Britain and around the world.

Race to success

The *Rocket*, designed and built by George and Robert Stephenson, convinced people that steam power was better than horse power. At the Rainhill Trials in 1829, the *Rocket* traveled 70 miles at an average speed of 15 mph.

Slow train to China

This Chinese locomotive is a KD class, which followed an American design. The Chinese did not make their own locomotives until they began to set up their own factories in the 1950s. Before then, locomotives had been imported from countries such as the USA, Britain, and Japan. Some Chinese trains are still steam-driven today, although diesel and electric ones are rapidly replacing them.

hot gases
pass through
to boiler

regulator valve   engine

boiler tubes
surrounded
by water

steam passes
through pipes
into cylinders

smokestack

smokebox

firebox

cab

steam
valve

piston inside
cylinder

driving wheels   coupling rod   connecting rod   leading truck

Steam traction

A steam engine converts the energy released from combustion into kinetic energy or movement. First, fuel (most often coal) is burned in a firebox to produce hot gases. The gases pass through boiler tubes that run the length of the water-filled boiler. The hot, gas-filled tubes heat the surrounding water and turn it into steam. This steam passes into cylinders, each of which contains a close-fitting piston. The steam pushes the piston along. The steam then escapes via a valve (one-way opening), and the piston can move back again. Rods connect the piston to the wheels. As the piston moves back and forth, it moves the rods, which, in turn, make the wheels go around.

FACT BOX
• Steam locomotives need about 26 gallons of water for every mile they travel. It takes 26–55 pounds of coal—equivalent to seven or eight times the weight of the water—to turn the water into steam.

Big wheels
The Stirling Single locomotive had only one pair of large driving wheels (third in from the left). The driving wheels are driven directly by the piston and connecting rod from the cylinder. Most steam locomotives had two or more pairs of driving wheels linked by coupling rods. The Single, designed by British engineer Patrick Stirling in the 1870s, reached speeds of 80 mph.

The Big Boys
In the 1940s, American engineers were designing huge steam locomotives such as this Union Pacific Challenger. At more than 130 feet, the Union Pacific's Big Boys were the world's longest-ever steam locomotives—more than five times the length of the Stephensons' *Rocket*. They could haul long passenger or freight trains speedily across the USA's vast landscape.

BEARING THE LOAD

Staying power
The coupling rod that connects the driving wheel to the other wheels is the lowest of the three rods in this picture. The connecting rod just above links the driving wheel with the cylinder. To stop train wheels from slipping sideways and falling off the rails, there is a rim called the flange on the inside of each wheel. This is a little different from the wheels you will make in this project, which have two flanges so that they sit snugly on the model rails from the *Making Tracks* project.

T HE VEHICLE and machinery carried by a modern locomotive's underframe and wheels may weigh up to 110 tons. As bigger and more powerful locomotives were built, more wheels were added to carry the extra weight. Early steam locomotives such as the Stephensons' *Rocket* had only two pairs of wheels. Most steam locomotives had two, three, or four pairs of driving wheels, all of which turn in response to power from the cylinders. The cylinders house the pistons, whose movement pushes the driving wheels around via a connecting rod.

The other wheels are connected to the driving wheel by a coupling rod, so that they turn at the same time. The pair of wheels in front of the driving wheels are called the leading truck. The ones behind are the trailing wheels. Locomotives are defined by the total number of wheels they have. For example, a 4-4-0 type locomotive has four leading, four driving, and no trailing wheels.

MAKE AN UNDERFRAME

You will need: sheet of stiff card (22 x 17 in.), pencil, ruler, pair of compasses, scissors, glue and glue brush, masking tape, four 4-in. lengths of ¹⁄₁₆-in. diameter dowel, four pieces of 2 x 2-in. thin card, silver and black paint, paintbrush, water pot, four map pins.

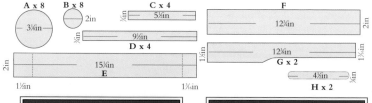

1 Draw and cut out the templates from the stiff card. Use a pair of compasses to draw the wheel templates A and B.

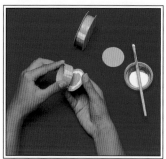

2 Roll the rim templates C and D into rings. Glue and tape to hold. Glue each small wheel circle onto either side of a small ring as shown. Repeat for big wheels. Leave to dry.

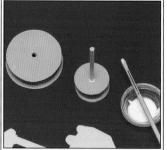

3 Use a pencil to enlarge the compass hole on one side of each wheel. Glue one end of each piece of dowel. Push the dowels into the holes of two big and two small wheels.

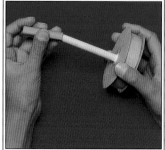

4 Roll the 2 x 2-in. card into sleeves to fit loosely over each piece of dowel. Tape to hold. Make wheel pairs by fixing the remaining wheels on to the dowel as described in step 3.

5 When the glue is dry, paint all four pairs of wheels silver. You do not need to paint the dowel axles. Paint two coats, letting the first dry before you apply the second.

6 Use a ruler and pencil to mark eight equal segments on the outside of each wheel. Paint a small circle over the compass hole, and the center of each segment black.

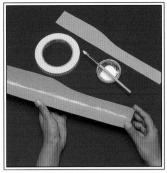

7 Fold along the dotted lines on E. Glue all three straight edges of template G and stick to template E. Repeat this for the other side. Secure all joins with masking tape.

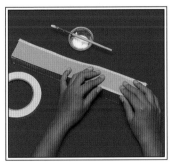

8 Glue the open edges of the underframe. Fit template F on top and hold until firm. Tape over the joins. Give the underframe two coats of black paint. Leave to dry.

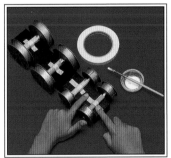

9 Glue the card sleeves on to the base of the underframe. Small wheel axles go 1⅜ in. and 2¾ in. from the front, big wheels 1⅜ in. and 5 in. from the back. Tape to secure.

10 Give the coupling rods (H) two coats of silver paint. Let the paint dry between coats.

11 Press a map pin through each end of the coupling rods, about ³⁄₁₆ in. from edge. Carefully press the pin into each big wheel about ⅜ in. beneath the center.

12 The wheels on this underframe are arranged for a 4-4-0 type locomotive. You will be able to run the underframe along the model tracks you made in the *Making Tracks* project. The wheels will fit on the rails just like those of a real train. In real locomotives, however, the wheels are mounted on swiveling units called trucks. When the train comes to a curve in the track, the trucks move to allow the train to follow the curve. Each truck has four to six wheels.

DIESEL AND ELECTRIC POWER

Today, most high-speed trains are either diesel, electric, or a combination of the two. Diesel and electric trains are far more fuel-efficient, cost less to run, and can stop or speed up more quickly than steam trains. Electric trains are also better for the environment, because they do not give off polluting exhaust fumes.

The first electric locomotive ran in 1879 at an exhibition in Berlin in Germany. However, it was another 20 or so years before railroad companies began to introduce electric trains into regular service. Similarly, the first reliable diesel engine was demonstrated in 1889 by its inventor, the French-born German Rudolf Diesel. It took a further 25 years for railroad engineers to design the first practical diesel locomotives. Diesel trains entered regular service during the 1920s in the USA, and during the 1930s in Britain. Steam locomotives were last used regularly in the USA in 1960, in 1968 in Britain, and in 1977 in West Germany.

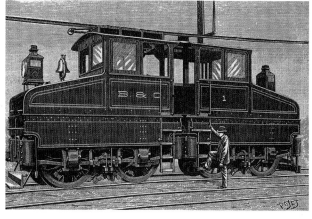

Electric pioneer
In 1895, the B&O *No. 1* became the world's first electric locomotive to run on a mainline track. It entered service in Baltimore in the USA (B&O is short for Baltimore and Ohio Railroad). The route of the B&O *No. 1* took it through many tunnels. One of the advantages of electric locomotives is that, unlike steam trains, they do not fill tunnels and cars with steam and smoke.

Beautiful Bugattis
Racing-car designer Ettore Bugatti designed this diesel train for the French *État* and Paris Lyons *Mediterranée* railroads. In the early 1930s, Bugatti's first trains were diesel or gas single railcars (self-propelled passenger cars). Instead of being hauled by a locomotive, the railcar had its own engine. The railcar-and-car combination shown left was a later introduction. Bugatti came up with the train's streamlined shape by testing his designs in wind tunnels. In 1935, one of Bugatti's trains reached 122 mph, setting a world diesel train speed record.

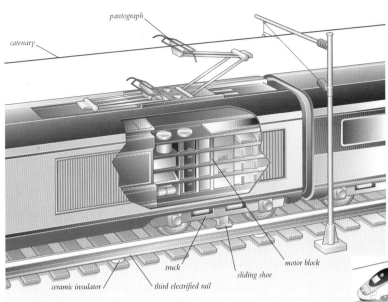

catenary

pantograph

Picking up power
Electric locomotives are powered in one of two ways. Some draw electricity from a catenary (overhead cable). This is connected to the locomotive by an "arm" called a pantograph on the roof. Others draw power from a third rail. The locomotive connects to the rail by a device called a shoe. The Eurostar trains that operate in Europe can use either power source depending on what country they are traveling through.

truck

motor block

sliding shoe

ceramic insulator

third electrified rail

Long-distance runner
Australian National Railways' diesel-electric engines work the long Indian Pacific route. This transcontinental railroad runs between Perth, on the Indian Ocean, and Sydney, on the Pacific Ocean. These locomotives belong to the CL class that was introduced in 1970. This class was based on one that originated in the USA but was built in Sydney, Australia.

Dutch double decker
Dutch Railways' IRM (*InterRegio Materiel*) electric trains are double-decked to cater for high levels of traffic in the densely populated Netherlands. Passenger traffic is expected to rise rapidly, and so the Netherlands is investing heavily in its railroads. Speeds on existing lines are limited to 87 mph, but new lines are being built for speeds of up to 137 mph.

Cisalpino Pendolino
Italy has developed a tilting train, or pendolino, called the ETR (*Elletro Treni Rapidi*) 470 Cisalpino. These dual-voltage trains are operated by an Italian-Swiss consortium (group of companies). Services began in September 1996 between Italy and Switzerland. The ETR 470 Cisalpino has been developed to be able to use existing rail networks at higher speeds by tilting into the curves as it travels. As a result, the top service speed of these trains is 155 mph.

MAPPING THE RAILROADS

Trains cannot easily climb mountains or cope with sharp corners. Planning and mapping the route of a railroad is not simply a matter of drawing a straight line between two destinations. New routes have to be worked out carefully, so that difficult terrain is avoided and time and money will not be wasted on tunnel- or bridge-building. Geographically accurate maps are made before work starts to show every bend of the planned track and the height of the land it will run through. Once construction starts, separate teams of workers may be building sections of track in different parts of the country. The maps are essential to make sure they are all following the same route and will join up when the separate parts meet.

Passengers do not need such detailed maps. They just need to find out which train to catch to get to the place they want to go. They do not need to know each curve or bridge along the way, just the names of the stations. Passenger maps provide a simplified version of the railroad routes, or sometimes a diagram.

Railroads in the Wild West

You can see how the railroads often followed a similar route to the wagon trails, passing through mountain passes or river valleys. After the first east-to-west-coast railroad was completed (the Central Pacific Railroad joined the Union Pacific Railroad in 1869), people could cross the continent in just ten days.

Early American railroad

A train runs along the Mohawk and Hudson Railroad, New York State, in the USA. This railroad line opened in 1831 and was built to replace part of the 40-mile route of the Erie Canal. This section of the canal had several locks, which caused delays to the barges. The journey took half the time it had taken by canal.

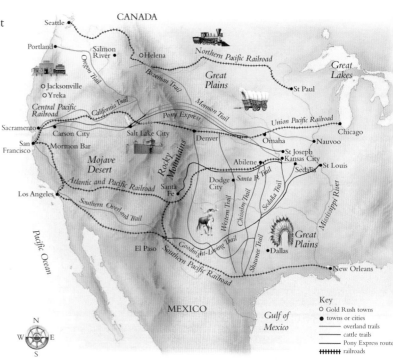

Neat networking

India's massive railroad network was one of the best planned in Asia thanks in large part to the British influence in the region. The Great Indian Peninsular Railway (GIPR) company was the first to open a line, a 25-mile stretch between Bombay and Thana in April 1853. India is a vast country, and railroad engineers had to plan routes for thousands of miles of track. They also had to find ways of taking railroads across every kind of difficult terrain, from boggy marshes to arid deserts, high mountains and deep ravines.

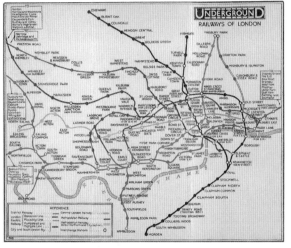

Designing ideas

Apart from the color-coded routes, the 1927 map of the London Underground (at left) looks very different from the one of today (shown above). Early route maps were hard to follow because they tried to show the real geographical route of lines. More abstract, diagrammatical maps were the brainwave of British engineering draughtsman Henry C. Beck. His 1933 redesign of the London Underground map was inspired by electrical circuit diagrams. It makes no attempt to show the real geographical route and is not drawn to scale.

Surveying railroad lines

Today, computer programs are used to plan and design new railroad routes. Data collected from on-the-ground surveying equipment (shown here), or the latest high-tech global positioning systems, is fed into a computer. The information is analyzed to insure that the new rail route is feasible. The most direct route is not always the cheapest. Surveyors must consider factors such as difficult terrain, environmental benefits, and existing rail networks when planning new routes.

BUILDING RAILROADS

THERE WERE no automatic tools or building machines in the 1800s when the first railroads were built. Everything was done by hand. Gangs of laborers moved mountains of earth using nothing but picks, shovels, and barrows. Horses pulled the heaviest loads. Never before had so much earth been shifted, or so many bridges or tunnels built.

The challenge for the engineers who planned the railroads was to construct tracks that were as level as possible. In the early days, locomotives had difficulty climbing even the slightest slope.

Channels were dug or blasted through low hills, while mounds of earth and rock were piled into embankments to carry tracks over boggy or low ground. The railroad routes had to avoid crossing high mountains and deep valleys. Sometimes, though, there was no getting around these obstacles. In the late 1800s, engineers such as Isambard Kingdom Brunel in Britain and Gustave Eiffel in France, began to design tunnels and bridges that were longer and stronger than the world had ever known.

Army on the march
Railroads were carved out of the landscape during the 1800s by gangs of strong laborers. Originally, these workmen built navigations, or channels, equipped with little more than picks and shovels. Gangs often moved from place to place, as one track, tunnel or bridge was completed and work on a new one started up. Some of the workers lived in temporary camps, while others rented rooms in nearby towns. The laborers had strong muscles, but many were also skilled carpenters, miners, stonemasons, or blacksmiths.

The best route
Millions of tons of earth and rock were blasted away for channels and to make railroad routes as level and as straight as possible. Even modern trains slow down on hills. Early steam locomotives just ground to a halt. Sharp curves would cause trains to derail. Alfred Nobel's development of dynamite in 1866 made blasting safer. It was more stable than earlier explosives.

FACT BOX
• At nearly 34 miles long, the Seikan Tunnel in Japan is presently the world's longest railroad tunnel. The Alp Transit Link between Switzerland and Italy will beat this record by 2 miles. This tunnel is due to be completed in 2012.

• The world's longest double-decker road and railroad suspension bridge is also in Japan. Called the Minami Bisan-seto Bridge, its main span is just over 1,200 yards long.

Bridging the valleys

There is not one perfect design for any bridge. In each case, an engineer has to take many factors into consideration before making the decision. These include the weight and frequency of traffic over the bridge, whether the underlying rock is hard or soft, the bridge's appearance in the landscape, and the overall cost of the project.

Suspension bridges can be the longest bridges of all. The weight of the bridge platform is carried by steel wires that hang from thick cables. The cables are held up by concrete towers and anchored firmly at the valley sides.

The beam bridge is made up of a horizontal platform supported on two or more piers (pillars). Sometimes a framework of steel girders is added. The girders act as a brace to strengthen and support the beam bridge between its piers.

The arch bridge can be built over very steep valleys or fast-flowing rivers, where it would be difficult to build piers. Steel or reinforced concrete supports press toward each other in the arch shape, making a very strong base for the bridge platform.

Building workers

Thousands of skilled workers are involved in the manufacture of locomotives and rolling stock (passenger cars and freight cars). There are whole factories that specialize in making particular parts of the engine or carriage, such as buffers or electric motors. At this factory, wheels and axles are being put together to be fitted to the truck. Today, much of the work is carried out by machines, but some tasks, such as precision welding (joining of metal parts), still have to be done by hand.

Machines lighten the load

A Paved Concrete Track (PACT for short) machine is one way of taking the sweat out of laying railroad track. It lays a trackbed of continuous concrete. Then, when the concrete is dry, other machines lift and clip the metal rails on top. In another automated method of track-laying, complete sections of track are made in factories with the rails already fixed to concrete ties. They are then transported to the site and lifted into position by cranes. Machines that could do such jobs automatically were introduced in the mid-1900s. They allowed the work to be done much more quickly, involving fewer people and a lot less effort.

LOAD-BEARING TUNNEL

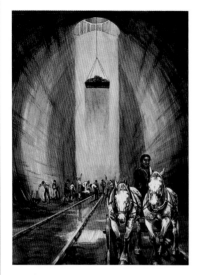

Tunnels often have to bear the weight of millions of tons of rocks and earth—or even water—above them. One way of preventing the tunnel collapsing is to make a continuous brick arch run along the length of the tunnel. Wedge-shaped keystones at the peak of the arch lock the whole structure together and support the arch and everything else above it. An arched roof is much stronger than a flat roof, because any weight above the tunnel is passed down through the sides of the arch and out toward the ground.

Between 1872 and 1882, a 9½-mile-long railway tunnel was driven through Europe's highest mountains, the Alps, to link Switzerland to northern Italy. The St. Gotthard tunnel was the greatest achievement in tunnel engineering of the time. Today, a long, train-like machine is used to build tunnels such as the Channel Tunnel. A big drill carves out the hole, sending the spoil backward on a conveyor belt. Behind it, robotic cranes lift precast concrete sections of the tunnel into place.

Keystone is key

Before a tunnel is built, engineers have to make sure the rock and soil are easy to cut through but firm enough not to collapse. A framework is used to build brick arches. The bricks are laid around both sides of the framework up toward the center. When the central keystone is in place, the arch will support itself and the framework can be removed.

SUPPORTING ARCH

You will need: two wooden building blocks or house bricks, two pieces of thick card (width roughly the same as the length of the blocks or bricks), a few heavy pebbles.

1 Place one of the pieces of card on top of the building blocks. Place pebbles on top as shown above. You will see that the tunnel roof sags under the weight.

2 Curve a second piece of card under the flat roof as shown. The roof supports the weight of the pebbles because the arch supports the flat section, making it stronger.

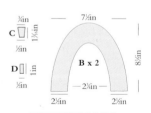

KEYSTONE

You will need: masking tape, piece of thick card measuring 18 x 10½ in., two sheets of thick card measuring 14¼ x 12 in., ruler, pencil, scissors, piece of thin card measuring 17¼ x 16 in., newspaper, cup of flour, ½ cup of water, acrylic paints, paintbrush, water pot, piece of thin card (11 x 8½ in.), glue and glue brush.

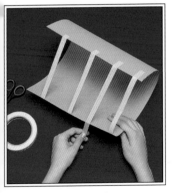

1 Tear off about four long strips of masking tape. Curve the 18 x 10½-in. rectangle of card lengthwise. Use the tape to hold the curve in place as shown above.

2 Copy the two templates A on to two 14½ x 12-in. pieces of thick card. Cut out the shapes. Attach each one to the sides of the tunnel and secure with tape as shown above.

3 Fold the 17¼ x 16-in. thin card in half. Copy the arch template B on to the card. Cut out to make two tunnel entrances. Stick these to the tunnel with masking tape as shown.

4 Scrunch newspaper into balls and tape to the tunnel and landscape. Mix the flour and water to make a thick paste. Dip newspaper strips in the paste. Layer them over the tunnel.

5 Leave to dry. When completely dry and hard, remove the tape and paint the tunnel and landscape green. Apply three coats, letting each one dry before you apply the next.

6 Paint the 11 x 8½-in. thin card to look like bricks. Draw and cut out templates C and D. Draw around C to make two keystones and D to make lots of bricks. Carefully cut the shapes out.

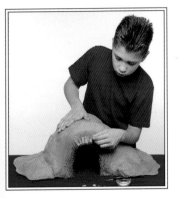

7 When the paint is dry, glue the keystones at the very top of each tunnel entrance. Then glue bricks around the arch either side of the keystone as shown. In a real tunnel, there would have been lots of central keystones running along the length of the tunnel.

8 Add finishing touches to your model using brown and green paints. Scrunch up newspaper into balls and dip them in the paste to make fake bushes. Leave them to dry and then paint them with brown and green paints. Do at least two or three coats. Leave them to dry between coats.

STATION STOP

ONCE PASSENGER trains began running in the 1830s, people needed special buildings where they could buy tickets and shelter from the weather while they waited to board. No one had ever designed or built train stations before. The owners of the new railroad companies wanted to make as much money as possible, so they had big, impressive mainline stations built to attract customers. Long platforms were essential for trains with many cars, so that passengers could get on and off trains safely. There also had to be waiting rooms and restaurants, as well as offices where station staff worked.

London's Euston Station was the first to have separate platforms for arrivals and departures. This train station was also among the earliest to have a metal and glass roof over the platforms. Euston was opened in 1838. From then on, most big train stations had glass and metal roofs. They were relatively cheap and easy to build, and they also let in a lot of daylight, which helped to save money on artificial lighting. In those days, lighting was provided by expensive gas lamps.

Housed in style
An early steam train puffs out of the first circular roundhouses, built in 1847 in London. Even the roundhouses where steam locomotives were housed for maintenance or repair were well designed. In the middle of these circular sheds was a turntable with short sections of track arranged around it, rather like the spokes of a wheel. Locomotives were parked on each section of track and released when they were needed for a journey.

Decorative ironwork
The iron pillars of stations in the 1900s were cast into a fantastic variety of shapes and then beautifully painted. At this time, cast iron was one of the latest building materials. Cast-iron pillars and arches were fairly cheap and quick to erect, as well as being a strong framework for station walls and roofs.

Temples of fashion
Bristol Temple Meads Station, Britain, looked like this in the 1800s. Engineers and architects tried to make their train stations stylish as well as be functional. During the 1800s, it was fashionable to copy the great building styles of the past. Bristol Temple Meads Station imitated the magnificent Gothic cathedrals and churches of medieval times. Small country stations, on the other hand, often looked like cottages or suburban villas.

Classical train station

The main station building of Washington Union Station in the USA is typical of train stations built in the early 1900s. It has a lofty vaulted ceiling and interiors made of paneled wood. It was opened in 1907 and was built by the Washington Terminal Company, which was specially formed by railroad companies serving the city.

German hub

Busy Cologne *Hauptbahnhof* (main train station) is at the center of Germany's vast rail network in the northwest of the country. The old steel-and-glass train shed was damaged during World War II (1939–45) but was later rebuilt. The front of the station has today been completely rebuilt with a more modern frontage.

Simple fare

Unlike the train stations that serve cities, country train stations are often very basic, such as this one at Pargothan, India. There are no platforms, and passengers climb into the trains from the track.

Single span

Atocha is the terminal of Spain's *Alta Velocita Española* (AVE) high-speed rail link between the capital, Madrid, and Seville in southern Spain. It was built in the early 1890s, and it serves all routes to the south, east and southeast of Madrid. It is Spain's largest train station and is famous for its single-span arched roof.

FACT BOX
• The world's largest train station is Beijing West Railway Station in China. It covers 133 acres and is bigger than the world's smallest country, the Vatican City in Rome, Italy.

• The world's highest train station is at Condor in Bolivia, South America. It is at 15,702 feet above sea level, 1,010 feet higher than the Matterhorn Mountain in the Alps.

• The world's busiest train station is Clapham Junction in south London, Britain. More than 2,000 trains pass through the station every 24 hours.

SHRINKING WORLD

BEFORE THE coming of the railroads, the fastest way to travel was on horseback. Even though the swiftest racehorse can gallop at more than 37 mph, it cannot keep this speed up for longer than a few minutes. Trains, on the other hand, can travel at high speed for hours on end. They can also transport hundreds of people at a time, or tens of carloads of freight, across vast distances. As more and more railroad lines began snaking across the countryside, life speeded up and the world seemed to grow smaller. People and goods could reach places they had never been to before.

During the 1800s, railroad technology spread from Britain all over the world. Tracks were laid between towns and cities at first. Later, railroads slowly grew to link countries and span continents. The world's first transcontinental railroad was completed in the USA in 1869. The expansion of the railroad system in the USA was rapid. Railroads were built through areas that had not yet been settled and played an important part in opening up many parts of the country.

Ticket to ride
Cheap, speedy trains meant that for the first time ordinary people, rather than the wealthy, could travel for pleasure. Train companies began offering day-excursion trips in the early 1830s. Outings to the seaside were particularly popular.

Ceremonial spike
On May 10, 1869, a golden spike was hammered into the track when the world's first transcontinental railroad was completed, linking the east and west coasts of the USA. The railroad was built by two companies, and the spike marked the meeting place of the two tracks at Promontory Summit in Utah.

FACT BOX
• With more than 149,000 miles of rail track, the USA has the world's longest network of railroads—just about enough to wrap around the Equator six times.

• It takes just over eight days to ride the entire length of the world's longest railroad, the Trans-Siberian line in Asia. This railroad, which opened in 1903, runs for 5,972 miles from Moscow to Vladivostok.

Desert runner
When surveyors planned the western section of Australia's transcontinental railroad, they plotted what is still the world's longest stretch of straight track. This 297-mile section lies within a vast, treeless desert called the Nullarbor Plain between Port Augusta and Kalgoorlie in southwestern Australia. The western section of this transcontinental railroad opened in 1917. The luxury Indian Pacific service was launched in 1969. Today, the 2,461-mile journey from Sydney to Perth takes just under three days.

Ruling by rail

A steam train passes over a bridge in India. During the 1800s, the British gradually introduced railroad networks to India and other countries in the British Empire. By speeding up the movement of government officials and the military, trains helped Britain keep control of its empire. Trade goods could be moved more quickly, too, which benefited British-owned companies. By 1939, India had more than 31,000 miles of track.

Keeping up with the times

The time in any place in the world is calculated from Greenwich Mean Time, which is the local time at 0 degrees longitude at Greenwich in London, England. Local time in other countries is calculated as either behind or in front of Greenwich Mean Time. Before the railroads, even cities within the same country kept their own local time, and accurate timetables were impossible. Timekeeping had to be standardized if people were to know when to catch their trains. British railroad companies standardized timekeeping using Greenwich Mean Time in 1847.

Coast-to-coast challenge

Pulled by diesel locomotives, passenger trains can today make the spectacular 2,890-mile journey across Canada in three days. When the Canadian Pacific transcontinental railroad was completed in 1887, the trip took steam trains about a week. The biggest challenge for the army of workers who built the railroad was taking the track through the Rocky Mountains—at Kicking Horse Pass, it climbs to 5,328ft.

A PASSION FOR TRAINS

IN 1830, a young British actress called Fanny Kemble wrote to a friend about her railroad journey pulled by a "brave little she-dragon … the magical machine with its wonderful flying white breath and rhythmical unvarying pace."

Over the years, all sorts of people—young and old, male and female, rich and poor—have caught Fanny's enthusiasm for trains. Some people love traveling on them, enjoying the scenery flickering past the windows and chatting to the strangers they meet on the journey. Others are happiest when they are standing at the end of a platform, spotting trains and noting down locomotive numbers. Other train buffs spend their spare time building their own private museum of railroad history. They collect anything from old tickets, timetables, and luggage labels, to early signaling equipment, station clocks, and locomotive numberplates. Some people "collect" journeys and take pride in traveling on some of the world's most famous railroads.

Museum piece
You can still ride a real steam train today, although in most countries only where short stretches of line have been preserved. Many classic locomotives of the past are on display in railroad museums. Visitors can usually get close enough to touch, and sometimes they are allowed to climb up inside the engineer's cab. You should never get this close when spotting working trains, however. Always stand well back on the platform, and never climb down onto the track.

Railroad mania
The walls of this train buff's room are decorated with prizes collected during years of hunting through junk shops and rummage sales, and attending specialist auctions. Lamps and many other pieces of railroad and station equipment came onto the market in Britain during the 1960s, when the government closed down hundreds of country railroad stations and branch lines.

Collecting signals

During the late 1900s, many old semaphore signals such as the ones in this picture were made redundant. They were replaced with color-light signals controlled from towers. Much of the old signaling was purchased by Britain's heritage railroads, but a few train buffs bought signals for their gardens. The ones in this picture are Great Western Railroad design signals, dating from the 1940s.

Museum pieces

The Baltimore and Ohio Museum was set up in the city of Baltimore, Maryland, by the Baltimore and Ohio Railroad in 1953. The main exhibits are displayed in a full-circle roundhouse in what used to be the railroad's shops. The exhibits feature a full range of locomotives from the last 180 years. They include a replica of the first American steam locomotive and a recently retired diesel passenger locomotive.

Tickets, please

Railroad tickets and timetables are all collectable items for those who are interested in trains and train journeys. A trainspotter's handbook and a set of railroad timetables are essential equipment for the serious train buff. In many countries, specialist bookshops sell handbooks that list all the working locomotives of the day.

WARNING BOX

- At stations, always stand well back from the platform edge.
- On bridges, never climb up walls or fences to get a better view—move somewhere else.
- Railroad lines sometimes have fences on either side of the track to keep people a safe distance from passing trains. Stand behind the fence—never climb over it.
- Modern trains are fast and make very little noise. If you disregard these simple rules, you will be risking your life.

Number crunching

Locomotives have number plates in much the same way that cars have license plates. The number plate is usually on the front of the engine, as can be seen on the front of this locomotive from the Czech Republic. In many countries, train buffs aim to collect the number of every working locomotive, but with so many locomotives in operation, it is a very time-consuming hobby.

TRAINS IN MINIATURE

MODEL TRAINS are just about as old as steam locomotives. The first ones were not for children, though. They were made for the locomotive manufacturers of the early 1800s to show how the newly invented, full-sized machines worked.

Although most toy trains are miniature versions of the real thing, they come in different scales or sizes. Most are built in O scale, which is ⅟₄₈ the size of the real train. The smallest are Z scale, which is ⅟₂₂₀th the size of a real train. Z-scale locomotives are small enough to fit inside a matchbox! It is extremely difficult to make accurate models to this small a scale, so Z-scale train sets are usually the hardest to find in stores and the most expensive to buy.

All the exterior working parts of the original are shown on the best model locomotives, from the smokestack on top of the engine to the coupling and connecting rods.

Smile, please
In the early 1900s, a few lucky children owned their own toy train. Some early toy trains had clockwork motors or tiny steam engines. Others were "carpet-runners." These were simply pushed or pulled along the floor.

Top-class toys
One British manufacturer of model trains was Bassett-Lowke, the maker of this fine model of *Princess Elizabeth*. Another manufacturer was Hornby, whose trains first went on sale in the 1920s. Hornby quickly grew into Britain's most popular model. Lionel is probably the leading manufacturer of miniature trains in the USA. All these companies produce many different models of real-life trains.

A model world
In the 1920s, toymakers began producing small-scale tabletop model railroads. Train stations and track took up less space than older, larger-scale models had needed. Many of these models were electric-powered and made from cast metal and tin plate by the German firm Bing. Today, these models are very valuable.

The German connection

Model trains are being made at the Fleischmann Train Factory, Nuremberg, Germany. Fleischmann produces highly detailed models of the full range of modern European trains. Like earlier model-railroad manufacturers, Fleischmann does not only make the trains. Collectors and model-railroad buffs can also buy everything that goes to make up a railroad, including signals and towers, lights and level crossings, roundhouses, bridges, and tunnels. There are even train stations and platforms with miniature newspaper stands, station staff, and passengers.

Model behavior

In the earliest train sets, miniature locomotives hauled cars on a never-ending journey around a circular track. Gradually, toymakers began selling more complex layouts, with several sets of track linked by points. Trains could switch from one track to another, just as in real railroads.

Ticket to ride

Model trains come in all sizes, including those that are large enough for children and adults to ride on. These miniature trains have all the working parts and features of their full-sized parents, including a tiny firebox which the engineer stokes with coal to keep the train chuffing along. In the USA in the late 1890s, small-gauge lines were appearing at showgrounds and in amusement parks. By the 1920s, longer miniature railroads were being built in Britain and Germany. Today, many theme parks feature a miniature railroad.

MODEL LOCOMOTIVES

A precision toy
As manufacturing techniques improved, so toy trains became increasingly sophisticated. Today, accurate, working, scale models have all the features of full-size working trains.

TOY TRAINS started to go on sale during the mid-1800s. Early toy trains were made of brightly painted wood, and often had a wooden track to run along. Soon, metal trains went on sale, many of them made from tin plate (thin sheets of iron or steel coated with tin). Some of these metal toy trains had windup clockwork motors. Clockwork toy trains were first sold in the USA during the 1880s. The most sophisticated model trains were steam-powered, with tiny engines fired by methylated-spirit burners. Later model trains were powered by electric motors.

Railroad companies often devised special color schemes, called liveries, for their locomotives and cars. Steam locomotives had brass and copper decoration, and some also carried the company's special logo or badge. Many toy trains are also painted in the livery of a real railroad company. The shape of the locomotive you can make in this project has a cab typical of the real locomotives made in the 1910s.

TOY TRAIN

You will need: *10¼ x 10¼-in. card, masking tape, scissors, ruler, pencil, 4 x 4-in. card, glue and glue brush, card for templates, paints, paintbrush, water pot, underframe from earlier project, two thumbtacks, 4½ x ½-in. red card, split pin.*

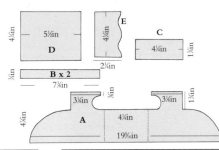

1 Roll the 10¼ x 10¼-in. card into an 3⅛-in. diameter tube. Secure it with masking tape. Cut a 2½-in. slit, 2 in. from one end of the tube.

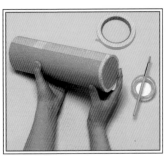

2 Hold the tube upright on the 4 x 4-in. piece of card. Draw around it. Cut this circle out. Glue the circle to the tube end farthest away from the slit. Tape to secure.

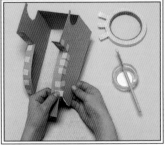

3 Copy and cut out templates. Fold template A along the dotted lines. Fold templates B across, 1¾ in. from one end. Glue both strips to the cab as shown and secure with tape.

4 When the glue is dry, gently peel off the masking tape. Now glue on template C as shown above. Hold it in place with masking tape until the glue dries.

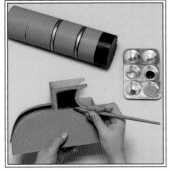

5 Apply two coats of green paint to the outside of the locomotive. Let the first coat dry before applying the second. Then paint the black parts. Add the red and gold last.

6 Glue around the bottom edge of the cab front C. Put a little glue over the slit in the tube. Fit the front of the cab into the slit. Leave the locomotive to one side to dry.

7 Give roof template D two coats of black paint. Let the paint dry between coats. Glue the top edges of the cab, and place the black roof on top. Leave until dry and firm.

8 Glue the bottom of the cylindrical part of the train to the underframe you made in the *Underframe* project. Press thumbtacks into back of cab and underframe.

9 Glue both sides of one end of the red strip. Slot this between the underframe and the cab, between the thumbtacks. When firm, fold the strip and insert the split pin.

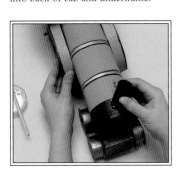

10 Paint one side of template E black. When dry, roll into a tube, and secure with masking tape. Glue wavy edge and secure to front of locomotive as shown above.

Just like a real locomotive, the basic color of your model train has been enhanced with red, black, and gold decoration. The locomotive is now ready to run on the railroad line you made in the Making Tracks project. The engineer and fireman would have shared the cab of the locomotive. The engineer controlled the speed of the train, following the signals and track speed restrictions. The fireman insured a good supply of steam by stoking the fire and filling the boiler with water.

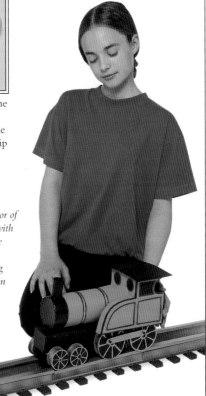

SIGNALS AND SIGNALING

THE EARLIEST railroads were single tracks that ran directly between one place and another. Later, more tracks were laid and branched off these main lines. Trains were able to cross from one line to another on movable sections of track called switches.

To avoid crashes, a system of signals was needed to show engineers if the track ahead was clear. The first signalers stood beside the track and waved flags during daylight or lamps at night. From 1841, human signalers were replaced by signals called semaphores on posts with wooden arms.

By 1889, three basics of rail safety were established by law in Britain – block, brake, and lock. Block involved stopping one train until the one in front had passed by. Brakes are an obvious safety feature on passenger trains. Lock meant that switches and signals had to be interlocked, so that a lever in the tower could not be pulled without changing both the switch and the signal.

Hand signals
The first people to be responsible for train safety in Britain were the railway police. The policemen used flags and lamps to direct the movements of trains. In the absence of flags, signals were given by hand. One arm outstretched horizontally meant "line clear," one arm raised meant "caution" and both arms raised meant "danger, stop."

Mechanical signals
A policeman operates a Great Western Railway disk and crossbar signal. The disk and crossbar were at right angles and rotated so the engineer could either see the full face of the disk, meaning "go," or the crossbar, meaning "stop."

Lighting up the night
Electric signals were not used until the 1920s, when color-light signals were introduced. Color-light signals look like road traffic lights. A green light means the track is clear, red shows danger, and yellow means caution. Color-light signals, such as these in France, are accompanied by displays showing the number of the signal, speed restrictions, and other information for engineers.

Signal improvements

This hand-operated signal frame features details dating from the 1850s, when a signaling system called interlocking was introduced. Signals and switches were interlocked (linked) so that a single lever moved a signal and the set of switches it protected at the same time. Tower levers were moved by hand to set signals and switches in those days. In many countries today, signals are set automatically by computers that are housed in a central signaling control room.

Safety first

Semaphore signals such as these made a major difference to railroad safety when they were introduced during the 1840s. At first, railroad companies throughout the world used semaphore signals with oil lamps behind colored glass to show if the track was clear at night (green light) or at danger (red light). From the 1920s, many countries upgraded their systems by introducing electric color-light signals.

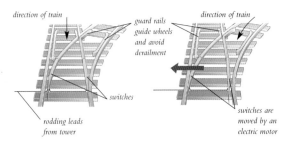

direction of train

guard rails guide wheels and avoid derailment

direction of train

switches

rodding leads from tower

switches are moved by an electric motor

Switches and humpyard

Trains are "switched" from one track to another using switches. Part of the track, called the blade, moves so that the wheels are guided smoothly from one route onto the other. The blade moves as a result of a signaler pulling a lever in the tower. The blade and lever are connected by a system of metal rods, and the lever cannot be pulled unless the signal is clear. From the late 1800s, railroad companies built humpyards. These made it easier to shunt freight cars together to make a freight train. As the cars went over a hump in the yard, they uncoupled. When they went down the hump, they could be switched into different sidings using a set of switches.

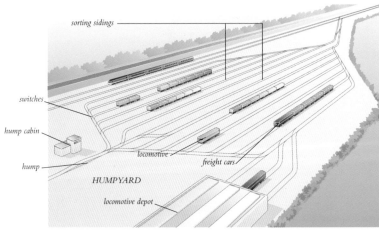

sorting sidings

switches

hump cabin

hump

locomotive

freight cars

HUMPYARD

locomotive depot

SAFETY FIRST

A CCIDENTS ARE a tragic feature of railroad travel today, but trains remain the safest form of land transport in most countries. Modern technology is largely responsible for the improvements in rail safety. In Britain, trains are fitted with an Automatic Warning System (AWS). If the signal indicates that the track ahead is clear, electric magnets between the rails send a message to equipment under the train. This causes a bell to sound in the engineer's cab. If the signal is not clear, the magnet stays "dead," and a horn sounds in the cab. If the engineer does not react, the brakes come on automatically. An improved system, called Train Protection and Warning System (TPWS), uses existing AWS but also provides an automatic stop at a red signal and a speed trap in advance of the signal.

A more advanced system is Automatic Train Protection (ATP). The train picks up electronic messages from the track, and they tell the engineer to slow down or stop. If he or she fails to respond, there is a warning and the brakes come on. ATP also slows or stops the train if it exceeds the speed limit.

On collision course
Head-on crashes were more common in the early days of the railroads, even though there were far fewer trains. On some routes, there was only a single-track line. A train heading toward a station was in danger of meeting another train leaving it. In most countries today, trains are timetabled so that no two are on the same line at the same time. This situation can only arise if a train passes a stop signal at a set of switches.

Japanese crash
A crane lifts a derailed train along the Hanshin Railway near Shinzaike Station. The accident was caused by an earthquake that devastated the city of Kobe on the Japanese island of Honshu in 1995. Several stations and several miles of elevated railroad lines were destroyed on the three main lines that run from Kobe to Osaka.

Control center

From the 1960s, signaling over large areas has been controlled from centralized towers. The towers have a control panel that displays all the routes, signals, and switches that the tower controls. Signalers set up safe routes for trains in the area by operating switches and buttons. Signals work automatically, and the switches change using electronic controls. This insures trains cannot get onto routes where there is an oncoming train. In the most modern signaling centers, the routes appear on computer monitors. The signaler uses a cursor to set up routes instead of using buttons and switches.

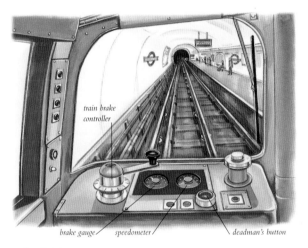

train brake controller

brake gauge / *speedometer* / *deadman's button*

In the driving seat

The control desk of a London Underground, or "Tube," train has a number of standard safety features. The train brake controller is a manual control to slow the train. The deadman's button must be pressed down continually by the motorman while the train is moving. If the motorman collapses, the button comes up and the train stops.

Onboard safety

In the event of an emergency, passengers will always find standard safety devices, such as fire extinguishers and first-aid kits, on board a train.

Buffer zone

Buffers stop trains at the end of a line. They are made of metal or wood and metal and are fixed to the track. They are strong enough to absorb much of the energy of a colliding train. Signals control a train's speed so that even if a train collides with the bufferstops, it is usually traveling slowly.

CABOOSE

F EW EARLY steam locomotives had brakes. If the engineer needed to stop quickly, he had to throw the engine into reverse. By the early 1860s, braking systems for steam locomotives had been invented. Some passenger cars also had their own handbrakes that were operated by the conductors. A caboose was added to the back of trains, too, but its brakes were operated by a brakeman riding inside.

The problem was that the engineer had no control over the rest of the train. When he wanted to stop, he had to blow the engine whistle to warn each of the conductors to apply their brakes.

The brakes on a locomotive and its cars or freight cars needed to be linked. This was made possible by the invention of an air-braking system in 1869. When the engineer applies the brakes, compressed air travels along pipes linking all parts of the train and presses brake shoes. Air brakes are now used on nearly all the world's railroads.

Coupling up

A locomotive is joined up to a car by a connection called a coupler. At first, chains or rigid bars were used to join cars. Later, a rigid hook at the end of one vehicle connected to chains on the front of the next. From the late 1800s, couplers made from steel castings and springs were used, but uncoupling was done by hand. Today, passenger trains couple and uncouple automatically.

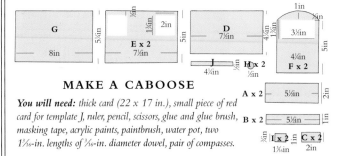

MAKE A CABOOSE

You will need: *thick card (22 x 17 in.), small piece of red card for template J, ruler, pencil, scissors, glue and glue brush, masking tape, acrylic paints, paintbrush, water pot, two 1⅟₁₆-in. lengths of ⁵⁄₁₆-in. diameter dowel, pair of compasses.*

1 Copy the templates on to card and cut them out. Glue templates A, B and C together to make the underframe as shown. Tape over the joins to secure them.

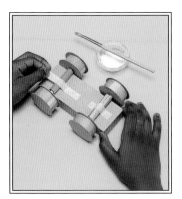

2 Make and paint two pairs of small wheels (2-in diameter) following steps 1 to 5 in the *Underframe* project. Glue and tape the wheel pairs to the underframe.

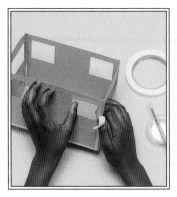

3 Glue the bottom edges of the caboose sides (E) to the caboose base (D). Then glue on the caboose ends (F). Secure the joins with masking tape until the glue is dry.

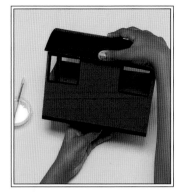

4 Paint the caboose brown with black details and the wheels and underframe black and silver. Apply two coats of paint, letting each one dry between coats.

5 Paint one side of template G black. Let the paint dry before applying a second coat. Glue the top edges of the caboose. Bend the roof to fit on the top of the caboose.

6 Apply glue to the top surface of the underframe. Stick the caboose centrally on top. Press together until the glue holds firm. Leave to dry completely.

7 Roll up templates I into two ¾-in. tubes to fit loosely over the dowel. Tape to hold and paint them silver. Paint the buffer templates H black and stick on each dowel.

8 Use compasses to pierce two holes 1 in. from each side of the caboose and ⅜ in. up. Enlarge with a pencil. Glue the end of each dowel buffer. Slot it into the hole. Leave to dry.

9 Cut a slot between the buffers. Fold red card template J in half. Glue each end to form a loop. Push the closed end into the slot. Hold it in place until the glue dries.

The caboose will also run on the tracks you made in the Making Tracks *project. You can also join the red-card coupler to join the caboose to the model locomotive you made in the* Toy Train *project. On old-style railroads, the caboose was at the back of the train so that the conductor could make sure that all the carriages stayed coupled. The caboose had one of two brake systems. One had hand-operated brakes that worked on the tread of the caboose's wheels. The other had a valve that allowed the brakeman to apply air brakes to all vehicles in the train.*

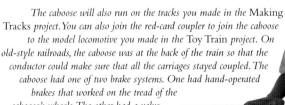

HAULING FREIGHT

Most of the traffic on the world's railroads is made up of freight trains that transport goods such as coal and iron ore from mines and cloth and other manufactured goods from factories. The earliest freight trains were slow because they did not have effective braking systems. Technical developments now mean that freight trains can run much faster than before.

Freight trains made a vast difference to everyday life as the rail networks expanded and brought the country nearer to the city. For the first time, fresh food could be delivered quickly from country farms to city markets. People could also afford to heat their homes. The price of coal for household fires came down because moving coal by train was cheaper and faster than by horse-drawn carts or canal.

In the mid-1900s, motor vehicles and airplanes offered an alternative way of transporting freight. However, concerns about congestion and the environment mean that freight trains continue to be the cheapest, quickest, and most environmentally friendly way of hauling a large volume of freight overland.

Four-legged freight service
The world's first public railroad opened in 1803—for horse-drawn freight cars. The Surrey Iron Railway ran for a little more than 8 miles between Wandsworth and Croydon near London. It went past a number of mills and factories. The factory owners paid a toll to use the railroad and supplied their own horses and cars.

Rolling stock
Freight cars were ramshackle affairs when the first steam trains began running during the 1820s and 1830s. They had metal wheels but, unlike locomotives, they were mainly built from wood. Their design was based on the horse-drawn carts or coal cars they were replacing. Waterproof tarpaulins were tied over goods to protect them from the weather.

Slow but steady
In the early 1800s, the first steam locomotives hauled coal cars called chaldrons from collieries to ships on nearby rivers. The locomotives were not very powerful. They could pull only a few cars at a time. Going any faster would have been dangerous because neither the locomotives nor the cars had much in the way of brakes!

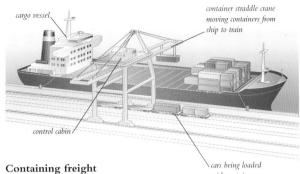

cargo vessel

container straddle crane moving containers from ship to train

control cabin

cars being loaded with containers

Mail by rail

Railroads first carried mail in the 1830s. A special mail car was introduced in Britain in 1838. Post Office workers on board sorted the mail for delivery while the train was moving. Modern versions of these traveling mail rooms still operate today.

Containing freight

From the 1960s, metal containers like giant boxes have transported goods by sea, rail, and road. They are a way of combining different methods of transporting goods in the most effective way possible. The containers are simply lifted from one vehicle to another using large cranes called straddle cranes. The trains usually have specially designed flatcars onto which the containers are locked into position. The containers remain sealed, apart from when they are inspected by customs officials.

```
FACT BOX
• Today, freight trains haul bulky loads, such as
coal, oil, and minerals, in purpose-built cars.

• As many as 10,000 freight trains crisscross the
USA every day.

• Some of the world's freight trains have
200 cars and can be up to 2½ miles long.

• Modern diesel and electric freight trains can
haul heavy loads at speeds of up to 75 miles.
```

Bulk transportation

Today, freight trains mainly transport heavy, bulky loads such as coal, iron ore, grain, or building materials. Smaller, lighter goods are usually sent by road or air. Railroad companies pioneered the idea of specially designed vehicles for different types of freight—tankers for liquids such as milk or chemicals, for example, and hoppers that tip sideways for unloading gravel or coal.

Chinese circle

From the mid-1900s, Chinese electric locomotives such as this hauled ore hoppers. The trains carried iron ore to be smelted in blast furnaces on an 50 mile circular line. The locomotives were based on a Swiss design. They had a sloping front so that the driver could see easily from the cab.

GOING UNDERGROUND

RAILROAD NETWORKS made it easier for people to travel from the country to cities and towns to shop or work. During the 1800s, the streets within cities became extremely crowded with people and traffic. One way of coping with the problem of moving around the cities was to tunnel underground.

The world's first passenger subway system opened in 1863. It was the Metropolitan Line between Paddington Station and Farringdon Street in London, Britain. Steam locomotives hauled the passenger cars, and smoke in the tunnels was a big problem. The locomotives were fitted with structures called condensers that were supposed to absorb the smoke, but they did not work properly. Passengers on the trains traveled through a fog-like darkness. Those waiting at the stations choked on the smoke drifting out from the tunnels.

The answer was to use electric trains, and the first underground electric railroad opened in London in 1890. Today, nearly every major city in the world has its own subway system.

Cut-and-cover construction
The first underground passenger railroads were built using a new method called cut-and-cover construction. A large trench—usually 33 feet wide by 16 feet deep—was cut into the earth along the railroad's proposed route. Then the trench was lined with brickwork and it was roofed over. After that, the streets were re-laid on top of the tunnel.

Tunnel maze
This cross section of the underground system in central London in 1864 shows the proposed route of the new Charing Cross line beneath the existing Metropolitan Line. Deep-level subways were not built until 1890, when developments such as ways of digging deeper tunnels, electric locomotives, better elevators, and escalators became a reality.

Underground shelters
Londoners came up with another use for their city's warren of underground railroad tunnels during World War II (1939–45). They used them as deep shelters from night-time bombing raids. The electric lines were switched off, and people slept wherever they could find enough room to lie down. Canteens were set up on many platforms. More than 130,000 gallons of tea and cocoa were served every night.

Keeping up with the times

The Washington DC Metro in the USA was opened in 1976. It is one of the world's newest and most up-to-date subway systems. The trains have no motormen and the entire network is controlled automatically by a computerized central control system. Passengers traveling in the air-conditioned cars have a smooth, fast ride due to the latest techniques in train and track construction. The airy, 200-yard-long train stations are much more spacious than those built in the early 1900s.

Overground undergrounds

Work started on the first 6-mile-long section of the Paris *Metro* in 1898 and took over two years to complete. The engineers who designed early underground subways, such as the Paris *Metro,* often found it quicker and easier to take sections above ground, particularly when crossing rivers. The station entrances were designed by French architect Hector Guimard in the then-fashionable Art Nouveau style. They made the Paris *Metro* one of the most distinctive and stylish subway systems in the world.

Mechanical earthworm

The cutting head of a Tunnel-Boring Machine (TBM), which was used to bore the Channel Tunnel between England and France. The 26-foot-wide cutting head is covered with diamond-studded teeth. As the TBM rotates, the teeth rip through the earth. The waste material, or spoil, falls onto a conveyor belt and is transported to the surface. The cutting head grips against the sides of the tunnel and inches farther forward under the pressure of huge rams. As the tunnel is cut, cranes line the tunnel with curved concrete segments that arrive on conveyors at the top and bottom of the TBM.

RIDING HIGH

I N SOME of the world's cities, the solution to overcrowded streets was to build railway networks above ground level. The earliest kind of overhead trains ran on a twin-rail track. The track was raised above the ground on arching, viaduct-like supports. These "elevated railways" were built in several American and European cities from the mid-1800s onward.

Today, some overhead trains run along a single rail called a monorail. Some are suspended systems in which the train hangs beneath the rail. Others are straddle systems in which the train sits over the rail.

Twin-rail systems called Light Rapid Transit (LRT) are now more common than monorails. They are described as "light" because they carry fewer people and therefore need lighter-weight vehicles and track than mainline, or "heavy," railways. In many cities, LRT cars are like a cross between a streetcar and a train. They run on rails through town and city streets, as well as through underground tunnels and along elevated tracks.

Wonder of Wuppertal
The oldest working monorail in the world is located in Wuppertal, Germany. Almost 20 million passengers have traveled along the 8-mile-long route since it opened in 1901. It is suspended about 33 feet above the ground. The wheels run along the top of the rail.

Flying train
Inventor George Bennie's experimental monorail was one of the strangest ever built. The streamlined machine was named the Railplane. It had airplane propellers front and back to thrust it along. It first "flew" in July 1930, along a 44-yard-long test line over a railroad track near Glasgow in Scotland.

Climb every mountain
The Paris funicular climbs to the city's highest point, the top of Montmartre. Funiculars were invented during the 1800s and are used to move cars up and down hillsides or steep slopes. Usually, there are two parallel tracks. Each one has a passenger-carrying car attached. In the early days, each car carried a large water tank that was filled with water at the top of the slope and emptied at the bottom. The extra weight of the car going down pulled the lighter car up. Later funiculars have winding drums powered by electricity to haul a cable up and down.

Tomorrow's world

During the 1950s, American film producer Walt Disney wanted to have a monorail for his futuristic Tomorrowland attraction when he built his first Disneyland theme park in California. The monorail opened in 1959 and was an immediate success with visitors. Disney was trying to promote monorails as the transportation system of the future, but his railroad had just the opposite effect. For many years, monorails were seen as little more than amusement-park rides.

FACT BOX
• New Yorkers nicknamed their elevated railroad the "El." It opened in 1867. By 1900, more than 300 steam locomotives and 1,000 passenger cars were operating on its 36-mile-long network.

Not everyone's darling

The monorail system in Sydney, Australia, links the heart of the city to a tourist development in nearby Darling Harbour. It has proved to be popular since it opened in 1988, carrying about 30,000 people a day along its 2-mile-long route. Many people who lived in Sydney were concerned that the elevated route would be an eyesore, particularly in older parts of the city. Protesters tried hard to block the monorail's construction. Today, it has become part of everyday life for many people who live in Sydney.

London's LRT

The Docklands Light Railway in London opened in 1987. It was Britain's first Light Rapid Transit (LRT) to have driverless vehicles controlled by a computerized control system. However, it was not Britain's first LRT. That prize went to Newcastle's Tyne and Wear Metro, which began running in 1980. LRTs provide a frequent service, with unstaffed stations and automatic ticket machines. Many cities throughout the world have chosen to install them in preference to monorails because they are cheaper to run.

MONORAIL

MONORAILS DATE back to the 1820s. As with early trains, these early monorails were pulled by horses and carried heavy materials such as building bricks, rather than passengers. About 60 years later, engineers designed steam locomotives that hauled cars along A-shaped frameworks. However, neither the trains nor the cars were very stable. Loads had to be carefully balanced on either side of the A-frame to stop them tipping off.

Today's monorails are completely stable, with several sets of rubber wheels to give a smooth ride. They are powered by electricity, and many are driverless. Like fully automatic LRTs, driverless monorail trains are controlled by computers that tell them when to stop, start, speed up or slow down.

Monorails are not widely used today because they are more expensive to run than two-track railroads. The special monorail track costs more to build and is more of an eyesore than two-track lines. The cars cannot be switched from one track to another, and it is expensive to change or extend a monorail line.

Staying on track
Vertical sets of running wheels carry the weight of this modern monorail and keep it on top of the huge rail. Other horizontal sets of wheels, called guides and stabilizers, run along the sides of the rail. They keep the train on course and stop it from tipping when it goes around bends.

MODEL MONORAIL

You will need: sheet of protective paper, 28¼-in. length of wood (1½ x 1½ in.), acrylic paints, paintbrush, water pot, 26½-in. length of plastic curtain rail (with screws, end fittings and four plastic runners), saw, screwdriver, sheet of red card, pencil, ruler, scissors, double-sided scotch tape, 7-in. length of 1-in.-thick foam board, glue and glue brush, black felt-tip pen.

3¾in
¾in
7½in
7½in
2⅛in 1⅜in 2⅛in ¾in
¾in

1 Cover the work surface with paper to protect it. Then paint the block of wood yellow. Let the first coat dry thoroughly before applying a second coat of paint.

2 Ask an adult to saw the curtain rail to size if necessary. Place the track centrally on the wood and screw it into place. Screw in the end fittings at one end of the rail.

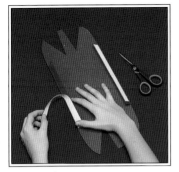

3 Copy the template onto the red card and cut it out. Score along the dotted lines and fold inward. Stick double-sided scotch tape along the outside of each folded section.

4 Remove the backing from the tape. Stick one side of the foam onto it. Fold the card over and press the other piece of double-sided tape to the opposite side of the foam.

5 Overlap the pointed ends at the back and front of the train and glue. Then glue the inside end of the top flaps, back and front. Fold them over and press firmly to secure.

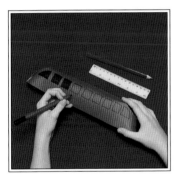

6 Pencil in windows along both sides of the train. Fill them in with a black felt-tip pen. Paint decorative black and yellow stripes along the bottom of the windows.

7 Put a dab of glue on the "eye" end of each plastic runner. Hold the train, foam bottom toward you. Push each runner in turn into the foam at roughly equal intervals.

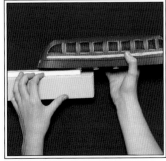

8 Stand the track on a flat surface. At the end of the track without an end stop, feed each plastic runner into the track. Run the train back and forth along the track.

The train you have made in this project is called a "straddle" system monorail. Monorail trains running on the straddle system rest on a single rail and are balanced and guided by side panels on either side of the train.

WORKING ON THE RAILROADS

A S THE railroads grew ever larger, so did the number of people employed to keep them running safely and on time. In Britain, for example, about 47,000 people worked for the railroad companies by the late 1840s. Today, about 95,000 people are employed on the British railroads—seven times less than during World War I (1914–18). One reason is that some jobs that were once done by people, such as selling tickets, are now done by machines. Automation has not been widespread, however. Most railroads around the world have little money to buy computers and control systems.

Stationmasters and train conductors are just some of the people who talk to passengers and deal with their needs. Most railroad employees work behind the scenes, however, and rarely meet passengers. Managers plan how many trains should run on a particular line, how often, and how fast. Engineering teams check and keep the tracks, signals, and other equipment in safe working order.

Standing on the footplate
Two men worked in the cab. They stood on the footplate because there were no seats. The engineer was in charge. He managed the engine controls and the main brakes and kept a sharp look out for signals and anything blocking the track. The fireman stoked the fire and insured the boiler contained enough water.

Laying track
Track workers check a section of track that has been newly laid with stone ballast, ties, and rail. Rails should be checked regularly for cracks and deterioration. The ground beneath the rail can also subside and twist the rails.

Building trains
Workers in a factory are assembling an aluminum-bodied diesel train. Modern trains are built of either steel or aluminum sections welded together into a strong single unit. Separate units such as the driving cab, air-conditioning engine, and restrooms are fixed on the car later.

In the driving seat

Compared to the older steam engines, life is fairly comfortable in the cabs of modern locomotives. For a start, the engineer can sit down. They are also protected from the weather inside fully enclosed cabs, and they do not have to stick their heads outside to see the track ahead. Today's engineers still manage the controls and brakes, and watch out for signals and obstacles on the track. They also have a lot of help from computerized railroad systems.

Insect debris

The windows of this train are being cleaned by hand, since this is the most effective way to remove the accumulation of flying insects on the cab windows. The bodies of most trains are cleaned in automatic washing plants using revolving brushes, high-pressure water jets, and powerful cleaning agents that meet high environmental standards. In most cases, trains are cleaned every 24 hours when they come back to their home depot for examination and routine servicing.

Chefs on board

Armies of chefs and kitchen staff play an important role in making sure passengers do not go hungry during the journey. Most cooked food is prepared onboard the train using microwave ovens and electric burners. Almost all long-distance trains have dining and lounge cars, where passengers can take refreshments during their journeys. Even smaller trains often have buffet cars or mobile buffet carts.

DRESSED FOR THE JOB

MANY DIFFERENT railroad workers began wearing special hats and uniforms during the 1840s, from train engineers to stationmasters. A uniform makes the wearer look smart and efficient and lets him or her stand out in a crowd. This is essential if a passenger is looking for help in a busy train station. Uniforms are issued by the railroad companies. Each company usually has its own special design for hat badges and uniform buttons.

In the past, different kinds of hat or badge often went with different jobs. The engineers of steam locomotives, for example, used to wear caps with shiny tops. Firemen were not issued with hats or uniforms. They wore overalls and often covered their heads with a knotted handkerchief. The first stationmasters wore top hats instead of caps to show how important they were. When they later switched to caps, the brim was often decorated with gold braid, similar to the one you can make in this project.

Dressed for the job
A stationmaster and conductor at Osaka Railway Station in Japan wear their distinctive dark uniforms, caps, and sashes. The stationmaster, or area manager, has an extremely important role in running the railroads. He or she is in charge of all aspects of running the station and must insure that trains arrive and depart on time.

STATIONMASTER'S CAP

You will need: *thin red card measuring 24 x 3½ in., masking tape, thin red card measuring 4¼ x 4¼ in., pencil, scissors, thin red card measuring 10¼ x 6 in., glue and glue brush, sheet of white paper, pair of compasses, black felt, black paint, paintbrush, water pot, 16-in. length of gold braid, extra card, gold paint.*

1 Wrap the 24 x 3½-in. piece of red card around your head to get the right size. Then stick the two ends together with masking tape to make the circular crown of the hat.

2 Place the crown on the 4½ x 4½-in. piece of red card. Hold the crown firmly and draw around it on to the flat piece of card. Cut out the circle to make the top of your hat.

3 Place the card circle on top of the crown of the hat. Join the two parts of the hat together using lots of strips of masking tape all the way around the join.

4 Place the hat over part of the 10¼ x 6-in. piece of card. Draw a semi-circle by tracing around the hat edge. Start from one end of the semicircle, and draw a crescent shape as shown.

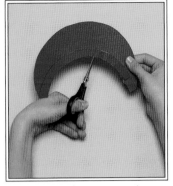

5 Use a pair of compasses to draw another semicircle ¾ in. in from the first. Cut out the crescent shape. Make cuts into the inner semicircle band all the way around to make tabs.

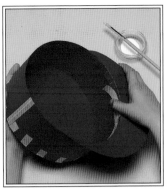

6 Fold the tabs up and glue around the edge of the crown where the peak will go. Fit the tabs inside the crown and stick them down. Cover the tabs with tape to hold firm.

7 Place the hat, top down, onto a sheet of paper. Draw and cut out a circle ½ in. wider than the hat. Pin it on the felt and cut out a felt circle. Glue this on to the top of the hat.

8 Cut a 24 x 4-in. piece of felt. Glue this to the side of the hat, folding under at the bottom. At the peak, make a ¾-in. cut in the felt, and trim off the excess as shown.

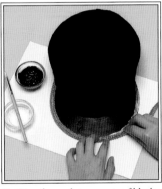

9 Give the peak two coats of black paint. Let the paint dry between coats. Then glue on a piece of gold braid as shown above.

10 Design your own hat badge or copy the one shown in the picture. Draw it on a small piece of card and paint it gold. When the paint is dry, cut it out. Glue it to the front of the hat.

If you have a whistle, you could attach it to a piece of gold ribbon and hang it around your neck to complete the outfit.

TRAVELING IN STYLE

IT WAS some time before traveling on a passenger train was as comfortable as waiting in one of the splendid stations. Before the 1850s, there were few luxuries and no restrooms, even on long journeys. The overall comfort of the journey depended on how much money you had paid for your ticket. First-class cars were—and still are—the most expensive and the most comfortable way to travel. Then came second class, third class, and sometimes even fourth class.

The pioneer of comfortable rail travel was a US businessman called George Pullman. In 1859, after a particularly unpleasant train journey, he designed a coach in which "people could sleep and eat with more ease and comfort." Pullman launched his sleeping car in 1864, and was soon exporting luxury sleeping and dining cars around the world.

First-class comforts
By the late 1800s, first-class passengers such as these elegantly dressed ladies enjoyed every comfort on their journey. There were soft, padded benches and armchairs and cloth-covered tea tables. The design of luxury railroad cars was based on that of top-class hotels. Windows had thick, plush curtains and fittings were made of polished wood and shiny brass.

Royal seal of approval
This luxurious railroad car was made specially for Britain's Queen Victoria, who reigned from 1837 until her death in 1901. It had padded walls, thick carpets, expensive paintings on the walls, and the finest decoration. Many European kings and queens had their own cars built so that they could travel in royal style. Queen Victoria's royal car included a sleeping compartment, and it is thought she enjoyed sleeping in it more than at her palaces.

The Blue Train
South Africa's Blue Trains run between Cape Town and Pretoria in South Africa and are regarded as the most luxurious trains in the world. Passengers benefit from a 24-hour butler and laundry service and two lounge cars, and all the suites are equipped with televisions and telephones.

Lap of luxury

The *Orient-Express* first graced the railroads of Europe in 1883. It formed a scheduled link between Paris, France, and Bucharest in Romania. The scheduled service stopped running in May 1977, and it was replaced by a new "tourist-only" *Orient-Express* in May 1982. Passengers can once again enjoy the comfortable sleeping cars with velvet curtains, plush seats, and five-course French cuisine in a Pullman dining car like the one shown above.

A rocky ride

The Canadian has a domed glass roof so that it offers spectacular views during the 2,776-mile journey from Toronto, on the east coast of Canada, to Vancouver, on the west. The journey lasts for three days and takes in the rolling prairies of Saskatchewan, Edmonton, and Alberta. It then begins the gradual ascent through the foothills of the Rocky Mountains.

Lounging about

Long-distance trains on the Indian Pacific line from Sydney, on the Pacific Ocean, to Perth, on the Indian Ocean, are well equipped for the 65-hour journey across Australia. Indeed, they are described as being "luxury hotels on wheels." Passengers can relax and enjoy the entertainment provided in the comfortable surroundings of the train's lounge cars. These trains also have cafeterias, smart dining cars, club cars, and two classes of accommodation. Passengers can eat, drink, and sleep in comfort. The trains are even equipped with a honeymoon suite and a sick bay.

ADVERTISING

I N THE early days of the railroads, radio and
television had not been invented. Rail companies
had to rely on printed advertisements to attract
passengers. Posters have long been used to attract
train travelers. At first, they were little more than
printed handbills—a few words with the odd
black-and-white picture. "The Wonder of 1851!
From York to London and back for a Crown," read
one British rail-company poster. A crown was
5 shillings (the equivalent of 35¢ in today's money).

Early posters were so basic because machines
for printing words and color pictures were not
developed until the late 1800s. Posters soon became
more colorful. For example, the French railroads
used eye-catching posters to advertise their new
electric services in the early 1900s. The pictures on
early railroad posters usually showed the destination
rather than the train—people travel on trains because
they want to go somewhere, after all. By promoting
new services and encouraging people to take
the train on vacation and on one-day trips, rail
companies helped to improve advertising methods.

Atlantic crossing
Britain's Southern Railway promoted both its own
train services and those of shipping company White
Star in this poster from the late 1920s. Passengers
could take the train to Southampton in England and
then join a White Star ship for the crossing to New
York in the USA. At that time, many railroads owned
shipping lines or worked with steamship companies.

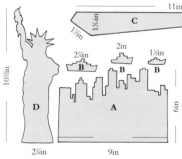

MAKE A POSTER

You will need: *protective paper, dark blue
card (10½ x 9 in.), acrylic paints, paintbrush,
water pot, glue and glue brush, cream card
(14¼ x 10 in.), light blue card (9 x 3⅛ in.
and 12 x 2 in.), pencil, ruler, scissors, large
sheet of black card, blue card (9 x 2¼ in.),
yellow card (12 x 4 in.), black pen.*

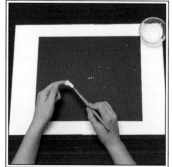

1 Cover the work surface and lay
the dark blue card on to it. Mix
some yellow and white paint, load a
paintbrush with paint and then flick
spots on to the card as shown above.

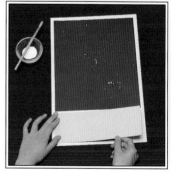

2 Glue the dark blue card onto
the cream card, leaving a ½-in.
border at top and sides and 3¾ in. at
the bottom. Glue the 9 x 3⅛-in. light
blue card at the bottom as shown.

3 Copy the New York skyline template (A) using the black card. Use the yellow-and-white paint mixture to make spots for lights in the windows. Cut the skyline out.

4 When the paint is completely dry, glue the back of the skyline template. Line up the bottom edge with the top edge of the light blue card and then press down firmly.

5 Copy and cut out the ship templates (B) using the black card. Use the yellow-and-white paint mixture to paint portholes on the ships. Leave the paint to dry.

7 Copy the statue template (D) or enlarge it on a photocopier and trace it onto yellow card. Add details with black felt-tip pen. Cut out the statue and glue it in position.

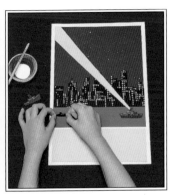

6 Glue the blue card onto the bottom of the skyline. Then glue on the ships. Copy and cut out the spotlight template (C) using the 12 x 2-in. light blue card and glue on the largest ship as shown above.

NEW YORK
BY TRAIN

Now that you know how to make a poster, you can design your own. Collect photographs and cuttings from magazines and tourist information leaflets of a town or a famous tourist attraction nearby. Photocopy them to the size you want and then trace them onto card in the same way you have done for this project.

TRAINS ON FILM

WHEN THE French brothers Auguste and Louis Lumière showed one of their short films in 1895 of a train pulling into a station, many of the audience fled. They were terrified that the train would burst out of the screen into the room. Hardly anyone had ever seen a moving picture before, and people found them frighteningly realistic.

Trains have had a starring role in the movies ever since. The climax of many early movies, for example, involved the "baddies" tying the heroine to a railway track, while the hero rushed to save her. Filmmakers have continued to use trains to keep audiences on the edge of their seats. Nearly all the best train movies have been adventure thrillers.

In the early days, filming moving trains was a risky business. The cameras were bolted on the locomotive, while the camera operator leaned out or rode on a train on a parallel track. Such risks in filming would not be taken today.

Poetry, please
Night Mail (1936) showed scenes of mail being dropped off, and collected, by the "Night Mail" train in Scotland. It was made to show how letters were carried on the mail train between England and Scotland. Later, the British-born American poet W. H. Auden was asked to write verse for a voice-over. His poetry echoes the noises of the train as it made its long journey through the night.

Tears on the train
In the 1945 movie *Brief Encounter*, two people (actors Trevor Howard and Celia Johnson) find romance in a railroad station. Their love is doomed, however, as both are married. Much of the action was shot at Carnforth Station in Britain.

Railway children to the rescue
When a landslide threatens to derail a steam train in *The Railway Children* (1970), the children save the day by turning red petticoats into a warning signal for the engineer. The movie used old engines and coaches on a heritage railway in Yorkshire, Britain. It gives an insight into how steam trains and local stations operated in the early 1900s.

Bond on board

Roger Moore plays the smooth British agent in the 13th James Bond movie, *Octopussy* (released in 1983). Like all Bond movies, it is packed with breathtaking stunts and chases. During a gripping sequence onboard a speeding train, Bond survives crawling below, along the sides, and over the roof of the cars. He also manages to jump off the train without getting hurt. Not something the rest of us should try! Sequences for the movie were shot on real trains moving at low speeds. Stunt men were used for the most dangerous scenes.

Smashing finish

A runaway train crashes through the walls of the station concourse in the thrilling climax to the 1976 action movie *Silver Streak*. Almost the whole movie is set on the train, during its two-and-a-half-day journey from Los Angeles to Chicago in the USA. Gene Wilder stars as the passenger who witnesses a murder on his first night and spends the rest of the journey battling off the baddies.

Animal mischief

Indiana Jones and the Last Crusade (released in 1989) opens with a thrilling flashback. Young Indie is trying to escape pursuers by clambering along the top of a steam train. Chases are the stock-in-trade of adventure movies, but this one is different. The steam locomotive is hauling circus cars. Indie falls into various cages, where he finds snakes, a rhinoceros, and even a lion!

Race to the death

A speeding freight train carrying a stolen nuclear weapon is the setting for the nail-biting closing sequence of the 1996 action movie *Broken Arrow*. The hero (shown left, played by Christian Slater) scrambles over and under the freight cars as he attempts to wrest control of the train back from the villain (played by John Travolta) and disarm the bomb before it explodes.

RECORD BREAKERS

Biggest, fastest, steepest—trains and railroads have been setting records ever since they were invented. Official speed records began when George and Robert Stephenson's *Rocket* reached a top speed of 30 mph in the 1829 Rainhill Trials. By the end of the 1800s, engineers were competing to produce a steam engine that could break the 100-mph speed record.

Timekeeping was inaccurate until speedometers were fitted to locomotives during the 1900s. An American *No. 999* locomotive may have briefly managed 100mph in 1893. The first steam trains capable of sustaining this kind of speed over long distances did not enter service until the 1930s.

World records are usually set over short distances, by locomotives hauling fewer carriages. When, for example, the 200-mph barrier was broken in 1955 by two French Railways electric locomotives, each one was hauling just three cars.

Claim to fame
The New York Central & Hudson River Railroad (NYC & HRR) built the 4-4-0 *No. 999* to haul its Empire State Express. On May 11, 1893, it was claimed that *No. 999* recorded a run of 112 mph between New York and Buffalo. The V-shaped "plow" at the front was one of the distinctive features of American locomotives. Since great lengths of the American railroads were not fenced off, it was essential to protect the front of the locomotives from wandering animals such as buffaloes. The plow performed this function very well.

Champion of steam
On July 3, 1938, Britain's A4–class Pacific *Mallard*'s sleek, streamlined bodywork helped it to set the world speed record for a steam locomotive. With engineer Joe Duddington at the controls, backed up by fireman Tommy Bray, it reached 125 mph—a world steam record that remains unbeaten today. *Mallard* was designed by British engineer Sir Nigel Gresley. It remained in everyday service up until the early 1960s.

• The world's fastest regular passenger trains are the *Trains à Grande Vitesse* (TGV) on the French national services and the Eurostar trains linking London with Paris and Brussels in Belgium. Their maximum speed is 185 mph. The trains being built for the Spanish railroads' new, high-speed Madrid-to-Barcelona line will go even faster—215 mph.

• The longest and heaviest freight train on record ran in West Virginia, USA, in 1967. The 500 coal cars weighed 46,200 tons and stretched a distance of 4 miles.

• The world's longest passenger rail journey is on the Russian service between Moscow and Vladivostok. The 5,972-mile trip takes seven nights and crosses eight time zones.

Steep slopes

The *Pilatusbahn* in Lucerne, Switzerland, is the steepest incline (rack-and-pinion) railroad in the world, climbing to a height of 6,791 feet above sea level. This system uses a rack laid between the rails. This links with a cog wheel under the engine as it drives the train up the steep 1:2 gradients (1 yard up for every 2 yards along).

Overcoming the obstacles

Mount Washington Railway in New Hampshire in the USA became the world's first mountain incline railroad when it opened in 1869. At this time, mountain climbing and sightseeing by steam railroad were great tourist attractions.

Shapes and sizes

. Scotsman Patrick Stirling's Single locomotives, dating from 1870, are particularly striking locomotives. The driving wheels of these steam engines were a massive 8ft in diameter.
. The fastest electric trains are the French TGV (*Train à Grande Vitesse*). A modified TGV unit set the current world speed record of 320 mph.
. By winning the Rainhill Trails in 1829, Robert and George Stephenson's *Rocket* put steam travel firmly on the world map, making this one of the most famous steam locomotives in the world.
. The world's largest and most powerful steam engines are undoubtedly the Union Pacific Big Boys, each weighing over 550 tons.

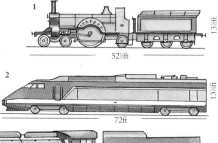

1

13½ft

52½ft

2

13½ft

72ft

3

16ft

24ft

4

132½ft

16ft

HIGH-SPEED TRAINS

THE RECORD-HOLDERS of today are the high-speed electric trains that whisk passengers between major city centers at 155–185 mph. These high-speed trains are the railroad's answer to the competition from airplanes and freeways that grew up after World War II (1939–45). High-speed trains can travel at well over the legal limits for road traffic. Although they cannot travel as fast as planes, they save passengers time by taking them to city centers. In some cases, high-speed trains even beat the flying time between major cities such as London and Paris.

The world's first high-speed intercity passenger service was launched in Japan on October 1, 1964. It linked the capital, Tokyo, with the major industrial city of Osaka in the south. The average speed of these trains—137 mph—broke all the records for a passenger train service. The service was officially named the *Tokaido Shinkansen* (new high-speed railroad), but the trains soon became known as Bullet Trains to describe their speed and the bullet-shaped noses of the locomotives.

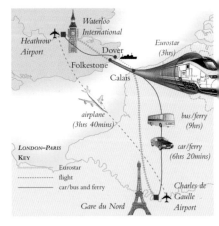

Market leader
The Eurostar has become the quickest way to travel between the city centers London, Britain and Paris, France. It cuts out time-consuming airport check-in and transfer periods. Ferry crossings dramatically increase the journey times by car and by bus.

Rocket on rails
The latest high-speed JR500 trains to operate on Japan's *Tokaido Shinkansen* are as streamlined as a jet plane. Today, they can haul their 16 passenger cars at 185 mph. The average speed of the trains in 1960 was 135 mph.

Stacking the odds

On some high-speed trains, such as this French TGV, passengers ride in double-decker cars. The initials "TGV" are short for *Train à Grande Vitesse* (high-speed train). The operational speed of these French trains is 185 mph. TGVs also hold the current world speed record for a wheeled train. On May 18, 1990, a TGV Atlantique reached an amazing 320 mph.

Swedish tilter

The Swedish X2000 tilting electric trains have an average speed of 95 mph and a top speed of 125 mph. Tilting trains lean into curves to allow them to travel around bends at faster speeds than non-tilting trains.

Melting the ICE

Germany's ICE (InterCity Express) high-speed trains reached speeds of more than 250 mph during tests, before they entered service in 1992. Their maximum operating speed is about 175 mph. Like other high-speed trains, they are streamlined to reduce the slowing effects of drag.

Spanish speeders

Spain's elegant high-speed trains are called AVEs (*Alta Velocidad España,* or high speed of Spain). Their average operational speed is about 135 mph. They entered service on Spain's first high-speed railroad, between Madrid and Seville, in 1992. The AVEs' design was based on the French TGVs. AVEs are made in France with some Spanish parts. Like all high-speed trains, AVEs take their power from overhead electricity lines.

INVESTING IN THE FUTURE

To accelerate to speeds of up to 185–215mph, trains need to run on specially constructed tracks, with as few curves and slopes as possible. The tracks have to be wider apart than was usual in the past. A speeding train stirs the wind into eddies, which can buffet a passing train and jolt its passengers. The ride is also smoother and faster if continuously welded rails are used. If they have their own, dedicated lines, high-speed trains do not have to fit in with the timetables of ordinary, less speedy trains that would slow them down.

Throughout the world, railroad companies are investing billions of dollars in building new lines or upgrading old track to carry their high-speed trains. In a few countries, people believe the future of land travel lies with an entirely different kind of train. Called maglevs, these trains "fly" less than an inch above the track, raised and propelled by magnetism.

Star performers
The Eurostar trains operate between England and Continental Europe. They can accelerate to 185 mph only when they reach the specially built, high-speed railroad lines in France. The speed of the trains through southern England is limited because they run on normal track. Work on a new, British, high-speed line, the Channel Tunnel Rail Link between London St. Pancras and Folkestone, is underway. It is expected to be completed in 2007 at a cost of more than $8 billion.

Scandinavian shuttle
These sleek, three-car, stainless-steel electric trains began running late in 1999 on a new railroad built to link the center of Oslo, the capital of Norway, with the new Gardermoen Airport, 30 miles to the north of the city. The maximum speed of these trains is 130 mph, which enables them to cover the journey in just over 19 minutes. The line includes Norway's longest railroad tunnel at just under 8½ miles.

Virgin express
Britain's Virgin Trains is investing a lot of money in new high-speed electric trains for its West Coast route between London and Glasgow. Work on upgrading old track to carry the trains is also underway. If all goes to plan, journey times between the two cities will be reduced from just over five hours in 1999 to just under four hours in 2005.

High-speed magnetism

Japanese maglev (short for magnetic levitation) trains have reached the astonishing speed of 343 mph on this specially constructed Yamanashi test line. This outstrips the world's fastest wheeled train, the TGV, by 24 mph. Maglevs are so speedy because they float above their track. They do not have wheels and they do not touch the rails. Rails solved the problem of the slowing force of friction between wheels and roads. Maglevs are the answer to reducing friction between wheels and rails.

Spanish AVE

Based on the design of the French TGV, the average operational speed of these trains is around 135 mph.

French TGV

A slightly modified TGV unit set the current world speed record for a train in a trial in 1990, reaching 320 mph.

British Pendolino

A new generation of British high-speed tilting trains, designed to reach speeds of 135 mph.

German ICE

A former world speed record holder in 1988, reaching 250 mph. These trains entered into service in 1991.

Italian Pendolino

These trains run at speeds of around 155 mph on the existing network in Italy, tilting as they travel around curves.

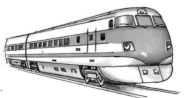

······ High-speed lines—existing or under construction
------ Planned high-speed lines

Oslo · Stockholm
Glasgow · Edinburgh · Göteborg
Belfast
Dublin · Liverpool · Copenhagen
Cork · Manchester
Cardiff · Hamburg
Bristol · London · Berlin
Hanover
Bonn · Leipzig
Rennes · Paris · Prague
Nantes · Strasbourg
Orléans · Munich Vienna
Bratislava
Bordeaux · Lyon · Zagreb
Bilbao · Turin · Milan · Ljubljana
Porto · San · Toulouse · Genoa
Sebastián · Marseille · La Spézia
Nice
Madrid · Barcelona · Rome
Lisbon
Huelva · Naples
Cádiz · Alicante · Brindisi
Málaga · Palermo

On the move in Europe

Many European railroads are planning to develop high-speed rail networks over the next few years. One of the fastest routes will be the high-speed link between Madrid and Barcelona in Spain. The line will have some of the world's fastest passenger trains in service, running at speeds of up to 215 mph. By 2007, Spain will have 4,500 miles of high-speed rail networks with a fleet of over 280 trains.

By 2004 in France, tilting trains will cut around 30 minutes off the journey time between Paris and Toulouse. Some of the fastest short-distance trains are running in Norway between Oslo and Gardermoen Airport. They travel at up to 130 mph and cover 30 miles in just 19 minutes.

FLOATING TRAINS

Maglev (magnetically levitated) trains need their own specially constructed tracks, called guideways, to move along. The trains are raised and propelled by powerful electromagnets. The special thing about magnets is that "unlike" poles (north and south) attract each other or pull together, while "like" poles (north and north, or south and south) repel or push apart. To make an electromagnet, an electric current flows through a wire or other conductor. When the direction of the current is changed, the magnetic poles switch, too.

A maglev train rises when one set of electromagnets beneath it repels another set in the guideway. The maglev is propelled by other electromagnets changing magnetic fields (switching poles). A set of electromagnets in the guideway ahead attracts electromagnets beneath the train, pulling it forward. As the train passes, the electromagnetic fields are switched. The maglev is repelled and pushed onward to the next set of magnets on the guideway.

The main advantage of maglevs over normal wheeled trains is that they are faster because they are not slowed by friction. In tests in Germany in 1993, a maglev train reached speeds of 280 mph. Maglevs are also quieter and use less energy than wheeled trains.

Maglevs get moving
The technology behind maglevs was developed in the 1960s. The world's first service opened at Birmingham City Airport in Britain in the mid-1980s. Japan and Germany now lead the field in developing the technology. When the German Transrapid maglevs start running between Berlin and Hamburg in 2005, they will provide the world's first high-speed intercity maglev service.

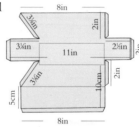

MODEL MAGLEV

You will need: yellow card, pencil, ruler, scissors, red card, green card, glue and glue brush, blue card, double-sided scotch tape, 12 x 4-in. wooden board, bradawl, two 3⅛-in. lengths thin dowel, wood glue, green and red paint, paintbrush, water pot, four magnets with holes drilled in their centers.

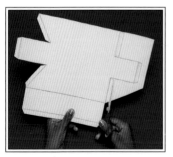

1 Copy the template on to a thin piece of yellow card. The tabs around the side of the template should be ½ in. wide. Carefully cut around the outline.

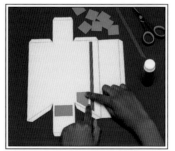

2 Cut two strips of red card and glue them to each side of the template as shown. Cut the green card into window shapes and glue them to the front and sides.

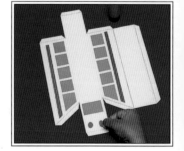

3 Continue to glue the windows to each side of the train to make two even rows. Cut two small blue card circles for headlights. Glue them to the front of the train as shown.

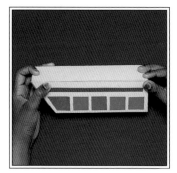

4 Leave the train template until the glue is completely dry. Then carefully use a pair of scissors and a ruler to score along the dotted lines for the tabs and the folds of the train.

5 Bend along the scored lines to form the basic shape of the train as shown above. Then cut small strips of double-sided scotch tape and stick them along each tab.

6 Stick the front and back sections of the train to the tabs on one side of the train. Repeat for the other side. Then stick the base section of the train to the opposite side.

7 Use a bradawl to pierce two holes in the wooden base, 3½ in. in from each end. Enlarge with a pencil. Put wood glue on the end of each piece of dowel and push one into each hole.

8 When the glue is dry give the base a coat of green paint. Paint two coats, letting the first dry before you apply the second. Then paint the dowel uprights a bright red.

9 Press the two magnets together so that they repel. These sides are the same poles—north or south. Use double-sided tape to fix the magnets to the base with like poles facing up.

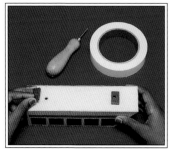

10 Hold the base of the train up to the dowel uprights. Mark two points in the center of the base the same distance as between the uprights. Pierce through the marks.

11 Push magnets over the dowel uprights to repel those on the base. Take them off and tape them over the holes in the train base so that these like poles face upward.

Push the train over the dowel uprights. Like poles on the wooden base and the train base face each other, making the train "float" in midair. You can feel the magnetic force if you push down on the top of the train.

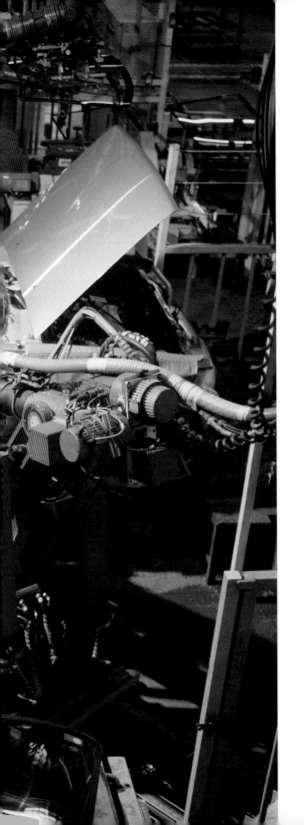

PART SEVEN

CARS

Millions of individuals and families in the
world own a car. Compared with trains,
boats and planes, motor cars are an affordable
means of independent, door-to-door travel.
They touch the everyday lives of ordinary
people—even those who do not own
one—in the way they have transformed both
city and countryside. This journey through
automobile history will make traveling by
car more interesting. You will not only
understand how a car works, but also learn
about the improvements that have been
made through the decades, see the changing
fashions in design, and go behind the scenes
of a Formula One event.

AUTHOR
Peter Harrison
CONSULTANT
Peter Cahill

THE JOURNEY BEGINS

CARS MAKE people mobile in a way that would have been impossible only a century ago. Then, a journey by road of just 30 miles could have taken an entire day. Today, we can travel this distance in half an hour. The ability to go where you want, when you want, quickly, makes traveling much easier. Millions of people all over the world use cars to travel to work or to go shopping, to go on vacation and to visit friends and relatives. Horse-drawn carriages and carts, and walking, were the main forms of transportation for thousands of years before cars. Many roads were in poor condition. Because cars moved under their own power, and encouraged better roads, they allowed people to travel much more.

Hold on tight
Very early cars such as this Velo, made in Germany in 1893 by Karl Benz, had no covering bodywork. When Benz's daughter Clara went driving, she sat high above the road with very little to hang on to if the car hit a bump in the road.

By the numbers
The tachometer (rev. counter), speedometer and clock from a Rolls-Royce Silver Ghost have solid brass fittings and glass covers. They were assembled by hand. The instruments on early cars were often made by skilled craftspeople. The Silver Ghost was made continuously from 1906 until 1925.

Bold as brass
A gleaming brass horn and lamp are proud examples of the detailed work that went into making the first cars. Early cars were made with materials that would be far too expensive for most people today. Seats were upholstered with thickly padded leather, because the cars had poor suspension. This prevented the drivers and passengers from being jolted up and down too much.

Old bruiser
This Bentley was built before 1931, when the company was taken over by Rolls-Royce. Bentley built powerful and sturdy sports cars, some weighing up to 775 pounds. They won many motor races in the 1920s and 1930s, such as the Le Mans 24-hour race in France. Big cars such as these were built on heavy metal chassis (frames). They had wood-framed bodies covered in metal and cloth, huge headlights and large, wire-spoked wheels.

Egg on wheels
In the 1950s and 1960s, car makers began to make very small cars, such as this German BMW Isetta. Around 160,000 Isettas were produced between 1955 and 1962. Manufacturers developed small cars because they were cheaper to buy and to run, and used less parking space. The Isetta, like so many of the microcars, was powered by a small motorcycle engine.

Cool cruisin'
Cadillac was an American company known for its stylish designs. This Cadillac from the 1950s, with its large tail fins and shiny chrome, is a typical example. Many cars from the 1950s and 1960s, including this one, are known as classic cars. People like to collect them and restore them to their original condition.

Redhead
The Italian car maker Ferrari has a reputation for making very fast, very expensive cars. This 1985 Testarossa has a top speed of 175 mph. Very few people can afford to own such a car. Even if they have the money, it takes great driving skill to get the best out of one.

Going nowhere?
The success of the car has its downside. Millions of people driving cars causes problems such as traffic jams and air pollution. Also, the building of new roads can ruin the countryside. These issues are being debated all over the world.

THE EARLIEST CARS

A MONG THE most important builders of early cars and car engines were the Germans Nikolaus Otto, Karl Benz and Gottlieb Daimler. In the late 1800s, they built the first internal combustion engines and found ways to link the engines to wheels. Car engines are called internal (inside) combustion

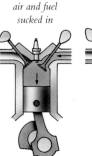

air and fuel sucked in

air and fuel mixture compressed

spark fires mixture and explosion pushes piston down

burnt gases blown away

(burning) engines because they burn a mixture of fuel and air inside a small chamber. People had long been trying to find ways to make engines for road transportation. In 1770, the Frenchman Nicholas-Joseph Cugnot made a steam engine that drove a three-wheeled cart. It was too heavy to use, however, and only two were built. The achievement of Benz, Otto and Daimler was to make a small engine that could generate enough power for road vehicles. In Great Britain, the earliest cars are known as veteran (built before 1905) and Edwardian (built between 1905 and 1919). They were not as reliable as modern vehicles, but sometimes more finely built.

Suck, squeeze, bang, blow
A car's piston (like an unturned metal cup) moves in a rhythm of four steps called the Otto cycle, after Nikolaus Otto. First, it moves down to suck in fuel mixed with air. Then it pushes up and compresses (squeezes) the mixture. The spark plug ignites the fuel. The bang of the explosion pushes the piston down again. When the piston moves up again, it blows out the burnt gases.

Trim trike
The 3-wheeled Benz Motorwagen was first made in 1886. It was steered by a small hand lever on top of a tall steering column. Karl Benz began his career building carriages. He used this training when he built his first car in 1885. By 1888 Benz was employing 50 people to build his Motorwagens.

Follow the leader
Soon after the first cars were being driven on the roads, accidents started to happen. Until 1904, there was a law in Great Britain requiring a person carrying a red flag to walk in front of the car. This forced the car driver to go slowly. The flag was to warn people that a car was coming.

Remember this

Important military gentlemen pose for photos with their cars. They are not in the driving seats, however. They had chauffeurs to drive the cars for them. Car owners in the early 1900s liked to show their cars off. They often posed for photographs to keep for souvenirs.

Look out!

The car horns that early drivers sounded to warn pedestrians were very different than those in modern cars. When the driver squeezed the rubber bulb, air traveled through the tube and made a noise when it came out of the end.

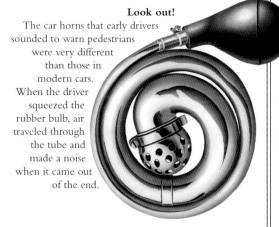

Snow disaster

Early cars were hard to control at times because their braking and steering systems were not very effective. When bad weather such as snow made the ground slippery, the car could easily run off the road. Even in modern cars with efficient brakes and steering, snow-covered roads are still dangerous.

All wrapped up

Drivers at the turn of the century wore thick goggles to protect their eyes, because their cars had no protective bodywork. The roads were not smooth and stones and dust were thrown up by the wheels. Cold winds felt even colder in a moving, open car, so thick caps and heavy driving clothes were worn to keep warm.

Nose to tail horses

This photograph from the late 1800s shows why the British talk about nose-to-tail traffic jams. Before cars were invented, most transportation was by horse-drawn carriage. City streets in those days could become just as jammed with vehicles as they do today.

WHEELS IN MOTION

BEFORE A CAR MOVES, the engine must change the up-and-down movement of the pistons into the round-and-round movement of a shaft (rod) that turns the wheels. With the engine running, the driver presses down the clutch and selects first gear in the gearbox. The engine turns a shaft called a crankshaft. The power from the turning crankshaft is then transmitted through the gearbox to the wheels on the road. The combined movement makes the wheels on the road turn forwards. The wheels turn backwards when the driver pushes the gear stick into reverse gear.

This project shows you how to make a simple machine that creates a similar motion, where one kind of movement that goes round and round can be turned into another kind of movement that goes up and down.

Wind up
The earliest motor cars did not have a starter motor. The driver had to put a starting handle into the front of the car. This connected to the engine's crankshaft to turn it. Turning the handle was hard work and could break the driver's arm if not done correctly. Button-operated starters began to be fitted in 1912.

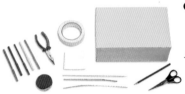

CHANGING MOTION

You will need: shoebox, thin metal rod about $1/8$-in. diameter, pliers, jelly jar lid, tape, scissors, 1 thick plastic straw, pencil, piece of stiff paper, at least 4 colored felt-tipped pens, 1 thin plastic straw

1 Place the shoebox narrow-side-down on a flat surface. With one hand push the metal rod through the center, making sure your other hand will not get jabbed by the rod.

2 Bend the rod at right angles where it comes out of the box. Attach the jelly jar lid to it with adhesive tape. Push the lid until it rests against the side of the box.

3 Carefully use the pliers to bend the piece of rod sticking out of the other side of the box. This will make a handle for the piston that will be able to turn easily.

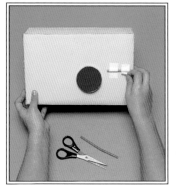

4 Cut a piece of thick plastic straw about 2 in. long and tape it to the side of the box close to the jelly jar lid. Make sure that it just sticks up beyond the edge of the box.

5 Draw a design in pencil on a piece of stiff paper. Copy the jester shown in this project or draw a simple clown. Choose something that looks good when it moves.

6 Using the felt-tipped pens, color the design until it looks the way you want it to. The more colorful the figure is, the nicer it will look on the top of the piston.

7 Carefully cut the finished drawing out of the paper. Make sure you have a clean-edged design. Try not to smudge the felt-tipped color with your fingers.

8 Use the tape to attach the thin plastic straw to the bottom of the drawing. About ³/4 in. of straw should be attached.

Place the box on end so the jester is at the top. Turn the handle on the left-hand side. As you turn, the jelly jar lid revolves and pushes the jester up and down, like a piston.

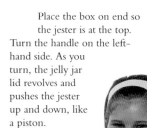

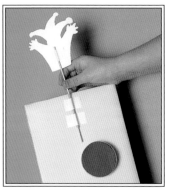

9 Slide the straw attached to the drawing into the straw taped to the back of the box. It will come out of the other end. Push down so that the straw touches the edge of the jelly jar lid.

MASS PRODUCTION

Once ways had been found to power a small, wheeled road vehicle, more and more people wanted to own a car. Having one made getting around so much easier. However, early cars were built by hand, piece by piece, which took time. In 1903, the inventor Henry Ford produced the Model A Ford, the first car designed to be built in large numbers. It gave him the idea to mass-produce all the separate parts of a car in the same place, then have his workers assemble many cars at the same time. This became known as the production-line method. By 1924, 10 million Ford cars had been built and sold. Today, almost all cars are built on production lines. Robots (automated machines) do much of the work. Some cars are still built by hand, but they can only be built very slowly. For example, the British sports-car maker Morgan made 11 cars a week in 1999. In comparison, the Ford Motor Company built about 138,000 cars a week in the same year.

Tin Lizzie
The Model T Ford was the world's first mass-produced (assembled on a production line) car. Millions were made and sold all over the world. Nowadays people collect examples of these cars, maintaining, restoring and repairing them, often to a gleaming state. It is unlikely that they would have been so well cared for by their original owners.

Herbert's big idea
The Austin Seven was one of the most popular cars ever. This version is a sporting two seater. Between 1922 and 1938 there were many versions, including racing cars and even vans. The Austin Motor Company was founded by Herbert Austin in 1903. The company allowed other car makers to build the Austin Seven in France, Japan, America and Germany.

Beetling about
In 1937, the German government founded a car company to build cheap cars. The car, designed by Dr Ferdinand Porsche, was called the Volkswagen, meaning "people's car", but it gained the nickname of the "Beetle" because of its unusual shape. Some people painted their Beetles for fun. By the 1960s, the car was popular worldwide. By 2000, over 21 million Volkswagens had been sold.

Next one, please

Modern cars are made with the help of machines in factories. Each machine does a different job. Some weld metal parts together, others attach fittings and secure fastenings, others spray paint. The car's metal body parts come together on a moving track that runs past each machine. Making cars like this means they can be put together quickly and in vast numbers.

Big yellow taxi

For people without a car, such as tourists, taxis are a convenient way of getting around in towns and cities. Taxi drivers try to find the best short cuts for an easy journey. Hiring a taxicab also means that people don't have to find a place to park. The bright yellow-colored "checker cabs" in New York became a symbol for the city all over the world, because everyone recognized them.

The people's servant

The Trabant was from East Germany. Many millions were built for ordinary people. Its name comes from a Hungarian word meaning "servant", and the Trabant served as a cheap, reliable car across Eastern Europe. This 601 model was first made in 1964.

Alec's big idea

Launched in 1959, the Morris Mini Minor was one of the most revolutionary cars of the last 50 years. It was cheap to buy and cheap to run, easy to drive and easy to park. Despite its small size, it could carry four people comfortably. The car's designer, Alec Issigonis, a British citizen of Greek parentage, also designed the Morris Minor, a budget car launched in 1948.

THE ENGINE

A CAR'S ENGINE is made up of metal parts. They are designed to work together smoothly and efficiently. In older cars, a valve called a carburetor feeds a mixture of air and fuel into the cylinder, where the mixture is burnt to produce power. Newer cars often use an injection system, which measures and controls the amount of fuel into the engine more accurately. To keep the engine cool, water is pumped from the radiator and circulated around chambers in the cylinder block. The waste gases created by the burned fuel are carried away by the exhaust system. The engine sucks in the air and petrol mixture and allows it to burn. To help the moving parts move against each other smoothly, they are lubricated with oil from the engine oil sump. A pump squirts the oil on to the parts.

A car's electrical power is driven by an alternator. The electrical current is stored in the battery. This provides the electricity for the spark that ignites the fuel mixture, for the car's electrical system, and for its heater, lights, radio, windshield wipers and instruments.

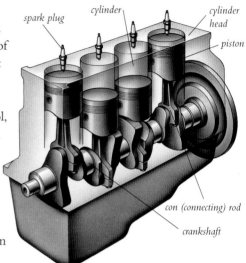

spark plug · cylinder · cylinder head · piston · con (connecting) rod · crankshaft

Working together
Most car engines have four cylinders. In each cylinder a piston moves up and down. Four rods, one from each piston, turn metal joints attached to the crankshaft. As the rods turn the joints, the crankshaft moves round and round. The movement is transmitted to the wheels, using the gearbox to control how fast the wheels turn relative to the engine.

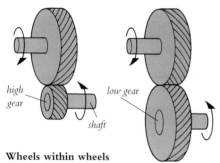

high gear · low gear · shaft

Wheels within wheels
The car's engine turns a shaft (rod) with different sized gears (toothed wheels) on it. High gears are used for more speed because when a big wheel turns a small one, it turns faster. The gear system is called the transmission, because it transmits (moves) the engine's power to the car's wheels. Many cars have five forward gears. The biggest is needed for slow speeds, and the smallest for high speeds. When the car goes round corners, its wheels move at different speeds. A set of gears called the differential allows the wheels to do this.

Turbo tornado
This 1997 Dodge engine can make a car go especially fast because it has a turbocharger that forces the fuel and air mixture faster and more efficiently into the engine cylinder head. Turbochargers are driven by waste exhaust gases drawn away from the exhaust system, which is a way of turning the waste gases to good use. Turbochargers are very effective at boosting engine power.

What you see is what you get
This vintage racing Bentley displays its twin carburetors mounted on a supercharger (a mechanically driven device similar to a turbocharger) in front of the engine. The water pipes from the radiator to the engine, electric leads, plug leads and large open exhaust pipes can all be seen.

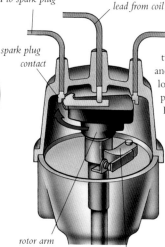

lead to spark plug *lead from coil*

spark plug contact

rotor arm

contact breaker

Power control
The distributor has two jobs. It connects and disconnects low-value electric power to the coil. It also supplies high-value electric power from the coil to each spark plug. This makes a spark big enough to ignite the air and fuel mixture at exactly the right time.

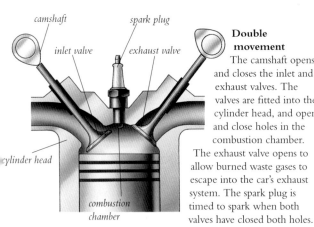

camshaft *spark plug*

inlet valve *exhaust valve*

cylinder head

combustion chamber

Double movement
The camshaft opens and closes the inlet and exhaust valves. The valves are fitted into the cylinder head, and open and close holes in the combustion chamber. The exhaust valve opens to allow burned waste gases to escape into the car's exhaust system. The spark plug is timed to spark when both valves have closed both holes.

See and be seen
The lights used on early cars usually burned either oil or gas. Oil was carried in a small container in the bottom of the lamp. Gas was created by dissolving in water tablets of carbide (carbon mixed with metal) carried in a canister.

Blow them away
Mercedes-Benz fitted a supercharger to this 1936 540K to add power to the engine. The German company first used superchargers on their racing cars in 1927. This method of adding power had first been used on airplane engines in 1915.

IN THE RIGHT GEAR

GEARS ARE toothed wheels that interlock with each other to transmit circular motion. They have been used in machines of many kinds for over 2,000 years. In a car gearbox, the gears are arranged on shafts so that they mesh with one another when they are selected. Cars have four, five or six forward gears according to the design, use and cost of the car. Several gears are needed because driving requires different combinations of speed and force at different times.

The largest gear wheel is first gear and turns slower than the higher gears. It provides more force and less speed for when the car is moving from stop, or going uphill. In fifth gear, less force and more speed is provided. This gear wheel is the smallest and rotates the fastest. The project connects two gears to show the beautiful patterns that gears can make. Then you can make your own three-gear machine.

Uphill struggle
Pushing a car up a steep hill in a 1920s car rally put a lot of strain on the low gears in a car. On steep slopes, first and second gears are often the only ones that a driver can use. Fourth gear is used for flat roads and fifth gear for cruising at high speeds.

DRAWING WITH GEARS

You will need: *compass, 8½ x 11-in. sheet of white paper, black pen, scissors, 8½ x 11-in. sheet of thin cardboard, 2 strips of corrugated cardboard, tape, 3 colored felt-tipped pens.*

1 Using the compass, trace a 5½-in. diameter circle on the paper. Draw over it with the pen and cut it out. On the cardboard, trace, draw and cut out another circle with a diameter of 4½ in.

2 Tape corrugated cardboard around the circles, as shown. Make a hole in the small circle wide enough for the tip of a felt-tipped pen. Turn the small wheel inside the larger. Trace the path in felt-tipped pen.

3 Make a second hole in the small wheel. Turn the small gear inside the larger using another felt-tipped pen. Make a third hole in the small wheel and use a third color pen to create an exciting geometric design.

THREE-GEAR MACHINE

You will need: compass, 8½ x 11-in. sheet of cardboard, pen, scissors, 3 strips of corrugated card, tape, 8½ x 11-in. piece of fiberboard, glue, 2½-in. piece of ½-in. diameter wood dowel, 3 push pins.

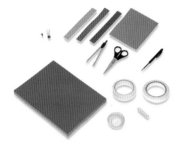

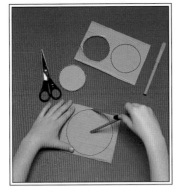

1 Use the compass to trace one 5½-in. diameter and two 4½-in. diameter circles in the cardboard. Draw around the circle edges with the pen and cut the circles out.

2 Carefully wrap the strips of corrugated cardboard around the circles, using one strip per circle, corrugated side out. Tape each strip to the bottom of the circles.

3 Place the largest gear wheel on the piece of fiberboard. Hold the gear down and glue the dowel onto the side of the gear base at the edge of the wheel. Set aside until it is dry.

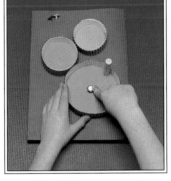

4 Position all three gears on the fiberboard, edges just touching each other. Pin each of them firmly to the fiberboard with a push pin but allow them to turn.

5 Gently turn the dowel on the largest gear. As that gear turns, the two others that are linked together by the corrugated cardboard will turn against it. See how they move in opposite directions to each other.

6 Now you have a three-gear machine where the energy from each gear is being transferred to the other, just like the gears in a car.

SAFE RIDE AND HANDLING

MOST MODERN cars have four wheels. The wheels tend to be placed one at each corner, which helps to distribute the car's weight evenly on the road. An evenly balanced car rides and handles well and has good road grip and braking. Engine power usually drives either the front or rear wheels. However, with the growth in off-road driving in farming and for pleasure, all-wheel drive has become increasingly popular. Driving safely at high speed in a straight line or round corners is a test of how well a car has been designed. Many cars now have power-assisted steering to make steering easier. Tires are an important part of good road handling. The tread pattern and grooves are designed to make the tire grip the road efficiently, especially in wet, slippery conditions.

Big bopper
The French tire manufacturer Michelin has been making tires since 1888. The Michelin brand has been known for many years by the symbol of a human figure that looks as though it is made out of tires.

Gripping stuff
Tire tread patters have raised pads, small grooves and water-draining channels to grip the road surface. There are different kinds of tires for cars, buses, trucks and tractors. Tire makers also make tires for different road conditions. Examples include winter tires and special self-sealing tires that stay hard even when they are damaged.

Dig deep
Tractor tires are very deeply grooved. This allows them to grip well in slippery mud. The width of the tires spreads the weight of the heavy vehicle over soft ground. The tires are high so that the tractor can ride easily over obstacles such as big rocks on the ground.

Burn the rubber

Race car tires are wide so that the car can go as fast as possible while maintaining grip and stability on the road. They are made in various very hard mixtures of rubber to cope with different amounts of heat generated by racing in different conditions. Ordinary tires would melt.

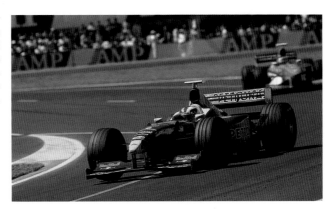

Out for a spin

Until very light alloy wheels became available in the last 20 years, sports cars often had wire-spoke wheels. These combined strength with lightness, which are both important features in a sports car. When a sports car brakes or turns sharply, modern wire-spoke wheels are strong enough to take the strain.

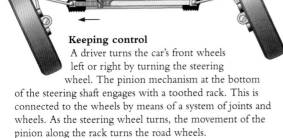

Keeping control

A driver turns the car's front wheels left or right by turning the steering wheel. The pinion mechanism at the bottom of the steering shaft engages with a toothed rack. This is connected to the wheels by means of a system of joints and wheels. As the steering wheel turns, the movement of the pinion along the rack turns the road wheels.

Monster trucks

Very large trucks that carry heavy loads use enormous tires to spread the weight. This flatbed truck has been equipped with earth-mover tires for fun. Look how much bigger they are than the car the truck's rolling over.

Strong grip

Traveling at high speed on a wet road can be dangerous. Water can form a film that is able to lift a tire clear of the road surface for several seconds. To prevent this, tire makers mold drain channels into the tire's tread to push the water away from under the tire as it rotates.

SPEED CONTESTS

RACE CARS against one another to test their speed and endurance has gone on for over 100 years. The American car maker Henry Ford, for example, designed and built race cars before he set up the Ford car factory in 1903. Many kinds of car races now take place, including stock-car, rally, speedway and drag racing. The FIA (*Fédération Internationale de l'Automobile*) makes rules about issues such as the tracks, the design and power of the cars, and the safety of drivers and spectators.

The fastest and most powerful kind of track racing is Formula One, also known as Grand Prix racing. The cars can travel up to 200 mph on straight sections of track. Because the races are so exciting, the best drivers are paid in the millions. Formula One winners, such as David Coulthard and Michael Schumacher, are international celebrities. Technological advances in production-line cars have often been developed and tested in Grand Prix cars.

GRAND-PRIX Dieppe de l'A·C·F·1907   NAZZARO su F·I·A·T·

Your move
When racing drivers complete a race and cross the finishing line, a race official waves a black and white flag known as the checkered flag. The black-and-white pattern of squares on the finishing flag looks like the pattern on a chessboard. It is known all over the world as the sign of motor racing.

Monster motors
Early Grand Prix cars, such as this 10.2 liter Fiat, had enormous engines. Grand Prix racing began in France in 1904 and slowly spread to other countries. The *Association Internationale des Automobiles Clubs Reconnus* (AIACR) set the rules for races until it was reformed as the FIA in 1946.

Furious Ferrari
The Italian car maker Ferrari has been making race cars since 1940. Here the German Michael Schumacher, driving the Ferrari F399, rounds a curve on the 7¹/₂-mi. Catalunya circuit at the 1999 Barcelona Grand Prix.

FACT BOX

• Between 1992 and the time of writing, the German driver Michael Schumacher has won 80 Formula One races, the highest number so far achieved by any driver.

• Ayrton Senna won the Monaco Grand Prix a record six times between 1987 and 1993.

• The racetrack at Indianapolis, Indiana, was known as "the brickyard" because it was paved with bricks until 1961.

Take-off

The speeds at which rally cars travel means they often fly over the tops of the hills on the course. The driver and navigator of this car in the 1999 Portuguese Rally are strapped into their seats to protect them from the tremendous thump that will come when the car's four wheels touch the ground in a second or two.

Take it to the limit

The heat generated by a Top Fuel drag racer's engine at the 1996 NHRA (*National Hot Rod Association*) Winternational makes the air vibrate around it. Drag races are short, like sprint races for athletes. The races take place over a straight course only 400 yds long, and the cars can reach speeds of 250 mph. The flat spoilers on the front and rear of the cars are pushed down by the air rushing past, helping to keep the car on the road.

The chase

Tight bends are a test of driving skills for Formula One drivers. The cars brake hard from very high speeds as they approach the bend. Drivers try not to leave any gap that following cars could use for overtaking. As the drivers come out of the bend they accelerate as hard as is possible without skidding and going into a spin.

Making a splash

Rally car driving is extremely tough on the cars and on the drivers. Cars drive over deserts, mud-filled roads, rivers, snow and many other obstacles. The cars follow the same route, but start at different times. The course is divided into separate sections known as Special Stages. There is a time limit for each stage. The winner of the rally is the car which has the fastest overall time.

Thrill becomes spill

The Brazilian Mauricio Gugelmin's car soars into the air at the 1985 French Grand Prix, crashing to the ground upside down. The driver survived and has since taken part in 74 Grand Prix races. Safety regulations have improved in recent years.

RACE TRACKS

Pᴇᴏᴘʟᴇ ʜᴀᴠᴇ been racing cars on specially designed public circuits (tracks) almost since cars were invented. The first race on a special circuit took place in 1894 in France. The Italian track at Monza is one of the oldest racing circuits. It was built for the 1922 Italian Grand Prix. Among the most well-known tracks are Silverstone and Brands Hatch in Great Britain, Indianapolis in the United States, the Nürburgring in Germany, and Monaco. Millions of people all over the world watch the races at these tracks and on television. The teams and the drivers compete furiously with one another to prove whose car is the fastest or can keep driving the longest. Sometimes the competition can be so fierce it is deadly. Ayrton Senna, a top Brazilian racing driver, died in a fatal crash at Imola in Italy in 1994. In this project, you can build your own race track, specially designed to let your cars build up speed on a steep slope, and race against a partner to see whose car is the fastest.

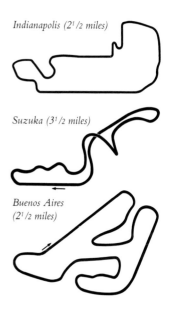

Indianapolis (2^1/2 miles)

Suzuka (3^1/2 miles)

Buenos Aires (2^1/2 miles)

TESTING GROUND

You will need: 10 in. of 3-in.-diameter cardboard tube, scissors, small paintbrush, blue paint, 10 strips of colored paper 2^1/2 x ^{3}/4 in., tape, 2 strips of white paper ^{1}/2 x 3 in., pencil, red and black felt-tipped pen, pieces of colored and white paper, toothpicks, 8^1/2 x 11-in. sheet of stiff red card stock, ruler, 2 small model cars.

Twist and turn

All racetracks, such as those shown above, test the skill of the drivers and the speed and handling of the racing cars. They combine curves with straight stretches. Sharp curves are known as hairpin curves. Most tracks are between 2^1/2 and 3^1/2 miles in length.

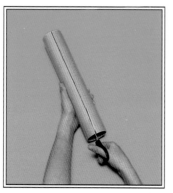

1 Use the scissors to carefully cut the cardboard tube in half along its length. Hold the tube in one hand but make sure you keep the scissor blades away from your hands.

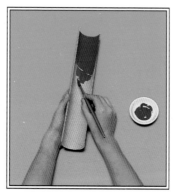

2 Use the paintbrush to apply a thick coat of blue paint to the insides of both halves of the tube. For a more intense color, paint a second coat after the first has dried.

3 Use tape to stick the ten narrow strips of colored paper together. Tape them along their widths to make a flexible seam. This joins the racetrack together.

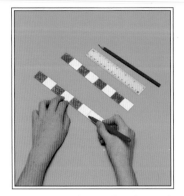

4 Now take the flexible curve you have made from strips of paper. Tape it to one end of one of the painted halves of the tube. Use small pieces of tape.

5 Use a pencil to mark eight equal ½-in. strips on both of the strips of white paper. Color in alternate red blocks with a felt-tipped pen to make striped crash barriers.

6 Color in a 1½ x 3-in. piece of paper with ½-in. black and white squares. Cut the other paper pieces into pennants (forked flags). Tape the flags to toothpicks.

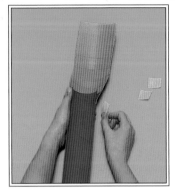

9 Tape the second half of the tube to the end of the flexible curve. Put in the crash barriers. Now you are ready to roll your toy car down the death-defying slope of your racetrack. Make another racetrack with a friend and you can race each other's cars.

7 Cut three 3-in.-wide strips from the sheet of stiff card stock. Use scissors to cut a semicircle out of the top of each of the strips.

8 Measure with a ruler and cut the three strips to varying heights of 8 in., 5½ in. and 2¾ in. Tape them to the bottom of half of the tube, fitting them on at the semicircle shapes to support the half tube in a gradual slope.

Popping the cork
Race winners Canadian Jacques Villeneuve and Frenchman Jean Alesi celebrate by showering each other with champagne at the Luxembourg Grand Prix in 1997.

COLLECTING

The cars that were made many years ago have not been forgotten. In Great Britain, they are known as veteran (made before 1905), Edwardian (1905–1919), vintage (1919–1930) and classic (1930 onward). Enthusiasts (people with a special interest) all over the world collect and maintain old cars. They value them for many reasons, such as the great care that went into making them, their design, their engine power and their rarity. Clubs such as the AACA (Antique Automobile Club of America) and FIVA (*Fédération Internationale Véhicules Anciens*) exist for the collectors of old American and European cars. There are also specific clubs for owners of particular models of car. Owners like to meet up and compare notes on maintaining their vehicles. Their clubs organize tours and rallies in which owners can drive their cars in working order.

Annual get–together
English veteran cars (built before 1905) parade along the sea front in Brighton, England. The London-to-Brighton veteran car run has been held every year (apart from during the wars) since 1904. It celebrates cars being driven without someone with a red flag walking in front to warn of their approach.

Who stole the roof?
Early vehicles were built on the frames of horse-drawn wagons, so they had little protective bodywork. Drivers and their passengers had to wrap up well when driving.

Room for two?
Frenchman Louis Delage built cars of great engineering skill. The engine of this 1911 racing model was so big that there was little room for the driver. The huge tube under the hood carried exhaust gases to the back of the car.

High roller

The Rolls-Royce Silver Ghost is one of the great early vintage cars. It was first built in 1906. Almost 8,000 were made before production finally stopped in 1925. By that time, fewer people were able to afford such large, expensive cars. Individual buyers could have the car's specification and equipment altered according to their own needs. Several Silver Ghosts were produced as armored cars to protect top British Army generals during World War I.

Mighty midget

The 1930 MG Midget was a powerful small car and clearly deserved its name. The Midget was the first car that the MG company sold in large numbers. Its success allowed the firm to expand and become more widely known.

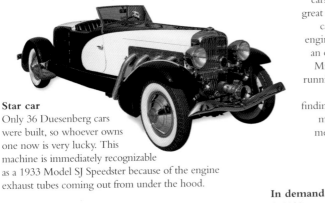

Star car

Only 36 Duesenberg cars were built, so whoever owns one now is very lucky. This machine is immediately recognizable as a 1933 Model SJ Speedster because of the engine exhaust tubes coming out from under the hood.

Mint condition

The owners of old cars have to give a great deal of loving care to the car engines. Keeping an original MG Midget engine running demands patience in finding spare parts, maintaining old metal and making regular tests.

In demand

A 1930s race car combines style and power, qualities that still give Alfa Romeo its strong reputation. Collectors today value race cars of the past just as much as old passenger cars. The Italian car maker Alfa Romeo has been building fast cars since 1915.

Starry Ferrari

The Italian company Ferrari is one of the world's greatest car makers. Owning a Ferrari has always been seen as a symbol of wealth and success, so the cars are favorites with film stars and sports stars. This 166 Ferrari is from the late 1940s.

OFF-ROAD VEHICLES

MOST CARS are designed for driving on smooth roads. There are specialized vehicles, however, that can drive across rough conditions such as mud, desert and rocky terrain. Usually called off-road vehicles (ORVs) or All-Terrain Vehicles (ATVs), cars of this kind often have four-wheel drive, large tires and tough suspensions. They stand high off the ground and have strong bodywork. The earliest ORVs were the American Jeep and the British Land Rover. The Jeep, made by Ford and Willys, started life in World War II. It was designed to travel across roads damaged by warfare. The Land Rover, built by the Rover company in the late 1940s, was based on the idea of the Jeep. It was intended for farmers, who have to drive across difficult terrain. The Land Rover proved useful in all parts of the world where roads were poor or non-existent. Traveling off-road is still a necessity in many places. But in recent times, it has become a popular leisure activity for some drivers, who like to test their driving skills in difficult terrain.

Seaside fun
Driving on beaches is difficult because wheels can sink into the wet sand. Vehicles for driving on beaches are built to be very light, with balloon tires to spread the vehicle's weight over a wide area.

Tough cookie
At the start of World War II the United States Army developed a vehicle with a sturdy engine, body and chassis. The wheels were at the corners for stability over rough ground. The GP (General Purpose) vehicle became known as the Jeep.

No traffic jams
The Lunar Rover, carried to the Moon by *Apollo 17* in 1971, was powered by electricity. The low gravity of the moon meant that it would not sink into soft ground. A wide track and long wheelbase stopped it from turning over if it hit a rock.

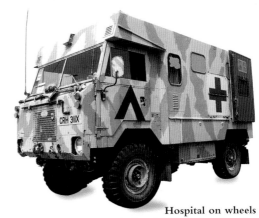

Angel of mercy

Vehicles such as Jeeps help doctors to take medical aid to people living in remote areas where there are few roads. A four-wheel drive vehicle, it can cross shallow rivers and rough terrain. A specially strong underbody protects against damage from water.

Hospital on wheels

Aid agencies such as UNICEF and *Mèdecins Sans Frontières* use specially adapted trucks equipped as mobile hospitals. They help to save lives in times of war and natural disaster. Heavily reinforced bodywork protects patients and fragile medical supplies.

Electric caddies

A typical game of golf involves traveling 3 miles or more. Golfers need an easy way to carry heavy golf clubs around the course. Golf carts (also called golf buggies) are simple, light vehicles powered by electricity. They have enough battery life to carry golfers and their clubs from the first to the last hole on the course.

FACT BOX

• The 7,000-mile Paris-Dakar-Cairo Rally is one of the world's best-known off-road races. Founded in 1978 by the French driver Thierry Sabine, the year 2000 race had 600 team members driving 200 motorcycles, 141 cars and 65 trucks.

Get tracking

Half-tracks played an important part in World War II, and still do in modern warfare. They have tank tracks in the rear to allow them to travel over very broken surfaces such as roads filled with shell holes and debris. The wheels at the front give half-tracks added mobility that tanks do not have.

Big boss

Large, high, sports-utility cars such as the Mitsubishi Shogun and commercial SUVs grew increasingly popular from the 1980s. They had four-wheel drive, which made driving on rough ground much easier.

CUSTOM-BUILT

SOMETIMES SERIOUS car enthusiasts decide to adapt a standard model. They might alter the engine to make it run faster, or change the body to make it look different. Specially adapted cars like this are known as custom cars. Custom cars have become very popular since the 1950s, particularly in the United States. The wheels may be taken from one kind of car, the body from a second, the mudguards and engine from others, and the different parts are combined to make a completely original car. The end result can be dramatic. These unusual cars have many different names, such as mean machines, street machines, muscle machines and hot rods. Racing custom cars is a popular activity. Stock cars are production-line cars modified slightly for races. Drag racers are incredibly fast and powerful cars built for high speed races over short distances.

Water baby
Surf's up and the muscle machine is on the beach. This cool dude has fitted big, wide tires on a sports car body to spread the car's weight on soft sand. He has been busy with a paintbrush, too, adding flames to his body paint.

Made to order
This car is a mixture of styles. The driver's cab and steering wheel have been made to look like those in a veteran car. The modern engine is chrome-plated, with all the parts visible. The exhaust-outlet tubes resemble those from a 1930s race car. The front wheels are bigger than the rear ones.

Soft furnishings
Some people change the insides of their cars to create a truly luxurious look. They replace the standard features, for example, with soft leather seats, padded dashboards and chrome-covered gear shifts.

Really smokin'
The grille on the hood of a customized hot rod is the turbocharger. It can boost the engine to speeds of 250 mph. When the car brakes at high speed, its tires make lots of smoke because they are burning from friction with the road.

FLUFFY DICE

You will need: *square box at least 4¹/2-in. square, 2 sheets 8¹/2 x 11-in. white paper, tape, scissors, 7³/4-in. length of string, 31-in. square of furry fabric, pencil, awl, glue, circle stencil.*

1 Stick white paper around all six surfaces of the box with tape. Use a small piece of tape to stick 1¹/4 in. of the end of the length of string to one side of the box.

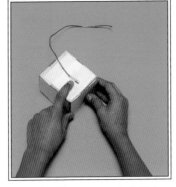

2 Place the fabric furry-side down. Place the box at one edge and draw around it. Then roll the box over and draw around it again. Do six squares like this to form a cross.

3 Cut out the cross shape. With an awl, carefully make a hole in the fur. Place the box face down on the fur where the string is attached. Pull the string through the hole.

4 Spread glue evenly on the inside of each square of the fabric, one at a time. Press the glued material squares on to the box faces.

5 Choose a medium-sized circle shape from the circle stencil. Using a pencil, draw 21 of the same circles on the piece of white paper.

6 Cut out the circles. Glue them on to the furry side of the fabric. Put six dots on one face, five dots on the next, then four, three, two and finally one dot. You could use a real dice to see the correct arrangement.

7 Make a second dice and hang them in the car for fun. Put them in a place where they will not distract the driver. They should not hang on any of the windows.

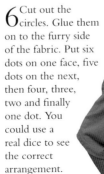

UNUSUAL DESIGNS

CARS ARE often adapted (have their design changed) to suit different needs, or just for fun. Three-wheeled cars, a kind of microcar, are cheap to operate and take up less road space than the conventional four-wheeled cars.

Amphibious vehicles that can operate on land and water were built in World War II for fighting. Since then, specialized German, British and Chinese manufacturers have gone on building small numbers of these cars for use in regions with many rivers.

Films studios often create sensational special effects around cars that appear to have special powers. Then there are the real but completely wacky cars, made by people who want to create cars that defy the imagination. These have included cars that split down the middle, cars that are covered in fur, and cars that look like sofas and hot dogs.

Frog face

The microcars produced in in the 1950s and 1960s were for driving in towns. This 1959 Messerschmitt had a tiny engine and was just 9 feet long. Even so, it had a top speed of 65 mph. The top of the car swings over to allow the driver entry. The car was also very cheap to operate. It used only one gallon of gas every 60 miles, almost half the fuel consumption of an average modern car.

Garden car

This car may look like a garden shed, but in order to travel on a public road it needs to conform to all the regulations of the road. It will have passed an annual inspection for safety and road-worthiness. Headlights, turn signals and safety belts are all installed.

Supermarket beep

A giant supermarket cart has been constructed and fitted with a car engine. This vehicle is strictly for fun. Lacking basic safety features such as proper seats, lights and bumpers, it is not allowed to be driven on public roads.

Only in the movies

The 1977 James Bond film, *The Spy Who Loved Me*, featured a car that behaved as though it was also a submarine. It was a British Lotus Elite car body specially altered to create the illusion.

Magic car

Ian Fleming, the creator of James Bond, also wrote a book about a magic car. This became the 1968 film *Chitty Chitty Bang Bang*. The car was an old one that the book's hero, Caractacus Potts, discovered in a junkyard. After restoring it, he discovered it could fly and float.

FACT BOX

• One of the amphibious vehicles used in World War II was called a "duck" after the initials DUKW given it by the manufacturer, General Motors. It had six wheels and moved through the water powered by a propeller.

• Microcars, such as the BMW Isetta and the Heinkel Trojan, were also known in the 1950s and 1960s as bubble cars because of their round shapes and large window spaces.

• Race tracks such as Le Mans in France, and Monza in Italy, hosted race meetings in the 1950s and 1960s where microcars such as the British Berkeley and the Italian Fiat Bianchina raced against each other.

Kit car

This 3-wheeler Triking, a modern replica (copy) of a 1930s Morgan, is a kit car that has been put together. The owner is supplied with all the different body panels and engine parts, and builds the complete car. Kit cars are cheaper than production-line cars, because the costs of assembly and labor are saved.

Web-toed drivers

Cars that can cross water are useful, especially in places where there are rivers but no bridges. Between 1961 and 1968, the German Amphicar company made almost 4,000 amphibious cars. They could reach a speed of 7 mph in the water, pushed along by two small propellers. On land they could reach 70 mph.

COOLING SYSTEM

T HE EXPLOSIONS in a car's engine, and the friction caused by its moving parts, create a great deal of heat. If the heat were not kept down, the engine would stop working. The metal parts would expand, seize up and stop. To cool the engine, water from a radiator is pumped through chambers in the cylinder block. The moving water carries heat away from the hottest parts of the engine. The radiator has to be cooled down too. A fan blows air onto it, to cool the water inside. The fan is driven by a belt from the engine crankshaft pulley. This project shows you how to transfer the energy of turning motion from one place to another. It uses a belt to move five reels. In the same way, some of the turning motion of an engine is transferred by a fan belt to the fan.

Rear engine

The air-cooled rear-engined Volkswagen Beetle was designed with an aerodynamic front and no need for a front-mounted radiator. Instead, the engine is cooled by a fan driven by a fan belt, like the one shown here. Engines of this kind are useful in cold climates, where low temperatures can freeze water in radiators.

FAN BELT

You will need: ruler, 6¹/4-in. square of thin cloth, scissors, 5 spools of thread, 8¹/2 x 11-in. wooden board, glue or glue stick, pencil, 5 flat-headed nails 1¹/2-in. in length, hammer, 3-ft length of 1-in.-wide velvet ribbon, tape, compass, 5 pieces of 6-in.-square colored card stock, 5 wooden skewers.

1 Using the ruler, measure five 1-in.-wide strips on the thin cloth. The height of the spools of thread should be more than 1 in. Use the scissors to cut out each strip.

2 Wrap one of the fabric strips around each of the five spools. Glue each strip at the end so that it sits firmly around the spool and does not come loose.

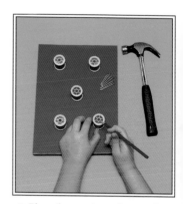

3 Place the spools on the wooden board as shown above. Trace the outlines with a pencil. Put the nails through the center of the spools and carefully hammer them into the board.

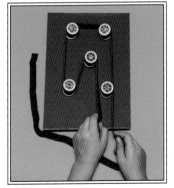

4 Wind the ribbon around the spools with the velvet side against four of the spools. Cut the ribbon at the point where you can join both ends round the fifth spool.

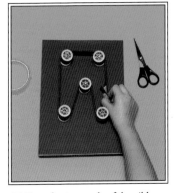

5 Tape the two ends of the ribbon together firmly. Make sure that the ribbon wraps firmly around all of the five spools, but not so tightly that it can not move.

6 Use the compass to draw circles about 2³/4 in. in diameter on the pieces of colored card stock. Then draw freehand spiral shapes inside each circle.

7 Use the scissors to cut each spiral out of each of the pieces of colored card stock. Start from the outside edge and gradually work your way in along the lines of the spiral.

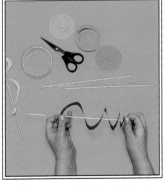

8 Tape one end of the spiral to the end of a skewer. Wind the other end of the spiral around the skewer a few times. Tape it close to the opposite end of the skewer.

10 Now you are ready to turn the belt. Like a fan belt in a car, it turns the fans around. This is a five-fan machine. You can add more fans if you like.

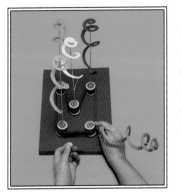

9 Put a small amount of tape on the end of each skewer. Place each skewer into one of the empty holes in the top of each spool of thread.

ENVIRONMENT MATTERS

CARS ARE convenient, but their effect on the environment causes concern. The manufacture and the driving of cars both use up precious natural resources such as metals and oil. The emissions (waste gases) that gas-powered cars produce pollute the atmosphere. One of them, carbon monoxide, is thought by many scientists to be contributing to problems such as global warming (the warming of the world's climate because of gases trapped in the atmosphere).

Although the environmental problems associated with cars are many, car makers have made many improvements to their models during recent years. Cars are much lighter than they used to be, so smaller amounts of raw materials are needed to make them. Because of their lighter weight, and improvements in their engine efficiency, they can drive many more miles per gallon of fuel than previously. In many countries, the emission of carbon monoxide into the atmosphere is actually lower now than twenty years ago, despite their being many more cars.

Costly accident
The gasoline that cars burn is extracted from oil pumped out of the ground or from under the sea. The oil is transported in enormous ships to refineries where the gasoline is extracted. Occasionally, a tanker sinks or springs a leak. When this happens, oil seeps into the sea and forms a slick on the surface, killing and injuring fish and birds.

FACT BOX

• Ford launched the Ford Ka in 1998, and the Ford Fiesta in 1976. Both are small everyday cars. But the exhaust gases of the 1976 Ford Fiesta contained fifty times more pollutants such as carbon monoxide and nitrogen oxides than the 1998 Ford Ka.

Traffic reports
Traffic police may gradually be replaced by computerized technology called Telematics. In-car navigation systems and traffic messaging (radio messages on traffic conditions) enable drivers to use the best route. This can reduce journey times, and gasoline consumption, by 10 percent.

Going nowhere fast

There are too many cars in the world. Traffic congestion is a common experience for many. Transportation experts are trying to link public transportation with car use to reduce the problem. For example, park-and-ride schemes allow drivers to park near a town, then catch a free bus downtown.

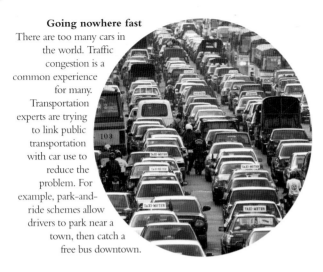

Rubber bounces back

The treads (gripping patterns) on tires wear away until the tire is too smooth to grip the road. Car owners throw away the old tires and buy new ones. Like metal and plastic, rubber does not biodegrade (decay naturally) easily. Tires can be reused by being shredded and turned into tiny chips of rubber. These can be melted down to make asphalt for covering roads.

Plug-in car

Electric cars create much less pollution than gas-powered cars. They use electricity stored in batteries. The batteries need to be recharged regularly by being plugged into the main electricity supply. In parts of California, drivers can find recharging stations in public places. Seven hours of charging will allow a car to travel a distance of about 100 miles.

In the dump

Most of the materials used in cars can be recycled. Car companies are using more and more recycled materials in their new cars, such as old batteries to make new batteries, and plastic accessories to make new plastic-based parts. But it is still very expensive to recycle the metal, so many old cars end up in the dump.

Lights in the smog

Fumes from cars cause smog over the city of Los Angeles. This is dangerous to people's health. Scientists are constantly researching alternative fuels. CNG (compressed natural gas) cars, which are already on sale, produce 20 percent fewer emissions than gas-powered cars.

BRAKING SYSTEMS

Cars have two types of brakes. Parking brakes lock the rear wheels when the car is standing still. They are controlled by the handbrake lever inside the car. Brakes used when the car is moving are usually made of steel discs attached to each wheel. They are called disc brakes and are controlled by the brake pedal inside the car. The disc brakes attached to the car's road wheels work just like the model disc brake in the project. Putting the brakes on too sharply when a car is moving can cause a skid, when the wheels lock and the tires slide on the road surface.

Antilock braking systems (ABS), now used in many cars, measure the road surface conditions and stop the car from going into a skid. This is done by making the disc brakes turn on and off very quickly, so that the wheels cannot lock.

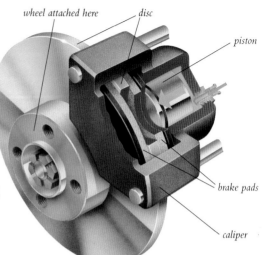

wheel attached here — *disc* — *piston* — *brake pads* — *caliper*

Squeeze, please
The disc brake unit's disc is attached to a turning hub. This is bolted to the road wheel. When the driver presses the brake pedal, fluid is squeezed down a tube to the piston on the side of the disc brake. The piston presses together two pads, one on either side of the disc, gripping it firmly and stopping it from turning. As the disc slows, so does the car wheel.

Ready, set, go
A stock car (modified production-line car) speeds up from standing very quickly. The driver builds up the power in the engine. When the engine is near full power, the driver quickly releases the brakes. Because the wheels suddenly start spinning incredibly quickly, the tires roar and whine against the hard ground, and burn with the heat of the friction (rubbing) against the road. The burning rubber turns into smoke which billows in dark clouds around the rear wheels.

Water sports
Rally drivers have to deal with extreme conditions such as dirt tracks, mud, snow and water. Powerful brakes help them to keep control of the cars. After going through water, a rally car's brakes would be wet. This makes them less effective because there is less friction. The brake pads slip against the wet disc. The driver has to press the brake pedal with a pumping action to get rid of the water.

DISC BRAKE

You will need: *scissors, 16-in. length of fabric, circular cardboard box with lid, tape, pencil, 8-in. length of 1/4-in. diameter wood dowel, glue, 3 x 5-in. piece of medium sandpaper, 2 1/2 x 4-in. wood block, two plastic cups, insulation tape.*

1 Use the scissors to cut a 16-in. long strip from the fabric. You may have to use special fabric cutting scissors if ordinary scissors are not sharp enough.

2 Take the strip of fabric you have cut out and wrap it around the rim of the circular cardboard box. Secure it firmly in place with small pieces of tape.

3 Make a hole in the center of the box's lid with a pencil. Twist the pencil until it pierces the bottom of the box. Now gently push the wood dowel through both holes.

4 Spread lots of glue onto the sandpaper's smooth side. Wrap the sandpaper carefully over the top of the wood block, pressing to attach it.

6 Spin the lid fast on the dowel. As it spins, bring the sandpaper into contact with the edge of the lid and see how it stops the lid turning. Test your brake disc and see how quickly and how gradually you can stop the lid.

5 Stand two plastic cups upside down on a flat surface. Rest either end of the wooden dowel on each cup. Cut two small pieces of insulation tape. Use them to attach each end of the dowel firmly to the cup tops.

SAFETY ISSUES

Traffic accidents are a constant danger. As the number of cars on the roads increased in the first half of the 1900s, the number of accidents to pedestrians and drivers increased also. During the last fifty years, ideas were put forward to reduce the scale of the problem. Gradually, most countries have decided that a driver must pass a test in driving skills. Governments have created safety regulations for road builders and car makers to follow. In many places, drivers and passengers are required by law to wear seat belts, and driving while under the influence of alcohol is forbidden in most countries.

New cars often have built-in safety features such as car body parts that resist crushing, and airbags that inflate to lessen the impact of collisions. Emergency road services deal more quickly with injured people. All these advances mean that in many countries there are now fewer road deaths than there were twenty years ago, even though there are more cars.

Safe and sound
If a car traveling at the relatively slow speed of 20 mph stopped suddenly, a child could be thrown forward and injured. To prevent this, a child can be strapped into a specially designed chair or seat that is fixed securely to a car seat. It also stops the child from distracting the driver.

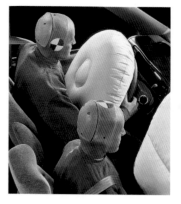

Bags of life
Experts who test cars for safety use crash-test dummies that react just like human bodies. These dummies are being protected by airbags, which were introduced into European production-line cars by Volvo in the 1980s. Airbags act as a kind of life-saving cushion, protecting a person from being thrown into the dashboard or the seat in front. The airbags inflate with gases as soon as sensors detect the first moment of a collision.

Not a care in the world
In the early days of driving, people were much less aware of road safety as there were very few cars. In this 1906 drawing, a rich young man–about–town leans over the back of his car seat. He does not have to worry about where he is going because he has a chauffeur to drive him. Yet even the chauffeur is careless and narrowly avoids hitting a pedestrian in front of the car.

Pain in the neck

When a car stops suddenly, a person's head is jolted forward and then sharply backward. This can cause damage to the neck called whiplash. It often results in serious injury. Car manufacturers have invented seats that slide backward and then tilt. The pictures show (1) the seat in normal position, (2) the seat sliding back, and (3) the seat's backrest tilting over. Combined with the headrest at the top, this seat design helps reduce whiplash.

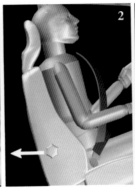
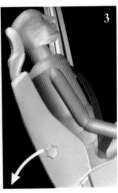

Traffic control

Before traffic control measures were introduced, accidents were common. In 1914, the first electric traffic light was installed in Cleveland, Ohio. Traffic lights control the flow of cars through intersections.

Grand slam

When cars collide with each other at high speed their bodywork (outer metal shell) smashes and twists. Safety engineers test the strength of a car's bodywork by hitting sample cars with powerful robot sleds. Wires attached to the car detect information about safety weak points. This information is used to improve the safety of materials and designs used in cars.

Major obstruction ahead

When a large truck tips over and spills its cargo, it creates all kinds of problems. Fire crews rescue anyone who is trapped in a vehicle, and medical teams treat any injured people. The police and fire crews direct the removal of the spilled cargo. Heavy cranes are needed to shift the truck. Although drivers are diverted to other roads, traffic jams build up that can stretch for long distances.

GOOD DESIGN

CAR MAKERS use large teams of people to create their new cars. Designers, design engineers and production engineers combine with the sales team to develop a car that people will want to buy. But before the new car is announced to the public, models are made. A quarter-sized clay model is tested in a wind tunnel to investigate the car's aerodynamics (how air flows over its shape). Finally, a prototype (early version) of the car is built and tested for road handling, engine quality and comfort.

Sleek and shiny
CAD (computer-aided design) software allows car designers to create a three-dimensional image of a new car design that can be looked at from any angle.

Painting on wheels
An old Mini Minor has been painted in exciting bright designs.

MODEL CAR

You will need: 2 sheets 8¹/₂ x 11-in. cardboard, scissors, glue, brush, awl, 6-in. square piece of colored card stock, pliers, 4 paper clips, 2 x 4-in. lengths of ¹/₂-in. diameter wood dowel, tape.

Wire basket
Three-dimensional, wire-frame (see-through) computer images allow designers to see how the shapes of the car fit together.

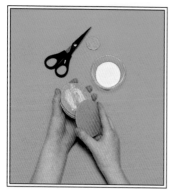

1 Cut out four 1-in. and eight 2¹/₂-in. diameter cardboard circles. Glue the 2¹/₂-in. circles together to make four wheels. Glue a 1-in. circle to the center of each wheel.

2 Use the awl to make a hole in the center of each wheel. Cut four ¹/₈-in. strips of colored card stock. Wrap one around each of the wheel rims. Glue the overlapping ends.

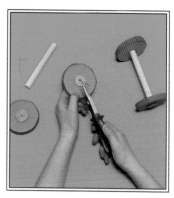

3 Push straightened paper clips into the holes and bend the ends with the pliers. Attach the wheels to the two pieces of dowel by pushing the paper clips into the ends.

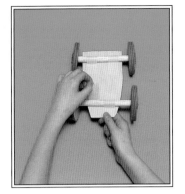

4 Cut a piece of cardboard to 3 x 6 in. Fold one end to make it 2½ in. wide. Tape the two axles to the board, one at each end. Leave space for the wheels to rotate freely.

5 Cut a piece of cardboard 3 x 14 in. Fold it over and bend it into a cab shape. Tape the two loose ends together. Stick the bottom of the cab shape to the car base.

6 Cut two cardboard shapes 6 in. long x 4 in. high. Trim them with the scissors to the same shape as the side of your car cab. Attach the sides to the cab with tape.

DECORATE YOUR CAR

You will need: acrylic paints in 2 colors, medium paintbrushes, pencil, 3 pieces of 6 x 8½-in. colored card stock, 1 piece of white card stock, felt-tipped pens in 2 colors, scissors, glue.

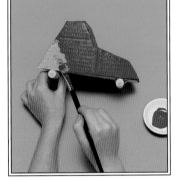

1 Remove the wheels from your car. Paint the sides and top of the cab with one of the two colors of paint. Paint two coats and let dry.

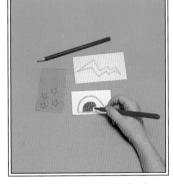

2 Draw exciting designs for the sides of the car, and a driver to go behind the windshield. Color them in with the felt-tipped pens.

3 Let the paint dry for a couple of hours. Cut the designs out of the card stock. Glue them to the sides and back of the car. Paint the wheels with the color of paint not yet used.

4 Replace the wheels when they are dry. Now your car looks just like a real street machine. Cut photographs of cars from magazines for ideas for new designs.

FRICTION AND OIL

WHEN THE parts of an engine move, they touch and create friction (rub against one another). The more quickly and often they move, the more friction there is. This makes the engine parts grow hot, but if they become too hot they expand and no longer fit properly. When this happens, the parts jam against one another and the engine seizes up.

Oil, a slippery liquid, lubricates the car engine. It is stored in the oil pan, from where it is pumped onto the moving parts. Eventually the oil gets dirty with soot and bits of dirt from outside. The dirty oil must be drained, and clean oil put in at regular intervals. Ball bearings help other moving parts of the car turn against each other. The project shows you how marbles can behave like ball bearings to reduce friction.

Oil giant
Car ownership grew steadily in the 1930s. This created a big demand for new car products. People wanted to keep their cars running smoothly and safely. Most of all, car owners needed engine oil that was always high quality, wherever and whenever they bought it. Oil companies spent a lot of money on advertisements, telling people that their oil was the best.

Sea changes
Oil rigs drill deep into the sea-bed to find crude (natural) oil. Car lubricating oil is made from this. Pumps in the rig draw the crude oil up from the sea-bed into pipes leading to refineries on land. Impurities are removed from the crude oil in the refineries. This makes it light enough to use in car engines.

Extra Jag
High-performance sports cars such as the Jaguar E-Type of the 1960s need a particularly light oil. Otherwise their powerful engines will not run smoothly. The E-Type engine in this car has six cylinders (most car engines have four). They generate the power needed to accelerate to a top speed of 150 mph. Over time a thick oil would clog the oil lines, leading to friction and wear and tear of many engine parts.

Luxury lines

Large luxury cars need a lot of oil. This 1958 Lincoln Continental has a huge 8-cylinder engine to lubricate. During the 1950s oil was very cheap. American car makers had less reason to think about the costs of running cars as carefully as they have in more recent years.

Beetle's brother

Between 1955 and 1974, Karmann produced the Karmann Ghia cabriolet for the car maker Volkswagen. It has a special body on the chassis (frame) of a Volkswagen Beetle. Like the Beetle, it has a rear engine.

BALL BEARINGS

You will need: 8¹/₂ x 11-in. sheet of stiff card stock, scissors, tape, 5 ¹/₂ x 8-in. strips of corrugated cardboard, 16 glass marbles.

1 Cut two strips of stiff card stock, both ¹/₂ in. wide. The first one should be 8 in. long and the second 4 in. long. Make both into circle shapes. Tape the ends together.

2 Use the strips of corrugated cardboard to line the inside of the larger card stock circle. Put all five strips in, and make sure that they are packed very closely together.

3 Place the smaller circle inside. Try to turn it against the corrugated cardboard. The corrugations create friction so it is not easy to turn the smaller circle.

4 Take the smaller circle and the corrugated strips out of the large circle. Now line the inside of the larger circle with the marbles until there are no gaps between them.

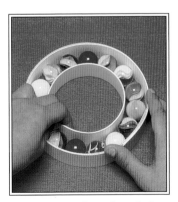

5 Place the smaller circle inside the larger one again. Turn the small circle. It moves very easily. The smooth surface of the glass marbles creates much less friction.

CLASSIC MODELS

IFFERENT PEOPLE collect different kinds of cars. Those who are looking for style collect classic cars (built after 1930, and at least twenty years old). Often the cars come from the 1950s, 1960s and 1970s. Owners take pride in the exceptional design and quality of the vehicles. For example, Rolls-Royces of any era look distinctive, and their engines and other mechanical parts were made with unusual care and the very best materials. High-performance classic sports cars such as the 1954 Mercedes-Benz Gullwing, the 1968 Aston Martin DB4, the 1960s Ford Mustang and the 1988 Porsche 959 are popular, too.

One of the greats
Few sports cars are as eagerly collected as the 1949 Jaguar XK120. It combines high speed with good looks. Its six-cylinder engine has double overhead camshafts (to control the valves in the cylinder heads). It can reach speeds of up to 120 mph.

Collectors of classic cars often belong to specialized clubs. The clubs help them to find the spare parts needed for their cars and to meet people who are interested in the same models. Motor museums such as the Museum of Automobile History, the National Motor Museum in the United Kingdom and the Porsche Museum in Germany exhibit classic cars for people to look at and enjoy.

Bumper beauty
American car makers of the 1950s such as Cadillac created cars that shone with large areas of chrome (shiny metal). Bumpers and radiator grilles were molded into streamlined shapes to catch the eye.

Fly me to the Moon
The Mercedes-Benz 300SL sports car was built by hand, so only 1,400 of them were ever made The car has one very striking feature. Its passenger and driver doors open upward from the roof of the car. The unusual design gave the car its nickname "The Gullwing," because the open doors look like a seagull. It is not very easy to get in and out of the car. Once inside, the driver and passenger sit close to the ground. The engine of the Gullwing was also set very low, to make sure that the driver could see over the top of the long hood.

Air-cooled cool

The 911 series Porsche Carrera was first made in 1964. The Porsche first appeared in 1939, as a higher-powered, streamlined, variation of the Volkswagen Beetle. Like the Beetle, the Porsche engine was air-cooled. Then, in 1997, the firm produced its first water-cooled car, the 928.

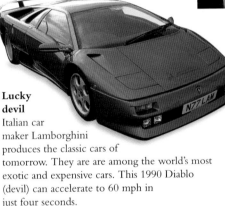

FACT BOX

• The classic Jaguar E-type was Britain's fastest production car in 1961. Its top speed 150 mph.

• The 1968 Ferrari 365GTB4 Daytona is still one of the world's fastest production cars. It has a top speed of 175 mph.

• A 1926 Bentley 3-liter four-seat tourer was auctioned for about $60,000 in 2000.

Lucky devil

Italian car maker Lamborghini produces the classic cars of tomorrow. They are are among the world's most exotic and expensive cars. This 1990 Diablo (devil) can accelerate to 60 mph in just four seconds.

Classic car, classic film

The 1997 film comedy *Austin Powers* used many different examples of 1960s style. They all helped to recreate the fun-loving, swinging image of that period. In this scene, the hero of the film, played by Mike Myers, is standing up in the seat of a 1960s Jaguar E-Type. The bullet shape of this car is a classic design of the period.

Classic performance

The British car maker Jaguar made many classic models in the past, such as the XK120 and the E-Type. The cars it makes today are also of top quality and performance. This 150-mph XKR convertible's engine is supercharged to give extra power.

Super-streamlined

Modern sports-car maker Marcos designs cars such as the Mantis that are destined to become classics of the future. They have luxurious interiors and powerful engines to match any of the old greats. The streamlining on the front of this Mantis gives the car a look that stands out from other sports cars.

SPORTS CARS

SPORTS CARS, also known as roadsters, are made for speed, not comfort. Their engines are more powerful than those in everyday cars. In addition, they usually have only two seats. That way they carry less weight than ordinary cars. A French Delage super-sports car made an international record in 1932 with a speed of 110 mph. In 1996, the British Lotus Esprit V8 arrived on the scene with a top speed of 170 mph. Sports cars are driven on ordinary roads but they can also be driven in races. The 1972 Italian Lancia Stratos won the Monte Carlo Rally five times. The engines and bodies of sports cars are often developed from race cars and have been tested under tough conditions. The Le Mans 24-hour race in France is used as a gruelling testing ground for sports car engines.

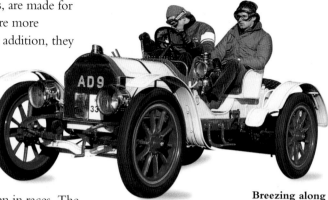

Breezing along
A 1904 Mercedes was no car to drive if you caught colds easily. There was no such thing as a convertible (a car with a folding roof) in 1904. But this Mercedes was still built for speed. A restored model shows the beautiful headlights and coachwork (bodywork) created for this masterpiece of early car engineering.

Friend of frogeye
This is a Big Healey, one of the larger models produced by the British car maker Austin Healey. The company are also known for their small sports car, the Sprite, nicknamed Frogeye because of its bulbous headlights. Austin Healey ceased production in 1971, but their cars are favorites with collectors.

FACT BOX

• Jaguar produced their first sports car, the SS90, in 1935.

• The 1968 Aston Martin DB5 was the favorite car of James Bond

• The Chevrolet Camaro was first produced in 1967 and is a powerful sports car, still popular today among collectors. The 1989 model had a V-8 engine that could reach 150 mph.

• The MG sports cars are so-called because the company that made them was originally called Morris Garages.

Red bullet
The 1961 Jaguar E-Type's engine was developed from the one used in Jaguar's D-Type race cars. Jaguar regularly took part in race car events in the 1950s. The D-Type was a truly great race car. It won the Le Mans 24-hour race four times between 1953 and 1957.

Pushy Porsche

The rear wing sticking out of the back of the Porsche 911 Turbo improves the flow of air over the back of the car when it travels at high speed. It works by flattening out the air flow as it moves over the top of the car and down the rear. This helps to keep the car's body firmly on the road and the driver in control on tight curves.

Cool bug

The Volkswagen Beetle was developed as an inexpensive family car. Then the 1968 Cabriolet appeared and surprised everyone. Volkswagen had made the engine more powerful to bring it into the same speed range as other small sports cars. It also had a flexible roof that could roll back in hot weather. Cars like this are called convertibles. This sporty Beetle is one of many changes the design has gone through since it was first produced in 1939.

Silver speeder

The Bugatti company started building high-quality sports and race cars in 1909, first in Germany and then in France. When the firm was sold in 1956, people feared it would never make cars again. In 1991, however, the Bugatti EB110 appeared, hoping to keep the glory of the past alive. Its design, 12-valve engine and four-wheel drive were praised widely. In 1994 Bugatti closed again, but the company was later bought by Volkswagen.

Beautiful beamer

The BMW (*Bayerische Motoren Werke*) company has made cars and motorcycles in the German city of Munich since 1928. In the 1970s, they began to sell more of their cars outside Germany. By the 1980s, BMWs were popular throughout the world. Although this 3-series convertible from the 1990s has four seats, its 115-mph top speed means it is still seen as a two-door sports car.

FUEL CONTROL

THE CONTROLLED flow of fuel into a car's engine is very important, because it affects how the car performs. If there is too much fuel and not enough air, the engine floods with gasoline and will not start. If there is not enough fuel, the engine will run in a jerky way. The mixing of fuel and air occurs inside the carburetor. A piston goes down as a valve opens to let the fuel and air mixture in. The valve closes and the piston goes up, compressing (squeezes) the fuel and air mixture. The spark plug fires to ignite the fuel mixture, pushing the piston down again. The piston rises again and the exhaust valve opens to release the waste gases.

The project shows you how to make a model that works in the same way as the camshaft. It opens one valve and then, as it closes the first valve, a second valve opens.

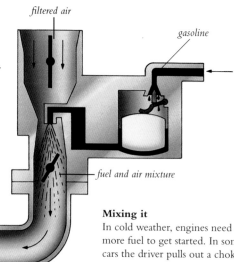

filtered air

gasoline

fuel and air mixture

Mixing it
In cold weather, engines need more fuel to get started. In some cars the driver pulls out a choke. This causes the carburetor to increase the amount of fuel in the fuel and air mixture. Many modern cars have automatic chokes. Internal computers work out the exact mixture of fuel and air that will suit the weather conditions.

AC 868 DV

Double trouble
Very powerful cars such as the Lamborghini Diablo need to generate a lot of energy to accelerate (increase speed) quickly. They have 12 cylinders in their engines, burning much more fuel than an ordinary 4-cylinder car. The burned fuel creates a large amount of exhaust gas. The Diablo has four exhaust pipes at the rear of the car. Most ordinary cars have only one exhaust pipe.

ROCK AND ROLL CAMSHAFT

You will need: scissors, 2¹/₂-in. square stiff card stock, masking tape, cardboard tube with plastic lid, pencil.

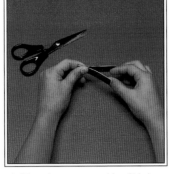

1 Use scissors to cut a ¹/₂ x 2¹/₂-in. strip from the stiff card stock. Fold it over in the center. Hold it with your fingertips. Bend the two ends of the card stock away from one another.

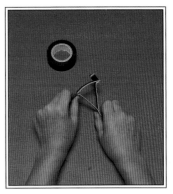

2 Cut a ¹/₂ x 1¹/₂-in. strip from the original piece of card stock. Use masking tape to fix the card strip to the folded bottom ends of the first piece. This makes a triangle shape.

3 Use the scissors to cut out two small circle shapes from the original piece of card stock. Use masking tape to secure them to the bottom piece of the triangle you have made.

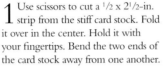

4 Put the triangle on top of the cardboard tube. The circles should touch the plastic lid. With a pencil, mark where the circles sit on the lid.

5 Using the scissors, carefully cut around the pencil marks you have made in the plastic lid of the tube. These form an inlet and an outlet.

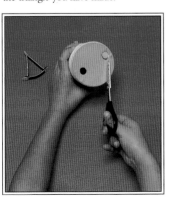

6 Now you can rock the triangle back and forth to cover and uncover the two holes one after another. This is just how a camshaft opens and shuts the intake and exhaust valves in a car's cylinder.

SUSPENSION

THE EARLIEST cars used coach wheels made of wood and metal. They provided a very bumpy ride. In the early 1900s, the French company Michelin made a rubber tire with an inflatable inner tube. The idea came from the inner tube tire that John Dunlop developed in the late 1800s for bicycles. The outer part of the tire was made of rubber. Inside it had a tube filled with air. The air cushioned the car's contact with the road and driving became much more comfortable. All car tires had inner tubes until the 1950s. From then on, more tubeless tires were made. In these, air is held in a web of cords and an inner tire that fits very tightly on the wheel rim. Cars use suspension systems, as well as air-filled tires, as cushioning. Suspension systems are attached to a car's wheels to absorb impacts from the road. In modern cars these are usually either coiled springs, shaped rubber cones or gas-filled cylinders.

Thick and thin
The engines on hot rods (cars with boosted engines) drive the rear wheels. These wheels often have thick tires. This means there is a lot of contact between the road surface and the tire surface, helping the car to grip the road when accelerating.

Suspension
A car's suspension system makes driving comfortable. It prevents the car from being bumped up and down too much on bumpy roads. In the early 1900s, car suspension was the same as the suspension in horse-drawn carriages. Modern cars use much more sophisticated systems. The Jaguar XKR Coupe shown here has a coiled spring system. The suspension system is attached to each wheel. If the car goes over a 2-inch bump, the wheel will go up 2 inches too, but the car's body will move up less distance. The suspension system absorbs the impact. After going over the bump, the car's body will sink down slowly, too. Hydraulic cylinders (cylinders full of a liquid or gas, such as oil) do this. The cylinders are called dampers, because they damp down the effect of the bump.

Taking off

Rally cars travel so quickly that when they come over the top of a hill they can leave the ground for a second or two. Then they come back down to earth with a stomach-churning bump. A hard landing can shatter a car's axles and put the car out of the competition. Rally cars take this kind of punishment hour after hour, day after day. They have to be fitted with extra-strong suspension systems

Early tires

A 1903 Mercedes-Benz sports car is equipped with tires made of rubber casing. Inside these were rubber tubes filled with air, just like the inner tubes in bicycle tires. Tire manufacturers stopped including inner tubes in car tires from the 1950s onward. Drivers were having too many flats.

Extreme machine

Four truck wheels have hijacked a pickup truck to provide a well-cushioned ride. In the quest for ever more bizarre effects, someone has put a pickup truck on top of a metal frame. The frame is then specially linked to the type of tires normally seen on enormous road vehicles such as earth-moving trucks. Suspension on this scale allows the truck to travel over extremely uneven surfaces, such as an uneven quarry floor.

Big smoothie

Limousines look spectacular and provide exceptional levels of comfort. Stretch limousines are the most luxurious of all. They are often used for weddings and other important events. Very long cars like this have what is known as SRC (Selective Ride Control) suspension to make for an extra-smooth ride. Computers control chambers filled with gas that is pressurized by a pump. The compressed air absorbs shocks from the road.

HOME FROM HOME

Long way from home
Long-distance truck drivers, who drive thousands of miles every year, often travel through regions where there are very few towns or villages. At night the driver finds a safe place to park, then sleeps in a built-in bunk behind the driver's seat.

THE GREAT advantage of setting off on an adventure by car is that you can go where you want, when you want. It is even possible to travel to places where there may be no towns or people. Once you're there, however, what do you do when you want to go to sleep at night? One solution is to drive a special car such as a multi-purpose vehicle (MPV) or a recreational vehicle (RV). They are built to provide sleeping space. Smaller ones have car seats that will lie flat to make a bed. Larger RVs have cabins with built-in bunks, kitchens and sitting areas. They may also have televisions, music systems, microwave ovens and all the high-tech equipment that can be found in a conventional house. The interiors of top-of-the-range RVs can be built according to the buyer's preferences.

Open-air life
Campers are mobile living units that can be towed from place to place by cars. Towing a camper requires a lot of extra power from the car, so larger vehicles are the most suitable. Drivers have to keep their speed down when pulling a camper, because the camper could easily flip over.

Time for a drink
Rolls-Royce built the 1960 Phantom as a touring car for people who wanted to travel to the countryside and eat when they arrived. The small seats fold down when the car is moving and pull up in front of the liquor cabinet when the car is stopped. Cars like this were often driven to outdoor events such as horse races, where eating a picnic from a car is a tradition.

SCENTED CAR AIR FRESHENER

You will need: 7 fl oz water, mixing bowl, 1 cup all-purpose flour, wooden spoon, baking sheet, pencil, bottle of essential oil, paintbrush, four colors of acrylic paint, 18-in length of string.

1 Pour the water into a mixing bowl. Stir in the flour slowly with a wooden spoon. Continue to stir until the paste thickens into a dough mixture that you can mold.

2 Place the dough mixture on a baking sheet. Mold the dough into a bell shape that bulges out at the bottom. Roughly shape a roof at the top and wheels underneath.

3 Wet the rough shape so it is easy to mold a design on it. Smooth your fingers over the top area to make a windshield. Shape the wheels more accurately.

4 Make small holes in the car and one larger hole in the top. Sprinkle essential oil in the holes. Bake in an oven for 45 minutes at 300°F. Let cool.

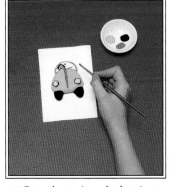

5 Once the car is cool, place it on a sheet of paper. Paint the hood first, then the details, such as a driver's face. Add lines around the headlights.

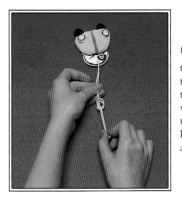

6 Allow the paint to dry. Thread the piece of string through the hole in the top of the car's windshield. Double the string back and knot it to make a noose.

7 Your air freshener is all ready to go in a real car. Now you can put it on the dashboard, hang it from the back of a seat or put it on the shelf in front of the rear window. It will make any car smell fresh and clean.

FUEL CONSUMPTION

THE AMOUNT of gasoline a car uses depends on the weight of the car, the speed it is traveling, and the size and efficiency of the engine. Pressing on the accelerator pedal lets more fuel flow into the engine's cylinders, speeding the car up. Most ordinary cars have four cylinders. A few extremely economical cars have two cylinders, and some powerful cars have six or even eight. Today, cars of all engine size are designed to use as little fuel as possible. This is because the oil from which gasoline is made is much more expensive than it was in the 1950s and 1960s. The average modern car can travel 35 to 50 mph on one gallon of gas. Gas guzzlers such as the Cadillac Fleetwood could only drive 10 miles on a gallon of gas.

Roaring oldie
Super Street hot rodders often take the bodies of old cars and combine them with modern parts. The 1950s car body here has been joined to big tires by a complicated suspension system. Some hot rodders use special chemical fuels such as ethanol and nitromethane. When they burn, they get much hotter than gasoline. The extra heat helps them to accelerate to very high speeds.

FACT BOX

• Rising oil prices in the late 1900s led to the creation of gasohol, a mixture of lead-free gasoline and ethanol. Ethanol can be made from plants such as grain and potatoes.

• Traces of the metal lead in car exhaust fumes are harmful. It is thought that many people suffered lead poisoning. Now, lead-free gasoline has been developed and is widely available.

Where's the car?
Members of the Eddie Jordan pitstop crew swarm over the Jordan 199 at the Australian Grand Prix in 1999. In the center, a team member holds the hose that forces fuel into the car's gas tank at high pressure. Up to 25 gallons of fuel can be pumped into the car in about 10 seconds. Speed is essential. Every second in the pit lane is equal to about 60 yards lost on the track.

Two-carb Caddy

The Cadillacs of the 1950s are reminders of a time when gasoline was cheap and car makers could make big, heavy cars. In the 1970s, the price of oil rose dramatically, so gas became much more expensive. The 1955 Cadillac Fleetwood had two carburetors, even though most cars built at that time would have had just one. The second carburetor was needed because the Fleetwood used so much gasoline.

Pink Thunderbird

The sleek rear fins and supercool spare-wheel holder made the 1957 Ford Thunderbird a car that people remembered long after Ford stopped making the model. This restored T-Bird is a convertible. When the cars were first sold, buyers were given both a hard top and a convertible top. They could use whichever one they wanted. In 1998, the 1957 Thunderbird's good looks earned it a Lifetime Automotive Design Achievement Award from the Detroit Institute of Ophthalmology.

Twice as much

Cars that use a lot of gasoline may have two or even four exhausts. Twin exhausts extract waste gases from the engine in a more efficient way than a single exhaust could, which allows the engine to perform more efficiently, too.

Flying flatbed

Flatbed trucks such as this are favorites for customizing enthusiasts. They take an old truck and turn it into an ORV (Off-Road Vehicle). An ORV consumes lots of gasoline as it drives across rough country, often far from any gas stations. They carry large cans of gas in case they run out.

SPEED RECORDS

I N MORE than a hundred years of car building, cars have reached faster and faster speeds. In 1899, the Belgian inventor Camille Jenatzy was the first person to drive a car faster than 60 mph. The car, designed by Jenatzy himself, ran on electricity. In the same year Sir Charles Wakefield created his Castrol Motor Oil company. The company awards the official trophy for the land-speed record to drivers who break the record. The trophy was first won in 1914 by the Englishman L.G. Hornsted. He reached a speed of 175 mph in a car from the German car maker Benz. Since then 38 other people have broken the record. The last person to succeed was the RAF Tornado pilot Andy Green, on October 13, 1997. His car, powered by two jet engines, broke the sound barrier (sound travels at a speed of 760 mph reaching 761 mph.

Electric with excitement
Between December 1898 and April 1899, there were no less than six attempts to beat the land-speed record. All of them were made by drivers in electric cars. The fastest, in April, was the Belgian Camille Jenatzy who reached 65 mph. He called his car *La Jamais Contente* (Never Satisfied) because he had already tried to set the land-speed record twice before.

Gas-powered wheels
Finding a long, flat, hard surface to travel on is very important when trying to set a speed record on land. Donald Campbell thundered across the Lake Eyre Salt Flats in Australia in 1964. He reached a speed of 402 mph in his gas-turbine powered car Bluebird. He was following in the footsteps of his father Malcolm, who set nine land-speed records.

Golden goer
The Golden Arrow set a land-speed record of 230 mph on March 11, 1929. The enormous, streamlined car was powered by a Napier-Lion airplane engine. It flashed along the hard, white sand at Daytona Beach, Florida. The driver was Major Henry Seagrave. After setting the land-speed record, Seagrave went on to set the World Water Speed Record.

Goodbye, Mr Bond

In the 1974 James Bond film *The Man with the Golden Gun*, the character James Bond performs many death-defying feats. His car takes at least as much punishment as the Secret Service Agent himself. To fly across the river, the car would have had to be traveling at 125 mph when taking off from the ramp.

Pushy guy

The Black Rock Desert in Nevada was the scene for another record-breaking attempt in 1983. On this dried lake bed, in blistering desert heat, Richard Noble set a new record of 631 mph. He was driving a specially made jet-engine powered Thrust 2. Making a speed record attempt costs a lot of money. The advertisements plastered all over the car are for businesses that sponsored this record attempt.

Head for the horizon

Ever since commercial movies started to be made in the early 1900s, car chases have formed part of the action. The cars are usually driven by stunt men and women specially trained in fast driving. In the 1991 film *Thelma and Louise*, shown above, the two heroines are chased by dozens of police cars. In the end, the two women drive off a cliff.

Supersonic car

In 1997 Andy Green drove the Thrust SSC at an incredible 761 mph. He did not just set a new world land-speed record, he traveled faster than the speed of sound (760 mph). Until then, speeds greater than that of sound had only been possible in flight. Andy was used to the speed because he was a jet pilot for the British Royal Air Force.

ROADS AND HIGHWAYS

BEFORE THE 1800s, most roads were just earth tracks. Some roads in cities and towns were made of stone and wood blocks, which gave a rough ride. Macadam roads (roads covered in a hard layer of tiny stones) were a great improvement in the 1800s, but with the invention of cars at the end of the 1800s, new road surfaces were needed. Roads made of asphalt (a mixture of bitumen and stone) and concrete offered the hardness and smoothness that cars needed to travel safely and quickly.

The first highway was completed in 1932 in Germany, between Cologne and Bonn. As car ownership grew during the second half of the 1900s, road building programs followed. Some people think there are too many roads. They protest against the building of more roads because they want to protect the countryside.

Multi-lane moves

Car ownership and use has grown relentlessly, and highways and freeways have grown too. In the last 30 years the freeways have increased in size from 4 lanes to 12 lanes, and even to 16 lanes on some stretches.

Pay as you go

The enormous costs of building highways can be partly paid for by charging drivers a toll (payment for using a road) when they travel on the new roads. The road owners set up barriers through which a car must pass to drive onto the road. Drivers crossing the Queen Elizabeth Bridge in Dartford, England, stop at toll booths to buy tickets that allow them to drive over the bridge.

Keep calm

Traffic calming is the name given to the different ways of slowing down traffic speed. Building speed bumps is one example of traffic calming. The speed bumps force drivers to slow down in areas where there is a lot of housing. Slower car speeds help to prevent accidents.

Going places

Modern countries need well-built roads so that goods and people can travel easily between cities and towns. This is Interstate 35 approaching Minneapolis. It is part of the vast interstate highway system that links the entire United States.

Major to minor

Road networks are often much easier to understand from the air. A cloverleaf links two major highways. Long curving roads such as these allow drivers to switch between major roads without having to stop at an intersection. The roads that link up major roads are called access roads.

Night guide

Small glass reflectors called Catseyes help drivers to see the road at night. The Catseyes are set at regular intervals in the middle of the road. They gleam brightly when a car's headlights shine on them. The British inventor Percy Shaw invented the device in 1933, after noticing how a cat's eyes shine at night.

The long and winding road

There are still many narrow old roads in remote areas. They twist and turn for miles through beautiful countryside. There is much less traffic on country roads, and they offer an enjoyable test of driving skills. Four-wheel drive vehicles handle particularly well on the tight corners and steep slopes.

Conic section

Modern roads carry a lot of traffic and need constant repair and maintenance. They cannot simply be shut down while that happens. Instead, some lanes are closed for repair while others remain open. The long lines of plastic cones on this stretch of highway have restricted traffic to one lane on one side and two lanes on the other side.

ORNAMENTS AND MASCOTS

Leading lady
All Rolls-Royce cars carry a winged figure mascot on the hood. It is called The Spirit of Ecstasy and was created by the sculptor Charles Sykes. The figure first appeared on Rolls-Royce cars in 1911. In modern Rolls-Royces, the mascot folds down backward into the hood during an accident to avoid injury.

Car Manufacturers take pride in the work that goes into the machines that they make. They put hood ornaments or symbols on their cars to show which company made the car. There are many different car makers all over the world, and they each make a different hood ornament. The instantly recognizable designs of the most prestigious companies, such as the Silver Lady on Rolls-Royces or the three-spoked circle on Mercedes cars, suggest elegance or power. Other celebrated symbols are the rearing horse on the front of cars made by the Italian Ferrari company, and the VW symbol used on Volkswagen cars. Sometimes these hood ornaments are called mascots, perhaps because car makers see them as a symbol of good luck. When people identify a car's hood ornament, they immediately know the name of the car maker. In this project, you can make your own hood ornament to symbolize the kind of car you like.

HOOD HERO

You will need: 8$\frac{1}{2}$ x 11-in. sheet of cardboard, pencil, scissors, tape, awl, glue, matchstick, newspaper, fork, 1 cup all-purpose flour, 7 fl oz water, tin of silver spray paint, fine paintbrush, black paint.

1 Cut a piece measuring 6 x 8 in. from the cardboard. Use a pencil to draw the outline of the shape you want to put on your car hood on the cardboard sheet.

2 Use the scissors to cut roughly around the ornament shape. Then cut around the outline accurately. Be careful not to cut off any of the detail in your drawing.

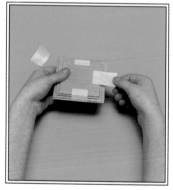

3 Cut three square pieces from the cardboard, one 2 in., one 2$\frac{1}{2}$ in. and one 3 in. Tape the smallest on top of the next largest and those on top of the largest as a solid base.

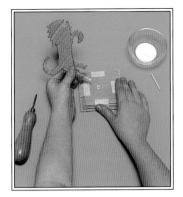

4 Make a hole in the center of the base with the awl. Put a glued matchstick in the bottom of your ornament. Insert it into the hole in the base so the ornament stands upright.

5 Tear strips of newspaper. Mix flour and water to make a thick paste. Use your fingers to dip the paper in the mixture. Apply the wet paper to the ornament in three layers.

6 When the newspaper is dry, spray your ornament with spray paint. Be careful to point the can downward, away from you. Put a piece of paper under the ornament.

7 Use the paintbrush to apply black lines on the ornament where you want to show more detail. For example, this one shows detail of the lion's mane, tail and paws.

Speeder's shield

The ornament on Porsche cars is like a coat of arms from medieval times. In the past, important people made decorations on shield shapes to tell others who their ancestors were and where they came from.

8 Your finished ornament could form the start of a great collection. You could copy all your favorite car ornaments. There are many more to choose from.

Roar of power

Jaguar cars have used the model of the leaping jaguar as their hood ornament for many years. More recent models do not have the statuette on the hood. They have been declared illegal because they could cause injury to pedestrians in an accident.

THE FUTURE

THE CARS of the future already exist, but only as the unrevealed designs of car makers. The use of in-car computers will be one of the main ways in which cars will change. These already control engine performance, navigation aids and air temperature. In future, a computer chip may apply the brakes automatically when the car in front is too close, or flash up HUDs (Heads Up Display) messages on the windshield about road conditions ahead.

Designers and engineers will continue to develop fuel-efficient cars (ones that use as little gasoline as possible), such as the Toyota Echo. They will also look at the potential of alternative power sources such as electricity, natural gas (a gas found underground), solar power (power from the sun's energy) and hydrogen (a gas in the earth's atmosphere). Of all the many developments that will occur, one is almost certain. There will be even more cars on the roads.

Hot item
Cars powered by energy from the sun (solar power) would be better for the environment than gas-powered cars. Photo-electric cells on the back of the car turn energy from the sun's rays into electricity. This energy is stored in batteries inside the car. The batteries then supply power to the engine. At the moment this method can only store enough energy to power small cars. Scientists are trying to find a way to use solar power in bigger vehicles.

FACT BOX

• The American car manufacturer General Motors is developing a car that will change its shape from a sedan to a pickup truck by means of voice-activated commands spoken by the driver in the front seat.

• Car makers are building concept (future idea) cars in which each seat has its own LCD (liquid-crystal display) screen. Passengers will be able to send and receive e-mail, browse the internet, make phone calls and read maps.

Take me home
GPS (Global Positioning System) navigation aids are already standard features in top-range cars. A radio antenna in the car sends a signal to one of the 24 GPS satellites that orbit the earth. The satellite sends a signal back to the car giving its exact position on the earth. The data is sent to a computer that reads maps stored on a CD-ROM. A small screen on the dashboard of the car displays a map of the road network and the position of the car on the map. If the driver inputs the destination, the screen displays the best route.

Neat package
Car makers produced classic microcars such as the BMW Isetta in the 1950s and 1960s. In the future, they will continue to make very small cars. They are ideal for short journeys in developed areas. The number of cars in towns and cities continues to grow. Extra-small vehicles such as the Smart car could be the answer to parking problems. It is so short (8 feet) that it can park not just along the edge of the road, but facing the sidewalk.

Snappy mover
Research has shown that on most journeys, the average number of people who travel in a car is two. Car makers now know that two-seater cars like the one shown here make a lot of sense for many drivers. Less metal is needed to make them, they use less fuel, and they are cheaper to buy. A car as small as this is also much easier to maneuver in the tight spaces of modern cities.

Three-wheel dream
One-person cars seem an obvious answer to many traffic problems. They are not always a hit with drivers, however. The British inventor Sir Clive Sinclair produced the electric-powered Sinclair C5 in 1985. The vehicle was not very popular, and was soon taken out of production.

Future taxi
Will the four-wheel yellow cabs of New York today be replaced by three-wheel taxis in the future? The 1992 science-fiction film *Freejack* showed great imagination in guessing what the taxicabs of tomorrow might look like.

PART EIGHT

AIRCRAFT AND FLIGHT

More than any other form of transport, aircraft have been inspired by the natural world. The very first flying machines, as well as the jumbo jets and supersonic warplanes of today, all have design features gained from studying birds and insects in flight. Here, you will find out the technological secrets of powered flight by looking at all the different types of aircraft, past and present, and follow some of the challenges that have faced pioneers throughout the history of aviation.

AUTHORS

Peter Mellett and John Rostron

CONSULTANT

Chris Oxlade

WHAT IS FLIGHT?

THINK ABOUT flight and you may think about birds and insects, paper darts and airplanes, bullets and footballs. All of these can move swiftly through the air, but are they all really flying? To answer this question, imagine you are launching a paper dart into the air. It glides away from you and finally lands back on the ground. Now throw a ball in exactly the same way. It hits the ground much sooner than the paper dart. We say that the paper dart was flying, but the ball was not. This is because bullets, footballs, stones and arrows are all projectiles. They do not really fly because they have nothing to keep them up in the air. Birds, aircraft, rockets and balloons do fly—they stay off the ground longer than something that is simply thrown.

Animal power
Birds, insects and bats all have wings. These animals use their wings to hold themselves up in the air and move along. Muscles provide power for take-off.

Balloons
This balloon is filled with a gas called helium that is seven times lighter than air, so the balloon floats upward, just like a cork floats upward in water. Airships are also filled with helium to keep them airborne. Before airplanes were invented, lighter-than-air craft, such as these, were the only way people could make a sustained flight.

Spaceflight
The space shuttle is launched into space by powerful main engines and booster rockets. It uses smaller engines, as part of the orbital maneuvering system, to increase speed, in order to reach an orbit about 185 miles above Earth. The force of Earth's gravity acts like a tether, keeping the shuttle in orbit, while the shuttle's speed prevents it from falling back to the ground.

Airplanes

Like birds, airplanes have wings to hold them up in the air, but they also have engines. Engine power is needed to help them take off from the ground and push them through the air. Most long-distance airplanes fly at great heights because as air becomes less dense with height, drag is reduced so less thrust is needed to maintain speed, and the power and fuel needed to push them through the air is much less than at ground level. More fuel is needed during take-off, as engines work at maximum thrust to gain height as quickly as possible.

Gliders

Since gliders have no engines, they have to be towed into the air by small airplanes or by machines on the ground. The towline is then released, and the gliders' wings hold them up. In still air they will glide slowly back to the ground in a gentle spiral. The pilot controls the glider's flight by searching for rising air currents, called thermals, and by altering the shape of the glider's wings. Most gliding is done in a hilly landscape where the hills cause the air to rise. By using these air currents, a glider pilot can keep his plane aloft for many hours, as long as these rising currents persist.

Flying a kite

A kite is lifted into the air by a blowing wind. A long string called a tether holds the kite at an angle to the wind. The air rushes against the kite, pushing it upward and keeping it in the air. If the wind drops or the tether breaks, the kite will fall back to the ground.

BIRDS IN FLIGHT

MUSCLE-POWERED flight is very hard work. In the past, many people have tried to fly by flapping artificial wings, but no one has succeeded. Birds, however, are very light and powerful compared to us, and are perfectly designed to stay up in the air. Birds' wings are covered in feathers— one of the strongest and lightest natural materials known to man. The airfoil shape of their wings provides lift, while tail feathers help with steering and braking. Birds flap their wings hard to take off and climb into the air, and need enormous flight muscles to provide enough power for flight. These muscles account for nearly a quarter of the weight of some birds, for example, eagles. To make sure plenty of blood is pumped to the muscles as they work, birds also have a large, fast-beating heart. If humans were to fly, they would need a chest the size of a barrel, arms 10 feet long, legs like broom handles, and a head the size of an apple—as well as thousands of feathers!

barb

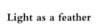

Light as a feather
Every feather has a hollow tube running down its center. Microscopic hooks lock each barb together so that air cannot pass through.

Eagle in flight
A soaring bird such as a vulture or an eagle has spread-out feathers with slots in between. Each feather acts as a tiny airfoil, lifting the bird as it flies through the air.

primary feathers

Flying feathers
The large primary flight feathers on the end of each wing produce most of the power for flight. These feathers can be closed together or spread apart to control flight. Smaller feathers on the inner wing form the curve that provides lift and are known as secondary flight feathers. The innermost feathers keep the bird warm and shape the wing into the bird's body, helping to prevent turbulence in flight.

secondary feathers

On the wing

This sequence of pictures shows how an owl flies through the air. A bird's wings bend in the middle as they rise upward, and the feathers open to let air pass through the wings. On the powerful downstroke, the primary flight feathers slice through the air and the feathers close up again. This pushes the air down and back and pulls the bird upward and forward.

flight feathers

wing bone

flight muscles

breastbone

A bird's body

Flight feathers are connected to thin bones at the end of each wing. Bird bones are light— most are hollow and filled with air. The large flight muscles are anchored to the breastbone at the front of a bird's chest.

Deadly speed

Peregrine falcons are the fastest animals in the world. They fold back their wings to reduce drag, then dive at their prey at speeds up to 215 mph. The force of the impact breaks the victim's neck instantly.

HOW BIRDS FLY

Move your hand across and back in a tank of water, with the palm flat. Now tilt your thumb side downward as you move it across. You can feel the forces pushing against your hand.

As you bring your hand back, tilt the thumb side upward. The forces are now pushing in different directions. In each case, a force pushes the thumb-edge forward.

L OOK AT a large bird, such as a goose, in the sky. Can you describe how its wings are moving? Flying birds do not simply flap their wings up and down. Their wings are not stiff and flat—instead, each wing has a joint like an elbow in the middle. This joint allows the wing to twist upward on the downstroke and downward on the upstroke. The feathers on the part of the wing corresponding to your hand are called the primary or flight feathers. On the downstroke, the front edge of the hand is tilted downward, so that the effect of the air flow is to generate a forward thrust as well as to produce lift. On the upstroke, the front edge is tilted upward. One effect of this is to produce a downward force (called anti-lift), but it also produces forward thrust. Thrust propels the bird forward.

A BIRD OF YOUR OWN

You will need: *sheets of stiff paper, tape, scissors, glue stick.*

1 Start by making the bird's short legs. Fold one piece of paper in half lengthwise. Fold it again several times until the paper is about 1 in. across.

2 Fold the strip of paper in half, as shown, and make a fold at each end for the feet. Tape the feet to your work surface to help keep your model stable.

3 To make the body of your bird, roll a piece of paper into a tube and secure the edge with tape. Use some more tape to stick the body to the legs.

4 To make the wings, fold a piece of paper twice lengthwise so that it is about six times longer than it is wide. Fold it into a W shape.

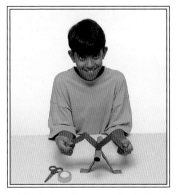

5 Stick the wings onto the body. You have now made a model bird. To mimic how a bird flies, hold one wing tip in each hand.

6 Move your hands in circles— one going clockwise, the other counterclockwise. At take-off, a bird's wings make large, round circles.

7 During the upstroke, notice how the bird's wings bend in the middle. Some birds raise their wings so high at the top of the upstroke that they bang together.

8 During the downstroke, the wings become flatter. To see how a bird's wings move when the bird is flying level, place your hands farther apart and move the wings in small, flat circles.

AMAZING FLYING ANIMALS

B ATS ARE the only animals that can fly, apart from birds and insects. They have wings that can push downward to create lift. Unlike birds, most bats are nocturnal—they fly at night and sleep in the day. Some other animals can glide through the air, but cannot control or power their flight with flapping wings. Instead, animals such as flying frogs, honey gliders, lizards, snakes and squirrels glide down. They jump outward from high places like trees and cave walls, moving forward through the air as they parachute downward. These animals usually have loose flaps of skin attached to their bodies. The flaps of skin act like the envelope of a parachute, catching the air and enabling controlled descent. Flying fish escape from their enemies and predators just below the ocean surface by sailing through the air above. Their gliding flight only lasts a few seconds, but it is faster than the fish's swimming speed.

Wings and fins

Flying fish swim very fast, close to the surface of the water. With wing-shaped fins stretched out, they leap upward and forward into the air, thrashing the water with their tails until they reach take-off.

Parachute tactics

Flying frogs have enormous webbed feet. They use their feet as parachutes when they jump down from trees in search of insects. They alter the shape of their feet to control their flight. There are sticky pads on their toes to help them climb. Using these pads, they can cling to the smoothest leaves and branches in the rainforest.

FACT BOX

• Some flying fish can glide along at 30 mph for several hundred yards. The longest recorded flight for a flying fish lasted 90 seconds and covered more than ½ mile.

• Flying foxes are actually a type of large fruit-eating bat. There are more than 2,000 species, or types, of bat living in the world.

• Flying snakes are able to flatten their bodies to help them glide from tree to tree.

• Some flying frogs jump from a height of 130 feet. They glide along, covering about 95 feet in only 8 seconds.

• The colugo, or flying lemur, can easily glide for at least 320 feet between trees.

Life-saving spines
A flying lizard has flaps of
skin along each side of its
body. These are supported
by spines hinged to the
ribs. When danger
threatens, the spines stick
out, and the lizard
glides away.

**Tree
gliding**
Flying squirrels have folds of thin skin
between their front and rear legs. They
glide from tree to tree by stretching
out their legs to spread the skin wide.

Smooth as honey
Honey gliders (*Petaurus breviceps*) are
small mammals that sail through the
rainforests of Queensland and New
Guinea. They eat sweet sap (sucked
from trees) and nectar (from flowers).

Flexibility
A bat's wing is a sheet of
flexible skin stretched between its
fingers, the side of its body and the back
of its legs. Bats can alter the shape of their wings much more than birds.
They can twist and turn like acrobats in the air as they chase insects for food.
The largest bats have wingspans up to 6 feet, but weigh only 2 pounds.

THE HISTORY OF FLIGHT

SINCE ANCIENT times, human beings have wanted to fly. The first people to get off the ground were the Chinese, who used kites to lift people into the air over 700 years ago. In the 1760s, lighter-than-air balloons carried their first passengers and in 1852, the world's first airship flight occurred. But it was not until the invention of the gas engine in the 1880s that true powered flight in a heavier-than-air machine became possible. In 1903, the Wright brothers made the world's first powered, controlled and sustained flight in their aircraft, *Flyer 1*. The basic structure of an airplane as devised by the Wright brothers has continued to the present day, although many details have changed. The designs of today are thanks to a mix of modern strong and lightweight metals (alloys) used to make planes, and improvements in fuel and engines.

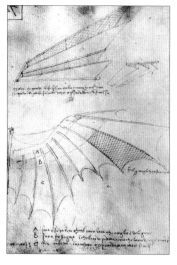

Ahead of time
Over 500 years ago, the Italian artist and inventor Leonardo da Vinci drew designs for flying machines. His ideas about flight were basically correct. However, a human would not have been able to provide enough power to make his machines work.

Clément Ader
In 1890, Ader's steam-driven aircraft *Eole* became the first full-sized airplane to leave the ground. It managed to hop 160 feet. However, it was not considered true powered flight because it was uncontrolled. Before the Wright brothers' success, aircraft wings were modeled on those of birds and bats. These wings are able to twist and move because they are made of separate bones. Such a mechanism does not work when scaled up to a size big enough to carry a man.

Otto Lilienthal
In the 1890s, German experimenter Otto Lilienthal built hang gliders from reeds covered with shirt material. He made over 2,000 flights and showed how curved airfoil wings work better than flat ones. He was the first person to make repeated, controlled flights, but while making a test flight, Lilienthal crash-landed and was killed.

Orville and Wilbur Wright

On December 17, 1903, American inventor Orville Wright flew *Flyer 1* for 118 feet at a height of about 10 feet. This was the first controlled, powered take-off, flight and landing. The Wright brothers continued to improve their aircraft, and eventually their planes could fly for around an hour. Within six years, they were being used by pilots in France and the United States.

Louis Blériot

The Frenchman Louis Blériot designed and built a series of planes. In 1909, he became the first person to fly across the English Channel. At an average speed of 37 mph the journey took 37 minutes. He reported that he had to wrestle constantly with the controls to keep his monoplane flying steadily. Shortly after his flight, a new engine allowed faster speeds and greater stability. The picture shows a modern replica of his plane.

FACT BOX

• 1908 Orville Wright made the first sustained, powered flight lasting one hour.

• 1937 the jet engine was designed by British engineer Frank Whittle.

• 1939 American engineer Igor Sikorsky designed the first helicopter.

• 1947 the first aircraft flew at supersonic speed in the United States

• 1952 the first jet airliner, the De Havilland Comet, entered service in the United Kingdom.

• 1970 Boeing 747 jumbo jet entered service.

• 1976 Concorde started transatlantic service.

Charles Lindbergh

In 1927, American Charles Lindbergh was the first person to fly alone and non-stop across the Atlantic Ocean in his tiny Ryan monoplane, *The Spirit of St Louis*. He took 33 hours and 39 minutes to fly 3,600 miles from New York to Paris, at an average speed of 107 mph. Lindbergh's feat paved the way for transtlantic passenger services. He became an advisor to the United States Air Force and to commercial airlines.

WINGS AND LIFT

However much you flap your arms up and down like a bird, you cannot take off because you are not designed to fly. Humans are the wrong shape, and their muscles are not strong enough. Birds have wings and powerful muscles that enable them to fly. Flapping provides a force called thrust, which moves a bird forward through the air. A bird's wings are a special shape, called an airfoil. In an airfoil, the top side is more curved than the underside. This helps keep a bird up in the air, even when its wings are not flapping.

When an airfoil wing moves through the air, it creates an upward push. This push is a force called lift. It counteracts the weight of the object (due to the force of gravity), which pulls an object down toward the ground. There are many different shapes and sizes of birds, gliders and airplanes, but they all have airfoil wings.

If you blow across a sheet of paper it reduces the pressure of the air above the paper. The stronger pressure beneath lifts the paper up.

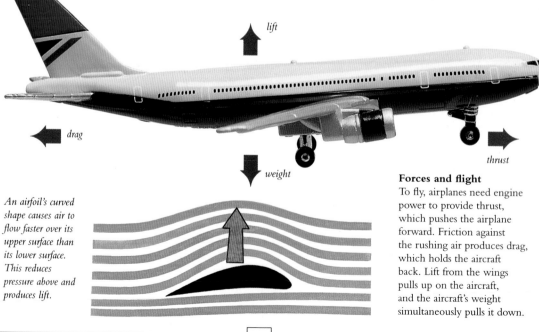

lift

drag

weight

thrust

An airfoil's curved shape causes air to flow faster over its upper surface than its lower surface. This reduces pressure above and produces lift.

Forces and flight
To fly, airplanes need engine power to provide thrust, which pushes the airplane forward. Friction against the rushing air produces drag, which holds the aircraft back. Lift from the wings pulls up on the aircraft, and the aircraft's weight simultaneously pulls it down.

Wings and soaring

A Lammergeyer can soar through the air without flapping its wings. As its wings slice through the air, the force of lift pushes up on them. The faster the bird's speed, the greater the lift. It is able to glide like this for many hours provided that it can maintain speed. Many seabirds can use the updraft near cliffs for this. Birds of the open ocean, such as the albatross, use variable air currents near the water surface, where the wind is slowed by contact with the water.

Rotation

Helicopters have long thin airfoil wings called rotor blades. Powerful engines whirl the blades to produce lift. Helicopters can hover, or fly forward, backward and sideways, as well as straight up and down. The pilot can position the angle of the blades to control lift and make the helicopter go in any direction. Because the rotor blades are continually spinning in one direction, the helicopter tends to rotate the other way. Most helicopters have a small propeller at the end of their body to help prevent this. Large helicopters may have a set of rotor blades at each end of the aircraft.

Taking off

Most airplanes need long runways to take off. They speed along, faster and faster, until the lift pushing up is greater than the weight pulling down, letting them leave the ground.

CURVE AND LIFT

FLY A FRISBEE

You will need: a large plate, thick card stock, pencil, scissors, ruler, tape.

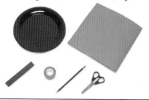

1 Place the plate face down on the card stock and draw around it with a pencil. Cut out the circle of card stock. Draw slots ¾ in. deep around the edge and cut these as shown.

2 The cut slots around the edge will make tabs. Bend the tabs down slightly. Overlap them a little and stick them together with small pieces of tape.

BIRDS, GLIDERS and airplanes all have wings. Their wings can be all sorts of different shapes and sizes, but they all have the same airfoil design. This means that the top side of the wing is more curved than the underside. The airfoil shape provides lift when air moves over it. Air flows faster over the curved upper surface than over the flatter, lower surface. This reduces the air pressure above the wing and lets the higher air pressure underneath lift it up.

You can make and test a model airfoil by following the instructions in these projects. They will show you how moving air lifts wings upward. In the first, disk-shaped frisbee project, the curve at the top and bottom is the same, but because the top curves outward, air can move faster over the top of it. The frisbee spins as it flies. The spinning motion and speed help to steady it.

3 Fly your frisbee outside, away from people. Hold it at the front and spin it away from you and up. It should glide through the air smoothly as the air pressure above it is reduced. Play toss-and-catch games with your friends and even have your own championship match. Commercial frisbees were introduced into the United States in the 1950s.

AIRFOIL ANTICS

You will need: *paper, pencil, ruler, scissors, tape, glue, plastic drinking straw, thick cotton yarn.*

1 Measure a rectangle of paper about 6 in. wide and 8 in. long. Carefully cut out the shape.

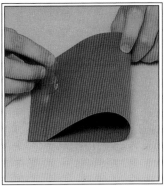

2 Fold the paper over, approximately in half. Use tape to stick the top edge ½ in. away from the bottom edge.

3 Cut out and stick on a small fin near the rear edge of your wing. This will keep the wing facing into the airflow when you test it.

4 With a sharp pencil, poke a hole through the top and bottom of your wing, near the front edge. Push a straw through the holes and glue it in place in the middle.

5 Cut a 3-ft long piece of thick cotton yarn and thread it through the straw. Make sure the cotton can slide easily through the straw and does not catch.

6 Hold the cotton tight and blow air from a fan or hair dryer over the wing. Watch it take off! This happens because you are decreasing the air pressure above the wing.

AIR RESISTANCE

WHEN YOU are swimming, you push your way through the water. All the time, the water is resisting you and slowing you down. In the same way, things that fly have to push their way through the air. Air also clings to their surfaces as they rush through it. The result is a backward pull called drag, or air resistance. Drag is the force that works against the direction of flight of anything that is flying through the air. The amount of drag depends on shape. Fat, lumpy shapes with sharp edges create a lot of drag. They disturb the air and make it swirl around as they move along. Sleek, streamlined shapes have low drag and hardly disturb the air, as they cut smoothly through it and fly fastest of all.

Whatever the shape, drag increases with speed. Doubling the speed creates four times the amount of drag. The result is that drag limits how fast aircraft, birds and insects can fly, increasing the amount of thrust needed.

Trapped air
Parachutes fall slowly because air is trapped beneath them. They are deliberately designed to have very high drag.

When an aircraft is in flight, the angle the wings make to the airflow is called the angle of attack. If the angle of attack is increased, the amount of lift also increases— but so does the drag.

angle of attack

If the angle of attack becomes too great, lift drops suddenly. The smooth flow of air over the wing is broken, creating turbulence, increasing drag and reducing lift.

turbulence

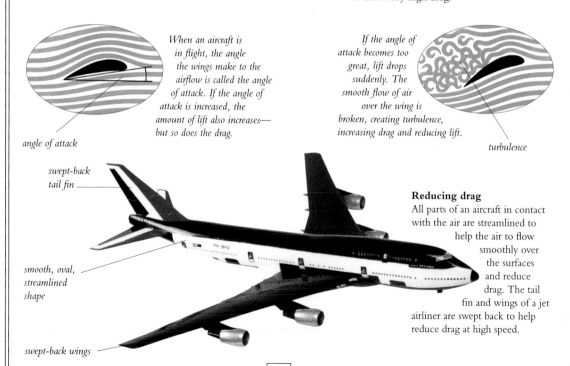

swept-back tail fin

smooth, oval, streamlined shape

swept-back wings

Reducing drag
All parts of an aircraft in contact with the air are streamlined to help the air to flow smoothly over the surfaces and reduce drag. The tail fin and wings of a jet airliner are swept back to help reduce drag at high speed.

Coming in to land

Birds must slow down before they land. This owl has tipped up its wings so that the undersides face forward. It has also lowered and spread out its tail feathers to act as a brake. Drag increases suddenly, lift decreases and the bird drops to its landing place.

High speed

Concorde could fly at a speed of over 1,200 mph. Its wings were swept back to reduce drag to a minimum. If its wings had stuck straight out they would have been ripped off at that speed.

Down to earth

Coming in to land, an airliner uses flaps on its wings to increase lift at low speeds. During flight, these flaps are retracted (pulled in) to reduce drag.

Parachute brakes

The Lockheed SR-71 lands at over 200 mph. A parachute helps it slow down, as ordinary brakes on its wheels would take too long.

SHAPED BY DESIGN

THINK OF a sleek canoe moving through water. Its streamlined shape makes hardly any ripples as it passes by. Streamlined shapes also move easily through air. We say that they have low drag, or air resistance. Angular shapes have more drag than rounded ones. For effective streamlining, think about the shape of fast-moving fishes that have to be very streamlined. A fish such as tuna has a blunt front end, is broadest about a third of the way along, then tapers toward the tail. This is more streamlined than a shape with a pointed front end and thicker at the other end because it creates less as it moves through water. It splits the water cleanly, allowing it to flow along each side of the tuna to rejoin without creating turbulence. In these experiments, you can design and test your own streamlined shapes, or make a model parachute with high drag to make it fall slowly.

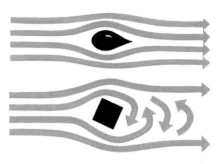

How it works
Air flows in gentle curves around the streamlined shape (top). Angles or sharp curves break up the flow and increase drag.

star   *square*   *teardrop*

Shape race
Make different shapes (*as shown on the right*) from balls of modeling clay all the same size. Race your shapes in water—the most streamlined shape should reach the bottom first.

Splash down
How much of a splash would you make diving into a pool? This diver's carefully streamlined shape will help her cut cleanly through the water to dive deeply.

MINI PARACHUTE JUMP

You will need: *felt tip pen, a large plate, thin fabric, scissors, needle, spool, tape, plastic cotton reel.*

1 Use the felt tip pen to draw around the plate on the fabric. Using the scissors, carefully cut out the circle to make what will be the parachute's canopy.

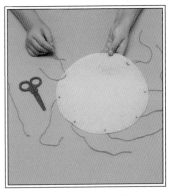

2 Make about eight equally spaced marks around the edge of the circle. Use a needle to sew on one 12-in. long piece of cotton thread to each point you have marked.

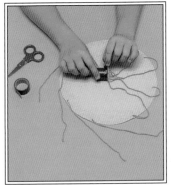

3 Use tape to secure the free end of each thread to a spool. Be sure to use a plastic spool, as a wooden one will be too heavy for your parachute.

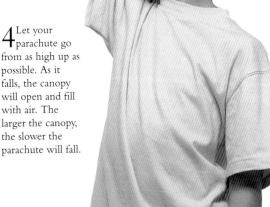

Holey parachute
Parachutes today have a hole in the center. This one brought two *Apollo 17* astronauts safely to land in the Pacific Ocean. The hole ensures that the air escapes evenly instead of at the sides, which would cause swinging.

4 Let your parachute go from as high up as possible. As it falls, the canopy will open and fill with air. The larger the canopy, the slower the parachute will fall.

GLIDING AND SOARING

Long, thin wings
A glider is towed into the air attached to a cable. Its long, thin wings give maximum lift and minimum drag for their size. If a glider flies level in still air, drag forces slow it down and the wings lose their lift. So, to keep up speed, a glider flies on a gradual downward slope.

WATCH A small bird as it flies. It flaps its wings very fast for almost the whole time. Large birds, however, often glide with their wings stretched out flat and unmoving. They can do this because their large wings create enough lift to keep them up in the air without flapping. Soaring birds, such as albatrosses and condors, glide for hours hardly moving their wings at all. They gain height by using thermals (rising columns of hot air) over the land and sea. Gliders are aircraft that do not have engines. Instead they have long, thin wings, similar to those of soaring birds. They are pulled along by small aircraft or by winches on the ground, until the lift generated by their wings keeps them airborne. Glider pilots also seek out thermals to lift their aircraft up.

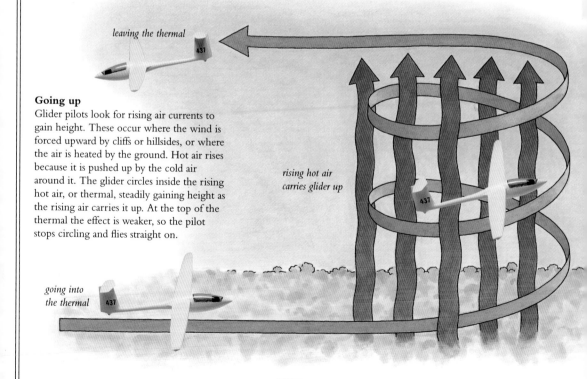

leaving the thermal

Going up
Glider pilots look for rising air currents to gain height. These occur where the wind is forced upward by cliffs or hillsides, or where the air is heated by the ground. Hot air rises because it is pushed up by the cold air around it. The glider circles inside the rising hot air, or thermal, steadily gaining height as the rising air carries it up. At the top of the thermal the effect is weaker, so the pilot stops circling and flies straight on.

rising hot air carries glider up

going into the thermal

Flying high

A paraglider's wing shape is made by air blowing into pockets on its leading edge. The pilot steers from side to side and can ride up thermals.

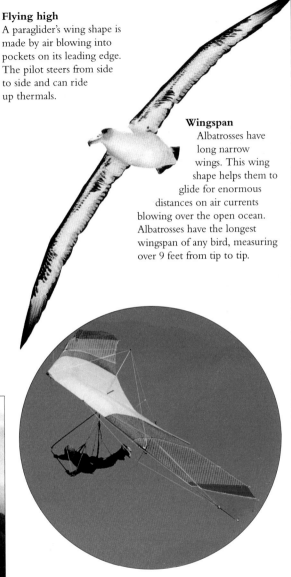

Wingspan

Albatrosses have long narrow wings. This wing shape helps them to glide for enormous distances on air currents blowing over the open ocean. Albatrosses have the longest wingspan of any bird, measuring over 9 feet from tip to tip.

Cockpit dials

This picture shows the inside of a glider's cockpit. The left-hand dial gives forward air speed. The middle dial shows the rate of climb or descent (how fast the glider is going up or down). The last dial on the right shows the glider's altitude (height above the ground).

Hang-glider

A hang-glider is made from strong, thin material stretched over a framework of aluminum poles and is very light. The material on the hang-glider's wing is stretched into an airfoil shape to produce lift. To steer the hang-glider, the pilot moves a control bar forward to climb and backward to dive. Hang-gliders are often launched by the pilot simply jumping off the edge of a cliff where an updraft of air will provide the necessary lift. Because of the pilot's all-around vision, hang-gliders are used for aerial surveys and observation.

KITES AND SAILS

WIND IS moving air that pushes against anything standing in its path. You can fly a kite because it is held up in the air by the force of the wind pushing against it. A string, called a tether, connects the kite to the person flying it and holds it at the correct angle to the wind. You can feel tension in the tether pulling on your hand. The tension is the result of the wind blowing against the kite and lifting it up. If the tether broke, the kite would no longer be held at the correct angle, and it would fall to the ground or blow away. When there is no wind, a kite can still be made to fly by pulling it through the air. A simple kite like the one below will also need a tail. This tail provides extra drag and ensures that the kite always faces into the wind at the correct angle so it can create lift. Traditionally, kite tails have many tassels along their length. These also add to the drag and mean that the tail does not need to be so long.

Open mouthed
Windsock kites may be flown from poles during festivals. They have open ends to catch the wind. Like all kites, they only fly when the wind blows against them.

Flying a kite
What makes a kite fly? Wind is deflected downward when it blows against a kite. This pushes the kite upward and creates lift. The tether keeps the kite at an angle to the wind (the angle of attack) with the nose higher than the tail. The kite's surface deflects the air downward. In a good breeze, a kite's weight is very small compared to the forces of lift and drag.

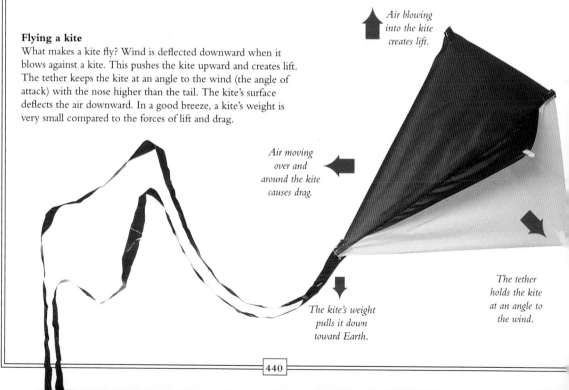

Air blowing into the kite creates lift.

Air moving over and around the kite causes drag.

The kite's weight pulls it down toward Earth.

The tether holds the kite at an angle to the wind.

Flat kite

The oldest and simplest kite is the plane surface, or flat, kite. It has a simple diamond shape and a flat frame. Kites like these have been flown for thousands of years. Flat kites look very impressive strung together to make a writhing pattern in the sky.

Box kite

A square box kite is more complicated to make than a flat kite. Its shape makes it more stable and gives it better lift. It does not need a tail to keep it upright. Box kites can be a combination of triangles and rectangles. Large box kites have been used to lift people off the ground in the past.

Parasail

A parasail is a kite that lifts a person into the air. It does not rely completely on the wind, but instead it is towed behind a boat or a car. A parasail looks like a parachute that has been divided into different parts, called cells. As the parasail is pulled along, air flows into each separate cell, inflating it to make a shape that creates lift. Parasails usually fly about 160 feet above the ground.

LET'S GO FLY A KITE

Or more than 3,000 years, people have been making and flying kites. The first ones were made from cloth or paper attached to a light wooden or bamboo frame. As time went by, the essential but simple secret of building a good kite was discovered. It must be as light as possible for its size, so that it catches as much wind as possible. Some kites can fly in remarkably gentle breezes. Their surfaces are wide so that the breeze has a large area to push against. Their low weight means that only a small amount of lift is enough to make them take off into the sky.

The Chinese have for long made some of the most elaborate and colorful kites of all. In Tibet and some other Himalayan regions, kite-flying is often a part of religious festivities. Competitions to see whose kite flies or looks best are now organized in many countries around the world. The kite design shown in this project has been used for many hundreds of years. Try flying it first of all in a steady wind. You might have to experiment with the position of the bridle and the length of the tail.

MAKE A KITE

You will need: *pen, ruler, two bamboo canes (one about two-thirds as long as the other), string, scissors, tape, sheet of thin fabric or plastic, fabric glue, colored paper.*

1 To make the frame, mark the center of the short cane and mark one-third of the way up the long cane. Tie the canes together crosswise at the marks with string.

2 Tape string around the ends of the canes and secure it at the top. This will stop the canes from moving, and it will also support the edges of your kite.

3 Lay the frame on top of the sheet of material or plastic. Cut around it, 1 in. away from the material's edge. This will give you enough to fold over the string outline.

4 Fold each edge of the material over the frame and stick the edges down firmly with fabric glue (or tape if you are making the kite from plastic). Let the glue dry.

5 Tie a piece of string to the long cane, as shown—this is called the bridle. Tie the end of the ball of string to the middle of the bridle to make the tether.

6 To make the tail, fold sheets of colored paper in zigzags. Tie them at about 10-in. intervals along a piece of string that is about twice as long as the kite. Glue or tie the tail to the bottom tip of the kite.

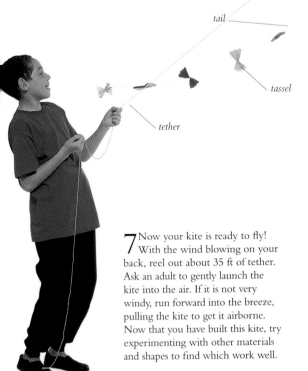

bridle

tail

tassel

tether

7 Now your kite is ready to fly! With the wind blowing on your back, reel out about 35 ft of tether. Ask an adult to gently launch the kite into the air. If it is not very windy, run forward into the breeze, pulling the kite to get it airborne. Now that you have built this kite, try experimenting with other materials and shapes to find which work well.

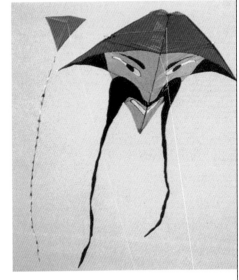

Flying faces
This kite has been made to look like a face with a long trailing moustache. Highly decorative designs can make the simplest kite look very effective.

LIGHTER THAN AIR

Hot stuff
A candle heats the air around it. Even after you snuff out the flame the smoke is carried upward by the hot air.

O IL FLOATS on water because it is the lighter and less dense of the two liquids. A bottle full of oil weighs less than the same bottle full of water. Water pushes upward on the oil with a force called upthrust. A similar process happens when smoke rises from a fire. Hot air is less dense than the cold air around it and is forced up by the cold air. It floats upward, taking the smoke with it.

A hot-air balloon is simply a huge bag full of hot air. It experiences upthrust from the cold air around it. The balloon takes off because the upthrust is greater than its own weight pulling it down. Airships are also lighter than the air around them. Modern airships are filled with a gas called helium, which is seven times lighter than air. The hot air in a balloon gradually escapes or cools down, however, so the pilot needs to regularly produce more by burning gas underneath it. The hot gases from a single gas cylinder can carry several people for half an hour.

Oil slick
Watch how oil floats on water because it is less dense than air. The water surrounding the oil pushes upward on it. This push is called upthrust. Try this with a glass of water and a teaspoon of cooking oil.

FACT BOX

• The first ever balloon passengers were not humans but a sheep, a duck and a cockerel, in 1782, at the Court of Versailles, in Paris. They were sent up to make sure it was safe to travel by this new form of transport.

• The first untethered balloon flight took place over Paris on November 21, 1783. It lasted only 25 minutes.

• Marie Elisabeth Thible became the first woman aeronaut. On June 4, 1784, she flew in a balloon over Lyon, France.

• One of the largest airships was the German *Hindenburg*, at 800 feet long. In 1937, it burst into flames on landing, killing 35 people.

The first aviators

In 1783, French brothers Joseph and Jacques Montgolfier built an enormous paper balloon and lit a fire on the ground beneath it. The air inside the balloon gradually cooled after take-off. The balloon sailed into the sky, safely carrying two people into the air for the very first journey by hot-air balloon. By 1784, refined versions of their balloon could carry six people.

Hanging baskets

Modern hot-air balloons are as tall as an eight-story block of apartments. They are made of nylon and can carry about five people in a basket hanging underneath. All hot-air balloons can only go where the wind blows them. This means pilots must have a landing site arranged downwind before setting off!

Danger

Airships in the 1930s were huge, being designed to carry passengers across the Atlantic in luxury. They were filled with hydrogen gas that easily burst into flames, making the airships very dangerous. Today airships use helium.

Modern airship

Unlike a hot-air balloon, this airship uses helium to float. It also has engines and propellers to drive it. The pilot steers by moving fins on the tail.

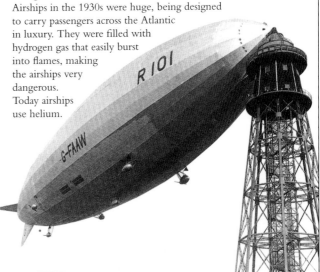

HOT AIR RISING

Hot air balloons rise into the sky because the air inside them is lighter than the air outside. The main part of the balloon is called the envelope. Hot air rises into the envelope from gas burners stored just beneath the envelope but above the basket. The number of gas cylinders stored in the basket depends on the journey time. The envelope fills with about 2.5 tons of hot air—about the weight of two cars. This hot air pushes cold, more dense air around the balloon, out of the way, producing enough upthrust to lift the balloon, its passengers and bottles of gas off the ground.

You can make and fly a model hot-air balloon to see it rise in exactly the same way. However, do not attempt to fill your balloon using flames of any kind. Modern hot-air balloons are made of flame-resistant fabric so that they do not melt or catch fire, especially during the process of filling the balloon with hot air. The best material for a homemade balloon is colored tissue paper. You can easily produce hot air without using flames by using a hair dryer.

A super challenge
Virgin *Challenger* is capable of flying journeys of thousands of miles. Once the balloon is high into the atmosphere, the strong winds of a jet stream (fast moving, high altitude winds) carry it along.

Stabilize a balloon
Try adding modeling clay to the string of a helium balloon until the balloon hangs steady. The force downward (weight) now equals the force upward (upthrust).

Gas burners
Roaring gas burners heat the air. The hot air rises to fill the balloon's envelope, which takes more than half an hour. When the envelope is full, the balloon is launched by untying ropes that hold it to the ground.

BALLOONING AROUND

You will need: *pencil, card stock, ruler, scissors, sheets of tissue paper, glue stick, hair dryer.*

1 Draw a petal-shaped template on card and cut it out. The shape should be 12 in. long and 4¾ in. across with a flat bottom edge.

2 Draw around your template on seven pieces of tissue paper. Be careful not to rip the paper with the tip of your pencil.

3 Use the pair of scissors to carefully cut out the shapes you have drawn. You should now have seven petals that are all the same size and shape.

4 Glue along one edge of a petal. Lay another petal on top and press down. Open out and stick on another petal in the same way. Keep going until the balloon is complete.

5 To fly your balloon, hold its neck open and fill the inside with hot air from a hair dryer. After ten seconds, switch off the hair dryer and let go of your balloon to launch it into the air.

WHAT'S IN A WING?

Triplane
This aircraft is called a triplane because it has three sets of wings. Early planes needed more sets of wings to provide enough lift as their speed was slow. Some very early planes were built with five or more sets of wings, but they were never successful.

T HE SMALLEST microlight aircraft carries one person and weighs less than 220 pounds. The largest passenger jet carries over 500 people and weighs nearly 400 tons. Whatever the size or shape, all airplanes have wings in common. Wings provide the lift they need to hold them in the air. The shape of the wings depends on how fast and high an aircraft needs to fly.

Narrow wings can reduce the amount of drag, and so are better for high-speed flight. Drag can also be reduced by having swept-back wings. However, wings like this are not as efficient when taking off and landing. To carry heavy loads, the airplane needs high lift, which is provided by a large wing area. Passenger and cargo planes have broad (medium-length) wings, slightly swept back. All wings have moving parts to help the airplane land, take off, slow down and change direction.

tail fin

wing

propeller

tailplane

NQT

fuselage

undercarriage

The parts of an aircraft
Each of the main parts of a small aircraft labeled here plays a part in helping the aircraft to take off, fly level, change direction and land. The body of the aircraft is called the fuselage, and the landing wheels are called the undercarriage. On many aircraft, the undercarriage folds up inside the body of the aircraft during flight to reduce drag. Hinged control surfaces on the tail and the wings are used to steer the aircraft from left to right as well as up and down.

Piper Cadet
Most airplanes today are monoplanes. A monoplane has one set of wings. The wings of small planes such as this Piper Cadet stick straight out from the aircraft's body, because at speeds of only a few hundred mph they do not need to be swept back, and this way they provide the greatest lift. These planes fly only short distances at a height of a no greater than a half a mile.

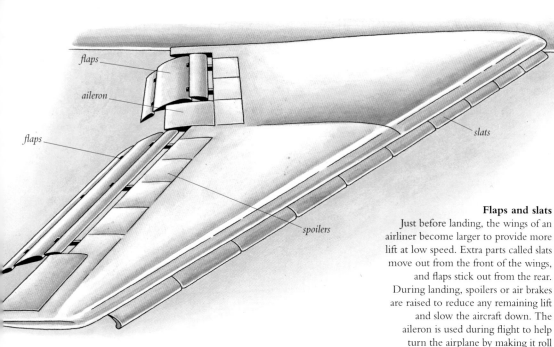

flaps

aileron

flaps

slats

spoilers

Flaps and slats

Just before landing, the wings of an airliner become larger to provide more lift at low speed. Extra parts called slats move out from the front of the wings, and flaps stick out from the rear. During landing, spoilers or air brakes are raised to reduce any remaining lift and slow the aircraft down. The aileron is used during flight to help turn the airplane by making it roll from side to side.

Boeing 747

Wide-bodied jets, such as this Boeing 747, fly high and fast. Large wings provide enough lift to carry nearly 400 tons, more than a third of which is the aircraft's fuel. The wings are tapered and swept back to keep drag low when flying at about 600 mph. Swept-back wings reduce lift, so a high take-off speed is needed, but by reducing drag they also reduce fuel consumption. Even so, in one hour, a Boeing 747's engines burn 2,100 gallons of aviation fuel, which is enough to run a family car for six years.

Swing-wings

Some military aircraft can move their wings. For high-speed flight, wings are swept backward in a low-drag triangle shape. To provide lift at lower speeds, the wings are swung forward.

TAKING FLIGHT

To make a car turn left or right, all you have to do is turn the steering wheel. To steer a light aircraft, you must move two sets of controls, one with your hands and one with your feet. Moving these controls alters the control surfaces on the plane's wings and tail. Control surfaces are small hinged flaps that affect how air flows around the plane. There are three main types of control surface. Ailerons are attached to the rear edge of each wing. Elevators are mounted at the rear of the tailplane, and the rudder is at the rear of the tail fin.

The pilot can also control flight by engine power—more power increases speed and so increases lift. So, an accelerating aircraft flying level will steadily gain height.

In a large or fast aircraft, controls are operated either electrically or hydraulically. The pilot can send electrical signals to small motors which operate the controls, or they can be hydraulically controlled by pumping fluid along pipes inside cylinders to operate them.

Double power
Biplanes have two sets of wings. They are strong, agile and easy to fly and are often used as trainer planes or in acrobatic displays. Biplanes with open cockpits and wings braced with wires and struts were the most common airplane design until the 1930s. Then, monoplanes (with single wings) replaced them in almost all functions.

Control surfaces
To turn the aircraft (yaw), the pilot turns the rudder to one side. To make the aircraft descend or climb (pitch), the pilot adjusts the elevators on the tailplane. To roll (tilt or bank) the aircraft to the right or left, the ailerons are raised on one wing and lowered on the other.

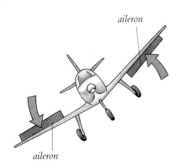

aileron

aileron

elevator

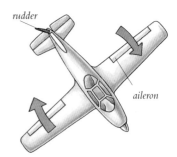

rudder

aileron

Roll
The ailerons operate in opposite directions to each other to tilt the aircraft as it turns. When one aileron is raised, the other is lowered. The wing with the lowered aileron then rises while the wing with the raised aileron automatically drops.

Pitch
The elevators on the plane's tail are raised or lowered to alter the pitch of the plane. Lowering the elevators causes the aircraft's nose to drop, putting the plane into a dive. Raising them causes the aircraft to climb.

Yaw
The rudder works with the ailerons to adjust the yaw. When the yaw is swiveled to one side the aircraft moves to the left or the right. Whichever way it points, the aircraft's nose (at the front) is turned in the same direction as the yaw.

Bank on it

When an aircraft turns, it moves much like a cyclist going around a corner. It banks as it turns, which means that it leans to one side with one wing higher than the other. This means that some of the lift from the wings is used to turn the aircraft.

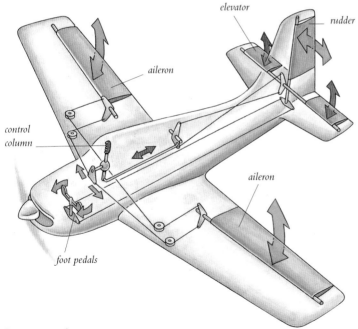

In the cockpit

Inside the cockpit of a modern airliner, the pilot moves throttle levers to control engine power. The control column and pedals move the control surfaces. Dials and gauges give information such as fuel consumption, flight direction, altitude and how level the plane is flying.

elevator

rudder

aileron

control column

aileron

foot pedals

In command

To control the aircraft, the pilot moves the control column from side to side to operate the ailerons. Moving the control column backward or forward operates the elevators. The foot pedals move the rudder from side to side.

MODEL PLANES

Paper airplanes
You can make model planes with
nothing but paper. They can vary
from a simple paper dart to a glider
with separate wings and a tailplane.
To make a successful paper plane,
you need to use stiff paper (not
cardboard), so that it will hold its
shape. You can also cut ailerons in
the rear edges of the wings to
adjust the flight as described in
the project below.

W̶E HAVE seen how the control surfaces on the wings and the
tail of an aircraft work—they change the way air flows over
the aircraft, allowing the pilot to steer the aircraft in different
directions. Working together, the ailerons and rudder make the
plane turn to the left or right. Moving elevators on the tail make
the nose of the plane go up or down. Although a model is much
smaller than a real full-size aircraft, it flies in exactly the same way.

The scientific rules of flying are the same for any aircraft, from
an airliner weighing 350 tons to this simple model made from
pieces of paper, tape and a drinking straw. Making this model
plane allows you to see how control surfaces such as the aileron,
rudder and elevators work. The flight of any plane, including your
model, is very sensitive to the angle of the controls. They need be
only a slight angle from their flat position to make the plane turn.
Too big an angle will make the model unstable.

GLIDE ALONG

You will need: pencil, set square,
ruler, paper, scissors, glue, tape,
drinking straw, paper clip.

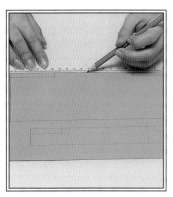

1 Draw two paper rectangles,
8¾ x 4 in. and 8 x 1½ in. Mark
ailerons 2½ x ½ in. on two corners of
the larger one. Mark two elevators
1½ x ½ in. on the other. Cut them out.

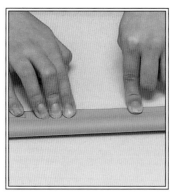

2 To make the wings, wrap the
larger rectangle over a pencil and
glue along the edges. Remove the
pencil and make cuts along the ½-in.
lines to allow the ailerons to move.

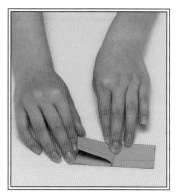

3 To make the tail, fold the rectangle
in half twice to form a W. Glue its
center to make the fin. Cut along the
two ½-in. lines. Make a ½-in. cut on
the fin to make a rudder.

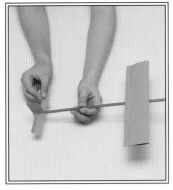

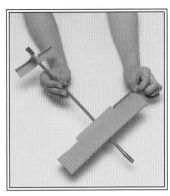

4 Use tape to stick the wings and tail to the straw (the plane's fuselage or body). Position the wings about one quarter of the way along the fuselage.

5 Try adjusting the control surfaces. Bend the elevators on the tail slightly up. This will make the plane climb as it flies. Bend the elevators down to make it dive.

6 Bend the left-hand aileron up and the right-hand aileron down the same amount. Bend the rudder to the left. This will make the plane turn to the left as it flies.

8 Launch your plane by throwing it steadily straight ahead. To make it fly even farther, use paper clips or modeling clay to weight the nose.

7 Bend the right-hand aileron up and the left-hand aileron down. Bend the rudder slightly to the right and the plane will turn to the right. Can you make it fly in a circle?

PROPELLERS

ALL AIRCRAFT need thrust to push them through the air. A propeller whirling at high speed creates thrust. Propellers have two or more blades, each of which is shaped like a long, thin airfoil wing. The blades generate lift in a forward direction as they move through the air. Modern propellers have variable-pitch blades, which means the pilot can alter the angle at which they bite into the air. Changing the pitch of a propeller is like changing gears on a bicycle. For take-off, the front of the blades point forward and the engine spins very fast to generate maximum thrust. Less thrust is needed when cruising, so the blades are set at a sharper angle and the engine spins more slowly. This arrangement makes for the most economical use of fuel.

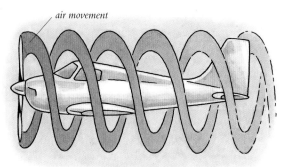

air movement

Air strike
Propellers screw their way through the air, in the same way a screw goes into wood. For this reason, aircraft driven by propellers are often known as airscrews. As the propeller turns, the blades strike the air and push it backward. This produces thrust and moves the aircraft forward.

Early racers
Sir Geoffrey De Havilland designed many early aircraft. The De Havilland DH-88 Comet took part in a race from England to Australia in 1934. It is shown here after it was restored for the fiftieth anniversary of the race. Each propeller is driven by a separate engine. Each one is like a huge car engine and is fueled by gas.

DH-88 Comet

Wooden propellers
The first airplanes had propellers made from layers of wood that were glued together. The pilot would spin the propeller by hand to start the engine. This was a very dangerous job because there was a chance that the pilot might be hit by the fast-spinning propeller.

Microlight

If you attach an engine-driven propeller to a hang-glider, the result is a microlight. The engine in this microlight aircraft develops about the same power as a small family car. The twin-bladed propeller is less than 3 feet across. It pushes the plane along at around 40 mph. Microlight aircraft are often used for survey work in remote parts of the world. The aircraft can be carried by road and then launched to survey areas far from the road.

Training planes

The Piper Seneca has four seats, so it can carry a pilot and three passengers. Aircraft like these are typically used for learning to fly. Like a car, they can be equipped with dual controls for trainer and learner. The propellers each have two blades. They are twisted at an angle like the blades of a fan. As the propellers spin, the blades force air backward.

Piper Seneca

Lockheed Hercules

Heavy-duty carriers

This aircraft carries military supplies. Each propeller has four variable-pitch blades. The propellers are driven by a turboprop engine, a type of jet engine in which the hot gases drive a turbine, which in turn drives the propeller. There is also some thrust provided by the fast-moving exhaust gases.

PROPEL YOURSELF

Back and forth
A boomerang is a special form
of spinner. Each of the two arms
is an airfoil shape. When it is thrown
correctly, a boomerang will fly
in a circle, eventually returning to
the thrower.

Propellers work in two different ways. When a propeller
spins, it makes air move past it. At the same time, the moving
air makes the propeller spin. Propeller-driven aircraft use this effect
to produce thrust. These projects look at propellers working in
these two ways. In the first you can make a simple paper propeller
called a spinner. As the spinner falls, moving air rushes past the
blades, making it revolve. This acts just like the fruits and seeds
of maple and sycamore trees which have two propeller blades.
As they drop from the tree, they spin and catch the wind, and
are carried far away.

In the second project, you can make a spinning propeller fly
upward through the air. The propeller-like blades are set at an angle,
like the blades of a fan. They whirl around and make air move.
The moving air produces thrust and lifts the propeller upward.
Children first flew propellers like these 600 years ago in China.

IN A SPIN

You will need:
thin paper, ruler, pencil,
scissors, paper clip.

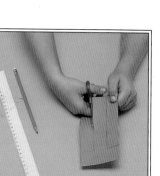

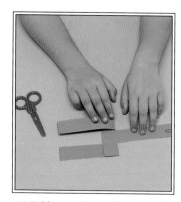

1 Take a piece of paper,
6 x 3½ in., and draw a T shape
on it, as shown in the picture above.
With a pair of scissors, cut along the
two long lines of the T.

2 Fold one side strip forward and
one backward, as shown above,
making two blades and a stalk.
Attach a paper clip to the bottom.
Open the blades flat.

3 Now drop the spinner—what
happens? Before dropping it
again, try giving each blade a
twist to make your spinner spin
around faster.

LET'S TWIST

You will need: *thick card stock, ruler, compass, protractor, pen, scissors, ½-in. slice of cork, awl, 3-in. length of ⅛-in. diameter dowel, model glue, spool, string.*

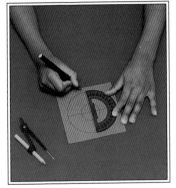

1 With the compass, draw a circle about 4 in. across on the card stock. Draw a smaller circle ¾ in. across in the center. With the protractor, draw lines across the circle, dividing it into 16 equal sections.

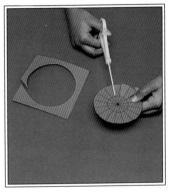

2 Carefully cut out the circle and along the lines to the smaller circle. Twist the blades sideways a little. Try to give each blade the same amount of twist, about 20 to 30 degrees.

3 Make a hole in the center of the cork slice with a awl. Put glue on the end of the dowel and push it into the hole. Stick the cork in the middle of the propeller.

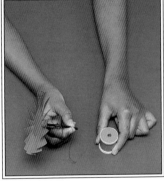

4 When the glue has dried, wind a long piece of string around the dowel. Drop the dowel into the spool launcher. You are now ready for a test flight.

5 Pull steadily on the string to whirl the propeller around. As the end of the string comes away, the blades produce enough thrust to lift the spinning propeller out of the launcher and into the air.

JET ENGINES

M OST LARGE modern aircraft are driven by jet engines. They fly faster than airplanes with propellers because they can fly high where the air is thin and drag is less. Jet engines have huge fans inside them that suck in air and compress it. Fuel burns in this air and produces a roaring jet of hot gases that blasts from the rear of the engine, producing thrust. Even more powerful turbojet engines are attached to some fighter aircraft, but they are noisy and use enormous amounts of fuel.

Passenger jets use turbofan engines that have an extra-large fan at the front of the engine. This fan produces most of the thrust by forcing air around the engine so that it joins up with the jet of exhaust gases at the rear. This surround of cooler air helps to muffle the roar of the jet.

Jet stream
An octopus uses jet propulsion to move along. It sucks in water and squeezes it out through a small hole. The jet of water pushes it along.

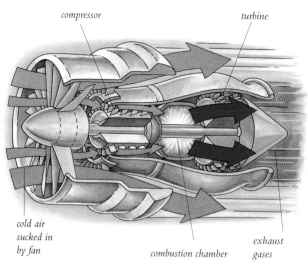

compressor

turbine

cold air
sucked in
by fan

combustion chamber

exhaust
gases

A turbofan engine
Jet engines are naturally tube-shaped because of the shape of the workings inside. Fast-spinning fans compress air into the engine. Fuel burns in the air and heats it. The exhaust gases spin the turbine, a set of blades that drives the compressor. Gases are forced out of the engine at over 6,500 feet per second and at 1,800°F. The blast of hot gases, together with the surrounding cold air, pushes the engine, and the aircraft, forward.

Inside a jet engine
A model of an aircraft's jet engine is shown with its protective casing removed so that the internal parts can be seen. The air is drawn into the engine from the left. The blades in the compressor unit then increase the air pressure before the fuel is passed further into the engine and ignited.

Lockheed Blackbird

Executive jet
A small commuter jet can reach speeds of 490 mph—nearly as fast as a large airliner. It is designed with the engines on the tail, rather than under the wings. The high tailplane avoids jet exhausts.

Reconnaissance
The Lockheed SR-71 Blackbird reconnaissance plane is powered by turbojet engines. In 1974, one flew from New York to London in 1 hour, 54 minutes—a still unbroken record of 2,070 mph. In the 1970s and 1980s, these airplanes were designed to fly fast and at high altitudes specifically for the use of the United States Air Force to take aerial photographs of enemy territory.

Jumbo jet
The Boeing 747 was the first wide-bodied jet airplane. It can carry 400 or more passengers. Since it was introduced in 1970, it has made international jet travel commonplace.

Turboshaft engine
This helicopter is powered by a type of jet engine without a stream (jet) of gases. Most of the energy from the engine turns the rotors, providing the thrust needed to keep it airborne. Only a tiny bit of energy pushes the helicopter forward.

Turboprop engine
The Vickers Viscount was one of the first and most successful passenger aircraft powered by jet engines that turned propellers. It was widely used in the 1950s and could carry 60 passengers.

ZOOM THROUGH THE AIR

A JET engine produces thrust from a roaring jet of super-hot gas. Its construction looks complicated, but the way it works is very simple. A powerful jet of gas moving in one direction produces thrust in the other direction. Imagine you are standing on a skateboard and squirting a powerful hose forward. Jet propulsion will push you backward. This reaction has been known about for nearly 2,000 years, but it was not until the 1930s that it was applied to an engine.

In the first experiment, you can make a jet zoom along a string. The jet engine is a balloon that produces thrust from escaping air. The second project shows you how to make a set of blades called a turbine. It uses hot air to turn the blades. These projects may seem very simple, but they use the same scientific principles that propel all jet airplanes through the air. When doing the turbine project, ask an adult to light the candles.

Water pressure
As the fruit of the squirting cucumber ripens, the contents become liquid. More water is drawn into it so that the pressure inside increases, like a balloon. Eventually it breaks off the stem and shoots away, squirting the seeds behind it.

BALLOON JET

You will need: long, thin balloon, scissors, tape, drinking straw, string.

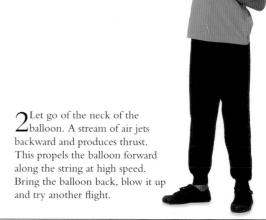

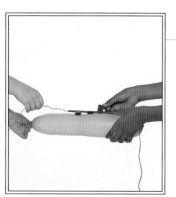

1 Blow up the balloon and, while a friend holds the neck, tape the straw to its top. Thread the string through the straw and, holding it level, tie it to something to keep it in place.

2 Let go of the neck of the balloon. A stream of air jets backward and produces thrust. This propels the balloon forward along the string at high speed. Bring the balloon back, blow it up and try another flight.

TURBINE LIGHTS

You will need: *aluminum pie pan, scissors, compass, protractor, ruler, dressmaking pin, 3-in. length of ⅛-in. diameter dowel, tape, bead, spool, modeling clay, plate, four night lights, matches.*

1 Cut out the bottom of a large aluminum pie pan as evenly as possible. Make a small hole in the center with the point of the compass.

2 Mark a smaller circle in the center. Mark 16 equal sections as in the spin project and cut along each one to the inner circle. Try to use just one scissor cut along each line.

3 Angle the blades by holding the inner tip and twisting the outer edges 20–30 degrees. The center of the inner tip should be in line with the center of the disk.

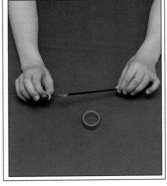

4 Tape the blunt end of the pin to one end of the dowel. Place the bead on the pin. This will allow the turbine to spin freely.

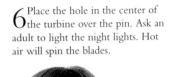

6 Place the hole in the center of the turbine over the pin. Ask an adult to light the night lights. Hot air will spin the blades.

5 Put the dowel in the spool and press the spool into the modeling clay in the center of the plate. Place the four night lights on the plate around the spool.

FASTER THAN SOUND

THE SOUND barrier is like an invisible wall that travels in front of a speeding aircraft. As an airplane flies, it sends out pressure waves through the air that are like the ripples streaming from a boat. The waves move away from the aircraft at the speed of sound. When the aircraft is traveling at this speed, the waves cannot outrun it. They build up and compress the air in front of the aircraft.

To fly faster than the speed of sound, the aircraft must fly through this barrier of dense air and overtake it. Wartime pilots, whose planes flew close to the speed of sound in a dive, reported that there seemed to be something slowing them down. The aircraft goes through the sound barrier with a jolt because drag suddenly increases and decreases again. Shock waves spread out and can be heard on the ground as a rumbling sonic boom. This boom represents all the sound energy that otherwise would be spread out in front of the aircraft, all arriving at once. We hear it as a rumble because of the distance it has traveled.

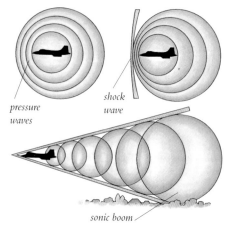

pressure waves

shock wave

sonic boom

Under pressure
As an aircraft flies along, it sends out pressure waves. At the speed of sound, a shock wave builds up in front of the aircraft. As the aircraft accelerates through the sound barrier, the shock wave breaks away to be heard on the ground as a sonic (sound) boom.

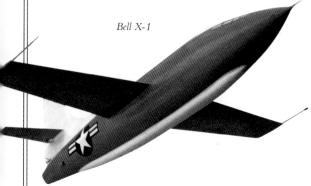

Bell X-1

Rocket plane
In 1947, the rocket-powered Bell X-1 was the first aircraft to travel faster than the speed of sound. The thin air at great heights reduces friction, but would not provide a propeller-driven engine with the oxygen in the air that it would need to burn its fuel. A rocket motor was needed for this.

Bombshell
The Bell X-1 rocket plane was dropped from a B29 bomber at 19,600 feet. This was the highest that a propeller-driven engine could reach. As the pilot accelerated and climbed to a height of 42,600 feet, the aircraft broke through the sound barrier.

Jet fighter

The Mirage flies at more than twice the speed of sound. It climbs almost straight upward, speeding faster than a rifle bullet. It can reach the same height as a cruising airliner in about one minute. The Mirage is used by air forces around the world. There are different models for use as fighters, fighter bombers or for reconnaissance.

Pilot's-eye view

A large transparent canopy gives the pilot a good field of view. Fighter pilots need an array of computers in the cockpit to cope with the enormous amounts of information they need to fly their jets safely.

Making waves

The wave created by the front of a boat (pushing through the water) is caused by the same process as the shock wave of a supersonic aircraft. The boat is traveling faster than the natural speed of the wave at the water's surface. The denser the air (or water), the quicker sound can travel through it. So speed of sound is greatest at sea level, where the air is most dense.

FACT BOX

• The speed of sound is described as Mach 1. The actual speed can change, according to air temperature and density. Sound travels faster in warm air. At sea level (68°F), Mach 1 is 761 mph, but at 39,300 feet (-58°F) Mach 1 is 658 mph.

• Subsonic speeds are below Mach 0.8 (jumbo jets). Transonic speeds are between Mach 0.8 and Mach 1.2 (breaking the sound barrier). Supersonic speeds are between Mach 1.2 and Mach 5 (Concorde and fighter jets). Hypersonic speeds are above Mach 5 (the space shuttle during re-entry).

• The first supersonic civilian aircraft to fly was the Russian Tupolev Tu-144 on the last day of 1968, two months before Concorde.

Breaking the sound barrier

The Concorde was the world's only supersonic passenger aircraft. It cruised at 1,351 mph, over twice the speed of an ordinary airliner, and could cross the Atlantic Ocean in just over three hours. Its engines were noisy and used a lot of fuel.

GOING UP

ATCH A bird taking off. It flaps its wings and up it goes! A modern airliner must hurtle down a runway as fast as a racing car. It has to travel up to 2 miles to reach take-off speed, when its wings lift it off the ground. Some special types of aircraft are designed to take off and land on a single spot. These are called Vertical Take-Off and Landing aircraft (or VTOL for short). Examples include the Harrier jump jet and an early prototype, nicknamed the *Flying Bedstead* because of its very peculiar appearance.

Helicopters are VTOL aircraft, but they are slow compared to airplanes and use a lot of fuel. Other aircraft are designed to use very short runways a few hundred yards long. They are called Short Take-Off and Landing aircraft (STOL). They can fly from inner-city airports or from remote airstrips in fields or deserts. Modern aircraft for use on aircraft carriers are now VTOL or STOL fighter planes. For this reason, the flight deck of modern aircraft carriers is much shorter than that of earlier ships. However, these aircraft still use up more fuel than conventional planes.

Up and away
The *Flying Bedstead* from the 1950s was built to experiment with ideas about vertical flight. Moving nozzles directed the thrust from a jet engine. Experiments with this machine helped finalize the design of the Harrier jump jet.

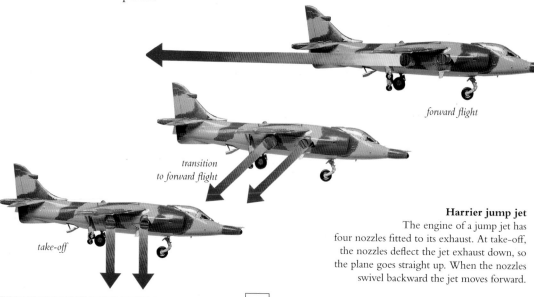

forward flight

transition to forward flight

take-off

Harrier jump jet
The engine of a jump jet has four nozzles fitted to its exhaust. At take-off, the nozzles deflect the jet exhaust down, so the plane goes straight up. When the nozzles swivel backward the jet moves forward.

De Havilland Dash
This aircraft is used on short runways in cities. It has four extra-quiet engines and can carry up to 54 passengers. Its large wings provide plenty of lift and are set high on its body to keep the propellers clear off the ground. The Dash can take off on a runway just 2,300 feet long.

Autogyro
The autogyro is a cross between an airplane and a helicopter. The helicopter-type rotor is not driven by the engine. During flight, rushing air spins the rotor, which provides most of the lift to keep the autogyro up in the air.

Bell-Boeing Osprey
The Osprey is known as a tilt-rotor aircraft. The giant propellers are called proprotors. These are mounted at the tips of the wings and tilt upward for take-off, like a helicopter. For forward flight, the proprotors swing into the propeller position of an airplane. The Osprey can fly about three times as far as a helicopter on the same fuel load.

Landing on water
Some modern aircraft carriers are much shorter than World War II carriers. They carry short take-off and landing planes such as the Harrier jump jet, which need the ski-jump ramp at the bow, for almost vertical take off. Some carriers catapult the planes as they take-off from the bow. Such planes land at the stern and are stopped by wires across the deck.

STRANGE AIRCRAFT

MANY AIRCRAFT have strange shapes. The Belluga looks like an enormous, fat dolphin with wings. The fabric used to make the wings of a pedal-powered aircraft is so thin that light shines through it. In each case, an aircraft's appearance is due to its being designed for a particular purpose such as speed or transportation. The Belluga is designed to carry large items that will not fit into the cargo hold of an ordinary transport airplane. The wings of pedal-powered aircraft are covered in thin plastic films to make them ultralight.

The people who design new planes are called aeronautical engineers. They can design planes for all sorts of different purposes—to carry enormous loads, to fly super-fast or even to fly nonstop around the world. All aircraft, however, have certain common requirements—they all must be able to take off, fly straight and level, and to land safely. Most aircraft are a compromise between many conflicting factors. They need to carry loads, fly fast and be efficient. Some aircraft have mostly been designed to be as effective as possible in just one of these ways at the expense of the others.

On the lookout
The *Optica* observation plane was designed for low-speed flight and to give a clear view. It is used to observe such things as problems with traffic flow or crop growth.

Pedal power
Gossamer Albatross was the first pedal-powered aircraft. It was made of thin plastic stretched on ribs only ¼ in. thick to make it light enough for a strong man to power.

World traveler
In 1986, the *Voyager* took nine days to fly Americans Jeana Yeager and Dick Rutan nonstop around the world without refueling. Each wing of the specially built plane was four times the length of the fuselage, providing the greatest lift with the lowest drag.

Invisible fighter

The F-117 "stealth" fighter is made up of flat, slab-shaped panels and special materials. These scatter beams from enemy radars and make the plane almost undetectable. Ordinary aircraft reflect radar beams straight back so they can be spotted. The F-117's low, flat shape reflects radar waves in directions other than back to the receiver, while special paint absorbs some of the radar waves.

A whale of a plane

The Belluga transport plane can carry almost 25 tons of cargo in its 26-foot-high hold. The Belluga is enormous, but it has the streamlined shape of a dolphin to help reduce drag. The hold is so enormous that it can carry a set of airliner wings from their manufacturers to the assembly point.

Sun strength

Solar Challenger was the world's first solar-powered aircraft. It flew across the English Channel in July 1981, in 5 hours and 23 minutes. Weighing 130 pounds, it is still the lightest powered aircraft. Solar cells on the wings change sunlight into electricity. An electric motor drives the propellers. A solar powered plane, based on the same ideas, has flown nonstop around the world.

FACT BOX

• In 1907, one of the first British powered flights was made in a bizarre-looking multiplane known as the *Venetian Blind*. It had nearly 50 sets of wings.

• The aircraft with the longest wingspan was a flying boat, the *Spruce Goose*. Designed by eccentric millionaire Howard Hughes, it had a wingspan of over 318 feet. It made its first and only flight in November 1947.

• A flying wing is an airplane with no tail or fuselage. The cabin and engines are inside the wing. The Northrop B-2 stealth bomber is an example of a flying wing.

Splash down

In areas near forests like this one in Canada, firefighting planes are used to carry water from the sea or a lake to put out forest fires. Some use an enormous flexible bucket suspended below the plane to pick up the water. Others, like this one, scoop the water directly into the body of the fuselage.

SPEEDING THROUGH WATER

WINGS CAN also work underwater. Some boats have underwater wings called hydrofoils. As the boat speeds along, the airfoil-shaped hydrofoils lift it out of the water. The hull of the boat is now traveling in the air, so drag is greatly reduced. Hydrofoil boats can travel at 60 mph, over three times as fast as an ordinary boat. Hovercraft seem to fly across the sea, just a few inches above the surface. Powerful fans blow air down through a rubber skirt to provide a cushion of air. This cushion cuts down the friction between the hovercraft and the water below. Propellers drive the hovercraft forward at up to 75 mph.

Many birds and even a few insects fly underwater. Penguins are birds that cannot fly in the air but can move so rapidly underwater that they can leap out of the water and even on to ice floes a yard or more above the surface. They don't flap their wings up and down to swim, but use a rowing action. Birds that can fly both above and below the water include auks, such as puffins and guillemots.

Sea skimming
Hydrofoils lift the hull of this craft completely clear of the water. At rest, it floats on the water like a normal boat. A small hydrofoil lifts a large boat because water is more dense than air, and so slower speeds create more lift.

HOW A HYDROFOIL WORKS

You will need: *the lid of a margarine container, scissors, stapler, awl, pliers, coat hanger wire (ask an adult to cut out the bottom section).*

3 Make sure that the hydrofoil moves freely on the wire. Try moving your hydrofoil in air—it will not lift up because air is far less dense than water. Pull it through water and it will rise up the wire. Water moves quicker over the hydrofoil than beneath it, reducing the pressure above. The higher pressure below pushes up the hydrofoil.

1 Cut a rectangle of plastic, about 2 x 4 in., from the lid of the margarine container. Fold it in half. Staple the ends together ½ in. in from the back edge.

2 Use a awl to make two holes in the front of the hydrofoil ½ in. away from the folded edge. Use pliers to bend ¾ in. of one end of the wire. Slide the hydrofoil onto the wire.

HOW A HOVERCRAFT WORKS

You will need:
styrofoam tray, pencil, balloon, balloon pump, button.

1 Use a pencil to poke a hole through the middle of the styrofoam tray. The hole should be about ½ in. across.

2 Blow up the balloon with the pump and push its neck through the hole. Keep pinching the neck of the balloon to stop the air from escaping.

3 Keep pinching with one hand, using the other hand to slip the button into the neck. The button will control how fast the air escapes.

4 Place the tray on a table. Air escapes steadily from under the tray's edges, lifting it up a few millimeters. Give the tray a gentle push and it will skate along.

Water spray
A hovercraft's rubber skirt is the black part just above the water. You can see how the air cushion makes the water spray about. Four large propellers drive the hovercraft in any direction. Hovercraft work best if the water is not too rough. They are used for travel along rivers and lakes, but some are still used on the sea.

ROCKET PROPULSION

Visions of the future
In the late 1800s, the French writer Jules Verne (1828-1905) wrote imaginative stories about the future. He predicted space travel many years before the first aircraft flew in 1903.

ROCKET engines are the only motors powerful enough to lift a heavy spacecraft into orbit and beyond. The earliest rocket propulsion worked by burning a solid fuel. This type of rocket is not suitable for spaceflight because it cannot be controlled—the fuel simply burns until there is none left. Solid fuel booster rockets are used to help provide extra power during the liftoff of the space shuttle and the launch of some modern rockets. For spaceflight itself, a controllable rocket is usually needed. This type of engine can be turned on and off and varied in power like the engine of a car. Liquid fuel rockets are used for spaceflight as they can be controlled in this way. They produce a stream of searing hot gas from the engine nozzle, usually by burning a mixture of liquefied oxygen and liquid hydrogen fuel in a combustion chamber. The gases rushing out in one direction create a huge amount of thrust, pushing the rocket in the opposite direction. Spacecraft carry a supply of liquid oxygen on board as well as liquid fuel to enable their rockets to function in the airless environment of space.

Father of rocketry
A Russian schoolteacher named Konstantin Tsiolkovsky was the first person to develop written theories on rocket-powered space travel. He proposed the use of multi-stage rockets and liquid fuel. His ideas were first published in 1903.

Liquid fuel rocket
American engineer Robert Goddard prepares to launch the world's first rocket propelled by a liquid fuel. Goddard's rocket was launched in 1926. Before this all rockets had been propelled by burning a solid fuel. Goddard's rocket soared to a height of 184 feet at a speed of almost 62 mph.

Rocket weapon
A V-2 rocket blasts off during the 1940s. It was the world's first supersonic guided missile. The weapon was developed in Germany during the Second World War (1939-45). One of its designers, Wernher von Braun, joined the U.S. space program after the war. He later headed the design team for the Saturn 5 rocket, which took astronauts to the moon.

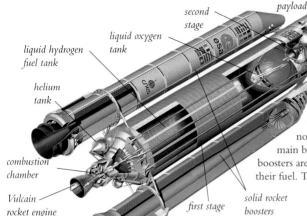

liquid hydrogen
fuel tank

helium
tank

liquid oxygen
tank

second
stage

payload

combustion
chamber

Vulcain
rocket engine

first stage

solid rocket
boosters

Inside Ariane 5

This illustration shows the inner workings of an Ariane 5 rocket, one of the largest launch vehicles of the European Space Agency's Ariane series. The Ariane rockets have launched many of the world's science and communications satellites. Ariane 5 is made of two rocket stages stacked on top of each other, with the payload housed in the nose cone. Two solid rocket boosters attached to the main body provide extra thrust. Each stage and both boosters are jettisoned (discarded) once they have used up their fuel. This reduces the weight of the rocket as it ascends.

nose cone
contains
satellite
payload

Ariane 5 launch sequence

Ready for launch

An Ariane 5 launch vehicle stands on its pad ready for liftoff. The rocket's nose cone contains two satellites, which it will launch into geostationary orbit around the Earth. Ariane 5 spacecraft can carry satellites with a mass up to 6.8 tons into space.

Launch

Liftoff! The main stage of the Ariane 5 burns about 130 tons of liquid hydrogen and 26 tons of liquid oxygen. Each of the booster rockets burns 237 tons of solid fuel as the Ariane 5 soars through the atmosphere.

Booster separation

At a height of 34 miles, only 129 seconds after liftoff, the two solid rocket boosters have exhausted their fuel supply. The rocket boosters are then jettisoned from the main body of the Ariane 5 vehicle.

Launching a satellite

At a height of 68 miles, the nose cone fairing of the Ariane 5 is jettisoned. The small second stage then carries the two satellites up into orbit. Finally, they are released into space.

ESCAPING FROM EARTH

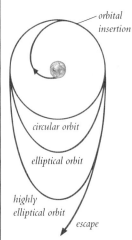

orbital
insertion

circular orbit

elliptical orbit

highly
elliptical orbit

escape

THE function of a rocket designed for spaceflight is to carry a satellite or astronauts into space. In order to do that, it has to overcome gravity (the force that pulls everything down to Earth). If the rocket's engines are not powerful enough, gravity will win and pull the rocket and its payload back to Earth. With more powerful engines, the rocket's attempt to fly into space is exactly equalled by the pull of gravity. With these two forces in perfect balance, a spacecraft will continue to circle the Earth. If the rocket is more powerful, it can fly fast enough to escape from Earth's gravity altogether and fly toward the moon or the planets. The speed that it needs to reach to do this is called escape velocity. You can demonstrate the speeds needed for escape velocity by trying out a simple experiment using a magnet and ball bearings. Then try launching your own cork model rocket from a plastic bottle.

Escape velocity

To go into orbit around the Earth, a spacecraft must reach a velocity of at least 17,700 mph. Depending on how fast it is travelling, the spacecraft may go into a circular, elliptical, or highly elliptical orbit. If it reaches a velocity of 25,000 mph, the spacecraft escapes from the Earth's gravity altogether.

LAUNCH A ROCKET

You will need: *baking soda, paper towel, water, vinegar, large plastic bottle, paper streamers, cork, push pin.*

A chemical reaction between the vinegar (representing liquid oxygen) and baking soda (representing fuel) produces carbon dioxide gas. The gas pressure inside the bottle pushes against the cork. The cork is blasted into the air like a rocket lifting off.

3 Push the cork in immediately so that it is a snug fit, but not too tight. Quickly take the bottle outside. Then move at least 10 ft away from it and watch what happens.

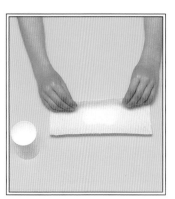

1 Place a teaspoon of baking soda directly in the middle of a 4 x 8-in. piece of paper towel. Roll up the towel and twist the ends to keep the baking soda fuel inside.

2 Pour half a cup of water and the same amount of vinegar into the bottle. Fix paper streamers to the top of the cork with a push pin. Drop the towel inside.

ESCAPE FROM GRAVITY

You will need: *thin card stock, ruler, pencil, scissors, magnetic strip, 4 x 2-in. piece of plastic, baking tray, modeling clay, tape, small steel ball bearings.*

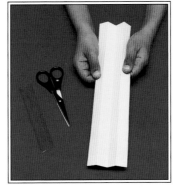

1 Measure out a 12 x 4-in. strip of thin card stock using a ruler. Cut it out with the scissors. Fold it lengthways into three sections to form an M-shaped trough.

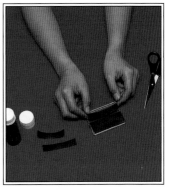

2 Cut the magnetic strip into 5 short pieces. Glue these short strips to the plastic base to make a large, square bar magnet, as shown above.

3 Fix the magnet firmly to one end of the tray with some of the modeling clay. Position it roughly in the middle. The magnet simulates the pull of the Earth's gravity.

4 Position one end of the trough over the edge of the magnet. Attach it to the magnet with tape. The trough represents the path of a rocket as it ascends into orbit.

5 Roll the remaining modeling clay into a round ball. Position the clay ball underneath the other end of the M-shaped trough. This raises the trough at a slight angle.

6 Place a small ball bearing at the end of the trough and let it roll down. The ball bearing sticks to the magnet. The velocity of the ball-bearing rocket along the trough's flight path is not fast enough to escape the pull of the magnet.

ball bearing escapes the pull of the magnet

7 Raise the trough and roll another ball bearing along it. The steeper angle increases the ball bearing's velocity. Keep raising the trough and rolling ball bearings until one shoots past the magnet. It has then achieved escape velocity!

THE FIRST SPACE FLIGHTS

AFTER the Second World War (1939-45), the United States and the Soviet Union raced each other to build a rocket powerful enough to reach space. On October 4, 1957, the world learned that the Soviet Union had won the race. It had successfully placed the first artificial satellite, *Sputnik 1*, in orbit. Getting a satellite of any sort into space successfully was an achievement because rocket launchers often failed. They frequently blew up or flew off course. As these early liquid fuel rockets were not very powerful, the first satellites had to be very small and simple. But soon, larger and more reliable rockets were built. They could launch bigger, heavier satellites. These satellites were designed to do different jobs. Weather satellites made weather forecasts more accurate, while science satellites carried out scientific research. Communications satellites relayed telephone calls and television programs around the world, and Earth resources satellites studied the planet. The space age had begun.

Artificial satellite
The first artificial satellite, *Sputnik 1*, was a metal sphere measuring 23 inches and weighing 185 pounds. Its radio transmitter sent a signal to Earth for 21 days. After 96 days the satellite re-entered the atmosphere and burned up.

V2 technology
A modified V2 blasts off from an American launch pad in 1950. V2 rockets captured in Germany during the Second World War were taken to America. They were used to develop rockets for the U.S. space program.

Chimp in space
Ham the chimpanzee was launched into space on January 31st 1961. His mission was to test the safety of the Mercury capsule, which would be used to carry the first American astronaut into space. Ham survived his flight, proving the capsule was safe for humans.

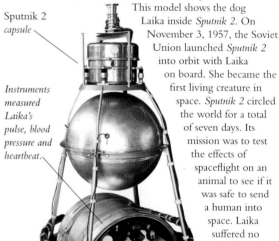

Sputnik 2 *capsule*

Instruments measured Laika's pulse, blood pressure and heartbeat.

Animal testing
This model shows the dog Laika inside *Sputnik 2*. On November 3, 1957, the Soviet Union launched *Sputnik 2* into orbit with Laika on board. She became the first living creature in space. *Sputnik 2* circled the world for a total of seven days. Its mission was to test the effects of spaceflight on an animal to see if it was safe to send a human into space. Laika suffered no ill-effects, but the capsule was not designed to return to Earth. She died when her supply of oxygen ran out.

Weather satellites

A TIROS satellite sits on top of a launch vehicle as it is fuelled for liftoff. A total of 10 TIROS satellites were launched between 1960 and 1965. They were the first weather satellites. Each TIROS satellite took 16 photographs of the Earth on every orbit. The photographs were then transmitted to Earth by radio when a ground receiving station came within range. The name TIROS stands for Television and Infra-Red Observation Satellite.

Explorer 1

The United States' first satellite, *Explorer 1*, clears the launch pad on January 31st 1958. The satellite's onboard instruments detected belts of intense radiation around the Earth. They were named the Van Allen belts, after the scientist who analyzed the satellite's data.

radio antenna

solar panels

Photographs from space

The satellite *Explorer 6* was launched on August 7, 1959. It sent back the first photograph of the Earth taken from space. For the first time in the history of humanity, people were finally able to see their homes as one world. More than 50 Explorer satellites were launched over the next 16 years, providing scientists with a great deal of valuable information about space and the sun.

Early Bird

The first privately owned communications satellite, or comsat, was called *Early Bird*. The satellite was also known as *Intelsat 1*. The orbiting spacecraft could be used to relay up to a maximum of 240 telephone calls or one television channel. *Early Bird* revolutionized international communications as it provided a regular service for the transmission of television pictures across the Atlantic Ocean.

MOON MISSION

THE 50-ton Apollo spacecraft needed the world's most powerful rocket, the Saturn 5, to send it to the moon and back. The Apollo spacecraft was made in three parts—the command module (CM), the service module (SM) and the lunar excursion module (LEM). The three-man crew lived in the tiny command module for the three-day flight to the moon and for another three days on the return journey. The service module attached to it provided electricity and air to breathe. The lunar module was the strange, spider-like craft used to make the moon landing. First, the Apollo spacecraft was checked out in Earth orbit by the *Apollo 7* mission. In December 1968, *Apollo 8* travelled to the moon, swung around behind it and returned to Earth. Two more practice missions followed. Then, in July 1969, *Apollo 11* made history by landing astronauts on the moon for the first time.

command module (CM)

service module (SM)

lunar excursion module (LEM)

instrument unit

third stage

third stage engine

second stage engines

second stage

first stage

first stage engines

stabilizing fins

The Saturn 5
This model shows the various components of the Saturn 5 launch vehicle. Its three rocket stages were jettisoned in turn as they used up their fuel. Only the third stage and the Apollo spacecraft modules reached the moon.

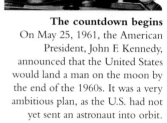

The countdown begins
On May 25, 1961, the American President, John F. Kennedy, announced that the United States would land a man on the moon by the end of the 1960s. It was a very ambitious plan, as the U.S. had not yet sent an astronaut into orbit.

Apollo 11 crew
Neil Armstrong, Michael Collins and Edwin (Buzz) Aldrin were selected to be the first Apollo crew to land on the moon. Armstrong was chosen as mission commander, in overall control of the spacecraft and crew. Aldrin had the job of flying the lunar excursion module (LEM). Collins was the command/service module (CSM) pilot, and remained in orbit while Armstrong and Aldrin walked on the surface of the moon.

Michael Collins

Neil Armstrong

Edwin (Buzz) Aldrin

Crawler transporter
The Saturn 5 rocket and Apollo spacecraft roll slowly from the assembly building to the launch pad on top of a crawler transporter. This strange vehicle weighed 3,000 tons and needed a crew of 15 to operate it.

Liftoff!
The *Apollo 11* mission gets underway as the mighty Saturn 5 rises off the launch pad. The escape tower on the top of the rocket was jettisoned once the Saturn 5 was safely in flight. The enormous power of its five first-stage engines made the ground beneath the Saturn 5 shake like an earthquake. The rocket was driven up by the rush of hot exhaust gases from the engines. Exhaust from four of the first-stage engines balanced the weight of the 3,000-ton rocket as the fifth engine provided the thrust required for liftoff.

Approaching the moon
The *Apollo 11* lunar module, called the *Eagle*, drops out of lunar orbit and heads for its landing site. The date is July 20, 1969. Inside it are Neil Armstrong and Buzz Aldrin. Shortly after touchdown, Neil Armstrong descends the lunar module ladder. As he places his foot on the lunar soil he says "That's one small step for a man —one giant leap for mankind."

FACT BOX

• The distance between the Earth and the moon is about 238,900 miles.

• During the lunar day the moon's surface temperature can be as high as 248°F. At night, the temperature is as low as -227.2°F.

• The moon completes one full orbit of the Earth every 27½ days.

Stepping out
Buzz Aldrin descends the *Eagle*'s ladder, becoming the second astronaut to walk on the moon. His spacesuit's Portable Life Support System (PLSS) backpack is clearly visible as he lowers himself down. As he looks around at the moon's lifeless surface, Aldrin describes the view as "magnificent desolation."

GOING TO THE MOON

Pᴸᴼᵀᵀᴵᴺᴳ a course to the moon is not as easy as travelling from place to place on a planet's surface. On Earth, people can navigate by following landmarks or natural features, such as hills, valleys and rivers. Pilots who fly at high altitudes navigate by using radio beacons on the ground or signals from satellites. The problem with travelling from the Earth to the moon is that both are moving. If you take off from the Earth with your spacecraft aimed directly at the moon, it will not be there by the time you arrive. The moon will have moved on around its orbit. If you aim at the moon and continually change your direction to follow its movements, you will use an enormous amount of fuel. The answer is to aim your spacecraft at the place where the moon will be by the time you get there. However, you also need to make sure you are not drifting off course on the way. Spacecrafts use one of the oldest navigation methods. They navigate by the stars. Try your hand at aiming at a moving target by following this simple project. You can also demonstrate staging by making your own two-stage rocket.

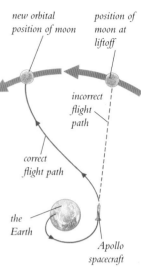

new orbital position of moon   *position of moon at liftoff*

incorrect flight path

correct flight path

the Earth

Apollo spacecraft

AIMING AT THE MOON

You will need: *string, ruler, scissors, masking tape, metal washer, book, small balls of paper.*

Moving targets
This diagram shows two possible flight paths for an Apollo spacecraft. Aiming directly at the moon does not take into account its movement as it orbits the Earth. The correct, efficient route compensates for the moon's orbital movement by aiming ahead of its position at liftoff.

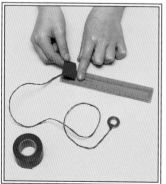

1 Measure out 24 in. of string with the ruler. Cut it off with scissors. Tape one end of the string to one end of the ruler. Tie a washer to the other end of the string.

2 Place the ruler on a table or box with the string hanging over the edge. Weigh it down with a heavy book. Try hitting the washer by throwing small balls of paper at it.

3 Start the washer swinging and try to hit it again with the paper balls. See how much more difficult it is to hit a moving target, like a spacecraft aiming at a moving moon.

MAKE A TWO-STAGE ROCKET

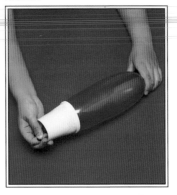

1 Using scissors, carefully cut the bottom out of a paper or plastic cup. This will serve as the linking collar between the two stages of the balloon rocket.

2 Partly blow up the long balloon with the balloon pump. Pull its neck through the paper cup. This balloon will be your two-stage rocket's second stage.

3 Fold the neck of the long balloon over the side of the cup. Tape the end of the balloon's neck to the cup to stop the air from escaping, as shown.

You will need: 2 paper or plastic cups, scissors, long balloon, balloon pump, tape, round balloon.

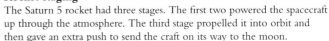

second stage fires

first stage jettisoned

second stage jettisoned

third stage fires

third stage powers command/service module (CSM) towards the moon

Rocket staging

The Saturn 5 rocket had three stages. The first two powered the spacecraft up through the atmosphere. The third stage propelled it into orbit and then gave an extra push to send the craft on its way to the moon.

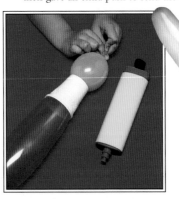

6 Peel the tape off the neck of the long balloon. Hold the rocket as shown. Let go of the round balloon's neck. Air rushes out, launching the first stage of the rocket. It then falls, launching the second stage balloon.

4 Carefully push the round balloon into the open end of the paper or plastic cup. This balloon will form the first stage of your two-stage balloon rocket.

5 Blow up the round balloon so that it wedges the neck of the long balloon in place inside the cup. Hold the neck of the round balloon to keep the air inside it.

SPACE SHUTTLE

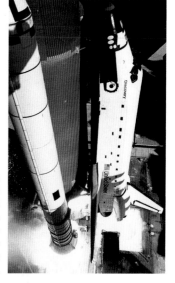

FOR the first 24 years of the space age, every rocket and spacecraft was custom designed for one mission only. Nothing was used a second time. This was an extremely costly and wasteful method of going into space. Scientists realized that if spaceflight was to become as common as other ways of travelling, spacecraft must be reusable, like aircraft or ships. The world's first reusable spacecraft, the United States' space shuttle Orbiter, was launched for the first time on April 12, 1981. The space shuttle Orbiter is a space plane. It is about the same size as a small airliner. The spacecraft is designed to take off like a rocket, complete its mission in space, return to Earth and land on a runway like an aircraft. Its short, stubby wings help it to glide down through the atmosphere. The U.S. Orbiter also has a large payload bay. It is used for carrying satellites or other structures into space or for bringing them back to Earth for repair. A similar spacecraft was developed by the Soviet Union in the 1980s, but it only made one orbital flight.

Shuttle transporter
The space shuttle is carried on the same crawler transporter that moved Saturn 5 rockets from the assembly building to the launch pad. Each shuttle will make this journey many times during its working life.

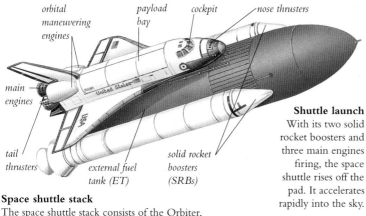

orbital maneuvering engines

payload bay

cockpit

nose thrusters

main engines

tail thrusters

external fuel tank (ET)

solid rocket boosters (SRBs)

Shuttle launch
With its two solid rocket boosters and three main engines firing, the space shuttle rises off the pad. It accelerates rapidly into the sky.

Space shuttle stack
The space shuttle stack consists of the Orbiter, an external fuel tank (ET) and two solid rocket boosters (SRBs). The Orbiter is attached to the giant external fuel tank, which supplies its three main engines with liquid hydrogen fuel and liquid oxygen during the launch. The SRBs are attached to either side of the ET to provide extra takeoff power. In space, smaller orbital maneuvering engines take over. Even smaller thrusters in the nose and tail are used to make adjustments to the shuttle's position.

Shuttle cockpit
The space shuttle is flown by the mission commander and pilot, who sit on the flight deck in the Orbiter's nose. They are surrounded by control panels and computer screens.

Lifting bodies

The HL-10 aircraft *(below)* is a lifting body, one a series of test vehicles built before the Orbiter was designed. Lifting bodies were designed to test how a vehicle with very short wings would fly. This shape was chosen as it would survive the heat of re-entry and could also be flown like a plane inside the atmosphere.

The X-15

During the 1960s, long before the space shuttle was built, another rocket plane was flying to the fringes of the atmosphere. The X-15 was an experimental plane used to study flight at very great heights. Results from the X-15 test flights were used to help design and develop the space shuttle.

Shuttle mission profile

Two minutes after launch, at a height of 28 miles, the solid rocket boosters fall away. Six minutes later, the main engines shut down and the external tank is jettisoned. The orbital maneuvering engines then fire twice to insert the shuttle in orbit about 250 miles above the Earth. When the mission is completed, the shuttle maneuveres for re-entry. It fires its orbital engines to slow it down (retro-fire), and then begins its descent. After re-entry, the shuttle glides to a landing, usually touching down at the Kennedy Space Center in Florida.

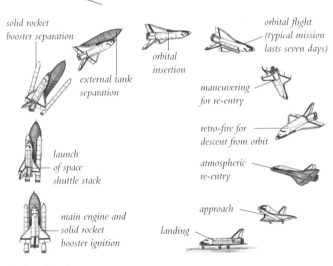

solid rocket booster separation

external tank separation

launch of space shuttle stack

main engine and solid rocket booster ignition

orbital insertion

orbital flight (typical mission lasts seven days)

maneuvering for re-entry

retro-fire for descent from orbit

atmospheric re-entry

approach

landing

Human spacecraft

Astronaut Bruce McCandless floats above the payload bay. He is wearing the manned maneuvering unit (MMU), a gas-powered jetpack that allows him to maneuver in space independently from the shuttle.

Soviet shuttle

This is the *Buran* shuttle built by the Soviet Union during the 1980s. Like the U.S. Orbiter, *Buran* was protected from the searing heat of re-entry by glassy silica tiles and fireproof cloth. The Soviet shuttle was only launched into space once, completing two orbits of the Earth in November 1988. *Buran* did not carry a crew on its flight and returned to Earth under automatic control.

ROBOT EXPLORERS

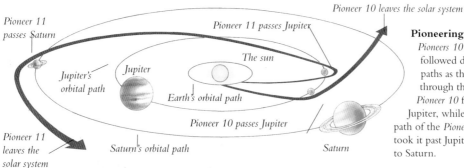

M ost of the solar system's planets are too far away from us to send astronauts to explore them. Instead, robot explorers are sent to be our eyes and ears in the distant reaches of the solar system. They have either landed on or flown past almost every planet in the solar system. On their travels, they have taken close-up photographs of the planets and their moons and taken measurements from their surfaces and atmospheres. *Luna 1* was the first space probe, heading out toward the moon in 1959. *Mariner* spacecraft then flew by Mercury, Venus and Mars. The *Venera* probes landed on the surface of Venus and the *Viking* landers touched down on Mars. The most widely travelled deep space probes are *Pioneer 10* and *11*, and *Voyager 1* and *2*, which have toured most of the solar system's outer planets. They used the pull of gravity from each planet they passed to change their course and speed them on their way to the next planet.

A message from Earth
Pioneer 10 carried a message from Earth to possible extraterrestrial life. Inscriptions on a metal plate fixed to the probe showed a man and a woman and the locations in space of the Earth and the sun.

Pioneer 10 leaves the solar system

Pioneer 11 passes Saturn

Pioneer 11 passes Jupiter

Jupiter's orbital path

Jupiter

The sun

Earth's orbital path

Pioneer 10 passes Jupiter

Pioneer 11 leaves the solar system

Saturn's orbital path

Saturn

Pioneering probes
Pioneers 10 and *11* followed different flight paths as they travelled through the solar system. *Pioneer 10* flew past Jupiter, while the flight path of the *Pioneer 11* probe took it past Jupiter and then to Saturn.

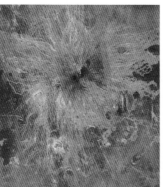

Volcanic activity on Venus
This radar image was taken by the *Magellan* probe in orbit around the planet Venus. It shows Ushas Mons, a volcano in the southern hemisphere that rises 1¼ miles above the planet's surface. Lava flows stretch for hundreds of miles away from the volcano.

Neptune flyby
Voyager 2 flew past the distant planet Neptune in 1989. The images sent back by the probe revealed a strange, inhospitable world. The surface is completely hidden from view by a blue haze of methane gas, and high, wispy white clouds made from frozen hydrogen sulfide.

Sojourner

In 1997, the *Mars Pathfinder* lander released the six-wheeled *Sojourner* rover on the surface of Mars. It moved around carrying out tests for three months. The rover's exploratory mission ended when the lander's battery failed.

Testing rocks

Sojourner was controlled by radio signals from Earth. Its mission was to drive up to nearby rocks and carry out tests on them. It moved from rock to rock, using an X-ray spectrometer to test what substances they were made of.

Galileo mission

As the *Galileo* spacecraft approached Jupiter in 1995, it sent a probe into the gas giant's atmosphere. As the probe descended into the clouds, it began sending back information to the orbiter. The orbiter in turn relayed the data back to receivers on Earth. The *Galileo* probe continued to transmit its data about Jupiter for 57 minutes. It was then destroyed by heat and the intense atmospheric pressure of the gas giant.

Galileo *orbiter*

Galileo *probe separates from orbiter*

Magellan probe

The *Magellan* space probe went into orbit around Venus in 1990. Its mission was to map the planet's surface. Radar was used to reveal the surface features, as radio signals can pass through the thick clouds that hide the planet's surface from view.

Mission to Saturn

Cassini-Huygens is a two-part spacecraft that reached the planet Saturn in June 2004 after a seven-year voyage. The *Cassini* craft will orbit Saturn for four years. In December 2004 the smaller *Huygens* probe will land on Saturn's moon Titan.

SPACE PLANES

integrated aerospike engines

tail fin

payload bay

stub wing

United States

X33

LOCKHEED MARTIN

VentureStar™

The future
This is an artist's impression of the U.S. VentureStar, a crewed, reusable future space plane. It will be a larger, more advanced version of an automated test vehicle called the X-33. The X-33 measures 65½ feet in length and 65½ feet across and weighs 124 tons. Results from X-33 test flights will be used in the development of the crewed, full-scale VentureStar spacecraft.

metallic thermal protection tiles

THE United States space shuttle has proved that crewed spacecraft can be used again and again to ferry people and materials between the Earth's surface and space. As space travel becomes more commonplace, more space planes will be needed, especially when the International Space Station is completed. A fleet of new space planes are being designed and developed around the world. Some of them will be launched with the help of extra rockets or a booster vehicle. Others will be more advanced single-stage-to-orbit (SSTO) craft that will take off under their own power and fly directly into space. Some will be controlled automatically while others will be flown by pilots. American designers are working on the X-33/VentureStar and a hypersonic space plane called Hyper-X. In Germany, a two-stage rocket-plane called Sänger is taking shape. British designers have also developed a plan for a space plane, which they have named Skylon. Several Japanese companies are developing designs for a range of advanced spacecraft including a space plane and an orbiting hotel.

FACT BOX

• VentureStar will be capable of carrying 23 tons of cargo to a height of 115 miles.

• The first rocket plane was designed by Dr. Eugen Sänger and Dr. Irene Bredt in Germany in the 1940s. The 100-ton craft was never built.

• Early space plane designs that were not built include the British MUSTARD and the U.S. Triamese, Bell Bomi and Dyna-Soar.

Launching satellites
VentureStar will perform similar tasks to the Space Shuttle, such as releasing satellites. It is designed to launch vertically using seven built-in aerospike rocket engines. The craft will return to Earth like a glider, using its fins to steer and its fuselage to create lift.

Hypersonic space plane

The experimental X-30 space plane stands in a hangar in this artist's visualization. The X-30 project studied the problems of flying at 25 times the speed of sound. It was cancelled in the mid-1990s, but the lessons learned from it are being used in a new project called Hyper-X.

Testing by computer

Computers are used to test the shape and performance of new aircraft and spacecraft. This avoids the expensive necessity of building scale models and prototypes at every stage. The computer simulation shown here uses false colors to show the stresses of flight on the Sänger space plane's fuselage.

Skylon

This is a model of a possible future spacecraft called Skylon. The Skylon project is a British concept for a pilotless, automated space plane. The vehicle is designed to take off and land horizontally, like a conventional airliner. Skylon's flight into orbit would then be controlled by an advanced neural-net computer. Its versatile wing-tip motors would operate as jet engines in the Earth's atmosphere and as rocket engines in space. The spacecraft's design would enable it to carry a 12-ton payload into orbit.

Sänger separation

The proposed Sänger space plane is designed to separate from its launch vehicle high above the Earth. The rocket-powered launch vehicle would then return to Earth to be prepared for its next flight. The launch vehicle could itself be developed into an airliner capable of flying at more than four times the speed of sound.

PART NINE

REFERENCE

This book has explored many hundreds of
inventions and discoveries throughout history.
The final part begins with a timeline,
putting the most important developments into
chronological order. From the beginnings
of civilization 2.4 million years ago until the
present day, the timeline shows when each
advancement occurred, and lists the most
important people associated with those
events. Next, a detailed glossary
provides an A–Z guide to technical terms.
From "accelerator pedal" to "zoom lens,"
there are many terms to discover which will
help you learn about how things work.

TIMELINE

Human beings have been creating tools and machines since their earliest beginnings on earth. This timeline shows some of the most important inventions in human history, from 2.4 million years ago through to the modern day.

EARLIEST TIMES

2.4 MILLION YEARS AGO The first simple stone tools are made by early human species.

1.6 MILLION YEARS AGO Early humans learn how to use fire.

400,000 YEARS AGO The oldest known wooden tool, a spear from Germany, is made.

300,000 YEARS AGO The oldest human structure, a simple hut made of branches discovered by archaeologists in France, is built.

hut made of branches

10,000 B.C.–5000 B.C.

c. **10,000 B.C.** The earliest pots are made in Japan.

c. **9000 B.C.** The first permanent houses are built, in the Middle East.

c. **6200 B.C.** The earliest known textiles are woven and the first copper tools and ornaments are made, both in Turkey.

first houses

500 B.C.–1 B.C.

c. **500 B.C.** Scissors are used in Greece.

c. **400 B.C.** The first cast iron is made in China.

280 B.C. The Pharos lighthouse is built at Alexandria in Egypt.

c. **100 B.C.** The Romans develop a system of central heating.

c. **50 B.C.** Spread of Roman architecture based on the use of arches and concrete.

Roman arch

A.D. 1–1000

A.D. 50 Watermills in use in the Roman empire.

A.D. 105 The Chinese invent paper.

c. **A.D. 130** The Chinese invent the wheelbarrow.

c. **A.D. 600** The windmill is invented in Iran.

c. **A.D. 900** Gunpowder rockets are invented in China.

gunpowder

1000–1250

c. **1000** The monk Eilmer of Malmesbury makes the earliest recorded flight using a primitive glider. Movable type printing is invented in China.

c. **1050** The magnetic compass is used by the Arabs and Chinese for navigation.

c. **1150** The first mechanical clocks are made in Europe.

c. **1200** Chinese ships are built with watertight bulkheads.

compass

1700–1750

1701 Jethro Tull invents the seed drill for the automatic planting of seeds.

1708 Thomas Newcomen designs a steam pump for draining tin mines in Cornwall, England.

1733 John Kay invents the flying shuttle, used for weaving cloth, beginning the mechanization of the textile industry in England.

1741 The first suspension bridge is built over the river Tees in England.

suspension bridge

1750–1775

1762 John Harrison perfects the chronometer for accurate timekeeping. It revolutionizes navigation.

1764 James Hargreaves invents the "Spinning Jenny" machine to make cotton thread.

1769 James Watt patents the condensing steam engine. This eventually makes possible the building of steamships and locomotives. Richard Arkwright invents a water-powered spinning machine.

1770 The first iron boat is built in England by John Wilkinson.

"Spinning Jenny" machine

1775–1800

1775 American David Bushnell builds the first working submarine.

1778 The flushing toilet is invented by Joseph Bramah.

1779 The first iron bridge is built over the river Severn in England.

1783 The French Montgolfier brothers make the first manned balloon flight in Paris.

flushing toilet

1795 The metric system of measurement is adopted in France.

5000 B.C.–3500 B.C.

c. 4500 B.C. The plow is used for farming in the Middle East.

c. 3650 B.C. The first wheeled vehicles are in use, on the Russian steppes (grassy plains stretching thousands of miles into Asia).

c. 3800 B.C. Bronze, a tough metal alloy made by adding tin or arsenic to copper, is made for the first time in the Middle East.

c. 3500 B.C. The first sailing boats are used on the river Nile in Egypt.

sailing boat

3500 B.C.–1750 B.C.

c. 3400 B.C. The earliest writing system, making pictures and symbols on wet clay tablets, is used in the Middle East.

c. 3000 B.C. Silk cloth is made in China.

c. 2550 B.C. The Great Pyramids are built at Giza in Egypt.

Egyptian pyramid

c. 1900 B.C. The spoked wheel is invented in the Middle East.

1750 B.C.–500 B.C.

c. 1700 B.C. Fast two-wheeled war chariots are invented in the Middle East.

c. 1600 B.C. The first alphabet is devised by the Canaanites in the Middle East.

c. 1500 B.C. Iron tools and weapons and glass are made for the first time in the Middle East.

c. 1100 B.C. Iron plowshares used in the Middle East.

c. 800 B.C. Iron-rimmed wheels are used for the first time in the Middle East.

two-wheeled chariot

1250–1500

c. 1280 The spinning wheel is invented.

1324 Earliest known use of cannons in Europe.

1364 First use of handguns in Italy.

c. 1436 Three-masted ships, permitting oceanic voyages, are built in Europe.

1455 Gutenberg builds the first printing press in Europe. The first book he prints is *The Bible.*

three-masted ship

1500–1600

c. 1525 Blast furnaces come into use for iron making.

1571 Leonard Digges invents the theodolite, making accurate surveying possible.

c. 1590 The microscope is invented.

1593 Galileo invents the thermometer.

Galileo

1600–1700

1608 Hans Lippershey patents the first design for a telescope.

1641 Blaise Pascal invents a calculating machine.

1668 Isaac Newton invents the reflecting telescope.

1688 Plate glass is manufactured for the first time.

1698 Thomas Savery patents the first working steam engine.

telescope

1800–1815

1800 Alessandro Volta invents the electric battery.

1802 The first steamship, the *Charlotte Dundas,* is launched in Scotland.

1804 Richard Trevithick builds the first steam locomotive, for use at a Welsh ironworks.

1808 The first practical typewriter is invented in Italy.

steam locomotive

1815–1830

1815 The first steamship crossing of the English Channel.

1816 Nicéphore Niepce conducts the earliest experiments in photography.

1823 Charles Macintosh invents waterproof rubber. One of its uses is to make raincoats.

1825 The Stockton and Darlington Railway opens in England. It is the first public railroad to use steam-powered locomotives. Aluminum is manufactured for the first time.

steamship

1830–1840

1831 The first electrical generator is built by Michael Faraday.

1833 *Royal William* becomes the first ship to cross the Atlantic Ocean by steam power alone.

1835 Charles Babbage invents the Analytical Engine, a mechanical computer.

1838 Louis Jacques Daguerre invents the daguerrotype, an early kind of photograph.

1839 Kirkpatrick Fleming invents the first practical bicycle.

Michael Faraday

1840–1850

1844 Samuel Morse builds the first telegraph line, between Washington and Baltimore in the USA. It allowed messages to be sent quickly through wires.

1845 Pneumatic tires, with inner tubes filled with air, are invented by Robert Thomson.

pneumatic tire

1846 Ether, a chemical which puts people to sleep, is used as an anaesthetic to stop patients feeling pain during surgery. Nitro-glycerine, the first high explosive, is invented.

1849 The safety pin and reinforced concrete are invented.

1850–1860

1851 The Crystal Palace, a prefabricated building of glass and iron, is built for the Great Exhibition in London. Isaac Singer makes a cheap and practical sewing machine.

1855 Henry Bessemer invents a revolutionary new furnace for steel making.

1856 Alexander Parkes invents celluloid, the first synthetic plastic material.

1858 The first transatlantic telegraph cable is laid.

sewing machine

1860–1870

1862 Pierre and Ernest Michaux invent the modern pedal-operated bicycle.

1863 The London Underground's Metropolitan Line opens. It is the first underground passenger railroad.

1867 Joseph Lister introduces antiseptic surgery, reducing the risk of wounds becoming infected.

1869 Completion of the first transcontinental railroad makes it possible for people to cross America in just 10 days. The first vacuum cleaner is invented.

use of antiseptic

1900–1905

1901 Guglielmo Marconi sends the first transatlantic radio message.

1903 The Wright brothers build and fly the first successful aeroplane.

1904 The fax machine, used for sending pictures down telephone lines, is invented in Germany.

fax machine

1904 The first Grand Prix motor race is held in France.

1905–1910

1905 The manufacture of the first artificial fiber, rayon begins in the UK.

1906 The first diesel-engined locomotive is built.

1907 The first electrical washing machine is made in the USA.

1908 Henry Ford introduces the Model T Ford, the first mass-produced motor car.

Ford motor car

1910–1920

1910 The neon light, used for street lighting and advertising signs, is invented.

1913 The first domestic refrigerators are made. Stainless steel is invented.

1915 The first tank goes into service with the British army during World War I.

1918 The first regular air passenger services begin in Russia and the USA.

1919 Alcock and Brown become the first to fly an aeroplane across the Atlantic Ocean.

army tank

1940–1950

1943 The British use Colossus, the first electronic computer for code-breaking during World War II.

1944 The first digital computer is made in the USA.

1945 The first atomic bomb is exploded.

1946 The first mobile telephone service is launched in the USA.

1947 American jet fighter plane becomes the first to fly at supersonic speeds. The Polaroid camera for instant photography is invented.

1948 The transistor radio is invented.

radio waves

1950–1960

1950 The photocopier is invented.

1952 The first jet airliner, the De Havilland *Comet*, enters service in the UK. The USA explodes the first hydrogen bomb.

1954 USS *Nautilus*, the first nuclear submarine, goes into service.

1956 The first nuclear power station opens at Calder Hall in the UK.

1957 The Russians place *Sputnik 1*, the first artificial satellite into orbit.

1958 Stereophonic long-playing records (LPs) become available.

submarine

1960–1970

1961 The Russian cosmonaut Yuri Gagarin becomes the first person to orbit the earth.

1962 *Telstar 1*, the first TV relay satellite, is launched.

1965 The first commercial communications satellite is placed in orbit.

1969 *Apollo 11* lands the first astronauts on the Moon. *Concord*, the first supersonic airliner, makes its first flight. The computer microprocesser (microchip) is invented. The first commercial video cassette recorder (VCR) is launched.

astronaut

1870–1880

1872 Edward Muybridge produces the first motion pictures, beginning the development of cinema.

1876 The telephone is invented by Alexander Graham Bell. German Nikolaus Otto patents the first internal combustion engine.

1877 The phonograph, the first machine for recording sounds, is invented by Thomas Edison.

1879 The first electric locomotive is built in Germany. The first electric light bulbs are invented by Joseph Swan and Thomas Edison.

phonograph

1880–1890

1882 The first skyscraper, the Home Insurance Company Building, is built in Chicago, USA.

1884 Thomas Edison builds the world's first electric power station in New York. George Eastman invents roll film for cameras.

1885 Karl Benz makes the first motorcycle.

1886 Gottlieb Daimler patents the motor car.

1888 Eastman produces the Kodak box camera.

1889 German Rudolf Diesel invents the Diesel engine.

motor car

1890–1900

1890 William Smith invents the first washing machine for clothes.

1895 Wilhelm Konrad von Röntgen discovers X-rays. The Lumière brothers open the first public cinema in Paris. The first mainline electric locomotive runs on the Baltimore and Ohio railroad in the USA.

1897 John P. Holland launches the first modern submarine in the USA.

X-ray

1920–1927

1922 The technicolor process, for making color films, is invented.

1923 The first diesel-engined lorry is built. The Leica compact camera popularizes the 35mm film format.

1926 John Logie Baird invents the first system for sending pictures by television. American engineer Robert Goddard launches the first liquid-fuelled rocket.

color film

1927–1930

1927 Charles Lindbergh makes the first solo flight across the Atlantic Ocean. *The Jazz Singer* is the first "talkie" (movie with sound).

1928 Alexander Fleming discovers penicillin, the first antibiotic drug. It was the first effective treatment for infections.

biplane

1930–1940

1930 Sir Frank Whittle invents the jet engine.

1934 The first electric refrigerator is made.

1935 Aircraft detection by radar is developed by Robert Watson Watt.

jet engine

1936 The BBC starts to broadcast the first public television service. Louis Breguet designs the first helicopter.

1937 Nylon is invented in the USA.

1938 The ballpoint pen is invented by Lazlo Biro.

1939 The Germans fly the first jet-powered aircraft.

1970–1980

1970 The Boeing 747 jumbo jet enters service. It weighs nearly 400 tons on take-off.

1975 *Viking 1* lands on Mars and takes photographs of its surface.

1977 The *Voyager* space probes are launched to explore Jupiter, Saturn, Uranus and Neptune. Apple launch the first commercial personal computer.

1978 The first test-tube baby is born in Britain.

1979 Mobile cell phones become commercially available in Japan.

personal computer

1980–1990

1980 The first Maglev (magnetic levitation) train service opens at Birmingham airport.

1981 The Space Shuttle is launched for the first time.

1982 Recordings on Compact Discs (CDs) go on sale for the first time in Japan.

1983 Tim Berners-Lee invents the World Wide Web (Internet).

1985 Microsoft introduces the Windows computer operating system. It becomes the world's most popular.

computer system

1986 The Russian *Mir* space station is built. It is permanently occupied until 1999.

1990–PRESENT

1990 The Hubble Space Telescope is launched.

1994 The Channel Tunnel opens, linking rail networks in Britain and France.

1997 RAF fighter pilot Andy Green breaks the sound barrier on land in *Thrust SSC*, a jet-powered car.

Channel Tunnel

1998 Construction of the International Space Station begins.

2001 The human genetic code is published.

2002 The world's first pet is cloned—a cat.

2004 The world's tallest building, Taepei 101, is completed in Taipei, Taiwan.

GLOSSARY

A

accelerator pedal A pedal beneath the driver's foot used to control the flow of fuel to a car engine.

aileron A movable flap on the trailing (rear) edge of an aircraft wing.

air pollution Where the air is tainted by gases such as carbon monoxide.

airbag A cushion that automatically inflates in a crash, protecting a car driver and their passengers from serious injury.

airbrake A mechanism that will slow a vehicle down using air resistance.

air-cooled An engine-cooling system in which the heat of the engine is carried away by air.

airfoil An object, such as a wing, that is shaped to improve efficiency of movement through air.

alloy A mixture of metals.

all-terrain vehicle (ATV) A car that can drive on surfaces other than smooth, tarmac roads.

amphibious car A car that travels both on land and in the water.

anchor A device that is dropped overboard to stop a ship from drifting.

angle of attack In aviation, the angle between the lower surface of an aerofoil and the direction in which it is moving.

A biplane has two sets of wings.

aperture A hole behind the lens which can be adjusted to let more or less light onto the film.

application Computer software designed for a specific type of activity, such as word-processing or graphics.

APS (Advanced Photographic System) camera Camera that allows the photographer to change the format for individual shots.

artificial Not achieved by natural means.

asphalt A mixture of bitumen and concrete used to give roads a hard, smooth, weatherproof surface.

astrology The belief that human lives are affected by the ways in which the planets and stars behave.

auger A large tool shaped like a corkscrew, for boring holes in the ground.

autofocus A feature on a camera which automatically adjusts the lens position to make sure a scene is in focus.

autopilot A computerized or mechanical system that senses changes in the direction of a vehicle, such as a ship or plane, and automatically adjusts the controls to maintain the original direction.

axle A bar which joins wheels together. Axles turn on bearings.

B

ball-bearing A hardened steel ball, often arranged with other ball-bearings around a turning surface, used to reduce friction.

bank To incline an aircraft at an angle, as part of a turn. When an aircraft banks to turn left, the right wing tip is higher than the left one.

battery A device that contains chemical substances that convert chemical energy into electricity.

belt drive A device that uses a belt to transfer a drive from one pulley to another.

beveled gears Gears with teeth set at an angle.

bifocal Having two points of focus.

bilge pump A means of pumping water that has collected in the bilges, or bottom of the hull, of a ship.

binary code The digital code computers use, made up of two numbers, "0" and "1."

bionic machine A machine that acts like a living thing.

biplane An aircraft with two sets of wings, one above the other.

bit The smallest amount of computer information such as a 0 or 1 in binary code.

bitmap An image that is built out of tiny dots of different color and tone. They can be edited dot by dot.

block and tackle A device that uses two sets of pulley blocks to help raise very heavy weights.

bodywork The outside body of a car.

boiler The part of a steam engine where steam is produced through the action of heat on water in the boiler tubes.

boom A pole to which the bottom of a ship's sail is attached.

bow The front part of a ship or boat.

brake A pad or disc that slows down a moving surface by pressing on it.

bridge The platform from where a ship's officers direct its course.

browser A piece of software such as Netscape Navigator and Internet Explorer, that finds and displays web pages.

bubble car The name given in the 1950s and 1960s to microcars such as the BMW Isetta because of their unusual, rounded shape.

buffer A rigid metal structure that absorbs the impact of a train to stop it at the end of the track.

bulkhead A solid, waterproof, airtight wall, ceiling or floor in a ship or aircraft that separates one section from another.

Bullet Trains The nickname for the high-speed, streamlined passenger trains that operate in Japan.

bumper The protective, wraparound metal or rubber barrier that protects the front and rear of a car.

buoy A float used to mark channels or dangerous waters in shipping lanes.

buoyancy tank A tank that can be filled with water to make a submarine sink or filled with compressed air to enable it to rise to the surface.

byte One letter or number in binary code. A byte is 8 bits.

C

cabriolet A car with a flexible roof that can be folded away into the rear of the car.

camera obscura A darkened box or room in which images of outside objects are projected.

camshaft A device that creates a regular, rocking movement, such as the opening and shutting of a valve on a car cylinder head.

canoe A light, narrow, open boat operated by human-powered paddles.

capstan wheel A revolving barrel in which the effort is applied by pushing against long horizontal levers.

car The part of a train that carries passengers, also known as a coach.

carbon monoxide A poisonous gas that is a by-product of burning petrol.

carburetor A unit that controls the fuel mixture entering the combustion chamber in an engine.

cargo Goods carried by a ship or plane.

catamaran A boat with two hulls.

catenary An overhead power cable supplying electricity to a locomotive through a pantograph attached to the top of the locomotive.

CD-ROM (compact disc read-only memory) A disk similar to an audio CD that stores data that can only be read.

cellular Things built out of single units (cells) joined together to make a whole.

centerboard A movable plate that can be lowered through the keel of a sailing boat to stop sideways drift when sailing into the wind.

chain drive A device that uses a chain to transfer a drive from one gear wheel to another.

checkered flag A black-and-white check flag that is waved as each car in a race crosses the finishing line.

chemical A pure substance present in the Earth that can be formed by or react to other substances.

chrome A shiny metallic finish from the metal chromium used, for example, on car fittings such as bumpers and handles.

classic car A car built after 1930, which is at least 20 years old.

A CD is used to store digital information.

clipper A fast sailing ship with large sails. The popularity of clippers peaked in the mid-1800s.

cockpit 1) The area around the seat of a pilot in an aircraft (usually at the front) containing the control panel and instruments. 2) The part of a small boat containing the wheel or tiller.

compass An instrument that enables people to find the right direction, especially one with a magnetized needle that swings to magnetic north so that true north can be calculated.

compressed air Air that has been squashed into a smaller volume than usual.

construction machine A machine, such as a digger, used on building sites.

converging (or convex) lens A lens that curves outward, like a magnifying glass.

CPU (central processing unit) The "brain" of the computer, containing the processing chips and electronic circuits.

container In transportation, an enormous metal box for carrying goods. Containers can be easily transferred from one means of transport to another, such as from sea to rail, in one journey.

convertible A car that can be driven with or without a roof.

coracle A small, oval boat made from the animal skins that are tightly strapped to a wickerwork frame.

coupler A connecting device that joins a locomotive to a carriage or wagon to make a train.

coupling rod A long, metal rod that connects the driving wheels on each side of a locomotive.

crankshaft The part of a car that transmits movement from the pistons to the road wheels. An axle that has parts of it bent at right angles so that the up-and-down motion is turned into circular motion.

cruise To fly at the most efficient speed and altitude for the design of a particular aircraft. The cruising speed and height is the one that uses least fuel for the distance covered.

custom car A car that has been adapted by the owner to make it look and drive the way he or she wants.

cut-and-cover construction An early method of building underground tunnels. A large trench is cut into the earth along the line of the tunnel, lined with brick and then roofed over.

cylinder In an engine, a hollow tube in which a piston moves.

D
dashboard The vertical surface that contains the instruments facing a driver inside a car.

data Pieces of information.

database An organized store of information.

deadweight The difference in the volume of water displaced by a ship when it is loaded and when it is unloaded.

deck A floor or platform in a ship or plane.

an early motor car

density A measure of how tightly the matter in a substance is packed together.

depth of field The distance in focus between the nearest and farthest parts of a scene.

desktop publishing (DTP) Creating printed material using a desktop computer and page-layout software.

desktop The main interface of the operating system that is shown on the screen after start up and before any programs are running.

dhow An Indian boat with one or more triangular sails.

die press A machine that squeezes metal into a shape using great force.

diffraction The scattering of light rays.

diffuser A filter than can be attached to a camera to soften light from a flash.

digital Any device that utilizes binary code. All computers are digital.

digital camera A camera that takes electronic images which are downloaded on to a computer to be viewed.

disk drive The device that holds, reads and writes on to a disk.

displacement The volume of water displaced by a ship when it is afloat.

diverging lens Lens that causes light rays to spread outwards.

document An electronic file.

downloading Copying files from the Internet to your computer's hard disk.

drag Resistance or force that acts in the opposite direction to motion.

drag racer A car specifically designed to take part in races at very high speeds over short, straight distances.

draftsman A person who makes drawings for specific purposes such as building a new house.

driveshaft A shaft that transmits power from an engine to the propeller in a ship or plane, or to the wheel in a train or car.

driving wheel The wheel of a locomotive that turns in response to power from the cylinder.

drug A substance used for fighting illness.

dry dock A dock that can be pumped dry so that the part of a ship's hull that is normally underwater can be repaired.

dug-out canoe A canoe made by hollowing out a log.

E
effort The force applied to a lever or other simple machine to move a load.

electricity The form of energy produced by the movement of electrons (charged particles) in atoms.

electron A tiny part of an atom that has an electric charge.

electronic circuit A circuit that consists of transistors.

elevator A movable flap on the tailplane or rear wing of an aircraft that causes the nose to rise or fall.

e-mail (electronic mail) A way of sending messages from one computer to another using the Internet.

The Internet allows us to send e-postcards.

endoscope A camera attachment that goes inside the body to take pictures of internal organs relaying the images to a computer screen.

engine A device that provides turning power.

exposure time The time it takes for the camera to take a picture.

exposures Photographs on a film.

F

fathom A way of measuring the depth of water in units of 6 feet.

fax machine A machine that can send and receive words and pictures that have been changed into electrical messages.

file A document in digital form that is stored either on the computer's hard disk or on an external disk.

fill-in flash Using the flash to light up certain areas of your photograph, but leaving natural light in the background.

filter Transparent material fitted to a lens that alters the color of the light or the way the light rays pass through it. Also a special effect that can be applied to a graphics image, such as a texture.

first-class lever A simple lever such as a see-saw, in which the pivot is between the two ends.

fish-eye lens A very wide-angle lens that collects light from 180 degrees. The center of the scene looks much bigger.

flange A rim on the inside of the metal wheel of a locomotive that stops the wheels slipping sideways and falling off the rails.

flash A bulb attached to the camera that provides a quick burst of light so that a picture can be taken in darkness.

fleece The coat hair of animals that is spun into yarn and woven into cloth.

floppy disk A portable data-storage disk. Floppies only hold about 1.4MB of data and are useful for storing text files.

focal length The distance between the center of a lens and the focal point—the point where light rays come together.

focal plane The area at the back of a camera where the exposed film is held flat.

focus A camera is in focus when the light rays from an object meet on the focal plane to form a sharp image of the scene.

folder A storage place for computer files. Folders can store anything from applications to your personal work.

force A push or a pull which results in an object moving faster or slower.

format The size and shape of a print and the way it can be viewed.

Formula One A class of racing car that has the most powerful engine specification of all. Also known as Grand Prix.

four-wheel drive A car in which power from the engine can be transferred to all four wheels simultaneously, not just to either the front or the rear wheels.

frame The area seen through the viewfinder of a camera.

freight Commercial goods transported by rail, road, sea or air.

friction A rubbing action between two surfaces that stops or slows movement.

fuel A substance, such as gasoline, that is burned to provide energy.

fuel efficient Designed to use as little fuel as possible while ensuring normal speed and power.

funicular A type of railroad that operates on steep slopes. Two cars move up and down the slope simultaneously as a cable attached to each carriage winds around an electrically powered drum.

fuselage The main body of an aircraft to which the wings and tail are attached.

G

gas A non-solid, non-liquid substance.

gasoline The easily burned liquid made from oil that is the main fuel for internal combustion engines.

gauge The width between the inside running edges of the rails of a railroad track. In Britain, the USA and most of Europe, the gauge is 4 feet 8 .

gear A toothed wheel designed to interact with other toothed wheels to transfer motion in a controlled way.

gearbox A set of gearwheels of different sizes that can turn wheels at different speeds and with different mechanical advantages.

a bicycle gear system

A sailboat uses the wind to propel it along.

germ A micro-organism that, once it is inside the human body, can cause illness.

gigabyte One billion bytes or characters.

glide To fly through the air in a controlled way using air currents (rather than an engine) as the power source.

gravity The pulling force between all masses.

groove A channel cut in a pulley wheel to keep a belt drive in place.

H
hang-glider A simple gliding aircraft consisting of a wing with a framework beneath for the pilot.

harbor A sheltered port for a ship.

hard disk A computer's main storage disk, which holds the operating system and application files.

hardware Equipment that makes up a computer—disk drives, processor, monitor, keyboard, printer, mouse etc.

helium The second lightest of all gases, used for filling lighter-than-air balloons.

helmsman The person who steers, or helms, a ship or boat.

hertz The name for the frequency of an electromagnetic wave.

home page An introductory page that contains links to other pages on a web site.

hovercraft A vehicle that can travel across land or sea on a cushion of air.

HTML (hypertext mark-up language) The computer code that makes text and graphics appear on a web site in an interactive way.

HTTP (hypertext transfer protocol) The language computers use to transfer web pages over the Internet.

hull The main body or outer shell of a ship.

humpyard An area beside a main rail route where freight wagons can be sorted to make a freight train.

hydraulics The use of water or other liquids to move pistons and other devices.

hydroelectric power Electricity generated by turbines that are driven by the force of falling water.

hydrofoil A type of boat with wing-like attachments on the bottom of the hull. At high speed, the force created by these foils lifts the boat clear of the water.

hydrometer An instrument for measuring the relative density of a liquid.

I
icon A tiny picture on which you click to make your computer do a task. Icons also tell you that your computer is busy.

incline (rack-and-pinion) railroad A railroad that operates on steep slopes. A cogwheel underneath the locomotive engages in teeth on a central rail that runs up the slope.

inclined plane A slope up which heavy objects can be moved more easily than by raising them vertically.

infection An attack on cells in the body by germs that cause people to fall ill.

inner tube A rubber tube filled with air inside the tyres of bicycles and older cars.

internal combustion The burning of fuel in a closed chamber to generate mechanical power.

internal combustion engine A motor that burns petrol or diesel in cylinders to supply hot gases to push pistons.

Internet A worldwide computer network that is made up of many smaller networks of computers that can all communicate with each other.

inventor A person who finds a new way to make human knowledge useful in people's everyday lives.

ISO (International Standards Organization) rating International rating system for film which tells you their speed.

ISP (Internet Service Provider) One of the companies through which Internet connection is made.

J
jet ski A small, self-propelled boat that resembles a scooter.

jib Any triangular sail set before the foremast of a boat.

joystick The control stick of an aircraft or other vehicle.

jumbo jet A passenger aircraft that can carry several hundred people. It is wide-bodied, with ten or more seats across.

junk A Chinese sailing vessel.

K
kayak A canoe-like boat with an enclosed cockpit.

keel The narrow point of a hull that runs between bow and stern, and from which the hull is built up.

keystone The central stone in the arch of a bridge or curved part of a building.

kilobyte 1,000 characters or bytes.

knot A unit of speed. One knot equals one nautical mile per hour.

L
laptop A portable computer that is powered by a rechargeable battery.

laser A device that produces an intense beam of light.

lateen A triangular sail.

latent image Invisible image made by light hitting the silver crystals in the film.

lathe A machine that spins an object against a cutting tool.

layout The way text and pictures are arranged on a page.

leading truck The pair of leading wheels at the front of a locomotive.

leaf shutter A camera shutter that is made up of a number of plates that overlap and retract to open.

lens A transparent material curved on one or both sides. It bends rays of light and directs them on to the film.

lever A long bar that is used against a pivot to help move a heavy object.

lift Force generated by an aerofoil that counters the force of gravity and keeps a flying object in the air.

light spectrum The colors that light can be split into.

limousine Luxurious closed-bodied car, featuring a glass partition between the driver and the passengers behind.

liner A passenger ship or aircraft.

load The weight moved by a lever or other machine.

locomotive An engine powered by steam, diesel or electricity used to pull the cars or wagons of a train.

longship A narrow ship with a square sail used by the Vikings.

lubrication The smoothing of friction between the parts of an engine, usually with oil.

M
macro lens A close-up lens with a very short focal length.

maglev train A high-speed, streamlined train that moves as a result of the action of powerful electromagnets.

magnet A piece of iron or other material that attracts other pieces of iron.

man-of-war A warship.

mass The amount of material in an object. Mass is measured in pounds and ounces.

mast Any vertical spar that supports sails, rigging or flags above the deck of a vessel.

mayday An internationally recognized signal of distress.

mechanical advantage The number of times by which the load is greater than the effort.

megabyte (MB) One million characters or bytes.

microcar A particularly small car, designed for use in cities to minimize traffic congestion.

microchip A device with thousands of electronic circuits on one silicon sliver.

micromachine A very small machine.

micro-processor A single chip containing all the elements of a computer's CPU.

microwaves Radio waves, often used to cook food quickly.

mill To grind or cut metal, stone, wood, grain, etc, using a machine with a turning motion.

modem (modulator/demodulator) A device that allows computer data to be sent down a telephone line.

monitor A screen used to display the computer's visual output.

monochrome Black-and-white film or photographic paper, which shows colors as shades of black/grey.

monohull A ship or boat with a single hull.

monoplane An aircraft with a single pair of wings, one either side.

monorail A train that runs along a single rail.

mortar A mixture, usually of sand, cement and water, which is used in building to fix bricks or blocks of stone firmly together.

mold A kind of fungus in the form of a woolly growth, often found on food.

mouse A computer input device that translates its movements into the movement of the cursor on the screen. It received its name because it is roughly mouse-size and has a "tail" wire that links the device to the computer.

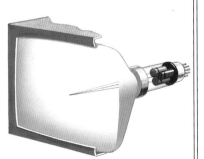

Electrical impulses create television pictures.

mudguard The wide wing of metal around a car wheel that prevents mud and stones from flying up off the road.

multimedia A combination of text, graphics, sound, animation and video.

multi-purpose vehicle (MPV) A vehicle that has more than one use, for example, one that has space for passengers as well as goods.

N

nanotechnology The study of how to make and use micromachines and other very tiny devices.

navigation The skill of planning and directing the route of a plane, ship or car.

nuclear power Power, usually electrical, produced by a nuclear reactor.

negative The photographic image on the developed film from which photographic prints are made. The colors in a negative are reversed, so that dark areas appear to be light and light areas appear to be dark.

neon A gas found in the air that glows when it has an electric current passed through it.

Nobel Prize Prizes that are awarded each year to eminent world scientists, writers and peacemakers.

nut A piece of metal, usually hexagonal, that fits onto a screw.

O

oar A long pole with a flattened blade at one end, used for propelling a boat through water.

oil A thick, black liquid found under the surface of the Earth, from which gasoline and other products are made.

organism An animal, plant or fungus.

OS (operating system) The major software that is needed by all computers to allow them to function properly.

outrigger A framework sticking out from the side of a boat to give the vessel more stability.

over-exposure A photograph that looks washed out as too much light from the subject has hit the film.

oxygen A gas in the Earth's atmosphere. Oxygen is essential for the survival of most animals and plants.

ozone layer The layer of the upper atmosphere, about 12 miles above the Earth's surface, where ozone is formed. It filters ultraviolet rays from the Sun.

P

paddle A short pole with a flat, broad blade used for propelling a small, light boat, such as a canoe, through water.

paddlesteamer A riverboat powered by giant wheels made up of broad, wooden blades. The blades push against the water as they turn in response to power from a steam engine.

panning Moving a camera to follow a moving subject.

pantograph An assembly attached to the top of some locomotives that collects electricity from an overhead power supply.

parachute A device made of a light material, with a harness attached beneath, to allow a person or a package to descend from a height at a safe speed.

pendolino A train that tilts from side to side, enabling the train to move around curves at higher speeds than non-tilting trains.

pendulum A swinging mass hanging from a thread or bar. Pendulums were used in old-fashioned clocks to help keep regular time.

periscope A system of prisms or mirrors that allows people, such as submariners, to view things above eye level.

pickup A small truck with a driver's cab at the front and a flat platform over the rear wheels.

pilot A person who flies an aircraft or spacecraft or navigates a ship into harbor.

piston A disc or cylinder that fits snugly inside another cylinder and is forced to move up and down by the pressure of gas or water. The up-and-down movement is then transferred to the wheels of the vehicle to make them turn.

pitch 1) A change in the vertical direction of flight, either up or down. 2) The angle at which a propeller blade on a ship or aircraft is set.

pivot The point about which a lever turns.

pixels Tiny dots that make up a digital image.

plastic A durable, synthetic material that is easily molded or shaped.

plow 1) A large blade used in farming that cuts through soil and turns it over. 2) A sloping, V-shaped plate attached to the front of American locomotives. Plows clear cattle and other obstructions from the line.

A steamship with sails to propel it when the wind is blowing in the right direction.

pneumatics The use of air or other gases to move pistons and other devices.

Polaroid camera A type of camera that can take and develop individual prints immediately as it has developing chemicals inside.

poop deck The raised deck at the stern of a ship.

port 1) The left-hand side of a boat or aircraft when facing forward. 2) A town with a harbor.

positive A print or slide showing a photographic image with colors or tones which are the same as in the original scene.

power station A group of buildings that house powerful machines which convert energy from fuels like coal into electric power.

primary colors There are three primary colors—red, blue and yellow, also known as cyan, magenta and yellow. When these colors are mixed together in varying proportions, they make any other color.

prism Specially shaped glass used to split white light into the spectrum, or to reflect and light rays away from their normal path.

production line A way of building machines in which the parts are added, one by one, in a continuous process.

propel To push or drive forward.

propeller A device with angled blades arranged around a hub. When turning at speed, it propels a plane through the air or boat through water.

prototype The first attempt to build a working model of a machine following the design.

pulley A mechanism for lifting and lowering weights by means of a wheel over which a rope or chain can be slung.

Pullman A car where passengers can eat and sleep in luxurious surroundings.

punt A long, flat-bottomed boat.

pylon A tall structure of metal struts designed to carry electric power lines high above the ground.

Q

quay A platform that projects into the water and is used for loading and unloading ships.

R

radar A system for detecting the position of distant objects using high-frequency radio waves.

radiator A container of water from which the water is pumped around an engine to prevent overheating.

raft A simple, flatwater craft, usually made of lengths of wood lashed together.

railcar A driverless passenger vehicle powered by diesel or electricity.

RAM (random access memory) Computer memory that holds data temporarily until the computer is switched off.

ratchet A device that allows movement in one direction only.

reconnaissance Surveying and searching over an unknown area, especially with a view to guiding others who might follow.

recreational vehicle (RV) A combination car and camper, with living and sleeping accommodations.

reflectors A sheet of reflecting material or umbrella used to light a subject.

refraction The bending of light rays.

reservoir Resources, such as water, that are frequently stored to use in times of scarcity.

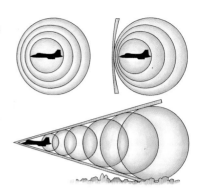

An aircraft breaking through the sound barrier.

resistance A force that acts against an object, causing it to slow down or stop.

resolution The number of shades of color a computer monitor can display.

reversal film or slide film A film that when developed gives a positive image, known as a transparency.

rigging The system of ropes and wires that support and control a ship's sails and masts.

roll A sideways, tilting movement of an aircraft or ship.

rolling stock The locomotives, wagons, cars and any other vehicles that operate on a railroad.

ROM (read-only memory) Computer memory that holds information permanently.

rotor A set of angled blades that radiate from a central block and which rotate at speed to form a rotating motor.

rotor rudder A device for controlling the direction of a ship or plane. The rudder works by cutting into the flow of water or air.

S

satellite A celestial or artificial body orbiting around a planet or star. Artificial satellites are used for communication, exploration and photography.

scaffold A skeleton structure made out of poles put up to help in erecting or repairing a building.

scanner A device used to scan data.

screw A spiral thread on a metal bar that can be used to join objects or raise a load.

screw jack A device that uses a screw to help raise a weight from below.

second-class lever A lever, such as a wheelbarrow, in which the pivot is at the end of the bar.

sewage Human and animal waste mixed with water.

sheet In sailing, a controlling rope attached to the lower edge of a sail.

shutter Camera mechanism, which controls the amount of time light is allowed to fall onto the lens.

silicon A non-metal which as an oxide forms quartz.

silicon chip A small piece of silicon on which are etched thousands of tiny electrical circuits.

slipway A ramp for launching boats.

SLR (Single Lens Reflex) A design of camera that allows you to see exactly what the lens sees.

software Applications that enable computers to carry out specific tasks.

sonar A system used to find out the location of underwater objects.

speedometer A dial that displays the speed at which a vehicle is traveling.

spoiler An airbrake formed from a hinged flap on the rear edge of an aircraft wing.

spoke A piece of metal that joins the rim of a wheel to the hub.

sports car An open or closed car built for speed and performance, usually with two seats.

starboard The right-hand side of a boat or aircraft when facing forward.

steam engine An engine powered by the steam (water vapor) created by heating water.

steel A hard, long-lasting metal made by blowing pure oxygen into molten iron.

stern The back part of a ship or boat.

stills photography Photography showing a single image (as opposed to photography taking moving images with a cine camera).

stock car An ordinary car that has been adapted to make it suitable for racing.

stokehole The room containing a ship's boilers.

streamlined A shape that moves through air or water in the most efficient manner, with the least frictional resistance.

submarine A vessel designed for underwater travel.

submersible A small watercraft that can travel on or below the water's surface. Submersibles are used for underwater research, exploration and repairs.

supersonic An air speed faster than the speed of sound.

suspension system The springs and other shock absorbers that cushion the movement of wheels on the ground.

switches Rails that guide the wheels of a train onto a different section of track.

synthetic An artificially produced version of a natural substance.

T

tailplane The small, horizontal wings at the rear of an aircraft.

telegraph A device that receives messages sent as electrical impulses.

telephoto lens A lens which takes a close-up picture of a distant scene.

thermal A rising current of air formed when part of the ground surface is heated by the sun.

third-class lever A lever in which the effort is applied between the pivot and the load.

throttle A valve that regulates the amount of steam or fuel going into an engine. As a result, the throttle also regulates the speed at which the engine operates and therefore how quickly the vehicle moves.

thrust The force that pushes any flying object forwards.

tie A horizontal, concrete beam supporting the rails on a railroad track.

tiller The steering arm in a cockpit that turns the rudder of a boat.

tonnage The space available in a ship for carrying cargo, measured in tons.

tooth The part of a gear wheel that fits into a chain in a chain drive.

A torpedo being fired from a submarine.

transistor A miniature device which amplifies or switches electric signals.

treadmill A wheel that can be turned by an animal or a person walking on the inner rim of the wheel.

trimaran A boat with three hulls.

triplane An aircraft with three sets of wings, one above the other.

truck A unit underneath a locomotive that guides a train around curves in the track. Four or six pivoted wheels are mounted on one truck.

tug 1) A small boat used for towing larger boats or oil platforms. 2) An aircraft that pulls a glider into the air.

tungsten film Film designed to be used inside. It reproduces light from a lamp or indoor light as if it was white so the pictures do not look yellowy.

Tunnel-Boring Machine (TBM) A giant tunnel-making machine that grinds through soft rock, such as chalk, using a giant, rotating, cutting head.

turbine A rotor that is moved by fast-moving gas currents. In aircraft, this air current is generated by burning fuel to produce hot, fast-moving gas.

turbofan A jet engine in which much of the turbine rotation is used to drive a fan that pushes air round the central engine. The thrust comes from the turbine jet exhaust and the fan-driven air.

turbojet A form of jet engine in which the turbine jet provides all the thrust.

turboprop A form of jet engine in which most of the rotation of the turbine is used to drive a propeller which then propels the aircraft.

turboshaft A form of jet engine in which all of the rotation of the turbine is

used to drive a rotor which then propels an aircraft such as a helicopter.

turbulence Air movement that consists of tiny wind currents flowing in random directions, with no smooth flow of air.

type The metal letter shapes used until the late 1970s to print books.

U
undercarriage The landing wheels of an aircraft. In some aircraft, the undercarriage can be lifted during flight to reduce drag.

underexposure A photograph that looks dark because not enough light rays from the subject were hitting the film at the time the shot was taken.

upthrust The force that makes a ship float or an aircraft take off.

URL (uniform resource locator) The address of a web site on the Internet.

V
valve A device that allows liquids or gases to flow in one direction only.

veteran car Any car built before 1905.

viewfinder The window you look through to see what will be in your photograph.

vintage car Any car built between 1919 and 1930.

virtual reality (VR) The process by which computers are used to create an artificial place that looks real.

volt A way of measuring the strength of an electric current.

W
web page A computer document written in HTML and linked to other web pages.

web site A collection of web pages.

welding Joining two pieces of metal together by heat or under pressure.

wide-angle lens Lens with an angle of view that is wider than normal for the human eye.

winch A wheel on which rope is wound at the top of a framework, in order to lift heavy weights.

wind tunnel A large chamber in which powerful drafts of air are blown over a car to test and measure how much air resistance the car shows.

windsock A tubular kite on a short tether that is used to indicate wind direction and strength.

WWW (World Wide Web) A huge collection of information that is available on the Internet.

X
X-ray A kind of electromagnetic wave that passes through the body and is picked up on specially prepared film.

X-ray photographs Pictures taken of the inside of our bodies, used to show broken bones.

Y
yaw A change in the horizontal direction of flight, either left or right.

Z
Zip disk A portable data storage disk that comes in two storage sizes—100MB and 250MB.

zoom lens A lens with a variable focal length, which is altered to get close to a subject.

A compact camera with a zoom lens.

INDEX

ACKNOWLEDGEMENTS

The publishers would like to thank the following children, and their parents, for appearing in this book:

Nana Addae, Tyrone Agiton, Mohammed Afsar, Katie Appleby, Rees Arnott-Davis, Emily Askew, Anthony Bainbridge, Sara Barnes, Emma Beardmore, Daniel Bill, Maria Bloodworth, Erin Bhogal, Maria Bloodworth, Joseph Brightman, Anum Butt, David Callega, Jessica Castaneda, Liliana Conceicia, Shaun Liam Cook, Gary Cooper, Diane Cuffe, Sheree Cunningham-Kelly, Stacie Damps, Joe Davies, Aaron Dumetz, Louisa El-Jonsafi, Amaru Fleary, Laurence de Freitas, Alistair Fulton, Ricky Edward Garrett, Africa George, Anton Goldbourne, Brooke Griffiths, Eleshia Henry, Francesca Hill, Sung-Kiet Hoang, Sasha Howarth, Thomas James, Carl Keating, Sarah Ann Kenna, Lee Knight, Shadae Lawrence, Jon Leming, Eddie Lengthorn, Alex Lindblom-Smith, Sophie Lindblom-Smith, Gabrielle Locke, Laura Masters, Emma Molley, Jessica Moxley, Aidan Mulcahy, Fiona Mulcahy, Seán Mulcahy, Robert Nunez, Ifunanya Obi, Joshua Parris, Nicky Payne, Kim Peterson, Mai Peterson, Emily Preddie, Jamie Pyle, Susy Quirke, Elen Rhys, Zoe Richardson, Jamie Rosso, Ajvir Sandhu, Jasmine Sharland, Paul Snow, Kisanet Tesfay, Nicola Twiner, Kirsty Wells, Joe Westbrook and Amber-Hollie Wood.

PICTURE CREDITS

Key: b = bottom, t = top, c = centre, l = left, r = right

INVENTIONS AND DISCOVERIES

Ancient Art and Architecture Ltd: 18tl, 48tr; Barnaby's Picture Library: 26br; BBC Photographic Library: 45tl; Bridgeman Art Library: 22tl, 52bl, 54tl; Paul Brierley: 49tr; Contour Colour Ltd: 12br; Corbis Images: 13br, 14tr, 14bl, 19r, 20tl, 21bl, 21br, 29br, 33bl, 48br, 52bl; E.T. Archive: 14br, 18bl, 20bl, 22bl, 32tr, 33br, 37tl, 49tl, 52tl; Mary Evans Picture Library: 35bl, 40tr, 41tl; G. D. A. Ltd: 23cr; Hoover European Appliance Group: 19c; Hulton Getty Picture Library: 49b; National Maritime Museum: 53tr; Oxford Scientific Picture Library: 15tl; Panasonic: 45br; Ann Ronan Picture Library: endpaper, 13bl, 23t, 28tl, 28bl, 28br, 29tl, 32br, 33tl, 36tl, 43b; Science and Society Picture Library: 12bl, 15tr, 16tr, 17br, 18l, 20br, 21tl, 21tr, 22br, 23cl, 25b, 26tl, 27tl, 29tr, 36bl, 37bl, 40bl, 40br, 41c, 41br, 42tl, 44tr, 44br, 52br, 53c, 53bl, 53br; Science Photo Library: 27tr, 27bl, 27br, 29bl, 56tr, 56bl, 56br, 57tl, 57tr, 57br; Spectrum Colour Library: 24tl, 46tr; Tony Stone Images: 30tr, 50tr; Zefa Pictures: 23b, 45bl.

MACHINES

Ancient Egypt Picture Library: 74tr, 74b; Bruce Coleman Ltd: 88bl, 88br, 89tl; /M Borchi 71tr; /G Clyde 81c; /Gryniewicz 108bl; /J Jurka 67c; /H Lange 61tr; /N McAllister 71cl; /HP Merton 109bl; Ecoscene: 88c, 103bl; /N Hawkes 75bl, 102bl; /W Lawler 76cl; /M Maidment 105tl; /Towse 106br; E.T. Archive: 71tl, 80b, 102tr, 107bl;

Mary Evans Picture Library: 93br, 96tr; Holt Studios: /I Belcher 104bl; /A Burridge 78c, 107br; /N Cattlin 102br, 104br, 104tr, 105tr; /J Hall 76c; /W Harinck 103tr; /P McCullagh 63bl; /P Peacock 108tl; /I Spence 81bl, 105c; ICCE: /M Boulton 61bl; Image Bank: 75tr; Powerstock: /Alex Bartel 89bl; Quadrant: 64br, 71br, 71c, 75tl, 80bl, 81br, 93tr, 95c, 97bc, 103c; Planet Earth Pictures: 61br, 75br; Science Photo Library: 110cl, 113c; /M Bond 84c; /M Fielding 61t; /V Fleming 85br; /P Fletcher 92tr; /Food & Drug Administration 108b; /A Hart-Davis 81tr; /S Horrel 89br; /M Kage 110bl; /J King-Holmes 94tr; /S Ogden 111bl; /A Pasieka 86c; /Rosenfield Images Ltd 109cv; /V Steger 108c, 110cl, 111cl; /US Department of Energy 112tr; Science Museum/ Science & Society Picture Library: 70br, 85bl, 92bl, 93c, 99tr; Tony Stone Images: 95tl; /Agri Press 68bl; /W Bilenduke 96c; /S Egan 61c; /B Lewis 105br; /P McArthur 99bl; /A Meshkinger 99c; /C Thatcher 99tl; /T Vine 82c; Superstock: 60tr, 61tl, 62br, 82tr, 89c, 103br; Zefa Pictures 95bl.

CAMERAS

The Publishers would like to thank Keith Johnson and Pelling Ltd for the loan of props. Aardman Animations Ltd: 166br; Allsport: 135tr; Mary Evans Picture Library: 116bl, 164c; Galaxy Picture Library: 171tr; Tim Grabham: 167br; Nigel Cattlin/Holt Studios International: 149tl, tr; 165bl, 170br, 173tl; Robin Kerrod: 171tl; Microscopix: 170c; Laurence Gould/Oxford Scientific Films: 163cr; Scott Camazine: 171b; Chris Oxlade: 159tr; Papilio Photographic: 164bl, 173bl, br, c; The Projection Box: 166tl, 168tr;

Science Photo Library:
Phillipe Plailly 161bl; Sinclair Stammers 170tl; Francoise Sauze 171cl; George Bernard: 171cr; L Weinstein, NASA: 170bl; Science and Society Photo Library: 121c, 135tr, 145tr, 166bl, 169br; Sony: 164cr; Tony Stone Images: 167cr; Lucy Tizard: 154tl; Zefa Pictures: 117bl, br, 146bl, 159bl, 160bl, 161t.

COMPUTERS

Adobe: 193 (x3); Courtesy of Apple Computers, Inc.: 178br, 181cr, 181bcr, 187t, 187b, 192c, 193tr, 193bl, 193tr (x2), 224, 225; Casio: 235tl; Corbis: AFP: 227b; /Kevin Fleming 196b, 231bl; Diablo II: 213bl; Getty One Stone: Chad Slattery: 231t; /Peter Dazeley: 176c & 177c (in monitor), 187bc (in monitor); /Peter Poulides: 188bc; Hulton Getty: 181bl; Iomega® Zip: 176bc, 189br; Louvre Museum: 228b (x3), 229t (x4), 229c (x2); ©Photo RMN/R. G. Ojeda: 228tr; Mary Evans Picture Library: 180bl; Mattel Interactive: 215t; Microsoft Corporation: Microsoft® Word: 192bl (x4); /Microsoft® Windows®: 193bc, 193tl (x2); /Microsoft Clip Art: 198b (x4); Netscape Communications: 193 (x1); Olympus Cameras: 202c; Powerstock Photo Library/Zefa: 212tl; Robert Partridge: The Ancient Egypt Picture Library: 228c; Science and Society Picture Library: Bletchley Park Trust: 181tl; /J.-L. Charmet: 180tl; Science Museum: 180cl, 181tr, 181tcr, 196t; Science Photo Library: 231c; /Alex Bartel: 176c, 177c; /Caida: 222c; /CS Langlois /Publiphoto Diffusion: 220bl; /D. Parker: 227c; /Damien Lovegrove 216b; /David Ducros: 222bl; /De Renpentigny /Publiphoto: 230br; /Gable Jerrican: 223; /Hank Morgan: 216c, 220tr;